Casebook in
Family Therapy

Casebook in Family Therapy

Edited by

David M. Lawson

Frances F. Prevatt

Brooks/Cole • Wadsworth

I(T)P® *An International Thomson Publishing Company*

Belmont • Albany • Bonn • Boston • Cincinnati • Detroit • Johannesburg
London • Madrid • Melbourne • Mexico City • New York • Pacific Grove
Paris • Singapore • Tokyo • Toronto • Washington

Sponsoring Editor: *Eileen Murphy*
Editorial Assistant: *Julie Martinez*
Marketing Team: *Liz Poulsen and Christine Davis*
Marketing Representative: *Ragu Raghavan*
Production Editor: *Janet Hill*
Manuscript Editor: *Jennifer McClain*
Indexer: *Patricia Lowe*

Permissions Editor: *May Clark*
Cover & Interior Design: *Christine Gerrigan*
Art Editor: *Lisa Torri*
Composition: *Omegatype Typography, Inc.*
Cover Printing: *Webcom*
Printing and Binding: *Webcom*

For more information, contact

WADSWORTH PUBLISHING COMPANY
10 Davis Drive
Belmont, CA 94002
USA

International Thomson Publishing Europe
Berkshire House 168–173
High Holborn
London WC1V 7AA
England

Thomas Nelson Australia
102 Dodds Street
South Melbourne, 3205
Victoria, Australia

Nelson Canada
1120 Birchmount Road
Scarborough, Ontario
Canada M1K 5G4

International Thomson Editores
Seneca 53
Col. Polanco
11560 México, D.F., México

International Thomson Publishing GmbH
Königswinterer Strasse 418
53227 Bonn
Germany

International Thomson Publishing Asia
60 Albert Street #15-01
Albert Complex
Singapore 189969

International Thomson Publishing Japan
Hirakawacho Kyowa Building, 3F
2-2-1 Hirakawacho
Chiyoda-ku, Tokyo 102
Japan

Printed in Canada

10 9 8 7 6 5 4 3 2

Library of Congress Cataloging-in-Publication Data

Casebook in family therapy / edited by David M. Lawson, Frances F.
  Prevatt.
      p.   cm.
    ISBN 0-534-34415-1
    1. Family psychotherapy—Case studies.   I. Lawson, David M.
  II. Prevatt, Frances F., [date].
  RC488.5.C369   1998
  616.89'156—dc21   98–40610

To Bruce, my husband and best friend.
Frances F. Prevatt

To Peggy, Paul, and Joel for their patience and support
David M. Lawson

Contents

Contributing Authors

Harlene Anderson, Ph.D., Founding Member and Faculty, Houston Galveston Institute, Houston, Texas

Barbara Anger-Dìaz, Ph.D., Research Associate, Mental Research Institute, Palo Alto, California; Staff Member, Brief Therapy Center; Co-Director Latino Brief Therapy Center

Insoo Kim Berg, MSW, Brief Family Therapy Center, Milwaukee, Wisconsin

J. Paul Burney, Ph.D., Faculty, Houston Galveston Institute, Houston, Texas

Andrew Christensen, Ph.D., Professor, Department of Psychology, University of California, Los Angeles, California

Catherine Ducommun-Nagy, M.D., Associate Director, The Institute for Contextual Growth, Ambler, Pennsylvania

Kathleen Eldridge, M.A., Doctoral candidate in Clinical Psychology, Department of Psychology, University of California, Los Angeles, California

Andrew Fussner, MSW, Adjunct Professor, Graduate School of Social Work, Rutgers and Bryn Mawr College; Consultant, Head Start Project, Philadelphia School District; Senior Clinician and Senior Faculty Member, Philadelphia Child Guidance Center, Philadelphia, Pennsylvania

Constance J. Fournier, Ph.D., Assistant Professor, Department of Educational Psychology, University of Missouri, St. Louis, Missouri

Herbert Goldenberg, Ph.D., Professor, Department of Psychology, California State University, Los Angeles, California

Irene Goldenberg, Ed.D., Professor, Department of Psychiatry and Biobehavioral Sciences, University of California, Los Angeles, Neuropsychiatric Institute and Hospital, Los Angeles, California

Jolanta Jachimczyk, M.A., MSW, CSW[1], Social Worker, Residential Treatment Center

Neil S. Jacobson, Ph.D., Professor, Department of Psychology, University of Washington Center for Clinical Research, Seattle, Washington

Jim Keim, LCSWC, Family Therapy Institute of Washington, D.C., Rockville, Maryland

Sylvia Kamenoff, Ph.D.[1], Clinical Coordinator, Residential Treatment Center

Herb Klar, MSW, Kaiser Permanente, Department of Psychiatry, Pleasanton, California

Edith Lawrence, Ph.D., Center for Clinical Psychology Services, University of Virginia, Charlottesville, Virginia

David Lawson, Ph.D., Associate Professor, Counseling Psychology Program, Department of Educational Psychology, Texas A&M University, College Station, Texas

Susan B. Levin, Ph.D., Executive Director and Faculty, Houston Galveston Institute, Houston, Texas

Bruce C. Prevatt, Ph.D., Director, Employee Assistance Program, Florida State University, Tallahassee, Florida

Frances F. Prevatt, Ph.D., Co-ordinator, School Psychology Program, Florida State University, Tallahassee, Florida

William A. Rae, Ph.D., Assistant Director, Department of Psychology, St. Louis Children's Hospital, St. Louis, Missouri

Karen Schlanger, MFCC, Senior Research Fellow, Mental Research Institute, Palo Alto, California; Assistant Director, Brief Therapy Center, MRI, Co-Director Latino Brief Therapy Center; Adjunct Faculty, University of San Francisco, School of Education

Douglas K. Snyder, Ph.D., Professor, Director, Clinical Psychology Program, Department of Psychology, Texas A&M University, College Station, Texas

[1]Affiliation withheld to protect the confidentiality of the families

Preface

The *Casebook in Family Therapy* reflects our goal of producing a text that is practical, empirically and theoretically based, and current with the contemporary practice of family therapy. Given the rapid rate of change in the field of family therapy, it is critical that we stay abreast of the evolution of the various models of therapy and that we accurately represent their application. A number of these changes are particularly relevant to the *Casebook*.

One such change has been the proliferation of therapy models based on postmodernist and social constructivist perspectives (for example, solution-focused therapy, collaborative language systems, narrative therapy). Although distinct differences separate these approaches, their authors largely view themselves as participant-observers who engage their clients in a collaborative effort to construct a more workable reality.

Another change in the family therapy field is the increasing number of integrative approaches, which blend together various existing therapy models based on empirical research and practical experience (for example, integrative couple therapy, pragmatic couple therapy, integrated intergenerational family therapy). As we talked with several authors about their approaches to therapy, we often encountered the comment, "Well, yes, what I do is based on such and such a theory, but it's really evolved into a combination of several approaches." Thus, while "stand-alone," distinct theories of family therapy still are the standard, many of the newer approaches exhibit greater convergence conceptually and technically.

It appears that the established approaches, such as strategic therapy, structural therapy, family-of-origin therapies, and communications approaches (that is, MRI, Satir), will continue to evolve and influence the emerging and integrative approaches. As such, it would not be surprising if family therapy models continue to evolve much like individual therapy models. As research and practice identify common factors across approaches, more integrative models likely will emerge in an attempt to be more effective with a wider range of clients.

Most of the previously mentioned approaches have been addressed to varying degrees in the literature. Several excellent texts exist that present an overview of current theories of family therapy. There are also several texts and articles that present brief descriptions of case studies or in-depth case studies of specific approaches (for example, Jacobson and Gurman, 1995; Coleman, 1985; Kaufman, 1984; Papp, 1977; Gurman, 1985). However, we saw a need for a text that presents detailed case studies with verbatim transcripts covering a broad range of established, emerging, and integrative approaches to family therapy.

In selecting the theories to include, we relied heavily on introductory survey texts such as *Family Therapy: An Overview* (Goldenberg and Goldenberg, 1996). It was our belief that students would be well served by beginning their studies with a solid basic text, which could then be supplemented with a companion text that would provide extensive verbatims and commentaries detailing how these theories are implemented. We sought to obtain a variety of couple and conjoint family cases that would represent typical cases seen by practitioners.

In planning the *Casebook,* we debated whether it would be advantageous to present one case that all authors would discuss, thus increasing the continuity between chapters and allowing for a more direct comparison of theories. However, we ultimately decided that actual cases with verbatim transcripts would be superior to discussions of one common case by all authors. Merely presenting a description of how a clinician *might* work with a case often overlooks the ebb and flow of the actual therapeutic process over time. For trainees and beginning therapists as well as experienced therapists who wish to better inform their practice, following a case through the therapy process, with abundant session verbatims, greatly enhances the instructive nature of the case study. In addition, where appropriate, we selected authors who had an affiliation with the major training center where specific theories have evolved (for example, the MRI Institute, the Houston Galveston Institute, the Philadelphia Child Guidance Center, the Brief Family Therapy Center, the Family Therapy Institute of Washington, D.C.). In all cases, we selected authors with extensive clinical and empirical experience in their selected theory.

The Approaches

The family-of-origin approaches are represented by contextual therapy and integrated intergenerational family therapy. In Chapter 1, Catherine Ducommun-Nagy presents a thorough discussion of contextual therapy. Her presentation follows closely the longtime work of Ivan Boszormenyi-Nagy that emphasizes the importance of trust, justice, and fairness in relationships. Family members are assisted in understanding and rebalancing the giving and receiving dimensions in their relationships. This emphasis on relational ethics is a major distinguishing characteristic between contextual therapy and most other family-of-origin approaches. The case study illustrates the application of contextual therapy with a family who presents with an adolescent daughter exhibiting psychotic symptoms.

In Chapter 2, David Lawson describes integrated intergenerational family therapy, which largely follows the theoretical principles of Bowen systems theory, Williamson's intergenerational family model, and, to a lesser degree, Beck's cognitive therapy. This approach places a primary focus on intergenerational relationships between parents and their adult children. An important goal in therapy is to assist adult clients in developing a balance between individuation and intimacy (personal authority in the family system) in their relationships with parents. It is believed that this renegotiation is necessary for most adults and necessarily generalizes to other relationships (partners, children, authority figures, and so on). Unique to this model is its integration with cognitive therapy. The tenets and methods of Beck's cognitive therapy are utilized to assist clients in becoming aware of and modifying problematic beliefs, which are often based on family-of-origin experiences. The case family includes a middle-aged female (who presents with anxiety and depression exacerbated by a recent divorce), her two children, and her father.

Two couple approaches are included in the *Casebook*. Both place particular emphasis on traditional, empirically derived research in the development of their models. In Chapter 3, Kathleen Eldridge, Andrew Christensen, and Neil Jacobson provide a thorough discussion of integrative couple therapy (ICT). This model evolved from Jacobson's longtime development of traditional behavioral couple therapy (TBCT) that emphasizes behavioral exchanges, communication skills, and problem-solving skills to produce change. The ICT model combines an emphasis on partner acceptance of each other's undesirable behaviors with the TBCT emphasis on behavior change. A major component of ICT is to produce change in partner reactions to each other's aversive behavior in addition to change in unacceptable behavior. The authors employ ICT in working with a couple who present with problems related to intimacy, negative emotions, and anxiety related to professional and parental roles.

Douglas Snyder discusses pragmatic couple therapy in Chapter 4. This approach holds that the sources and means of effectively changing distress vary greatly from couple to couple. Thus, it is critical to conduct a thorough assessment across multiple dimensions of the couple's relationship in order to construct an intervention plan that corresponds to the couple's unique needs. The concept of tailoring the therapist's approach to each couple is not unique to this model, but Snyder takes seriously the dependence on empirical literature to bring about this process. Consequently, effective treatment may employ a wide range of interventions drawn from numerous theoretical models and employed in a conceptually logical manner. In the case example, the author demonstrates his approach with a couple presenting with sexual and financial problems.

Structural family therapy (the subject of Chapter 5) has been best represented by the work of Salvador Minuchin. Structural family therapy differs from other systemic models in its use of spatial and organizational metaphors, both in describing problems and in identifying avenues for solutions. This approach also assigns an extremely active role to the therapist as an instrument of change. This chapter, written by Sylvia Kemenoff and Jolanta Jachimczyk and coauthored by Andrew Fussner of the Philadelphia Child Guidance Center, describes a wide range of concepts, including subsystems, boundaries, complementarity, hierarchies, alignments, and coalitions. The chapter presents four different cases, each depicting a different dysfunctional family structure. Case 1, a stepfather family with an aggressive child, illustrates a detouring triad. Case 2, a sexually acting-out child, illustrates diffuse boundaries and the lack of differentiation among family members. Case 3, a stepmother family with an aggressive child, illustrates unequal spousal power and the use of alignment and blocking. Case 4, a single-parent family plus grandmother with an aggressive, hyperactive child, illustrates a weak parental hierarchy and the use of unbalancing techniques.

Several authors describe their approaches as being modifications of communications theory. In Chapter 6, Karen Schlanger and Barbara Anger-Díaz describe the work currently being done at the MRI Institute in Palo Alto. This approach, evolving from the early work of Bateson, Jackson, Weakland, and Haley, focuses on the relational aspects of current problems. It is predicated on the notion that a change in behavior leads to a change in interactions, ultimately changing perceptions. Similar to several other theories, the focus is on the presenting problem rather than past history. The goal of therapy is to change attempted solutions by helping family members behave differently. The case involves a young adult son with vocational, interpersonal, and emotional difficulties.

A similar lineage led to the humanistic approach of Virginia Satir, which is outlined in Chapter 7. Edith Lawrence explains Satir's belief that individuals are inherently healthy and growth oriented. Unhealthy symptoms are merely adaptive attempts gone awry. The goal of therapy is to identify unhealthy communication patterns and make it safe to reveal true feelings. In this approach, the therapist is very active and direct, becoming coach, teacher, supporter, and challenger. The case involves a mother in denial over the sexual abuse of her daughter by the paternal grandfather.

A third approach heavily influenced by the early work of Gregory Bateson and the MRI group is Milan systemic therapy. In Chapter 8, Frances Prevatt describes the continuing evolution of this approach. In its early years, strategic concepts such as counterparadox and positive connotation were emphasized. Later, the Milan theory became more systemic; early glimpses of a social constructivist approach emerged, as the notion of a jointly constructed world view evolved. The chapter traces the split between the four original theorists and describes a case influenced more heavily by the Boscolo/Cecchin pair of theorists. The concepts of hypothesizing, neutrality, and circular questioning are illustrated in a case of marital distance and oppositional children.

In Chapter 9, Jim Keim presents the most current account of the Washington School of Strategic Therapy. From this perspective, it is the therapist's primary responsibility to plan a strategy for solving the client's problems. Most often, these interventions focus on the social context in which the problem is played out. Clear goals related to the presenting concern are a hallmark of this approach. With child problems, a particular focus is placed on hierarchy between parents and children. Keim demonstrates this approach with a family that presents with an oppositional child.

Three emerging theories share a background in social construction and narrative approaches. Herb Klar and Insoo Kim Berg describe solution-focused brief therapy in Chapter 10. This approach has drawn considerable interest and acceptance in the last few years. Greatly influenced by social constructivism, solution-focused therapists work collaboratively with clients in constructing a desirable outcome for therapy based on the identification of exceptions to the problem. Distinct from many traditional therapies, solution-focused therapy minimizes "problem talk" while emphasizing outcome, "solution talk." Therefore, therapist questions focus on eliciting client descriptions of outcome situations that define the client and the client's problems in an entirely different way than initially presented. The authors' clinical case describes working with a substance-abusing father and his family.

In Chapter 11, a postmodern collaborative approach to therapy is described by three members of the Houston Galveston Institute: Harlene Anderson, J. Paul Burney, and Susan Levin. This postmodern philosophy focuses on language as a social and cultural means by which groups create narratives that help them understand their world. Therapists become participants in the therapy system and take on the primary task of facilitating the conversational process. The conversation becomes a process in which new meanings and relationships are created. The case involves a nuclear family with a distressed father-daughter relationship and marital difficulties.

The work of Michael White is also characterized as postmodern constructivism, yet it bears some resemblance to the Milan group's use of circular questioning. Michael White tends to be much more focused and directive in his conversations, believing that he can help liberate families from narratives molded by the dominant culture with active guidance toward alternate stories. As described by Bruce Prevatt in Chapter 12, this model engages families in conversations designed to externalize their problems. A variety of specific letter-writing techniques are a hallmark of this approach. Externalization of the problem is exemplified in the case study, which involves a marital separation due to spousal alcoholism

The final model of family therapy, psychoeducational family therapy, is often omitted from many family therapy texts because it is not viewed as family therapy (McFarlane, 1991). However, this approach has been found to be effective with intractable disorders such as schizophrenia (Goldstein and Miklowitz, 1995). In Chapter 13, Constance Fournier and William Rae present the similarities and differences between psychoeducational family therapy and more traditional family therapies. Psychoeducational family therapy, while embracing many of the common concepts and skills associated with family therapy, places greater emphasis on disseminating information appropriate for the family followed by assisting the family in incorporating this information. The strong educational element is accompanied by an emphasis on health in addition to problem resolution. Psychoeducational family therapy is often associated with medical settings, although it is not limited only to this context. The case presentation illustrates working with a family whose child has been diagnosed with insulin-dependent diabetes mellitus. Therapy with the family occurs on both an inpatient and an outpatient basis.

In addition to the case studies, a final chapter written by Herbert and Irene Goldenberg addresses current issues and trends in family therapy. It provides an incisive look at four major areas in marital and family therapy: postmodern outlooks, population diversity, qualitative research methodology, and outcome studies. The reader receives an overview of each of these topics, followed by a glimpse of future directions in family therapy.

Acknowledgments

A number of individuals have made major contributions to the completion of this book. We would like to express our thanks to all of our contributing authors and all the staff at Brooks/Cole Publishing, in particular, our editor, Eileen Murphy, Janet Hill for her guidance through the production process, and the book production team. Finally, we thank Patricia Lowe for her meticulous work in preparing the index.

We also thank those who were involved in the reviewing of the manuscript, and who provided thoughtful and invaluable suggestions for improvement, including Susan Anzivino, University of Maine at Farmington; Joshua Gold, University of South Carolina; Herbert Goldenberg, Sepulveda VA Medical Center; Clarence Hibbs, Pepperdine University; and Sheryl Olson, University of Michigan.

David M. Lawson
Frances F. Prevatt

References

Coleman, S. (Ed.). (1985). *Failures in family therapy.* New York: Guilford Press.

Goldenberg, I., & Goldenberg, H. (1996). *Family therapy: An overview* (4th ed.). Pacific Grove, CA: Brooks/Cole.

Goldstein, M. J., & Miklowitz, D. J. (1995). The effectiveness of psychoeducational family therapy in the treatment of schizophrenic disorders. *Journal of Marital and Family Therapy, 21,* 361–376.

Gurman, A. S. (Ed.). (1985). *Casebook of marital therapy.* New York: Guilford Press.

Jacobson, N. S., & Gurman, A. S. (Eds.). (1995). *Clinical handbook of couple therapy.* New York: Guilford Press.

Kaufman, E. (Ed.). (1984). *Power to change: Family case studies in the treatment of alcoholism.* New York: Gardner Press.

McFarlane, W. R. (1991). Family psychoeducational treatment. In A. S. Gurman & D. P. Kniskern (Eds.), *Handbook of family therapy, Volume II* (pp. 363–395). New York: Brunner/Mazel.

Papp, P. (Ed.). (1977). *Family therapy: Full-length case studies.* New York: Gardner Press.

Casebook in
Family Therapy

Chapter One

Contextual Therapy

Catherine Ducommun-Nagy

The treatment of clients suffering from psychotic disorders has been both a challenge to the therapist and a source of controversy over the years. Are mental illnesses brain disorders, as the slogan of NAMI (National Alliance for the Mentally Ill) states, or the result of pathological sequences of communications, as some systemic family therapists would like to believe? Today it would be difficult to deny that biological factors play a role in the development of mental illnesses like schizophrenia or bipolar disorders. This does not mean, however, that we are about to reach an etiological understanding of these disorders. Every day brings new discoveries, yet we are unable to create solid bridges between the relevant bodies of knowledge (genetics, biochemistry, behavioral sciences, depth psychology, systems theory, and others). Given the complexity of the factors that affect human behaviors, we will have to accept gaps in our understanding of mental illnesses. Neither a simple biological hypothesis nor a simplistic view of relationships can answer all the questions that we face while treating clients with severe mental disorders. Thus, we need to present our clients with a comprehensive treatment approach.

Contextual therapy provides the clinician with a model of therapy that allows for the combination of several modalities of treatment under the guiding principles of relational ethics. Contextual therapy assumes four dimensions to relational reality: the facts (biology and sociohistorical givens), the individual psychology (emotional and cognitive elements), the transactions (systemic elements), and relational ethics (a balance of giving and receiving). This multidimensional

I would like to thank my husband, Ivan Boszormenyi-Nagy, M.D., for his constructive comments during the redaction of this chapter.

model gives therapists a practical framework for the assessment of complex clinical situations.

Contextual therapists can also provide clinicians with a reason for optimism without having to rely on unfounded claims. Therapists do not need to strive for the eradication of pathology but can aim at the mobilization of relational resources. Despite deep-seated pathologies, clients have a capacity to care for others that can be mobilized if we are willing to learn about the contextual theory of motivations.

Development of Contextual Therapy

Contextual therapy originated from the work of Ivan Boszormenyi-Nagy, one of the pioneers of family therapy. His clinical research has spanned more than four decades, and his writings have influenced, directly or indirectly, a large number of family therapists in the United States and worldwide. The broad recognition that Nagy has gained for his contribution to the field of family therapy does not preclude some misunderstandings of his work.

It is noteworthy that two of the concepts Nagy introduced to the field of family therapy (that is, loyalty and parentification) are now so widely used that their origin has been forgotten. This same process seems to be occurring with the concept of multidirected partiality.

Most authors who have written about the history of the family therapy movement have struggled in their attempts to find a place for Nagy's work in their respective classification systems. Most of them have categorized his work under the psychodynamic approaches to family therapy and, in doing so, have failed to recognize the fundamental originality of contextual therapy.

Goldenberg and Goldenberg (1991) have appropriately stated: "One of the foremost original thinkers in the field, Boszormenyi-Nagy emphasizes that to truly grasp human existence it is essential to understand both individual and relational realities, particularly intergenerational issues that permeate every family's life" (p. 103). Nonetheless, they have failed to clearly distinguish contextual therapy from psychoanalytic theory, which can misguide the reader about the foundations of contextual therapy. This approach is not based on an expansion of psychoanalytical principles of therapy; it does not have interpretation as its method and insight as its goal. Instead, contextual therapy is a true relational model of therapy based on an understanding of the dimension of giving and receiving in relationships. It has multidirected partiality as its strategy and earning of entitlement through due consideration for others as its ultimate therapeutic goal. These elements also clearly separate contextual therapy from other forms of family therapy (systemic-classical family therapy).

What critics generally fail to recognize is that contextual therapy addresses a dimension of human relationships that is neither psychological nor systemic—the dimension of relational ethics. The reader needs to remember that contextual principles can inform not only the family therapist but also individual and marital therapists.

It was Nagy's determination to find ways to help clients suffering from psychosis that led him to study medicine, to become a psychiatrist, and later to devote his life to the search of what constitutes effective therapy. In addition, his eagerness to study any elements that could lead to an understanding of schizophrenia brought him to invest several years in biochemical research before returning to his original interest in therapy.

In 1957, Nagy was invited to found a research department on schizophrenia at the Eastern Pennsylvania Psychiatric Institute. By the beginning of the '60s, Nagy and his co-workers were among the early practitioners of what became known as intensive family psychotherapy (Boszormenyi-Nagy and Framo, 1965). As Nagy's understanding of intergenerational family dynamics and interpersonal relationships grew, he started to define his approach as intergenerational dialectical family therapy (Boszormenyi-Nagy and Spark, 1973). This later evolved into contextual therapy (Boszormenyi-Nagy, 1978; Boszormenyi-Nagy and Krasner, 1986).

Nagy has more recently examined the implications of contextual therapy for society at large, including human survival and the prevention of mental and relational disorders (Boszormenyi-Nagy, 1987). In an era of dramatic societal changes, increased fragmentation of families, and decreased care for the vulnerable members of our society, he believes that the contextual principle of receiving through giving is one of the rare realistic antidotes available to fight rampant individualism. In addition, Nagy stresses the need for solidarity of action between individual and family therapists to protect the future of therapy at large. He also warns us that any exaggeration of claim to success, any pretense to etiological knowledge, can seriously endanger the scientific credibility of all psychotherapies.

Theoretical Underpinnings

Expanding the scope of psychotherapy to reach clients with psychotic disorders is rooted in the origin of the family therapy movement. In addition to an understanding of the psychological determinants that had been explored by the psychoanalysts, the pioneers of family therapy needed new tools to explain what they were beginning to observe in conjoint family sessions.

Nagy, like his colleagues, found in the general systems theory a useful framework to describe the dynamics of family systems at a time when pioneers of family therapy had no language to depict these processes. On the other hand, he has since contended that general systems theory cannot provide a conceptual model for the integration of system-based characteristics and individually based (dialogue-based) characteristics of families. Nagy's own answer to the challenge of finding a comprehensive model of family relationships was to look at them from a dialectic perspective informed by the philosophy of Friedrich Hegel and enriched by Martin Buber's philosophy of the dialogue. According to Nagy's dialectic view of relationships, each individual depends on another for self-delineation. Therefore, from a dialectic point of view, autonomy becomes a paradox because individuals need someone to relate with in order to assert their existence as a separate self.

Nagy's clinical experience with families convinced him that trust, justice, and fairness are at the core of the human experience and constitute one of the most powerful dynamics in interpersonal relating. He described this aspect of relational reality as the ethical dimension of relationships, the dimension of giving and receiving, or the dimension of trustworthiness in relationships.

Entitlement

Relational ethics refers to the principle that any action between partners is recorded as either an act of giving or an act of receiving. This sets in motion a balance of merits and obligations between the two partners. As I have received, I will be expected to repay my partner either in kind or at least by a fair consideration of his or her needs at a later time. In close relationships, unlike in commercial dealings, no one can expect an exact return for what has been invested in the relationship, but a fair response by the partner, that is, a willingness to be available in turn is required for the relationship to remain equitable.

As givers, individuals should expect a fair return for their giving, and even if this does not occur, they can derive a gain from the act of giving in the form of an inner satisfaction or, in contextual terms, a constructive entitlement. Inasmuch as individuals receive an indirect reward from giving, they can be generous to their partner without having to become altruistic. What is lost in direct returns is gained in the form of self-validation.

These views brought Nagy to define a new dialectic principle, the principle of receiving through giving, and to postulate that individual autonomy cannot be reached without a genuine consideration of others. To the extent that it represents giving, the child's offering of loyalty to the parents is not an obstacle to autonomy but a chance for self-validation.

Being wronged accumulates a destructive entitlement: The individual is owed a compensation, a repair for the incurred damage. If this individual cannot turn to the person who wronged him or her for compensation and instead makes a third party accountable to undo the damage, the individual commits a new self-injustice. To that extent, the original entitlement becomes destructive to others. In addition, the very fact that the person has a valid claim makes him or her blind to the damage that can be caused to others by using them as a source of compensation.

The perpetuation of exploitative patterns of relating over generations results from a combination of the child's loyal availability to the needy parent and from the parent's destructive use of the child as a source of compensation for past injustices. The exploitation of children can take two forms: Parents may expect the child to be available like a mature and trustworthy adult (parentification), or they can cripple children into a predictable availability through preventing their growth (infantilization). Both situations amount to the same level of exploitation and unfairness for the child.

To help parents decrease their reliance on destructive entitlement, therapists use a two-pronged approach. First, they offer partiality to the parents by acknowledging the injustices they incurred when they were children; then they ask the parents to consider the children's own interest. When parents experience that they can gain a new self-worth and inner freedom from meeting the needs of their children, they might decrease their reliance on past claims, that is, on their destructive entitlement, and start to earn constructive entitlement. Here, multidirected partiality gains a new definition: It is the capacity for the therapist not simply to offer due consideration to each family member but also to give a fair chance to each person to become a giver. As Nagy explains, a healing moment is found each time two or more persons can benefit from an action, one as the giver and one as the receiver. The therapist's optimism does not need to be anchored in a naïve belief in the good nature of people or in overlooking severe individual or relational pathologies. It lies in the understanding that an individual receives through giving and that all human beings can benefit from being offered a chance to give to others, no matter how disturbed or confused they are.

Finally, the belief that symptoms, though undesirable, can also serve a hidden purpose is not new. Psychoanalysts have long described how clients can derive secondary gains from their symptoms. What family therapists discovered is that symptoms may serve a hidden purpose not only for one person but also for other family members. The client who presents with symptoms is not always the one who suffers the most. For instance, a paranoid man may suffer from hearing disparaging voices, but his wife may suffer even more from his relentless accusations of betrayal.

The Therapeutic Contract

An important technique for contextual therapy is the therapeutic contract. The very idea of a contract implies a notion of individual responsibility for decisions and of personal accountability for their consequences. Any therapist can observe the unfolding of systemic rules in a given family system, but who other than individual family members can give the therapist permission to interfere with the family system's observed functioning? Contextual therapists rely on multidirected partiality to include in the therapeutic contract anyone who can be affected by the consequences of their interventions and to explore the conflicting interests of family members who engage in the treatment process.

When clients are not ready to address an issue, the therapist might offer them a moratorium, that is, a time to think about difficult issues or decisions. In doing so, the therapist retains the initiative in the treatment without having to become manipulative. The moratorium can also apply to the invitation of absent family members. The therapist is responsible to bring up the interests of absent family members and to recommend that they be invited, yet the therapist is not expected to decide who is going to attend a given session.

Contextual therapists tend to abide by a regular schedule for the treatment sessions, commonly once a week, for a fixed length of time.

The Case: Work with a Psychotic Client and Her Family

Among the many clinical situations I have encountered over the years, the story of Rita and her family demonstrates best the usefulness of contextual therapy in the treatment of clients with severe mental disorders. It is important for the reader to understand the nature of the therapeutic contract in contextual therapy and how it affects the course of interventions over time. This is why I have chosen to present several short passages of treatment sessions rather than to analyze one from beginning to end.

I would like to thank Rita and her relatives for their cooperation in presenting this chapter. Not only did they give me the authorization to relate their journey from pain toward healing and growth, but they made useful suggestions about my choice of passages to quote. To protect their privacy, I have changed their names and withheld some identifying data. In addition, I have left aside several elements of Rita's treatment that were important at the time but not crucial to the understanding of the sessions presented here.

Background

At the time of the first referral, Rita was a teenager who had two younger siblings, a sister Mary and a little brother Jo. The family had moved recently from a deteriorating ethnic neighborhood to a nice suburb and were well integrated in the new community except for Rita, who complained about missing her old surroundings and friends. Initially, the children attended a parochial school, but Rita requested a transfer to the local public middle school.

Both parents shared the same ethnic background and convictions. The father had his own business and was willing to adjust his schedule to be available to the family. The mother was working part-time and was very devoted to the care of her children. The parents described their marriage as strong and viewed themselves as being a good team when it came to decisions about the children. It was important that they could give more to their children than what they had received while they were growing up.

The mother was the oldest of three siblings. Her sister was married and had two young sons. She was close to Rita's family. Her brother was single and, at the time, unemployed. Rita's grandfather was a hardworking man who was a widower and who did volunteer work after his retirement. He lived part of the time with Rita's family and part of the time with his sister, who never married. This sister had lived with her parents until her mother died of cancer. The grandmother was described as a demanding and somewhat helpless woman who had experienced considerable hardship in her own growing up.

Rita's father was one of many children. His father, who was at times violent to his wife and children, died of alcoholism when Rita's father was 16 years old. Rita's father later developed a strong bond with his mother's partner, who played the role of a surrogate father and who remained a strong role model until his death. Rita's father visited his mother regularly but did not like to spend much time with his siblings. He reported that there was still alcoholism and violence in his family. He was proud of the fact that he did not drink, was even tempered, and was able to be a good parent. He reported feeling closer to his wife's family. Rita's mother also disapproved of the lifestyle of most of her in-laws.

Reason for the Referral

Initially, Rita presented with physical complaints and was treated by her family physician. As she started to isolate herself, to miss school, and to become increasingly depressed, several medical specialists examined her but could not agree about a diagnosis. Eventually, she was referred for a psychological assessment. Shortly after the initial consultation with a psychologist, Rita exhibited bizarre behavior and became increasingly suicidal. She stated that she did not want to live anymore and that her mother should kill her. Her condition deteriorated to the point that it became necessary to admit Rita to a psychiatric facility for her own protection and for a complete evaluation. Her symptoms included depression, compulsive behaviors, visual hallucinations, paranoid thinking, and delusions about imminent catastrophes. I was assigned to her treatment as the attending psychiatrist.

When I first met her parents, they had no idea what was happening to Rita, and they felt helpless in the face of the severity of her symptoms. They had no experience with any kind of therapy and simply hoped that the hospital team would know how to treat their daughter. Moreover, they had no information about contextual therapy. They were eager to cooperate with any treatment, but they could not see in what way talking about themselves and their families of origin could help their daughter get better. Rita was very active during the family therapy sessions and surprised her parents by bringing up several painful subjects from their own life history. Rita's siblings needed reassurance and support.

I had several functions in Rita's treatment. I led the family therapy sessions that were also attended by her social worker, I provided individual psychotherapy sessions in accordance with the unit policies, and I was also the prescribing physician.

Rita experienced negative side effects from her psychotropic medication. Soon it became evident that she had an atypical response to most of the commonly available drugs, which added to her belief that she would never get better.

Rita was also asked to participate in group therapy, and she made efforts to adjust to her peers. Additionally, she learned to rely on the unit staff members for support and reassurance. Progressively, she became less agitated, less delusional, and eventually stable enough to return home. As she appeared too fragile to return to a regular school program, she was referred to a specialized school.

After her discharge, Rita and her family resumed treatment with the referring psychologist, who asked me to remain involved in care. We worked in close collaboration, and I continued to see Rita and her family as needed. Initially Rita did well; however, she deteriorated abruptly during a family vacation. She became depressed, delusional, and agitated and, as a result, was readmitted to the hospital. Several changes were made in her medication without success; she remained delusional and depressed until one day when she developed a surprising response to a new compound. Rita became hypomanic and exhibited significantly increased social interactions with patients on the ward. Her hallucinations stopped and she reported feeling much improved. To everybody's surprise, this change created a crisis for her mother. The mother admitted with a remarkable openness that she was scared by her daughter's change and stressed by Rita's sudden need to meet with new people. After the medication was decreased, Rita returned to a more subdued way of interacting with others that was less challenging to her mother. At the time when Rita returned home, she was much more positive and much less delusional. The crisis had allowed her mother to become more open to the possibility of a connection between her own difficulties and some of Rita's symptoms. This provided a new impetus to the family therapy sessions.

For a period of several months, Rita remained labile, with occasional bouts of hallucinations. She continued to require considerable attention both in school and at home. The treating psychologist felt that Rita was too dependent on her parents for support and needed to develop a capacity to rely on other people. She recommended the involvement of a mobile therapeutic team not only to help Rita at home but also to support her in social activities outside of the home. The intention was to decrease the parents' need to spend all their time supervising her. At first, the family was thrilled with the offer but soon experienced the presence of the mobile therapist as a severe intrusion. This time, the father rejected the treatment recommendation. This resulted in a confrontation with the psychologist, who maintained the position that Rita needed help to become less dependent on the family. The parents then turned to me and asked me to take full charge of Rita's treatment. I was hesitant to accept their request, knowing that the psychologist had a valid concern. Furthermore, I felt that I was not equipped to deal with crisis interventions as well as the mobile team was. In response to my concerns, Rita volunteered a proposal. She would take upon herself to behave appropriately so that the family would not have to call on people for emergency interventions. In return, I would accept sole responsibility for her treatment and for family therapy. I decided to take her offer seriously. I felt that her effort to help the family at a moment of crisis needed to be supported. Since this time, Rita and her family have continued to see me as the sole therapist.

Despite some initial difficulties and brief recurrences of depression and psychosis (mostly during episodes of physical illness), Rita has improved steadily over time. She has now developed into a sophisticated teenager who is a good student and who is holding a part-time job. She is freer to express her concerns directly rather than through her symptoms. Her mother has become more aware of the link between her own parentification and some of the unfair expectations that she was placing on Rita (see session 1). Thanks to Rita's insistence, her father agreed to discuss more openly some aspects of his relationship with his father (see sessions 2 and 3). Both parents continue to require support in addressing issues related to Rita's new claim to independence. Her siblings are well-adjusted youngsters who have been substantially burdened by Rita's illness but who also have enjoyed the benefits of their parents' own growth and improved capacity to see their needs.

Contextual Assessment

The dimension of facts.   As previously mentioned, contextual therapists accept the notion that psychosis and depression have a neurobiological base. Contextual therapists welcome any intervention that can improve factual reality. If the use of psychotropic medications can bring a relief of symptoms, it is encouraged. The same is true of any psychosocial interventions (for example, coordination with the school, participation of the parents in a support group, use of a mobile team, and so on).

The dimension of psychology.   The second dimension of relational determinants is the realm of individual psychotherapy, of the cognitive or insight-oriented kind. Unfortunately, experience shows the limited impact of these approaches during the time when clients experience acute psychosis, as was the case for Rita. Rita's hallucinations are part of a private psychological experience that is not shared by others. Rita's cognitive distortions and, at the time, paranoid thinking were part of this dimension.

Rita's psychosis also brought an arrest to her normal psychological development. In her shattered inner world, there was no place for the emergence of her own adolescent sexuality and no place for the resolution of old oedipal conflicts. Instead of being able to experience ambivalent feelings toward her parents, she had to see them killed in catastrophes and to see herself as an abandoned orphan. As terrifying as these thoughts were, they were less threatening to her than the admission of feelings of jealousy toward her mother and the belief that her mother could retaliate. Given the delusional nature of her thoughts, a direct interpretation of the meaning of her fears would have not reached her. I had to limit my interventions in that dimension to supportive listening as she shared her inner experiences with me. My willingness to hear about her fears and despair without challenging her was reassuring for her and, to that extent, helpful.

The dimension of transactions.   The behavioral and systemic implications of Rita's symptoms were numerous; I will mention only the one that became significant over time. Communication patterns of the family changed when Rita became psychotic. Her psychotic episodes were accompanied by shouting, screaming, cutting people off when they were talking, or conversely trying to hide from any contact with others.

Rita's illness had also changed the boundaries between several subgroups in the family. Rita's mother did not feel comfortable around her in-laws, and conflict had often occurred around the father's need to visit his relatives. As Rita became ill, he had an excuse not to visit them without feeling guilty, which helped decrease some tension between his wife and him. Rita's symptoms also affected the boundaries between her parents and her. She could shut them out completely by her psychotic talking and, to that extent, create an artificial barrier between herself and her parents that substituted for her lack of an age-appropriate differentiation.

Nagy's description of what he calls the "collusive postponement of mourning" was helpful to understand some of the family members' behavior. Any new step in development can trigger an experience of loss, of mourning for the preceding situation in the mind of the person. Nagy observed that family members tend to protect each other from having to face such an experience of loss in a collusive fashion. As one family member becomes ready for a step toward individuation, another family member becomes anxious and responds negatively to the move. Eventually, no one is able to make a genuine step into a new stage of the family life cycle and no one can be individually blamed for causing the observed stagnation. There were many examples of such collusion in Rita's family. Rita stated on many occasions that she would never change to spite her parents; but when she started to improve, they became anxious and indicated that she was improving too rapidly.

Contextual therapists rely on multidirected partiality rather than prescription of behaviors to obtain changes. They deal with the collusion by asking each family member to take a position and to accept responsibility for their contribution to the given situation. In one example pertaining to Rita's medication, her mother was asked to tell Rita that she had asked me to decrease her medication and why she had become anxious. Rita was then asked if she would consider her mother's needs.

The dimension of relational ethics.   The last dimension to examine is relational ethics—the balance of giving and receiving in close relationships. Rita gave many examples of her restrained capacity to give, even at times when she was still delusional. She could also be extremely demanding, mostly toward her siblings. In her case, I suspected that the source of her destructive entitlement did not lie entirely in issues of transgenerational exploitation but partly stemmed from the very fact of being ill. Having to suffer from mental illness, to be different from her peers, and to experience negative side effects of her medications were all injustices caused by no one, but which nonetheless required compensation.

Both parents displayed a genuine devotion to Rita and remained available to each of the children despite the tremendous pressure caused by Rita's psychiatric decompensation. Even so, I noticed some early clues about the mother's possible destructive entitlement when she bluntly stated that she had always assumed that Rita would never grow into an independent adult and never leave home. Her destructive entitlement surfaced again with the issue of Rita's medications. She was implicitly communicating that her needs were more urgent than her daughter's need to improve. She denied having experienced many injustices in her growing up and felt that she was actually treated much better by her parents than was her sister. As I became more familiar with her family history, I was able to understand the sources of her destructive entitlement. Her mother idealized her as the perfect child, which set her apart from her siblings. She was also expected to act as a peacemaker between her mother and her father's single sister, who was living with the family. Both situations amounted to parentification. Rita's mother was now caught between her wish to be available to Rita and her need to be compensated for these past injustices. She was expecting Rita to accommodate her own unmet dependency needs and expected her daughter never to leave her. She was also hoping that Rita would not cause any problems that would force her to once more become a peacemaker. In that sense, Rita's occasional expression of jealousy vis-à-vis her siblings was more threatening to her mother than her delusional talking.

The transgenerational ledger of giving and receiving impacted Rita's father differently. He was generally free to give to his children and there were no obvious indications that he was counting on them to undo past injustices. However, he was not open to discussing his past family experiences with them. Rita was convinced that his exposure to violence when he was a child had affected his capacity to allow his children to express negative feelings and had sensitized him to any expressions of anger. Many times, Rita asked her father to explore these issues, and he remained adamant that he had not suffered from his father's violence. His attitude raised the question of possible invisible loyalty to his own father. Despite the fact that he seemed more loyal to his mother's male friend than to his father, he was ready to fight with his own children to protect his father's image. He refused to condemn him for his violence even at the cost of hurting his daughter. Later, it became more obvious that he had been deprived of a consistent support by his parents and was used as a referee in their fights. It was probably difficult for him to offer an answer to his daughter's questions while he was left alone with his worries when he was a child.

Treatment Plan

For Rita, the original goal of therapy was to achieve a decrease in her symptoms. Later, she expected support in reaching an age-appropriate level of autonomy. For the parents, the original goal was to find ways to help Rita improve and later to address past family issues that could have impacted their manner of parenting. The siblings expected support in their own needs and individuation processes. To reach these goals, I needed to offer partiality to each family member, including the absent and deceased members. This strategy is illustrated in the following session verbatims.

Since autonomy stems from a capacity for both self-delineation and self-validation, each family member was encouraged to take a position and to offer due consideration to others. Both parents needed to discover that they could gain something by allowing Rita to move toward an increased autonomy. What they might lose in Rita's movement toward independence they could gain in an increased self-esteem and freedom for their own lives.

Case Transcript

The following passages demonstrate how to use multidirected partiality to address issues of conflict of interest, destructive entitlement, and invisible loyalties in the course of therapy.

Session 1: Mother and Daughter

Therapist to both mother and daughter: Where are we today?

Rita: I had a good week. In school, I'm doing well. I'm fine. I don't really know what to talk about.

Therapist to Rita: Let me hear your mom.

In asking the parent to describe the current situation, the therapist does not put the child down but instead places the burden of the responsibility for the session on the adults. It also protects the child from having to take a position that could eventually become disloyal to the parent.

Mother: Rita was good for awhile, but we had a bad incident just a few days ago that upset me.

Therapist: What happened?

Mother: I took Rita and Mary to shop at a big outlet, and Rita got so upset on the way back that I'm really worried about her.

Therapist to Rita: Do you know what your mom is talking about?

Rita: Yes, I know what she's talking about, but I'm fine.

Mother to Rita: It's not true. You got very upset and out of control and that's not fine.

Mother to therapist: We spent the afternoon in R_____. Rita had not gone shopping with us there since she got sick. I thought that it would go well, but it didn't. The drive home was horrible; Rita was completely out of control. I was so exhausted when we finally arrived home! Rita fought with her sister the whole time we were driving back. I can't have her around me when I am driving if she can't contain herself.

Therapist: I guess I missed something. What was Rita fighting about?

Rita: We went to see a few places, and my sister spent a lot of time at one place. I asked Mom if I could go on another floor to look for stuff I wanted to buy. She said I had to wait. She didn't want me to leave her. I could have gone there by myself. It's not dangerous.

Mother: Rita, it's a big place; I didn't want you to get lost. Also, I wasn't sure that you would be OK. It was the first time that you were out in such a big place; maybe you could have gotten in a panic once you were alone.

Rita: I know, but I wouldn't have gotten lost. I don't know why I was expected to wait for Mary. You told me that I could buy what I wanted. Mary could have come with me. Why did you let her spend so much time trying to find her stuff? You knew that there would be no time left for my shopping. Why did you let her do what she wanted and not me?

Mother: I didn't want you to leave us. I don't know the place well either, and we could have spent forever trying to find each other. I really thought

that there was enough time for us to go together. I mean it, I didn't know
that the outlet was closing at 6 P.M.

Rita: You knew it!

Mother: No, I did not!

Therapist to Rita: At this point, can you believe your mother?

Rita: Yes, but if she was not sure, she could've asked someone and not allowed my sister to spend all our time looking for her stuff.

Mother: I'm sorry, Rita. I really wanted you to have a good time, and I didn't
think at all that we would be in a time squeeze.

Therapist: Do you believe your mom now?

Rita: I guess.

Therapist: So it doesn't sound to me that your mom wanted your sister to
have a better time than you did.

Rita: I guess.

The therapist expects that members of the family establish their subjective
point of view about the incident and try to clarify the areas of agreement and
disagreement. The goal here is to help each person toward self-delineation and
increased trust. Using multidirected partiality as a tool, the therapist makes
sure that both parties are given a fair chance at presenting their side.

Mother: Even if you didn't believe me then, why did you have to fight with
your sister in the car? Your behavior is not acceptable. I could hardly concentrate on driving. We could have had an accident.

Therapist to mother: How badly were they fighting? Were they hitting each
other?

Mother: No, they were just arguing. It lasted for more than an hour while we
were driving home. Rita couldn't stop. She became so agitated that I told
her that I would ask you about maybe increasing her medication.

Therapist: What do you think, Rita?

Rita: I already told you, I'm fine, and I don't like when my mom talks like
that. Finally, I'm not scared to go out anymore and she is angry with me.

Therapist to Rita: Honestly, were you starting to slip, to get agitated like you
can be sometimes? Your mother talked about maybe increasing your medication. Do you feel that you were starting to hallucinate again?

Here the therapist is partial to the mother by taking her concerns seriously.
At the same time, the therapist tries to give Rita the chance to define her own
position. This is another example of multidirected partiality. The therapist is not
frightened to discuss the issue of Rita's psychosis directly. In doing so, the therapist offers her partiality to Rita and respects her as a responsible human being.
Failing to discuss this subject openly with her would amount to considering her
too sick a person to have an opinion.

In asking this question, the therapist moves into both dimension 1 (facts)
and dimension 4 (relational ethics). The therapist wants to know if indeed Rita
could benefit from an increase of her medication (dimension 1) and extends her
trust and consideration to Rita (dimension 4).

Rita: No, I'm not getting sick again, I was just mad.

Mother: She couldn't control herself.

Therapist to mother: Do you agree that Rita wasn't getting psychotic again but that she was just mad?

Mother: That's right, she wasn't hallucinating like she does sometimes.

Therapist to mother: I know that you can handle Rita's hallucinations. Now you're asking me to maybe increase her medication around a more trivial issue. Granted that driving the car with the two girls bickering in the back isn't pleasant. Is it something to worry about? It sounds to me that it was quite an event that the three of you could go shopping together after such a long time when Rita refused to go anywhere.

Mother to therapist: I agree with you that I should be happy that Rita has come out of her shell. But she should be able to control her temper and be reasonable with her sister. I guess it's more difficult for me to deal with Rita when she's angry than when she's sick. When she's sick, I feel bad for her and I have a lot of patience. When she feels better, I expect more from her.

Mother to Rita: I should not have to deal with your fighting. You should be reasonable enough to not argue with your sister.

Therapist: Well, you just said that you expect more from her. Is it entirely fair, or are you expecting too much? I assume that any mother at some point would have to cut in and tell both girls to chill. Granted, it would be nice it they could have cooled down by themselves, although I'm not sure it's realistic to expect it.

Mother: I don't want to blame it all on Rita. Mary could have stopped too.

Therapist: I suppose so, but she has taken in a lot over the last years, and I could see her not being willing to budge. To me the issue is still, Who is responsible for setting a limit to the fighting, you or either of them?

Mother: I guess you are right; I should have said something myself.

Therapist: What blocked you from that?

Mother: I'm not sure. I was counting on Rita to stop by herself.

After helping mother and daughter clarify their positions, the therapist now explores what could be the source of the mother's blindness to her daughter's obvious need to be redirected. Rather than blaming her for her shortcomings or prescribing new behaviors, the therapist offers partiality to the mother by exploring the possible origins of her difficulties.

Therapist to mother: Well, is something missing in the picture? You agree that Rita is doing much better than you expected. Yet you're angry because she doesn't behave like you expected, and it hurts you. What's that? I start to think about what you told me about your growing up. I remember what you told me about you as a peacemaker, about being expected to listen to both your mother and your aunt and help them get along.

Mother: I remember that we talked about it. I don't see what it has to do with Rita and Mary in the car. I was a peacemaker, but it was like a second nature for me. It didn't bother me.

Therapist: You told me that it was easier for you when Rita had hallucinations than now that she's just fighting with her sister.

Mother: Yes, I didn't have to take sides; I knew that what she was saying wasn't for real, even when she was accusing her sister.

Therapist: If acting as a peacemaker is like a second nature for you, what bothered you that day? I start to wonder how often you did wish that someone else could have taken the burden of dealing with your mom and aunt when they were fighting; how much it hurt you that your father didn't try to protect you and didn't try to settle things between your mom and your aunt.

Mother: I never thought of it that way.

Therapist: Still you wished that Rita would stop her badgering so that you didn't have to become a referee between her and her sister.

Mother: I agree, it's how I felt.

Therapist: You sound like someone who has served her years of duty and deserves to retire or maybe like someone who had already served a round and doesn't want to be called back to the service a second time.

Mother: This is a funny idea.

Therapist: Is that how it feels?

Mother: You're right, it does.

Therapist: Well, it seems that now what happened on the trip makes sense. So we're pretty far away from where we started, including the discussion of the medication. My question would be just the same: Who carries the burden of stopping the acting-out? Do you have to tell Rita to calm down, or is it Rita, in trying to cool off maybe by having to take more medication? I don't know what is fair.

Here the therapist has moved the discussion of medication into the dimension of relational ethics. Contextual therapists who handle factual elements (medications, case management) must remember to explore the impact of each new move on the balance of giving and receiving between the family members. The therapist wants to offer the mother a new opportunity for earning entitlement, not just to decide from an objective point of view whether an increase of medication is justified.

Mother: I was very worried, but now I see why I was so angry. I see now that what happened has nothing to do with the medication.

Therapist: OK, then you two agree that there is no need for a change right now.

Mother: Yes.

Rita: I told you that I'm fine.

Therapist to mother: Coming back to what happened to you when you were a child, I can see that you would deserve some kind of retirement for having been available to your mother and aunt for all these years. The only problem is that Rita shouldn't have to worry about what happened to you in the past. She has a right to expect you to step in and help her when she struggles with her sister.

Rita: Yes, I think so. I wasn't doing anything wrong; I was just arguing with
   Mary, and you shouldn't have gotten angry with me.
Therapist to mother: I don't know what you two can do about this. This is the
   trap. No matter what you try, it will end up unfair. If Rita has to behave
   extra reasonably, it isn't fair to her and, on the other hand, if you accept to
   step in, you will have to do more than has been done for you.

The therapist has pointed out the injustice that was incurred in the mother's
growing up. Having been exploited, she is entitled to compensation. This entitlement is destructive because when the mother expects Rita to stop fighting
(which is the mother's need), she overlooks Rita's own entitlement to be addressed as a teenager rather than a responsible adult. The therapist acknowledges the impasse. The damage to the mother's justice cannot be undone. If she
renounces turning to Rita for compensation, she forgoes her chances for a fair
balance of giving and receiving. On the other hand, by relying on her destructive entitlement, she loses the option to give to Rita and to earn constructive entitlement by meeting Rita's own needs. The therapist helps her to consider both
options and their consequences. If the mother can become more generous to
Rita, what she loses in direct repayment for what she did in the past she would
gain in self-respect and inner freedom. It is her chance now to depart from her
reliance on destructive entitlement and to discover that she can also receive
from giving.

Mother: I can see it now, but I never thought about it before. It's true that I
   expect Rita not to cause troubles for me, but you're right; she should not
   have to be good just because of me.
Therapist to Rita: Now, do you understand where your mom is coming from?
Rita: I guess.
Therapist to Rita: Now, could you find ways to help your mom?
Rita: I could try to listen better to my mom.
Therapist: It sounds right to me; let me ask you mom. Would you be willing
   to tell Rita when things bother you and let her know that you would like
   her to listen to you?
Mother: Maybe it will be easier for me not to get upset now that I under-
   stand better what hurt me. I will try to tell her what I need before getting
   angry.
Therapist: It sounds good to me. Even just telling her that you're annoyed is
   giving her more than waiting for her to cool off by herself.

We know that children, bound to their parents by loyalty, may choose to
sacrifice their own interest for the interest of their parents. It is realistic to believe that Rita could meet her mother's need to avoid conflicts by regressing
into psychosis. No parents like to think that they wish for their child to be sick,
but here Rita's mother is surprisingly open to the fact that she indeed tolerated
Rita's hallucinations better than her bickering. Rita is therefore at risk of having to regress into psychosis to meet her mother's needs. The contextual therapist, instead of fighting against the parents on the child's behalf and blaming

the parents for their noxious influence, tries to offer partiality to both parents and children. The mother has a need that cannot be ignored but can be destructive for Rita. Rita is helped to see her mother's predicament so that she can exonerate her mother. In accepting the therapist's offer to try to understand her mother, Rita is giving to her. Later Rita is helped to find ways to remain available to her mother without sacrificing her own growth. Exploring ways by which a child can remain loyal to the parents via active and realistic giving rather than passive surrendering of growth is a core strategy in contextual therapy. Loyalty as an underlying determinant of parent and child relationships cannot be counteracted simply by asking the child not to care about the parents. Furthermore, the child would be caught in a loyalty conflict between the parents, who expect filial loyalty, and the therapist, who expects the child to choose for independence. In asking Rita to think about ways that she could help her mother, the therapist avoids both traps. Rita needs to see that her therapist is not an enemy of her mother and, at the same time, she should be able to see the therapist as an ally who supports her growth. By asking Rita to take the initiative in trying to meet her mother's needs, Rita is free to explore ways to meet her mother's needs that are compatible with her own interests. In choosing to meet some of her mother's needs, she earns entitlement and self-validation. This will help her in the move toward autonomy. In this instance, the therapist offers partiality to Rita in two ways: first, by asking her mother to consider Rita's needs (partiality based on the right of a person to receive) and later by offering Rita a chance to earn constructive entitlement (partiality based on the right to give).

Session 2: Parents, Rita and her siblings

Therapist: I'm glad to see all of you today. We talked for awhile about this session.

Therapist to Jo and Mary: You haven't been here in a long while. I know that you don't like to come here, but do you understand why you were invited?

Jo: Yeah! Mom told us to come to discuss how Rita is doing now. I don't want to stay for the session; I would like to read in the waiting room.

Therapist: If you want, but it's your chance now to tell us if you need something, and if you're in the waiting room we may talk about you, about things that could be improved between all of you, and you won't be able to have a voice. So maybe it is better if you stay for the whole time. You decide.

This is an example of the therapist's respect for each client's position, even when the client is a child. The therapist does not expect the parents to take a position at this juncture but indicates simply that Jo has to face the consequences of his choice. If the parents decide to override the child's choice, it is their privilege, but in turn, they would be expected to take responsibility for their preference.

Therapist to the parents: I'm telling Jo what I see, but I didn't ask you. Is it OK for Jo to stay with us for awhile and leave later if he wants to, or did you expect something specific from him?

Father: Nothing definite; he can leave later if he wants to.

Therapist to Mary: How are you doing?

Mary: Good. I get along better with my sister; she's also nice with my friends.

Therapist: I remember that you got hurt several times because they were asking you about her, maybe making fun of her. I also remember that sometimes she was rude to them. You're telling me that things are better now.

Rita: I try to be nice to them. Sometimes I'm jealous because I don't have friends and she has so many.

Therapist: Are you making some friends at the gym?

Rita: Not really; I'm the youngest and all the others are adults. I wish there were people my age.

Mother: I've told Rita to invite her cousin. They could go shopping together.

Rita: Mom, this is true but she lives far away. She can't visit very often.

Mother: She could take the bus.

Rita: Anyway, I wish I had friends near my home like my sister has.

Therapist to Rita: It's good that your mom is trying to help you. Maybe she will come up with other ideas. Let me ask your brother how he's doing in school these days.

Jo: Good, but sometimes I have trouble with my homework.

Rita: Since Mom comes back from work later, I help him.

Therapist: How does it work?

Jo: I like when she helps me! Before she would always need Mom and now it is different. Now she also plays with me.

Therapist: It sounds like things are moving along pretty nicely. Let me now ask your parents. What would you like to discuss today?

Father: I agree that Rita is much nicer with them. She really makes efforts to help them, but I don't like the way she treats her mother; sometimes she's very rude to her.

Mother: It's not that bad.

Father: It doesn't matter. She shouldn't be disrespectful. I don't want to hear her yelling.

Rita: Dad, I don't yell.

Father: Yes, you do.

Rita: Don't yell at me now.

Father: I'm not yelling, Rita. I don't like your attitude.

Rita: I'm frightened of you when you talk to me like that.

Father: Frightened of what? Doc, how can she talk like that?

Rita: I am frightened of you because you were abused.

Father: What are you talking about? First, I don't like when you tell me that I was abused. It's not true. That my dad hit me a few times is not abuse.

Therapist: Do you understand what upset her?

Father: I don't know what this has to do with my family. She's rude to her mother, and I don't want this. This talking about my father is a cop-out.

Rita: I can't trust my dad. He says he's not violent, but I'm afraid of him. [cries] He tries to say that he didn't suffer from what his dad did to him. I don't believe him. It means that he doesn't see what violence is and that's scary. Dad, I am afraid of you! [She screams again.]

Father: Rita, this is ridiculous. Doc, I have never hit anybody, and I'm the calmest person you can think of.

Rita: [screaming] See, it's not true. You can't discuss anything without yelling at me. I'm scared. Why do you do that? [Her face changes, she looks terrified and runs out of the room. She is now clearly responding to internal stimuli. Her siblings leave the room too, trying to help her, and her brother looks upset by the situation.]

Father: Do you see this, doctor? It's ridiculous, I cannot believe that she really means what she says. She's still sick.

Therapist: Well, would you gain to try understanding Rita's questions?

Father: What questions? I'm here for her treatment, not to talk about my father.

Rita has slipped into a psychotic agitation. This tells the therapist about the level of stress raised by that question and about Rita's remaining areas of fragility. In addition, is she now invisibly loyal to her father? Openly, she wants to expose his childhood, which is disloyal to him. In screaming and running away, she makes it difficult for anyone to pursue the issue that she has just raised, which indicates that she is indirectly willing to protect her father. The therapist is not discouraged by a moment of disorganization and tries to keep the focus on the original subject raised by Rita. In doing so, the therapist offers partiality to Rita despite the fact that she is absent from the room. Rita deserves the therapist's partiality because she is both the most courageous and the most vulnerable. The offer of partiality does not reward behaviors (that is, who behaves better or who tries to get the therapist's attention) but genuine contributions to the ethical balance. Rita is out of control. She does not deserve special attention for this but for her contribution in trying to help her father.

Therapist to father: I know that you don't like to discuss the past, but it might help Rita if she could ask her questions. In any case, I would like to tell you that we aren't here to blame your dad, to point the finger at him, but to understand his side too and to help Rita.

The therapist offers to base this exploration on loyalty rather than disloyalty to the deceased grandfather, hoping that this would enable the father to be open without having to become disloyal and to feel less guilty for revealing his own father's shortcomings to others. Here the therapist indicates her partiality to Rita, to her father, and to her grandfather.

Father: Do you really believe that it would help her if I were to tell her more about my childhood? I don't even know what I would tell her. She knows what happened to me already. I said it right here a long time ago.

Therapist: Well, this is what she is telling you. If you were willing to listen to her, I think it could help her to at least understand her questions. She is obviously very upset, and even if we are on a wrong track, it's worth trying.

Therapist to Rita (who has returned to the room with Mary and Jo):   I'm still talking with your dad about what you asked.

Father: I really don't believe that the whole thing makes any sense, but I if you think that it could make a difference for her it's OK. Would it really make a difference for you, Rita?

Rita: [still very loud] Yes!

Father: I have already told you many times that for me it doesn't change anything. I'm over it. I don't want to dwell on this. First, my dad was only violent when he was drunk. Otherwise, he was all right. It's just sad that he had to drink that much.

Therapist: I'm starting to think that it's not such a good idea to discuss your dad too much now. I'm sure that you wouldn't like us to judge him. As I told you before, I would like us to understand his side too.

The therapist lets Rita know that she cares about the grandfather's side and that she is going to move toward helping family members to exonerate him. The severity of the grandfather's pathologies is already known. The therapist can help the family members to discover redeeming elements in him and move toward exoneration and acceptance of a sad reality rather than anger or denial.

Mother to father: I think it would be good if you could talk about this. From seeing your brothers and how they behave, I'm sure that there was a lot going on, and I wonder what it has done to you.

Therapist to father: I'm worried now that everyone wants to push you and maybe it puts you in the middle. I remember you mentioned that it bothers you when your wife criticizes your family. You became defensive when she talked about them. It might be better for everybody to keep the discussion of your dad between you and the kids. Sometimes it is hard to talk about bad aspects of one's family even in front of a spouse, but children are born into it, so it is different for them.

Therapist to mother: How would you feel if we keep this discussion for a separate time?

Mother: I'm fine either way. I have no problems with that.

In general, it is advisable to discuss the shameful elements of an individual's family of origin only among family members who share the same loyalty context, not with spouses who are not part of it. Spouses would also hear information that they could use against one another, for instance, in a divorce. The initiative of a disclosure to a spouse should remain in the hands of the clients, not with the therapist.

Therapist to Mary and Jo: If Rita and your dad start to talk about his father, would you like to be included too?

Mary and Jo share the same loyalty context. Therefore, they should be invited even if they are not interested but, as indicated above, allowed to decline the invitation. If there is a risk that the children might end up caught between the parent who is present and the one who is absent, this would have to be addressed in advance by both parents. Here the mother has enough maturity and enough trust in her husband to accept that exclusion. She also recognizes that her negative attitude toward her husband's family of origin could block him from revealing more about his relatives.

Mary: No, I don't care. I know that my dad is completely different from his dad.

Jo: I feel the same. I don't understand why it's important for Rita.

Therapist: OK, if this is what you want, I'll see Rita and your dad next week and later we'll ask you if you're interested to hear about our meeting. Let's continue now with any other point that should be discussed today.

Session 3: Rita and father

Therapist: I'm glad to see you both. Did you discuss today's session before coming?

Father: No; I still am not sure why Rita wants me to talk about all that stuff in the past. I already told you that I'm not angry because of what happened with my dad. He didn't hit me more than just a few times, and after I got stronger than he was, he didn't even try anymore. He only did it when he was drunk. He was nasty then, but otherwise he wasn't a bad person. I have forgiven him. I was only 16 when he died, and my mother's friend treated me like a son. I was working for him [his mother's male friend] after school, and we got along great. It wasn't an easy life all the time, but he was good to me. I did miss him a lot when he died. Rita knows that. She doesn't remember him much, but he was like a real grandfather to her too. He never married my mother, but it made no difference for me.

Therapist: I hear what you say, but I now wonder about something else, how it was for you when your mom and her partner talked about your dad? Were they negative about him?

Father: They never criticized him. Sometimes, I had to protect my mom because my dad would start swinging at her, but after he died, she never talked about that anymore.

Therapist: I would be interested to know more about your dad's side. What happened to him that he ended up drinking that much?

The therapist wants to explore the possible sources of the grandfather's destructive entitlement that could account for his lack of sensitivity to others. To be able to be partial to the grandfather, the therapist needs to find elements of his life that can deserve consideration. Finding them would also allow Rita's father not simply to forgive the grandfather but also to truly exonerate him.

Father: I don't know too much about this. He was an only child when his dad died when he was about 4 years old.

Therapist: So you didn't grow up having a grandfather? What about your grandmother?

Father: She lived much longer, but nobody liked her. My mother didn't like her at all.

Therapist: Do you know why?

Father: In my dad's family, people used to say that she killed her husband!

Therapist: What did you make of it? Do you believe it yourself?

Father: She didn't really kill him like if she had shot him or something like that, but what she did was very bad. He was called to the army, and he lied so he didn't have to go. She gave him away, and he was picked up. He caught something at the army camp and died right away from disease. All his family blamed it on her. After that, there was a complete cut-off.

Therapist: It's a terrible story, and at this point it's hard to figure out what was really happening between her and her husband that made her do that. Do you have any clues about how it affected your dad? He wasn't just an orphan, but was he told that his mother was accused of a quasi murder? She did raise your dad, didn't she?

Father: I knew that story, so obviously he knew it too. Yes, she raised him.

Therapist: It must have been horrible for your dad to be caught in that. Hard for him to figure out who was telling the truth. I suppose that his mom had her own version of the story. She must have been quite desperate to end up denouncing the father of her own child. Do you have any thoughts about her side of the story?

Father: Not really, I just heard that his mother must have been quite awful, that is all.

At this point, the therapist sees split loyalty as a major factor at the origin of the grandfather's destructive entitlement. She wonders about his alcoholism as a response to deepen his despair over his origins, between a good-for-nothing father, as his mother must have described him, and a mother who people thought of as a criminal.

Therapist: I wonder how much this story contributed to your dad's drinking. He must have been caught in a horrible place, between a mother who must have tried to justify what she did and his dad's family who were telling him that she was a murderer. Even you talk about her like that. How could your dad not be caught? I don't know him, but it must have damaged him a lot. Who could he trust? By comparison, what happened to you while you were growing up was less tragic.

Father: I never thought about this part of his life. I guess you're right.

Therapist: In your case, things were not as bad, but maybe there were some similarities. When people were pointing the finger at your dad because he was a drunk, did you have to defend him? You certainly defended him last week.

Father: I never thought of that.

Therapist: Now, you told me last time that your mom didn't tell you bad things about him after he died. How was it earlier?

Father: I don't remember. I told you that when my dad was drunk, he could swing at my mom and it was a mess. We had to protect her and stop him from beating her. When he didn't drink, he was a nice guy. My mom never badmouthed him in front of us. I don't even think she would have divorced him if he'd lived longer. It's funny, something comes back to my mind about the way she used to talk about him. We had a talking bird at home, and it would imitate her; it would say "God bless you, John." It was so weird.

Therapist: It sounds like the bird was imitating your mom being sarcastic with your dad. What do you make of it?

Father: I guess that it was sarcastic.

Therapist to Rita: The bird must have heard your grandmom many times to be able to imitate her so well.

Rita: It's funny, a bird talking like that!

Therapist: It is quite a story. Now back to you. Do you believe that your mom was indeed sarcastic with your dad? To that extent, could you have been caught in the middle? In your eyes, I guess from what you told me, she was the victim in many ways. Did you feel bad for your dad also?

Father: I can't remember, but it's possible. I told you already, I don't remember very much.

The story of the bird gives the therapist some clues about the grandmother's possible contempt vis-à-vis the grandfather. Was the father caught in a predicament of split loyalty between his father and mother? Was his capacity to trust damaged by his parents' mistrust of each other? Was it the issue of mistrust between his parents that possibly blocked him from giving freely to either of them? To that extent, the father was right to state that the violence in the family was not a major issue for him. Rita's father was very reliable and trustworthy, but he had a tendency to count only on himself and to avoid asking anyone for help. Could this have been linked to a damaged capacity to trust?

Therapist: Do you remember times when you were lonely, when you were alone with your bad feelings? Who could you count on to tell when you were feeling upset?

The therapist tries to find out who was available for the father, who he was able to trust at the time.

Father: So many things come back to my mind today. I haven't thought about this in years, but I used to listen to songs. I had one favorite singer, and I was listening to him all the time. When I think of it, it's almost like he raised me, like he was a father to me. Doc, you should listen to some of his stuff. He had great songs. You should listen to some of them.

Therapist: Well, I hardly know any songs, but I would be interested to know what was in the content that you found so much connection with.

Therapist to Rita: Do you know this singer? Did your dad tell you about him?

Rita: No, but it makes me feel good. I'm glad for him that he had something he liked.

Therapist to Rita: How are things now? Do you feel better, or are you still scared that something about your dad's growing up could hurt you?

The therapist returns to Rita's initial request and gives her some space after the long time spent discussing her father's family of origin. She has received a lot through the father's willingness to explore the past. Clients learn that each person will be offered consideration in due time and they don't need to be concerned about the fact that a good part of a session can be spent on one person. Here it is even difficult to tell who had benefited the most from the earlier sessions. Did the father receive more because he was able to discover some avenues to exonerate his father and in doing so to earn entitlement? Did Rita receive more by hearing a lot of information about her father's family and his childhood? Would this knowledge help her to exonerate not only the grandfather who she saw up to now as the culprit but her father too? Could she now better accept some of her father's own limitations, for instance, his difficulty relying on others for help?

Rita: No, my dad doesn't scare me anymore. I'm glad, now I know my dad better. It feels good.

Therapist: Maybe your dad was right. The violence didn't bother him. Do you think that the feeling that he was cut off from his dad could have hurt him more than the fear of being hit? In that sense, it might be true that his mom's partner did make up for what he missed to a point, at least by being a good role model.

Rita: Yes.

Father: It sounds right, missing a role model that I feel bad about. I won't dwell on it, but it did hurt me.

Therapist: I'm impressed by the way you handled it, the idea you had of relying on those songs for direction in your life. It sounded almost like you were talking things over with this singer, like if he was a father to you too.

Therapist: All right! Let's finish. [to father] I'm sorry that Jo wasn't here today. It would've given him a new sense of you as a man. I'm sure that Mary would be interested too. Can you share some of what we discussed with them?

Father: Sure.

Therapist: It doesn't have to be in a session at this point. Well, without Rita's insistence, all this could have been missed.

Father: I know, doc, you're right! [laughs] [to Rita] It's true, there were things that I didn't remember, like how much I was relying on the songs, and I still listen to them; they still mean a lot to me.

Therapist to father: I'm glad you could talk about that part of your life. In addition, I feel that Rita is a lot better today. It was good that you could answer her questions.

Therapist: Some other thoughts may come to your mind later. For the time being, I'd be interested to hear if you would like to discuss other things.

Conclusions

In order to understand and design therapeutic interventions, most if not all other schools of therapy would follow the line of pathology to design the therapeutic agenda and the strategies used to reach that goal. The therapist would have approached the family through the pathology of behavioral patterns and would have tried to change them via strategies that vary from one school to the other. For instance, Rita's father could be seen as a captive of a two-generational pattern of parental abuse that could be diminished through insight and open revelation between father and daughter.

By contrast, contextual therapy does not focus on pathology but on the utilization of relational resources, that is, the exploration of possibility for each family member to earn entitlement through appropriate giving. Options for giving that have not yet been addressed are explored, with the therapist encouraging each family member to consider the interest of the other, for the benefit of the receiver. Pathology is addressed only indirectly. As people move through this process, they discover that they can reach a more satisfying level of functioning by giving consideration to others rather than in relying on their pathology to manipulate relationships. Contextual therapists strengthen relationships mainly through enabling family members to give and earn entitlement of a constructive nature.

In the last example, it is conceivable that Rita's grandfather's alleged violence was not as detrimental for her father as Rita believed but that her father incurred damage by being blocked in his capacity for open giving to his father due to a constellation of split loyalty. His daughter's urging and repeated questioning of the grandfather's attitude enabled the father to defend (give to) his father and to explore the sources of the grandfather's own destructiveness. Such efforts at exonerating a parent's own parents often lead to a broad-based earning of constructive entitlement by several family members. Ultimately, the greatest relief that children can find lies in the exoneration of their parents in their own eyes (Boszormenyi-Nagy and Spark 1973).

Study Questions

1. What is the main strategy utilized by contextual therapists?
2. What is your understanding of the concept of destructive entitlement?
3. Explain the relationship between parentification and destructive entitlement.
4. What interventions would be relevant to decrease the impact of parentification over several generations?
5. What does contextual therapy mean by the principle of "receiving through giving"? How is this related to the possibility of reaching autonomy?

References

Boszormenyi-Nagy, I. (1978). Contextual therapy: Therapeutic leverages in mobilizing trust. *The American family*. Report number 2. New York: Smith Kline and French Laboratories.

Boszormenyi-Nagy, I. (1987). *Foundations of contextual therapy: The collected papers of Ivan Boszormenyi-Nagy*. New York: Brunner/Mazel.

Boszormenyi-Nagy, I., & Framo, J. (1965). *Intensive family therapy.* New York: Harper and Row. (Reprint: Brunner/Mazel (1985).)

Boszormenyi-Nagy, I., & Krasner, B. R. (1986). *Between give and take: A clinical guide to contextual therapy.* New York: Brunner/Mazel.

Boszormenyi-Nagy, I., & Spark, G. (1973). *Invisible loyalties.* New York: Harper and Row. (Reprint: Brunner/Mazel (1984).)

Goldenberg, H., & Goldenberg, I. (1991). *Family therapy: An overview.* Pacific Grove, CA: Brooks/Cole.

Chapter Two

Integrated Intergenerational Family Therapy

David M. Lawson

Systemic family therapies view family problems as being influenced by interactions between family members (Goldenberg and Goldenberg, 1996). However, the various therapies place different emphases on which family members should constitute the focal family configuration for therapy. Family-of-origin approaches such as Bowen systems theory (Kerr and Bowen, 1988) and Williamson's intergenerational family therapy (1991) focus on relationships across and between the generations. Relational patterns are regarded as learned and transmitted across the generations, influencing present interactive patterns (Harvey and Bray, 1991). More specifically, the manner by which people relate occurs because of overt and covert influences and attributions by other family members. Specific behaviors become refined and regulated through reinforcement and modeling within the family (Harvey and Bray, 1991). Moreover, the influence of family members continues with or without contact with the family (Williamson, 1991). Thus, assessment and interventions focus on relationship patterns within and between family members and generations.

The therapy model utilized in this paper is an integrated intergenerational family therapy approach, largely based on the work of Bowen (1978), Williamson (1991), and Beck (1976). To a lesser degree, an interpersonal processing orientation is utilized on occasion (Teyber, 1992). Bowen's position that therapists remain emotionally low key in order to minimize emotional reactivity is employed more flexibly in the current integrated model. Emotions are viewed as critical indicators of clients' internal relational maps as well as important vehicles for change (Greenberg and Johnson, 1988). As a result, interventions are more active and directive than those espoused by Bowen.

Williamson's methods (1991) (for example, umailed letters, taped meetings with parents, conjoint sessions with parents) are utilized in preparation for conjoint sessions with clients and their parents and later for conducting the conjoint sessions. The tenets and methodologies of cognitive therapy (Beck, 1976; Bedrosian and Bozicas, 1994) (for example, collaborative empiricism, Socratic dialogue, guided discovery) are employed to assist clients in becoming aware of and changing problematic beliefs that were often rooted in learnings from their family of origin. The integration of elements from these approaches is based on the view that family dynamics directly influence the development of an individual's beliefs and personal story about self, others, the world, and relationships (Bedrosian and Bozicas, 1994; Williamson, 1991). Conversely, problematic relationship patterns are viewed as being influenced and maintained by distorted beliefs, which in turn are influenced by the individual's current emotional state and experiential organization; thus, interactions, cognitions, and emotions are viewed as mutually influencing one another.

Although limited, research regarding the effectiveness of intergenerational family therapy provides initial support for its effectiveness. Of particular relevance is the finding that intergenerational family therapy provides significantly more positive changes between clients and their parents than other systems approaches (Williamson, 1982; Bray, Williamson, and Malone, 1986). Conversely, cognitive therapy has a well-documented history of effectiveness with a variety of problems across many contexts (Baucom and Epstein, 1990; Hollon and Najavitis, 1988). Even though research pertaining to the integration of intergenerational family and cognitive approaches to therapy is largely nonexistent, the utilization of various family-of-origin concepts with cognitive therapy concepts is common in the literature (for example, Bedrosian and Bozicas, 1994; Lawson, 1996; Pinsof, 1995). Undoubtedly, continued and productive utilization of these approaches in combination will necessitate a body of research.

Theoretical Underpinnings

The intergenerational family view is based on the work of Williamson (1991), who was influenced by the work of Bowen (1978). Williamson extends the work and focus of Bowen's basic concepts, emphasizing the importance of individuation from parents or primary caregivers while simultaneously maintaining a voluntary connection with them. Many individual and family problems are the result of inappropriate relationships between younger adults and their parents. From a developmental perspective, the fourth and fifth decades of life are seen as significant periods for the development of a healthy balance between individuation and intimacy in significant relationships with parents (Williamson, 1991). A failure to achieve this balance for adults during this time indicates a dysfunctional hierarchy in the intergenerational family system (Bray, Williamson, and Malone, 1983). The intergenerational family constructs that have particular significance to the following case study are individuation, fusion, intimacy, triangulation, intimidation, and personal authority.

Individuation is similar to Bowen's concept of differentiation and refers to an individual's ability to invest himself or herself emotionally while functioning autonomously within an interpersonal context (Bowen, 1978; Bray and Williamson, 1987). Individuated persons are able to take control of their own thoughts and feelings, consider their judgment as an adequate basis for action, and take full responsibility. Individuation also includes the notion of intimacy with others or autonomy with voluntary closeness. Fusion is the opposite of individuation and describes people who lack a clear sense of self, are overly dependent on others, and are emotionally reactive. Personal authority is a more advanced type of individuation that is characterized by a peerlike relationship between the young adult and parents while simultaneously acting from a differentiated position.

In order to attain personal authority, adults must discontinue the hierarchical boundary between themselves and their parents and thus address intergenerational intimidation, which maintains the power inequity between the parent and the younger adult that is rooted in childhood dependency on the parent for physical and psychological needs (Williamson, 1991). Intergenerational intimidation and fusion are manifested behaviorally in triangulation, in which two people (for example, a couple) who are unsuccessful in negotiating intimacy or conflict involve a third party, often a child, to decrease the tension between the two of them. Failure to resolve triangulation patterns typically leads to lower levels of differentiation for the three participants and greater difficulty functioning in other intimacy-demanding relationships.

At the cognitive level, adults hold both positive and negative beliefs about their family-of-origin relationships (Williamson, 1991). These beliefs tend to engage without deliberation, and if unchallenged, they are often accepted uncritically as fact. Maladaptive beliefs act to distort current relationships to fit previously learned relationship patterns from the individual's family of origin (Bedrosian and Bozicas, 1994). However, individuals are often less attuned to these beliefs and more attuned to their immediate emotional experience.

In addition, many of these emotional experiences are central to affectional attachments between people. Therefore, they often act as barometers indicating a person's sense of security and trust in relationships (Shaver, Hazan, and Bradshaw, 1988). Taken together, clients' patterned thinking and affective experiences offer a salient assessment context as well as a vehicle for changing problematic behaviors that are relationally oriented.

The assessment process for the integrated family therapy approach is viewed as an ongoing, integral part of therapy. Standard family-of-origin assessment methods and instruments, such as the genogram (McGoldrick and Gerson, 1985), the family autobiography, and the Personal Authority in the Family System Questionnaire (Bray, Williamson, and Malone, 1984), may be utilized as the therapist becomes more focused on family-of-origin issues. However, these means of assessment are not necessarily employed with every client. A variety of other instruments can be employed (for example, the Beck Anxiety

Inventory, Beck Depression Inventory, Inventory of Interpersonal Problems, and Brief Symptom Inventory) and interpreted within a family/relational context.

The following case presentation illustrates various aspects of the integrated intergenerational family approach to therapy, including aspects of the underlying theories and representative interventions.

The Case: A Single Parent with Depression and Anxiety

A 38-year-old female, Sue, initially presented for therapy with stress-related symptoms (for example, sleep and eating disturbance, vascular headaches, hypervigilance) as well as depression, anxiety, being overweight, and having parenting difficulties. Sue had been an elementary schoolteacher for 12 years.

The exacerbation of these symptoms coincided with the initiation of divorce proceedings by Sue with Ray, her husband of 17 years. Ray had recently moved out of the home, leaving Sue and her 10-year-old son Jason and 7-year-old daughter Lisa. She reported that she and her husband had struggled in their relationship for the last ten years. She attributed much of their conflict to his abuse of alcohol and his lack of involvement in the family. His alcoholism had also interfered with his career advancements and salary increases over the years, often contributing to financial strain for the family. Sue also reported that Jason had become less interested in his academic work, resulting in B's and C's rather than his usual A's. In addition, Jason was engaging in more noncompliant behavior with regard to her disciplinary actions. Lisa reported less pervasive symptoms than either Sue or Jason but experienced some disruption in her sleeping and eating routine.

In addition to these problems, Sue had lost her mother, Joan, to a stroke less than a year before and was continuing to struggle with her grief over this loss. Her father, Albert, was currently in the process of selling the house in which Sue and her sibling had been raised and moving to a retirement center because of his failing health.

Sue's results on the Brief Symptom Inventory indicated scores in the clinical range on somatization, depression, anxiety, and interpersonal relationships. The PAFS-Q was administered after the second session and indicated a high degree of fusion with her parents, a consistent tendency to utilize triangulation with her children, and a high degree of personal intimidation experienced with respect to her parents.

Sue attended the first four sessions individually. Other sessions included her children and, toward the end of therapy, two sessions with her father for a total of 22 sessions.

The following verbatims are excerpts from approximately five months of weekly therapy with Sue and various members of her family.

Therapist: I know you shared a little bit about your situation on the phone, but I'm wondering if you could provide some more detail for me.

Sue: Sometimes I feel anxious, depressed, and just out of control. I mean, it's been really hard with the situation with Ray and all.

Therapist: You seem to be getting more anxious just talking about it. [pause] Can you tell me a little more about the situation with Ray?

Sue: He's why I'm so anxious and just kinda uncertain. We've been married 17 years and it's just not working out. His drinking has been a problem for a long time. I've put up with it for almost ten years. He's lived with us; he just hasn't been much of a husband or father. I've tried and tried to get him into counseling with me or even by himself over the years. He's just refused to do anything. He tried kicking the drinking on his own, but he just can't do it for long. I've filed for divorce. I just hope I've done the right thing with the divorce and all.

Therapist: You feel you've tried your best, but it just hasn't worked out. [pause] You also seem to be having some second thoughts about whether the divorce is what you want right now.

Sue: Really! But he hasn't given me much choice. I care for him, but I don't think I can ever love him like I did at first.

Therapist: Maybe some uncertainty at this time is OK. I mean, you've spent 17-plus years of your life with Ray. He's the father of your children. [pause] I guess I would be more concerned if you had no second thoughts at all. This is an important decision. [long pause] Can you tell me how you see your depression, anxiety, and other concerns are related to the situation with Ray?

Sue: Well, I guess I've always been a little anxious. I've always tried to please everybody, from my parents, especially my father, to my husband, my principal, everybody. My feelings change from day to day and sometimes minute to minute on the divorce. But with the divorce coming shortly, the realization of being alone and the fact that I guess in a way I've failed. It just makes it worse. Problems with the kids too.

Therapist: So the anxiety, the apprehension about pleasing others isn't new, but the fact of the divorce seems to mean failure to you.

Sue: Yeah! It just builds. And then I get depressed and down. I don't want to do anything but sit in front of the computer and play those stupid games.

Sue shares information about herself in a rapid fashion. She appears anxious, as indicated by her difficulty in maintaining eye contact, a quiver in her voice, and the almost constant rubbing of her hands. The description of her physical symptoms moves quickly into the current divorce proceedings with Ray. As she weaves in and out of related topics, the issue of her overly pleasing manner seems to be a common thread that warrants further exploration. She continues to confirm the possibility that for her, pleasing is an "only if" proposition rather than a choice, with such statements as, "As long as people are happy, it (the tendency to worry) is better." The life theme of pleasing (probably to an extreme) is a strong indicator of someone struggling with individuation issues. The stress of feeling as if she must please others to feel comfortable with herself along with the distress resulting from the divorce proceedings have pushed Sue's anxiety level quite high, probably accounting for at least some of the somatic symptoms.

In the next segment, the focus remains on obtaining a clearer picture of Sue's functioning in relationship contexts.

Therapist: Sue, I suspect you spend a great deal of your time and energy trying to do the right thing and then once you've done what you think is right, you worry about whether or not it was right and how other people will think about you.

Sue: Yeah. I know I do. My friends tell me I do. I just can't not do it. But it's better when I'm clicking; all's well with everyone.

Therapist: What about when it's not working, somebody's unhappy? What's it like for you then?

Sue: Well, it's kinda like it builds. Particularly at work. The other teachers, the principal, all know I can work with the kids that nobody else can or wants to. I can really do a good job with them. I can keep it up at school for awhile. It's like a high when I'm on, but when things come unraveled, I just kinda plunge.

Therapist: Sue, how do you know when you are and are not doing a good job?

Sue: I guess everything is clicking. I'm doing the right things and I sense others see it the same way. I can see it the way they look at me.

>•◄

Therapist: So with Ray, some pretty strong emotions can happen. The guilt in particular . . .

Sue: Well, yeah. I get angry with Ray, and then later I feel the guilt. Maybe that's what starts all the down, depressed times.

Therapist: Maybe there are some fairly predictable things that happen to lead to the depressed, anxious times?

In this segment of the first session, the client shares her views on the problem. The primary goals during this time are to begin establishing a working alliance with Sue by active listening and probes and to begin obtaining Sue's views of her problems. As she relates her story, it becomes apparent that relationships seem to be the context for many of her issues. Some of the more salient issues are problems with her parents, especially her deceased mother, a compelling "only if" pleasing paradigm that seems to function as a protection against her fears of rejection by others, a long history of varying degrees of anxiety and depression, and struggles with divorce proceedings that she recently initiated. Given her long and consistent history of a "pleasing till it hurts" style of interacting, I assumed Sue was lacking a clear individuated self. She has probably been able to manage her anxiety over the years by hard work and keeping very busy with others. Given her level of distress, I also assumed she would be prone to engage in triangulating patterns in an attempt to manage her anxiety. This was confirmed as I experienced her intense anxiety level in her rapid speech and intense emotionality. I felt she desperately wanted someone to listen to her, support her, and provide answers for her. Given this atmosphere, it was important for me to carefully monitor my own experiences to ensure that I did not attempt to simply move in and rescue her. It was important to allow her to experience her fears and concerns but also to provide some clarity on her own internal experience as it relates to her external reality. For example, I pointed out that she appeared to become more anxious as she talked about her anxiety and depression. I also asked Sue to talk about how her anxiety and depression were related to the situation with Ray. These interventions were intended to sow some rudimentary ideas about Sue's ability to exert greater control over her symptoms by suggesting that some tangible factors were related to her symptoms (that is, the way she talks and probably thinks about her anxiety and her perceptions of the divorce) and that her conflicted feelings were a useful and perhaps necessary experience for resolution.

Based on the information provided in this first session, I wanted to explore how Sue's children fit into the picture as well as the death of her mom and her current relationship with her father. This information might also help assess for triangulating patterns, intergenerational intimidation and intimacy, cognitive/emotional schemas supporting these dynamics, and the personal resources Sue employs to deal with the stressors in her life.

Therapist: Sue, in the last session you shared about your anxiety and depression; in particular, how they're related to the divorce with Ray and how you think others see your performance at work. Your wanting to please or at least not disappoint seems to be a real motivating factor for you.

Sue: Yeah, I feel it [that is, pleasing] more than I really think about it. I mean, it's kinda automatic.

Therapist: Sure, I think I understand. It's like a sense of urgency when you're around people. Particularly, if you sense you're on stage, having to perform.

Sue: Uh-huh. The performing thing seems to kinda hit home [pause] And I guess it happens a lot—at school, home, church, almost anywhere, to varying degrees.

Therapist: To feel you're expected to be in top form or close to it a lot of the time, I would think it would take a lot of energy to keep the edge.

Sue: Oh, it does. It's exhausting. My mind just starts racing and even after I'm away from whoever I've been with, it just keeps spinning. My feelings really get extreme. Sometimes it's good, like I can do almost anything, and other times it's bad—then the depression comes.

Therapist: Like it's sometimes hard to find a balance? Something in between the two extremes?

Sue: Yes! I can't find a balance. I'm either in overdrive or park, or at least it sure seems that way. I'm a mental and physical wreck.

Therapist: I can sense that as you think and talk about all the things you do or need to do, you can get revved up pretty quick. Your rate of speech quickens some. Your face seems to get a little flushed and your overall intensity increases. What's your awareness of this? [long pause]

Sue: [with a quivering voice] I can feel it. It happens a lot.

Therapist: Sue, how about right now, with me—now?

Sue: I'm OK. I'm just a little antsy.

Therapist: Might you be feeling that I'm pushing you or maybe criticizing you when I describe your reactions? [long pause] It's OK if you feel angry or. . .

Sue: [pause] Well, maybe not mad, but threatened.

Therapist: Can we talk about feeling threatened?

Sue: [long pause, sigh] Well, if I think someone is criticizing me, I get angry 'cause I think I'm doing my best most of the time. But also maybe I'm not doing as well as I thought I was.

Therapist: And that's how you're feeling now, here with me?

Sue: Well, yeah, a little.

Therapist: Like I'm not aware of or appreciate how hard you've worked to get where you are now? You're doing your best? [long pause]

Sue: Uh . . . both I guess. But I'm also just embarrassed that my frustration shows so clearly. I thought I could control it some.

Therapist: Trusting me with the less controlled side of yourself—maybe it's uncomfortable, a little? I have a hard time really trusting.

In this segment, we have identified some additional core issues for Sue—trusting herself and others. Furthermore, her sense of self is highly dependent on how she believes other people perceive her. She is overly attentive to others across contexts and less attuned to her own needs until the symptoms become too troublesome. This pattern seems to have a long history and has taken on an almost instinctual quality. This would confirm an earlier assumption that Sue is struggling with a distinct lack of individuation.

Many of my responses were intended to identify and clarify Sue's functional assumptions about herself and others; for example, "you sense you're expected to perform in some way." I also clarified how Sue attempted to deal with the depression and anxiety: "So you kept very busy." My hopes were that she would begin to get a clearer picture of not only what she does but also the negative consequences of what she does to feel better about herself. A therapeutic goal was to help her move to a more balanced interactive position between her intellectual and feelings systems (Knudson-Martin, 1994; Williamson, 1991). Relationally, individuation with intimacy was the goal (Williamson, 1991).

Several strategies are implemented in an attempt to achieve greater individuation. First, by helping Sue connect her own inner experience (for example, depression) with specific relationship contexts (for example, the perception that the principal is not pleased with her), previously inaccessible elements for change become more accessible and tangible. Second, it is hoped that our interaction will provide a different affective/cognitive experience for her in an intimacy-demanding relationship. By directly addressing her response to my description of her nonverbal behavior and giving her permission to feel angry or upset with me, new possibilities for relearning affectively and cognitively occur. She seemed uncomfortable with this direct discussion because she assumed she had failed to do somthing right—that is, she had not controlled her nonverbal responses as she talked about an upsetting situation. It is hoped that if Sue is allowed to share her negative feelings and they are accepted, this will begin to challenge old assumptions. It is important for her to have similar experiences with significant people in her life such as her children and father. Third, if Sue and I can interact around intense and meaningful issues, and if I can remain in affective contact with her while maintaining an individuated position, then she may take further steps toward individuation.

In the following segment, we continue to focus and expand on the issue of trust.

Therapist: Because if they know all about you, they may not like that other part of you?

Sue: Probably. I haven't really thought a lot about it. But I can feel it.

Therapist: You mean when people are trying to get closer to you than you're comfortable with?

Sue: Yeah.

Therapist: Right now, for example?

Sue: Yeah. A little. Fear is the main feeling.

Therapist: Fear that what might happen?

Sue: I guess it gets back to fear that I'm not doing what I'm supposed to do. They might not like it or something like that.

Therapist: What will happen if they see that less controlled, down side of you?

Sue: I guess that they won't have anything to do with me. I'll lose them.

Therapist: And then what will happen if they have nothing to do with you?

Sue: I don't know.

Therapist: You mean it's never happened to you?

Sue: Well, I've talked to a few people about these things.

Therapist: What did they do?

Sue: They mostly tried to encourage me. Probably too much. You know, like, "Do something for yourself. Go away for the weekend." Or some will tell me what they do when they get down or have gone through a divorce.

Therapist: Maybe I missed something, but I haven't heard you say someone cut themselves off from you because you shared your hurts and frustrations with them.

Sue: [with an anxious laugh] Well, no, that's never happened.

Therapist: I suppose the point I'm trying to make is that, first, one of your fears hasn't happened yet or at least it hasn't happened with someone that really mattered to you. Second, even if it did happen, even with one or two people, it wouldn't feel good to you and you would certainly regret losing two friends, but the consequences wouldn't be so dire that it would have to ruin your life. [pause] Would it?

Sue: No. I guess not.

Therapist: Sue, it seems that if you sense someone's not happy with you, whether that's an accurate perception or not, you tend to take the first salvo of blame. "It must be my fault. I screwed up!"

Sue: Oh, yeah.

This segment of the the session represents a shift to a more cognitive focus. I gently challenged the cognitive dimension of her fear that she will surely lose friends and loved ones if she doesn't do "the right thing." We continue addressing self-blame and methods she can utilize to identify and counter self-condemnation, such as being aware of potential self-blaming situations and substituting more accurate, functional beliefs for maladaptive ones.

After introducing the cognitive dimension, the following segment of the session shifts back to the influence of her family. The cognitive focus provides Sue with some tangible tools to address some of her immediate symptoms as related to her beliefs and feelings. However, based on Sue's age (38), lifelong pleasing behavior, and a brief allusion to her parents, I suspected that pursuing the family-of-origin experience might more directly yield important information as well as assist in deciding whether more focused family-of-origin work would benefit Sue.

Therapist: Is it possible that many of your current assumptions are the same or similar to the ones you learned when you were younger living at home?

Sue: Yeah, pretty consistent over the years. They just seem to have intensified recently. Like I still feel like Daddy's little girl when I go visit Daddy. I've always wanted to please him. I think I was his favorite.

Therapist: What about Mom? How did she fit in?

Sue: Mother was the critical one. I love her, but she seemed to always be looking for what we did wrong—never good enough for her. Daddy kinda balanced things. I don't remember them openly fighting, but they seemed to be apart more than together. Daddy was always wrapped up in the church. Mother supported him at church, but her life was primarily at home. She was the disciplinarian.

Therapist: In thinking about what you just said, I'm wondering if some of the overemphasis on pleasing and feeling bad if you're not pleasing could've been learned with your parents?

Sue: Oh, yeah, surely something. I was always a little anxious around Mother because I figured she was always looking for something to criticize me on.

Therapist: So the pleasing was functional for you? Avoided conflict with Mom.

Sue: Oh, yeah.

Therapist: Maybe it's outlived its functionality?

Sue: It seems like it. I mean it really causes problems now.

>•◄

Therapist: Your parents seemed to represent two distinct roles for you. You saw your dad as fun and adventurous while Mom was the authoritarian in the family. Mom let Dad be the good guy. And maybe he let her be the bad guy sometimes?

Sue: [long pause] I've never thought of it quite like that. I mean, that she let him or he let her. But their roles were definitely clear cut, no mistaking one for the other.

Helping Sue place her overpleasing pattern in the context of learned behavior was important to convey that change can occur. Her acceptance of this concept was personally empowering for her, given her previous view that others largely controlled her choices. Additionally, the idea was presented that her parents' behavior was to some degree mutually reinforcing, introducing the possibility of a new interpretation of Sue's polarized views of a stern, less caring mother and a loving, caring father.

It is interesting to note that Sue refers to her parents as Daddy and Mother. The use of "Mother" as compared to "Daddy" seems to represent a more formal and distant relationship that is reflected in Sue's discussion about her parents.

The following session segment explores Sue's views on how the children are being affected by the divorce and her style of relating.

Therapist: Sue, would you share with me how the kids fit into everything?
Sue: The kids are really great. They put up with a lot from Ray and me. Jason tries to help me sometimes 'cause I think he knows how much all this bothers me.
Therapist: Does that mean you talk about some of these things with Jason and Lisa?
Sue: Not all the time, but sometimes, particularly Jason. Anyway, when I talk with Jason, it's not like I plan it. The kids are really concerned about Ray and why he's not living with us. I try not to be critical of him, but when they keep wanting to know why their dad isn't here I have to tell them something. Sometimes I have a hard time keeping it in check.
Therapist: What's that like for you when you feel it building, I mean when you're talking about Ray with Jason or Lisa? Having to keep it in check?
Sue: Well, like I said, it kinda sneaks up on me before I know it. [long pause] I guess I feel angry, defensive, and guilty, all at the same time.
Therapist: Can you go back and re-create a recent situation where this happened?

At this point, I want information on triangulating patterns between Sue, Ray, and the children.

Sue: I think one happened on Monday. We were moving some things around in the garage, and Jason said somthing about wishing Dad were here to help. I was tired from teaching all day and heard his remark as a slam to me. I tried not to say anything, but Jason kept on. I finally told him that his dad wasn't here and wasn't going to be here on a regular basis. He asked why, and I countered with some tacky response. I don't remember exactly what I said, but I felt guilty about it. Later I tried to talk to Jason about it, but he was angry. Plus, we both seem to dump on Lisa during our little tiffs; almost like we're ganging up on her. More guilt.
Therapist: So it's not uncommon for you and Jason to talk about the divorce and end up arguing or just feeling bad after the discussion, and then both you and Jason seem to focus your frustration on Lisa.
Sue: Well, yeah; [pause] but it doesn't happen all the time.

Therapist: [Sue appears agitated] Sue, I'm wondering if you're feeling like I'm pushing too much or trying to catch you on something.

Sue: No; [pause] well, maybe a little.

Therapist: That's OK. Tell me how you're feeling when you sense me pushing you.

Sue: Uncomfortable to start [pause] and right now embarrassed.

Therapist: That maybe I'm not happy with you?

Sue: [pause] Well, yeah, I guess.

Therapist: Is it possible that many of your negative or uncomfortable feelings are related in some way to other people's opinions? Or what you think their opinions are?

Sue: [long pause] Maybe. At school, it's the principal and some teachers. At home, my kids and Ray

Therapist: And here, me?

Sue: Yes.

Therapist: What are you experiencing right now?

Sue: Kinda uncovered.

Therapist: Vulnerable?

Sue: Yes.

Therapist: Because I might do what?

Sue: Not you, but that I've done or said the wrong thing. It's really frustrating. [long sigh]

Therapist: And let's just say you do the wrong thing, whatever that is. What might happen? Here, now?

Sue: Well, nothing I guess.

Therapist: Yes, you're right. Nothing. You have a right to your feelings and thoughts even if I or others don't agree with them.

Sue: I just blame myself a lot.

Therapist: I know this is difficult to talk about, but let's stay with it just a little while longer to get a clear picture of the pattern. When you get down and in a self-blaming mode, how does it affect you at home with the kids?

Sue: [long pause, sighs] I get depressed, then withdrawn, and the kids know something's wrong. Lisa tries to cheer me up. [pause] Jason will sometimes seem to ignore me and other times try to talk to me. I think he gets irritated with me. I try to explain, but it usually ends up in a fight or we both get depressed.

The remainder of the session was spent discussing triangulation issues, including the often adverse effects on the participants if this becomes a regular pattern for dealing with problems. Sue seemed to understand the detrimental effects on her and the children. This led to a discussion of methods the family could utilize to share their feelings without anyone having to take responsibility for others or blame someone else. We also identified alternate strategies that were already in place that Sue could utilize to deal with some of her own daily stressors. Based on this discussion, Sue committed to engage in some form of exercise at least three times the following week as a stress reducer.

Although stress reducers such as exercise, of themselves, may not directly affect a person's level of individuation, they often reduce situational and chronic anxiety enough to lessen the tendency of the family projection process for the short run, making it easier for clients to engage in more demanding individuation work in a relational context. In Sue's case, her lower level of individuation combined with the situational stressors, especially the divorce, and family-of-origin issues were intense enough to engage the family projection process with the children on a regular basis.

We also addressed her symptoms of depression with regard to a need for psychotropic medications. She stated that she wanted to pursue therapy for awhile and see if it could help without the medications. I agreed with her conclusions but suggested we leave the possibility open.

The following is an excerpt from a session that was attended by Sue, Lisa, and Jason. This was our first conjoint family session.

Therapist: I appreciate everybody coming tonight. I'm hoping that both you guys [Jason and Lisa] can help me get a clearer picture of your family right now. You can tell me as much or as little as you'd like to. [pause] Jason, maybe you can start. [pause] How are things for you around the house?

Jason: Well, OK I guess. It's harder without Dad, though.

Sue: Jason, I'm really sorry, but you know what we've talked about before.

Therapist: Sue, it's OK to let him talk. Jason, is there anything you'd like to ask your mom about the situation between her and your dad? Maybe something you've not talked about? It's OK.

Jason: Yeah, why doesn't Dad come around much?

Sue: Jason, I'm very sorry that your dad doesn't spend as much time with you anymore. Even though I know it's not easy, maybe we can talk with him and work out something so you can see him more.

Jason: Yeah, but it's still not gonna be like he's living here.

Sue: You're right, it won't. But maybe we can make it a little better. I really want you and Lisa to be as happy as you can, even though I know this is hard.

Therapist: I think you're both right. It won't be like it was before. But maybe things can improve to where all three of you are feeling better about things at home. Can we talk for a minute about how the three of you can help each other during the sad times?

Sue: Jason, you know, we've talked some about this. How we can talk to each other when [sigh], when we're just feeling angry or sad or whatever.

Jason: I don't know, maybe like we've been doing.

Therapist: Jason, I know you guys know what you've been doing, but I really don't. It might help me to hear and even see how you all have been handling some of these times.

Sue: OK, somtimes the three of us will talk while we're driving someplace. It's easy to turn off the radio. I guess I seem to do most of the talking, but Jason and Lisa will sometimes talk.

The session continues as Sue, and to a lesser degree Jason and Lisa, talk about the divorce and its consequences. The three agree to continue talking and to start scheduling family conferences at least once or twice a week just to talk about family issues, including the divorce. Lisa seems to be the least negatively affected while Jason is struggling the most. We had a second conjoint session the following week and processed their previous week, with particular attention to the family conferences. They reported conducting three family conferences that week, with moderate interaction by the children. We had three more conjoint family sessions spread over the next two months. Much of these sessions focused on facilitating supportive interaction between the three family members and, secondarily, developing family problem-solving skills.

The following session excerpt focuses on Sue and her relationship with her parents. Sue had discussed her parents in an earlier session and acknowledged their influence on the manner in which she views herself in relationships. Sue attended this session alone.

Sue: I don't know if I can take what I know about all my stuff. I guess that's why I'm here. What's next? What can I do? [pause]

Therapist: What direction do you want to go?

Sue: My parents. Maybe even my father. You said one time it might help to talk to him sometime. Maybe I need to.

Therapist: What would you like to say to him?

Sue: That I love him. I want him to be happy. I know he's getting older and he's aware of that.

Therapist: You mean you're both aware that time is shorter for him now? There are some time limits as he's getting older?

Sue: Uh-huh. I mean, he's not in real bad health, but he's declining. He's in his 70s and with my mother gone, it's just a reminder of, well, maybe he's next.

Therapist: What will be important for you to say to your dad? For you and him?

Sue: Well, I know he worries about all of us [Sue, her brother and sister]. I wish he didn't worry so much.

Therapist: And if you knew he didn't worry so much, how would that affect you?

Sue: I guess I wouldn't worry about him so much or feel like I have to try and protect him from all the things that have happened to me.

Therapist: You could be less anxious, more relaxed around him or thinking about him?

Sue: Yeah, I think so.

Therapist: Can you talk about your worrying about your dad and being protective?

Sue: [pause] He's done a lot for me.

Therapist: Maybe it goes beyond love and appreciation to feeling obligated to protect your dad?

Sue: Well, yeah, I guess I do feel obligated. I mean, he's done so much for me and I owe him something. He's always been there for me.

Therapist: And maybe something beyond just feeling you owe your dad something? Not just that "I owe Dad so much" but also "If I don't show him I love and appreciate him, what would he think of me?" and maybe "I might lose him, or his love for me might be lessened in some way."

><

Therapist: The fact that you're here in therapy and willing to think about their relationship says to me you're willing to at least look at other views of your parents. How does it feel talking about it?

Sue: Now better than when we started a few sessions ago. I mean I don't have to do anything, just think and talk, right?

Therapist: It sounds like that personal choice issue is still a question for you. Like "I can choose, can't I?" A statement followed by a question about the statement. "Do I really have a choice?"

Sue: Well, yes, or at least that's what it feels like. I mean, I want the choice. To be able to say this is what I want and it's OK to have what I want.

Therapist: How does that feel to say that, "This is what I want and I can or should have it"?

Sue: It sounds better than it feels, at least right now. But I really want that. I guess I've lived my life afraid of not pleasing others or of feeling good about what I've done.

Sue is gradually becoming more open to seeing herself and her situations differently. I have also begun to challenge her self-perceptions of choice and personal power. For example, when she seeks my permission to choose in the session, I attempt to highlight this interaction and place that decision back with her.

From our discussion, we concluded that a reasonable homework assignment would be for Sue to be aware of those situations in which she moves into her "overpleasing" mode and to prepare herself through self-talk for those situations. At this point, it wasn't critical that she always respond in an ideal fashion but that she first begin to recognize those situations and, second, if possible, begin to respond differently in some small way.

In the following segment, we return to the issue of the conjoint session with Sue and her father. She seems to be in the midst of struggling with her own need for differentiation in the context of her relationship with her parents. Williamson (1991) would suggest that addressing intergenerational intimidation with parents and then establishing a sense of peerhood with them are critical tasks to achieve for individuals to engage others in an intimate but individuated manner. Sue appears to be approaching this juncture in therapy. In addition, we revisit the issue of intimidation by her father's goodness.

Therapist: As we've talked about your father, I often get this feeling that you are very careful about not sounding critical of him. Almost protective of the image you've portrayed to me.

Sue: [long pause] Well, I guess that's because there's not much to criticize. As I've said, he's done a lot for me and [pause] . . .

Therapist: And what?

Sue: [long pause] He's old and I don't want to upset his last few years. I mean, goodness, he just lost his wife of 52 years. Will criticizing him really help matters?

Therapist: Sue, might you be feeling that I'm criticizing your father?

Sue: It sounds a little like that. I mean, keeping up his image and not criticizing him.

Therapist: I appreciate your candor. I'm not trying or looking for something to criticize your father about. [pause] I guess, though, I'm feeling that in some respects you're not allowing him to be a fallible human being who makes mistakes. Maybe where you've placed him in your own mind is a long step up from you.

Sue: What do you mean, long step?

Therapist: I'm wondering if in your heart of hearts you're aware of your dad's weaknesses and fallibilities and yet he's been a solid fixture in your life. You need a degree of infallibility from Dad right now. Someone you can depend on through thick and thin. And yet with all the things that have happened to you and him in the last few months, maybe you're beginning to sense that Dad won't be there forever, and what then? Who can you depend on?

Sue: [long pause] I think I've been aware of my dependence on him for a long time. I guess I don't think so much in terms of infallibility as much as someone that I can depend on to give me good advice and who really cares about me. I know in a real sense his time is limited. That's sad and scary.

Therapist: Scary because?

Sue: I guess 'cause I'll be alone.

This segment continued with the intimidation issue as related to Sue's behavior toward her father. Note her feeling "scared" about changing the relationship with her father. This is a common expression by those facing the challenge of renegotiating the hierarchical boundary with a parent. Sue seems to equate change in the parent-child relationship with being alone and possibly with the emotional and eventual physical loss of her father. Giving up the need to be parented is often accompanied by some degree of disorganization of the self prior to reorganization at a higher level. The existential realization that one must ultimately turn to and be dependent on self alone is disquieting. And yet, paradoxically, it is only from this position that true intimacy with a parent and ultimately with others can occur (Williamson, 1991).

The remainder of this session and the three following sessions focused on Sue's relationship with her father. Session discussions included how she would like to relate to him differently and yet respectfully and lovingly. Her intimidation by his goodness was a consistent theme. On the one hand, she felt he loved her unconditionally, but on the other hand, she feared displeasing him would in some way diminish his love for her. She also expressed harboring resentment toward her mother and yet experienced guilt about it. This seemed to be based on her feelings of conditional love from her mother and often feeling aligned with her father against her mother (that is, triangulation) while growing up and on occasion as an adult. She described how her older brother and younger sister moved away from home shortly after graduation from high school because of her mother's "overbearing style of love." Sue was the only one of the three children to stay close to home after high school.

At this point, Sue was ready to prepare for a session with her father as well as to deal with her grief and anger concerning her mother. Our goal was for Sue to be able to interact with her father on an adult level, minimizing a sense of parental intimidation. From this position, Sue could freely express affection and gratitude toward her father as a matter of choice (that is, intimacy and individuation) rather than from a sense of coercion or obligation. Through a series of successive approximation experiences suggested by Williamson (1991) (for example, unmailed letters to her father, session role plays, autobiographical letters, phone conversations with her father, and home visits with her father), Sue prepared to address intimidation and hierarchy issues directly with her father and indirectly with her mother.

An excerpt from one of the three preparation sessions follows.

Therapist: Well, let's go back to something I think I mentioned several sessions ago, about your parents complementing each other. [pause] Is it possible that whatever each brought to the relationship made it easier for them to stay the same or harder for them to change because of the other's role?

Sue: [pause] You mean they were stuck in a role? They couldn't change?

Therapist: Well, it's not impossible to change. It just made it harder to change after functioning in complementary roles for so long. I guess what's more important than the roles they played is the possibility of you seeing them as human beings who made mistakes as well as doing many helpful things.

Sue: So can I see them as people who do both good and bad?

Therapist: Yes, both of them. And maybe reconciling the good and not-so-good is a little different for each parent. How can you humanize them based on their own past experiences; things that are unique to each one? Like, for example, your mother: How can you allow yourself to balance your view of her?

Sue: It's easier to do that in my head than heart. I mean, I've known her as a stern, structured, and tough lady. How can I just give that up?

Therapist: I'm not asking you to give it up. That's one way of seeing her. But go inside for a minute and with what you know about your mother, allow yourself to get behind that monolithic profile you have of her. What made it easier for her to be that way than other ways? What may have influenced that behavior? For example, think about how the home functioned with everybody there.

Sue: Well, no big surprise, Mother was the one who got us up and moving. I don't remember Daddy doing much of that. He was there primarily afternoons and church at night.

The focus of this segment is continuing to help Sue soften and expand some of her conclusions about her mother and father. It is important that Sue begin to see her parents as fallible human beings who could behave for better or for worse. The process of humanizing the parents is an important step toward resolving intergenerational intimidation. Conjoint sessions with parents provides the most direct manner to address this issue.

As the session continued, Sue became more open to viewing her mother's behavior as something learned and reinforced over many years across many contexts. During later sessions, we utilized the empty chair technique to allow Sue to begin to make peace with her deceased mother. This heightened her emotional experience of loss but also her sense of love and a different understanding of her mother's stern behavior. Forgiving her mother came to be viewed as much for Sue as it was for her mother's memory. Resolving negative emotions toward her mother was another step toward resolving intergenerational intimidation.

The two following sessions largely focused on Sue's preparation for a conjoint session with her father. This consisted of continued processing of a ten-page autobiography about her family, composing letters to her father that were never mailed, telephone conversations with him, and visits to his home. Additionally, several goals emerged for the sessions with Sue and her father. One was for Sue to share her feelings about both parents with her father. The intention was to allow Sue and Albert to process the loss of Joan and for Sue to begin delineating herself as an adult in the presence of her father. With regard to the process of the session, Sue wanted to engage in an adult-to-adult conversation with her father and communicate that she was progressing personally, regardless of the divorce and the loss of her mother. In addition, she wanted to communicate to her father that, although she loved him very much, she no longer expected him to always rescue her when a problem or crisis occurred. Using Williamson's term, Sue no longer needed to be parented. A more ambitious goal was for Sue to discuss with her father her life in the future when he was no longer around.

The following segment is approximately ten minutes into the first conjoint session. I have introduced myself to Albert and shared about some of what I do as a therapist.

Therapist: I can see you care deeply for your daughter and you're willing to help her. How do you think you can help?

Albert: Uh. Well, she and I talked about her mother's death and how difficult that's been for her and me. I think she wants to be able to handle things in her life without having to depend on me or others so much. I want her to do it, but I don't want her to think she has to do it by herself.

Sue: Daddy, I'm just at a point where something's got to change in my life. In my sessions, we've talked a lot about me and how I've gotten along so far. I need to break out of what I've been in for a long time. I need to do this for me, you, the kids, people I work with, almost everyone I'm around. You and I always got along. Mother and I didn't always, but that doesn't mean I didn't love her very much.

Albert: I know you did, hon. Your mother was a good woman and a good mother to you and your brother and sister and a good wife to me. She was just, just uh, a little stern in how she showed it. You know she had a tough life coming up.

Albert continued to share information pertaining to his wife's difficult childhood years. This historical perspective provided a broader context from which Sue could begin to rethink her relationship with her mother. This seemed to evoke sincere empathy from Sue for her mother. She and her father were also drawn together not only to grieve over their loss of her but also to experience her in a positive, caring manner.

The following segment focuses on the relationship between Sue and her father.

Albert: I've thought for a long time that you were more thoughtful about people than your brother or sister. I guess that's why sometimes I've felt closer to you than the other two [siblings].

Therapist: Do you think this ever caused any conflict for you and your wife? I mean with Sue in the middle?

Albert: Maybe. Sue was always right there and willing to go with me when I had church meetings, or visits, or later checking out rental property. It was hard for Joan to just drop everything and go with me, even though that's what I always wanted. I just think she felt that Sue got out of doing some things at the house or chores or something that she thought needed to be done.

Sue: Daddy, I don't remember being treated any different than Bill or Becky. I guess I thought Mother was pretty much the same with all three of us. I do think I would sometimes kinda rescue Becky or maybe distract Mother from chewing her out or something.

Therapist: Do you agree with your dad that you may have been closer to him than you were with your mother?

Sue: Oh, yes. Daddy was easier to talk to.

Therapist: And I guess it was a little easier to be supportive and sympathetic with your dad than your mom?

Sue: Yeah.

Therapist: I'm wondering if maybe we're at a growth point. A time to go to the next level in this relationship. Sue, you and I have talked about this before. Can you talk about this with your dad?

Sue: [long pause] Daddy, this is the part that's a little harder to talk about, but I think we need to talk about it some. I mean, it's hard because you and I have a real good relationship. But maybe we can add to it or give each other more choices or something.

Albert: Well, I know we've talked some about this when you've come by. Maybe I need to get a better picture of this. Can you . . . I mean, uh, what will be different? [long pause]

Sue: [tentatively] Well, Daddy, you know I've felt that I need to look at some things differently. Like how I sometimes have felt about Mother. I love her, but I've felt some real resentment toward her and I don't want to feel that way. I think I'm making some progress there, but with you and I, I mean, I've always felt we've had a pretty good relationship. But as I said before, I think I depend on you too much, at least in the way I think about things.

Albert: What do you mean? (pause) How do you think about things?

Sue: Well, I guess I think too much about how you might think about me. You and Mother did a great job raising me and gave me lots of what I know about getting along in the world. I'm thankful. But I want to be able to feel more comfortable with my decisions and my life and whatever else I'm doing. I just need to feel that I can do something and not question myself.

Albert: Honey, I hope your mother and I haven't caused you to feel this way. [Sue begins to cry.] Sue, I'm sorry.

Sue: But, Daddy you don't have to feel sorry. I'm OK. You haven't done anything. It's just I need to cry. [long pause] It's nobody's fault. This is maybe what I mean about you not feeling so responsible for me. [long pause; Albert looks puzzled]

As Albert and Sue converse, they seem to be describing a triangular relationship in which they team up and leave Joan out. This arrangement in all likelihood had an adverse effect on Albert and Joan's relationship. However, the process of individuation by Sue from Albert is viewed as more relevant and most likely to result in therapeutic movement at this point in time.

The next segment continues with the interaction between Sue and Albert. It illustrates a greater focus on Sue and Albert interacting in a different, more individuated manner than their previous history.

Therapist: Albert, maybe feeling responsible is a big part of being a parent. Perhaps that's part of what we're here for, to rethink responsibility issues. Sue, why don't you talk to your dad about this.

Sue: [pause, sigh] Daddy, I don't expect you to feel responsible for me, like now while I'm crying. I'm just at a point where I'm trying to change some things personally. I want to focus on the future and how I can improve myself. I don't want you to feel responsible for me like you did when I was little. Most of my situations and decisions are due to my choices, not yours.

Albert: And I know that, dear. I just want you to have what you want.

Therapist: Albert, how easy or difficult will it be for you to give up some of that responsibility Sue's talking about? It sounds like she's trying to let you off the hook for being a parent to her in the same way you were when she was much younger.

Albert: Well, I'll always be her father.

Sue: Oh, Daddy, of course. You and I have really been talking about this off and on for awhile. I guess, as I've been saying, I don't want for you to feel so responsible for me. I don't know exactly what that means in terms of what it looks like. [long pause]

Therapist to Sue: Well, what about a moment ago when you teared up and your response to your father's apology? Can we work with that some? What can be helpful for both of you?

Sue: OK, um, well, [to her father] maybe if you think I'm upset or I think you're upset or whatever's bothering either of us, uh, we could first check out what's wrong before we try to help.

Albert: OK, but sometimes, just because I don't say something doesn't mean I'm not thinking something, just not doing anything.

Therapist: So perhaps we're also looking at an attitude or the way you two think about each other. For example, believing that, say, Sue can handle this situation with the divorce. She may need your support from time to time, but you both know that you [to Sue] will make it through this situation. And that Sue can make good decisions but not always perfect ones. Albert, how could this fit for you?

Albert: Well, I know she makes good decisions. I just worry about her sometimes. You know, nobody wants their child to have to suffer or hurt.

Sue: Daddy, I really like that you worry and care about me. I just don't want you to do so much that you can't enjoy your life.

Therapist: Maybe that's the issue you both can agree on. That it's OK for each of you to worry, just not too much. Is this a possible point of agreement on this issue? Worrying but contained worry?

This was a fairly productive session. Sue and Albert discussed Joan's death and also began to rethink their relationship in the present. For example, Sue attempted to relieve her father of having to continue as the protective parent. The idea of "contained" worry was not planned but simply emerged from the discussion. Sue and Albert eventually agreed to worry 10–15% of their thinking time about each other rather than their usual 40–50%. This was not intended to be an exact percentage of "worrying" time but a clear commitment by each that they were willing to begin thinking about the other differently. This was a significant event for Sue. Having a face-to-face meeting with Albert provided an opportunity for her to address intergenerational intimidation directly without all the accompanying self-talk of self-doubt and self-criticism. The fact that her father supported this step toward differentiation provided a noticeable boost for Sue's confidence level in the next session with her father and in additional sessions. This step seemed to provide Sue with confidence for her interactions in other relationships. The change was gradual and continued in a progressive fashion over a period of months.

Sue was also able to experience her father as a fallible human being who makes mistakes. For example, Albert shared his regret about avoiding many of the home responsibilities and thus contributing to his wife's more instrumental role around the house.

In later sessions, Sue continued to struggle in establishing a clear parental boundary with her son. Much of this was related to Jason's struggle with a split sense of loyalty between his parents. In later conjoint sessions, Sue, Jason, and Lisa reported less triangulation behaviors than in the earlier stages of therapy. Sue also reported more compliance by Jason and that his grades were once again improving. I also made several attempts to involve Ray in a family or individual session, but he declined.

The final four sessions were extended over a two-month period of time. Much of the sessions' content revolved around the divorce, such as redefining friendships forged during her marriage, the possibility of dating at some point in time, and dealing with Sue's grief and differentiation regarding her deceased mother by visiting the gravesite (Williamson, 1978). We also explored the possibility of any connection between Sue's relationship with her father and her problems with Ray. As our sessions came to a close, Sue reported feeling greater certainty that the divorce was the best course of action.

Sue's presenting symptoms (that is, sleeping and eating disturbance, headaches, depression, and anxiety) diminished considerably, although she continued to have occasional periods of depression. She eventually tried a mild antidepressant that improved her mood and sleeping. Improved sleeping greatly improved her stamina and thus outlook on life. Although Sue was not totally symptom free, results on the Brief Symptom Inventory indicated that scores on somatization, depression, anxiety, and interpersonal relationships were all in the nonclinical range. The PAFS-Q also indicated a noticeable increase in individuation and decreases in triangulation with the children and with her experience of intimidation by her father and mother.

Conclusions

Although not appropriate for all clients presenting concerns, the client's age and client family history can be indicators that an integrated intergenerational family approach might be effective. The degree of success with this case was based to some extent on a good alliance between the therapist and the client and the fact that the client was motivated and regularly attended sessions and largely was cooperative and involved in the therapy process. The cooperative participation of Sue's father, Albert, was particularly critical for Sue's movement toward a greater degree of individuation. After therapy ended, Albert developed a relationship with a woman at his retirement facility. Sue and her brother and sister were supportive of this relationship, and it seemed to reinforce the developing individuation-with-intimacy relationship between Albert and Sue.

In cases where a parent or parents choose not to participate in conjoint sessions, informal home visits between a client and parents can be extended. This arrangement would involve more modest goals and a more gradual parent involvement.

In conclusion, the approach described here was an effective means of renegotiating the hierarchy between middle-aged adults and their parents. This renegotiation appeared to generalize to other relationships beyond Sue and Albert's, with little emphasis in therapy sessions.

Study Questions

1. How are individuation and personal authority related?
2. How do the methods and techniques employed in the sessions facilitate the individuation process?
3. Oftentimes, Williamson employs small group work with individuals addressing issues of individuation prior to conjoint sessions with parents. How could group work have helped or hindered Sue's preparation prior to her sessions with Albert?
4. Intergenerational family theory assumes that if triangulation is a predominant mode of relating in one generation, it will in all likelihood be utilized in the next generation. How is triangulation utilized in the case example?
5. Provide your reaction to the use of cognitive techniques with family-of-origin theory. What other theories and techniques might also be employed with the current integrated approach?

References

Baucom, D., & Epstein, N. (1990). *Cognitive-behavioral marital therapy.* New York: Brunner/Mazel.

Beck, A. (1976). *Cognitive therapy and emotional disorder.* Madison, CT: International Universities Press.

Bedrosian, R. C., & Bozicas, G. D. (1994). *Treating family of origin problems: A cognitive approach.* New York: Guilford Press.

Bowen, M. (1978). *Family therapy in clinical practice.* New York: Aronson.

Bray, J. H., & Williamson, D. S. (1987). Assessment of intergenerational family relationships. In A. J. Hovestadt & M. Fine (Eds.), *Family of origin therapy: Application in clinical practice* (pp. 31–44). Rockville, MD: Aspen Systems.

Bray, J., Williamson, D., & Malone, P. (1984). Personal authority in the family system: Development of a questionnaire to measure personal authority in intergenerational family processes. *Journal of Marital and Family Therapy, 10,* 167–178.

Bray, J. H., Williamson, D. S., & Malone, P. E. (1986). An evaluation of the effects of intergenerational consultation process to increase personal authority in the family system. *Family Process, 25,* 423–436.

Goldenberg, I., & Goldenberg, H. (1996). *Family therapy: An overview* (4th ed.). Pacific Grove, CA: Brooks/Cole.

Greenberg, L. S., & Johnson, S. M. (1988). *Emotionally focused therapy for couples.* New York: Guilford Press.

Harvey, D. M., & Bray, J. H. (1991). An evaluation of an intergenerational theory of personal development: Family process determinants of psychological and health distress. *Journal of Family Psychology, 4,* 42–69.

Hollon, S. D., & Najavitis, L. (1988). Review of empirical studies on cognitive therapy. In A. J. Frances & R. E. Hales (Eds.), *American Psychiatric Press review of psychiatry* (Vol. 7, pp. 643–666). Washington, DC: American Psychiatric Press.

Kerr, M. E., & Bowen, M. (1988). *Family evaluation: An approach based on Bowen theory.* New York: Norton.

Knudson-Martin, C. (1994). The female voice: Applications to Bowen's family systems theory. *Journal of Marital and Family Therapy, 20,* 35–46.

Lawson, D. (1996). Achieving personal authority in the family: An intergenerational family and cognitive approach for counseling with adults. *The Family Journal: Counseling and Therapy for Couples and Families, 4,* 116–126.

McGoldrick, M., & Gerson, R. (1985). *Genograms in family assessment.* New York: Norton.

Pinsof, W. M. (1995). *Integrative problem-centered therapy.* New York: Basic Books.

Shaver, P., Hazan, C., & Bradshaw, D. (1988). Love as attachment. In R. J. Sternberg & M. L. Baines (Eds.), *The psychology of love* (pp. 68–99). New Haven, CT: Yale University Press.

Teyber, E. (1992). *Interpersonal process in psychotherapy* (2nd ed.). Pacific Grove, CA: Brooks/Cole.

Williamson, D. S. (1978). New life at the graveyard: A method of therapy for individuation from a dead "former parent." *Journal of Marriage and Family Counseling,* January, 93–101.

Williamson, D. S. (1982). Personal authority in the family experience via the termination of the intergenerational hierarchical boundary: Part III. Personal authority defined and the power of play in the change process. *Journal of Marital and Family Therapy, 8,* 309–323.

Williamson, D. S. (1991). *The intimacy paradox: Personal authority in the family system.* New York: Guilford Press.

Chapter Three

Integrative Couple Therapy

Kathleen Eldridge, Andrew Christensen, and Neil S. Jacobson

Integrative Couple Therapy (ICT) is a promising new treatment for distressed couples. Although it has its origins in behavioral couple therapy (Jacobson and Margolin, 1979), it goes beyond the change focus of this approach to incorporate interventions aimed at fostering acceptance between partners. It incorporates interventions that resemble those from a number of other orientations, such as strategic, experiential, and ego analytic approaches, but conceptualizes these strategies within a behavioral framework. Independent reviewers have lauded the approach (for example, Hendrick, 1997). More importantly, three small unpublished studies have documented the effectiveness of the approach (see Christensen and Heavey, in press).

This chapter outlines the theoretical framework of ICT and describes the research relevant to its development. However, the main focus of the chapter is on a clinical case example that is used to illustrate ICT and to highlight common issues encountered by therapists working with distressed couples.

Theoretical Underpinnings

Couples seeking treatment are dissatisfied with their current relationship. Typically, this dissatisfaction takes the form of each partner wanting the other to change. The traditional behavioral treatment for couples, traditional behavioral couple therapy (TBCT) (Jacobson and Margolin, 1979), also known as behavioral marital therapy (BMT), proposes that changes in behavior will produce improvements in relationship satisfaction. Consequently, TBCT therapists attempt to create behavior changes in two ways. First, they directly instigate changes by encouraging partners to define the specific behaviors they would like their partner to exhibit and instructing partners to increase the frequency of those behaviors. Second, they create changes by teaching distressed couples communication and problem-solving skills they can utilize to produce those changes. Hence, TBCT focuses on improving relationship satisfaction by producing changes in behavior.

In contrast, integrative couple therapy (ICT) (Christensen, Jacobson, and Babcock, 1995; Jacobson and Christensen, 1996) recognizes that partners are not always able to make the changes emphasized in TBCT. Consequently, instead of relying solely on changes in behavior to improve relationship satisfaction, ICT attempts to produce changes in reactions to that behavior. In other words, ICT suggests there are two ways to solve problems in a relationship: by changing aversive behavior or by fostering acceptance of that behavior. The relative focus of change and acceptance depends on the needs and characteristics of each individual couple. In short, the primary difference between TBCT and ICT is the relative emphasis on change and acceptance. In TBCT the primary focus is change, whereas in ICT the dual emphasis is on change and acceptance.

ICT was developed because of the limitations TBCT demonstrated in clinical trials evaluating its efficacy. TBCT is the most extensively researched treatment for distressed couples and has garnered a tremendous amount of empirical support (Alexander, Holtzworth-Munroe, and Jameson, 1994; Jacobson and Addis, 1993; Lebow and Gurman, 1995). In numerous investigations, TBCT has significantly outperformed control groups that do not receive treatment for relationship distress (Hahlweg and Markman, 1988). However, despite its empirical success and the fact that it is the only couples therapy to be designated as an empirically validated treatment (Crits-Christoph, Frank, Chambless, Brody, and Karp, 1995), TBCT has some significant limitations. In general, about two-thirds of couples show relationship improvement with TBCT by the end of treatment, but some of these couples relapse (Jacobson and Follette, 1985). After one to two years posttreatment, only about one-half of couples who received TBCT have improved relationship satisfaction (Jacobson, Schmaling, and Holtzworth-Munroe, 1987).

Research has identified specific characteristics of couples who respond poorly to TBCT. Couples that fail to practice the acquired skills effectively in problem areas tend not to have favorable outcomes (Iverson and Baucom, 1990). This is not surprising, given the premise of TBCT that improving communication and problem-solving skills will improve relationship satisfaction. Other studies indicate that older couples, and/or those following more traditional gender roles are less likely to benefit from TBCT (Jacobson, Follette, and Pagel, 1986). Furthermore, studies indicate that severely distressed couples (Baucom and Hoffman, 1986) and emotionally disengaged couples (Hahlweg, Schindler, Revenstorf, and Brengelmann, 1984) are also at a disadvantage in TBCT. It is likely that the difficulty with these couples lies in their inability to make the changes emphasized in TBCT (Jacobson, 1992).

There are a number of reasons why TBCT is not always successful at producing long-term changes in behavior. First, many distressed couples may not lack communication or problem-solving skills. Instead, they are simply unmotivated or unable to use these skills due to feelings of anger or resentment. In other words, there is a performance deficit, not a skills deficit. Therefore, focusing on the acquisition and demonstration of skilled behaviors is not helpful for many couples. Rather, treatment needs to address the underlying emotions hindering the performance of positive behaviors. Unless partners are motivated to change their behavior, change is not likely to occur.

Second, the changes in behavior emphasized in TBCT are rule governed. Rule-governed behaviors (Skinner, 1966) are those that are performed to obey a rule, like a husband giving his wife a hug and kiss when he arrives home after work because the therapist instructed him to increase the positive behaviors leading to satisfaction in his wife. In TBCT, therapists foster rule-governed behavior by assisting couples in developing a set of rules about behavior and reinforcing partners for following these rules. Behaviorally speaking, rule-governed behaviors are reinforced when a rule is followed, and violations of the rule are punished. However, TBCT therapists hope that natural contingencies, like the experience of more satisfying interactions following the behavior, will maintain the initially rule-governed behavior. Unfortunately, this is not always the outcome. In several instances, the rule-governed behavior fails to promote natural reinforcement because it feels fake or superficial to the partner exhibiting the behavior and because it is perceived as forced and insincere by the partner "receiving" the behavior. As a result, the interaction is not naturally fulfilling or satisfying to either partner and is primarily reinforced by the therapist's acknowledgment and praise. Once the therapist is not present (either between sessions or after the couple terminates treatment), the reinforcement no longer exists and the behavior is extinguished.

A third limitation of TBCT is that it focuses on a circumscribed number of behaviors. Therapists in TBCT help couples define specific behaviors that will improve relationship satisfaction instead of identifying the theme or underlying purpose of those behaviors. For instance, a wife may want her husband to kiss her, ask her about her day, and listen attentively to her when she returns home from work. These specific target behaviors would be defined in TBCT, and the husband would be instructed to exhibit those behaviors. Unfortunately, what does not get explored in TBCT is the larger issue or theme—that the wife may feel ignored and may want her husband to be more attentive and caring toward her in general. This underlying theme would suggest a multitude of behaviors the husband could perform that would exhibit attentiveness and caring instead of just the ones defined by the wife. Since it is impossible to define every behavior that will serve that purpose, the husband is limited to the target behaviors defined by his wife and does not have other behaviors to choose from that serve the same purpose. The other behaviors left undefined may have come more naturally to the husband and may have been perceived as more genuine by the wife.

To account for these limitations of TBCT, Andrew Christensen and Neil S. Jacobson developed ICT, an innovative approach that integrates TBCT change strategies with new strategies to promote acceptance where changes are not feasible. This approach acknowledges that a number of couples are not able to make desired changes and emphasizes emotional acceptance when change does not occur. ICT suggests that changing the partner's aversive behavior is not the only way to decrease distress in the relationship. In addition to changing the aversive behavior, treatment can change the reaction to the aversive behavior so that it is experienced as less aversive. Often, changes in reaction to a behavior produce changes in the behavior itself (Jacobson and Christensen, 1996). ICT promotes both types of changes: change in the behavior, if possible, and change in reaction to the behavior if change in the behavior is not possible. Consequently, it has a dual focus—change and acceptance.

To promote changes in behavior, ICT suggests that three factors must exist. Partners must (1) know what behaviors to change, (2) have the skills to perform those behaviors, and (3) be motivated to perform those behaviors.

To address the first factor, ICT attempts to identify the underlying theme of a problem instead of simply defining some of the behaviors that may alleviate the problem. Elucidating this theme for partners increases their understanding of their problem and enables them to choose from several behaviors to solve the problem, instead of just those defined by their partner.

ICT also incorporates the second factor into treatment. If partners are lacking in communication and problem-solving skills, ICT therapists work to help them develop those skills. However, the emphasis is on fostering skills that are improved versions of preexisting skills rather than on completely changing how the couple interacts. Partners are taught to communicate and problem-solve in a way that comes more naturally for them but is still effective for the particular couple. In addition, instead of instructing partners to always use their skills when communicating about an issue, ICT therapists acknowledge that it is not always possible for couples to utilize the skills they learn but that it is beneficial to the relationship when they can.

Although it is necessary to address the first two factors to create change, ICT proposes that the most frequent barrier to change is the third factor— motivation. The acceptance interventions in ICT are designed to foster intimacy between partners, which increases motivation. Once greater intimacy is established, partners are less angry and resentful, less resistant to making changes, and more self-motivated to change their own behavior to improve relationship satisfaction. Positive behaviors are performed willingly without instruction and are perceived as more genuine as a result. These types of behavior changes are different from those emphasized in TBCT because they are contingency shaped (Skinner, 1966). In contrast to rule-governed behaviors, contingency-shaped behaviors are those performed because they are reinforced by natural consequences. In therapy, couples desire behaviors from their partner that are contingency shaped, not rule governed. For instance, a husband is more likely to want his wife to be attentive to him because she enjoys being attentive to him, wants to please him, and enjoys the satisfaction he expresses in response to her attention than because she was instructed to be attentive and is following these instructions whether or not she particularly enjoys it or finds it rewarding. Contingency-shaped behaviors are reinforced by the natural consequences stemming from the behavior. When both partners naturally feel good about the interaction, they are more likely to repeat it in the future even without the presence of a therapist. Theoretically, in ICT, emotional acceptance fosters intimacy, which can lead to spontaneous positive changes in behavior that are not rule governed like the TBCT changes. Because the spontaneous changes are more contingency shaped, they are expected to be experienced as more sincere and rewarding by partners (Christensen et al., 1995) and thus more durable.

Several interventions are utilized in ICT to foster emotional acceptance: empathic joining around the problem, detachment from the problem, tolerance, and self-care (Jacobson and Christensen, 1996). To promote empathic joining around the problem, the therapist reformulates couples' problems as deriving from basic differences between partners that cause painful reactions and that lead to unsuccessful attempts to solve the problem. In addition, the therapist encourages partners to talk openly about the painful, vulnerable feelings they are experiencing ("soft" emotions) in place of the angry, blaming feelings ("hard" emotions) that stem from these hurtful reactions. The purpose of this intervention is to evoke an empathic response from the partner to promote intimacy and understanding rather than the defensiveness provoked by anger and blame.

The second goal of ICT, detachment from the problem, is fostered by modeling for the couple how to discuss a problem without engaging in it, which means discussing it in a detached manner instead of blaming and accusing each other. The couple is encouraged to jointly describe their problem in an objective, descriptive way to increase emotional attachment and decrease blame. Ideally, the couple begins to see the problem as something they both share, not something the other is responsible for.

The third focus in ICT is on increased tolerance of negative behaviors. To promote tolerance, the therapist points out the positive features of negative behaviors and acknowledges the inevitability of lapses into negative behavior patterns. In fact, the couple may role-play a slip-up, when they are not feeling angry or defensive, so that they can discuss what their reactions would be and see how understandable their partner's reactions are. The final goal of ICT is to encourage partners to be more self-reliant, particularly when they are faced with aversive behavior from their partner. This way, the negative behavior is experienced as less painful and the ability of the partner to tolerate it can increase.

Although ICT also incorporates typical TBCT change interventions, they are not described or demonstrated here due to space limitations. These interventions, described by other authors (Christensen et al., 1995; Jacobson and Margolin, 1979; Jacobson and Christensen, 1996), include behavior exchange, communication skills training, and problem-solving skills training. The extent to which ICT therapists utilize these change interventions, in addition to the emotional acceptance interventions demonstrated in this chapter, varies depending on the characteristics of the couple. As described previously, research has demonstrated what sort of couples typically have less favorable outcomes with TBCT, and acceptance interventions are emphasized with these couples. Couples who are able to make the changes fostered in TBCT respond to both acceptance and change interventions.

The Case: A Distressed Couple with Intimacy Problems

The case material used to illustrate ICT comes from a couple who, after being married for four years, responded to an advertisement about a treatment outcome study involving two treatments for distressed couples and met criteria to be recruited into the clinical trial. The case will be briefly described, including the ICT case formulation and assessment data.

Ron and Leslie, a Caucasian couple in their 30s, have an infant daughter and a 4-year-old son. Ron works full-time in business administration and Leslie stays at home with their children. In addition, Leslie writes children's books and does some acting. The couple entered treatment with several complaints that fell into three general categories: (1) amount of intimacy, (2) coping with negative emotions, and (3) anxiety over professional and parental roles. Specifically, Leslie desired more intimacy from Ron in the form of more interest in sex, more initiation of sex, and more closeness, affection, and positive regard. Ron, on the other hand, had a lower desire for sex and intimacy than Leslie and found it very difficult to initiate sexual encounters with his wife. The second general issue was that both partners had become very angry, critical, and defensive and often exhibited out-of-control behavior in response to these emotions. Occasionally, this behavior escalated into physical aggression by both partners. The third issue was Leslie's confusion over career decisions and her defensive reaction to Ron's attempts to help her resolve these confusions. As strengths, Leslie and Ron were highly committed to making their marriage work and were able to work as a team in raising their children.

An important component of ICT is the case formulation. In fact, "if one were to generate a one-line description of the overarching goal in ICT, it is to get the couples to adopt our formulation . . . if they leave therapy with this formulation as a prominent part of their relationship history, they will in all likelihood have benefited greatly from therapy" (Jacobson and Christensen, 1996, p. 41). The case formulation consists of three components: (1) the theme, or main conflict, for the couple that pervades several seemingly unrelated conflicts; (2) the polarization process, or typical pattern of interaction between partners when they engage in the main conflict; and (3) the mutual trap, or final outcome, of the conflict that leaves both partners unable to resolve or recover from the argument. The therapist comes to a formulation after the initial assessments and evaluation sessions. This initial formulation is not written in stone; rather, the therapist presents it tentatively to the couple and elicits reactions to it. Further, the formulation is often modified during the process of therapy. The primary purpose of the formulation is to provide the couple with an organizing framework for their conflict that is not blaming but emphasizes the understandable hurtful reactions they each have to their differences. Having this formulation then enables the couple to accept or change those reactions instead of to blame one another for them. It is only necessary that the formulation be helpful in this regard, not that it be "true" in an absolute sense. Although the formulation is primarily meant to be therapeutic for the couple, it also guides the therapist in deciding which conflicts described by the couple should be the focus of a session. Typically, the therapist concentrates efforts on conflicts that relate to the formulation. Occasionally, if the couple does not make progress, the therapist alters the formulation and finds that the couple then makes improvements.

Often, the theme of the formulation revolves around a difference between partners that was once perceived as attractive but has become a source of distress. This was the situation with Ron and Leslie. Ron had initially been attracted to Leslie's energy level and enthusiasm for life. He found her fun and outgoing. Leslie liked Ron's stability and quiet optimism. Together, they felt her intensity and his rationality would be a good balance. However, this difference became a problem for them. Due to their different family backgrounds, Leslie had become accustomed to outspoken criticism, anger, and rejection, but Ron had little experience with expressed emotion and had learned to be the rational caretaker of the family. As a result, Leslie was comfortable outwardly expressing negativity, but Ron was fearful of her expressions of anger and would withdraw from them. Further, he had difficulty expressing positive and negative emotions to her. Leslie perceived his rationality and withdrawal as a lack of any emotion and felt rejected by him. Leslie responded to the feelings of rejection by criticizing Ron. In turn, Ron would be hurt and frustrated by her criticism and would retaliate or withdraw further. This theme was typically played out in a polarization process in which Leslie was angry, outspoken, and animated while Ron was withdrawn and avoidant. In response to Ron's withdrawal, Leslie's anger would escalate until Ron would eventually lose control and burst with anger and frustration. Afterward, they were mutually trapped by their hurt, anger, and inability to resolve their conflict. They both felt like attempts to resolve conflict were futile but did not want to give up on the relationship.

Prior to treatment, Leslie and Ron's scores on marital distress and satisfaction questionnaires, such as the Global Distress Scale of the Marital Satisfaction Inventory (MSI) (Snyder, 1979) and the Dyadic Adjustment Scale (DAS) (Spanier, 1976), indicated that they were in the maritally distressed range. Typically, the following scores are considered indicators of clinically significant marital distress: 59 or higher on the MSI (higher scores indicate more marital distress) and 97 or lower on the DAS (lower scores indicate more marital distress). Upon recruitment into the clinical trial, Ron was more distressed and less satisfied than Leslie. On the MSI and DAS, Ron scored 71 and 88, respectively. Leslie scored 58 on the MSI and 91 on the DAS.

Ron and Leslie also responded to an Areas of Change Questionnaire (ACQ) (Weiss and Birchler, 1975) modified by Christensen and Jacobson to assess the frequency and acceptability of partner behaviors. On this Areas of Change and

Acceptance Questionnaire (ACAQ), Ron reported a lower frequency of positive behaviors demonstrated by Leslie (5.9 per month) than the frequency reported by Leslie of Ron's positive behaviors (9.4 per month). In other words, Leslie thought Ron exhibited positive behaviors more frequently than Ron thought Leslie exhibited positive behaviors. The ACAQ also instructs partners to rate the acceptability of the current frequency of positive behaviors on a 10-point scale, with 0 being totally unacceptable and 10 being totally acceptable. Interestingly, Ron reported that the current frequency of positive behaviors exhibited by Leslie was more acceptable to him (7.5) than Leslie's acceptance of the frequency of Ron's positive behaviors (5.7). Simply, although Ron exhibited positive behaviors more frequently, Leslie reported that frequency less acceptable. Ron was more accepting of Leslie, even though the frequency with which she exhibited positive behaviors was lower.

Ron and Leslie presented with some interesting complaints that are frequently addressed in couples therapy. Specifically, they were physically aggressive, had different preferences for sexual intimacy, and had different desires for closeness. However, they were somewhat atypical in their roles in these issues. Following is a discussion of these three topic areas and how ICT incorporates these issues into treatment.

Physically Aggressive Couples

Research has indicated that nearly half of couples seeking therapy have experienced some form of physical aggression in their relationship during the year prior to obtaining therapy (O'Leary, Vivian, and Malone, 1992). Couples therapy is contraindicated if this aggression constitutes battering, which we will define as aggression that leads to injury and/or intimidation. In battering cases, couples therapy can precipitate violence by encouraging partners to talk openly about their feelings and problems, thereby potentially angering the batterer. Moreover, using the format of couples therapy for marital distress in battering cases can support a view that both partners are responsible for the violence, instead of just the batterer. Clinicians can only prevent these negative consequences if they assess violence prior to initiating couples treatment and make appropriate referrals for battering.

In ICT, therapists determine the severity and frequency of aggressive acts through self-report questionnaires and follow-up interviews. The Conflict Tactics Scale (CTS) (Straus, 1979), a self-report questionnaire filled out independently by partners about each other, is a well-validated questionnaire on violence. It has been found to elicit more reporting of aggressive behaviors from couples seeking marital therapy than either direct interviewing or open-ended written reports, indicating that, if only one measure is used, the CTS is the most informative (O'Leary et al., 1992). If it appears that either partner is aggressive, the partners are independently interviewed to clarify how frequent and severe the aggression is currently and was in the past. If it becomes clear that injury or fear of injury or aggression are currently present, marital therapy is not the appropriate intervention. Instead, the violent partner is encouraged to seek individual treatment to address the violent behavior. Depending on the circumstances, the victim may need assistance as well.

Frequently, couples will report that there is not violence in the relationship currently, but there was in the past, or that there is currently mild aggression in the relationship. If neither partner has experienced injury and is not afraid of the other, marital therapy may be appropriate. However, several steps must be taken to ensure that the treatment does not increase the amount of aggression in the relationship and that the amount of aggression does not reach levels at which couples therapy is no longer appropriate. In ICT, these steps are as follows:

1. A no-violence contract that explains that violence is not acceptable, outlines specific steps that can be taken to prevent violence (like time-outs), and indicates that violence will result in termination of couples therapy and commencement of individual therapy for the batterer (the contract is very specific about the behaviors that will result in these consequences)
2. Safety planning with the victim of violence to determine ways of preventing battering (that is, recognizing the cues the partner exhibits prior to becoming violent and having a plan for leaving when these cues are present)
3. Exploring with the victim possible deterrents to leaving when violence is likely or actually occurs
4. Educating the victim about community resources and legal options for victims of battering
5. Continued assessment for violence and for adherence to the contract throughout treatment

A national survey indicates that domestic aggression is equally prevalent in women and men (Straus and Gelles, 1990). However, other investigations have clarified that men are more likely than women to be batterers, and women are more likely than men to engage in aggression as self-defense and to be injured due to domestic aggression (Stets and Straus, 1990; O'Leary et al., 1992). In Ron and Leslie's case, Leslie was more physically aggressive than Ron, and Ron's aggression was typically in response to Leslie's attacks. Fortunately, the physical aggression between them did not lead to injury or fear of injury, so they remained in treatment. However, thorough assessments of the violence were conducted, and prior to the first treatment session a no-violence contract was put in place. Further, safety planning was conducted whenever necessary throughout treatment, and the therapist questioned the partners about physical aggression and time-outs throughout treatment.

Differences in Preferences for Sexual Intimacy

It is common for couples to have different needs and wants for sexual intimacy. These differences can be in the frequency, quality, and/or intensity of sexual activity in the relationship. Typically, men are motivated to engage in sexual activity to relieve sexual tension, whereas women engage in sexual activity to receive love and intimacy (Brown and Auerback, 1981). Consistent with this gender difference in motivation for sexual activity, male partners usually desire sexual activity that is physically arousing, whereas female partners desire sexual activities that demonstrate love and intimacy (Hatfield, Sprecher, Pillemer, Greenberger, and Wexler, 1988). Further, men initiate sexual interaction more often than women (Peplau, Rubin, and Hill, 1977; Brown and Auerback, 1981). However, even with these differences, heterosexual couples can usually create a sexual relationship that is mutually satisfying. Yet sometimes these differences become a source of distress in the relationship, and couples seek therapy with sexual differences as their primary problem.

Ron and Leslie's pattern of preferences for sexual intimacy was contrary to the typical pattern. Leslie wanted Ron to initiate sex more often and desired more arousing sexual activity than Ron. Their arguments around this difference fit with their formulation. Leslie would demand more sex or intensity from Ron, and Ron would withdraw due to fear of Leslie's anger and criticism of his performance. In turn, Leslie would feel rejected and her anger would escalate, causing Ron to withdraw further or burst with anger. Eventually, they would be too upset and exhausted to engage in any sexual activity.

In ICT, differences in preferences for sexual intimacy are viewed as a common difference between partners and are handled in the same way as other differences. Empathic joining around the problem is fostered by encouraging partners to discuss their "soft" feelings about the different sexual preferences and to discuss their emotional reactions to the conflictual interactions that result from these differences. Further, a detached view of the difference is fostered by enabling partners to see their different sexual preferences as a problem they share, not as a problem in their partner. In addition, tolerance of the difference is fostered by accentuating the positive aspects of partners' different desires for sexual intimacy, by role-playing conflicts over sex when the couple is not currently distressed, and by exploring with each partner ways to relieve the frustration when their partner demands or avoids sexual activity.

For some couples, differences in sexual preferences can lead to sexual dysfunction in either partner. One way this can happen is when one partner continually feels pressured to engage in sexual activity with their partner and eventually is unable to respond sexually under the intense demands. When sexual dysfunction is present, traditional sex therapy is conducted simultaneously with ICT.

Differences in the Desire for Closeness

It is common for couples entering therapy to have conflicts about the amount of closeness in the relationship (Greenberg and Johnson, 1986). Further, it appears the extent of conflict over closeness is strongly associated with the extent of marital dissatisfaction (Christensen, 1987, 1988). Typically, this difference in desire for closeness manifests itself in a demand-withdraw pattern where the partner desiring more closeness pressures, criticizes, and complains, whereas the partner satisfied with the level of closeness in the relationship withdraws from these demands to preserve the status quo (Christensen, 1988; Jacobson, 1989). Further, investigators have demonstrated a gender difference in this pattern, with women most often in the demanding role and men most often in the withdrawing role (Christensen, 1987, 1988; Sullaway and Christensen, 1983).

Although Ron and Leslie did not exhibit the typical pattern of physical aggression or desire for sex, they exhibited the typical demand-withdraw pattern. Leslie exhibited much more emotion than Ron and wanted not only more sexual activity from Ron but more romance and emotional expression as well. Consistent with their formulation, he would withdraw from her demands out of his fear of her anger and his discomfort with emotional expression, and she would respond to his withdrawal with anger, criticism, and more demands. The cycle would continue until they both exploded with rage. This difference in emotionality was the primary problem between Ron and Leslie. Consequently, it was the primary focus of ICT interventions.

Similar to the ICT view of sexual differences, differences in the desire for closeness are also viewed as a normal and common difference between partners in a relationship. Consequently, ICT therapists foster empathic joining around the difference, a detached view of the difference, tolerance of the difference, and self-care strategies when the difference causes painful feelings. With Ron and Leslie, the therapist encouraged them to describe their hurtful reactions to this difference. To do this, instances in which the difference caused an argument for them were explored and their emotional reactions to the conflict were elicited. When they expressed their hurt feelings, each partner naturally reacted with compassion, which increased the empathy and intimacy in the relationship. In addition, by describing the conflicts surrounding this difference in nonblaming and descriptive terms, the therapist modeled a detached way of thinking about and describing the conflict. This enabled Ron and Leslie to view the difference as a problem they shared and not as a deficit in the other partner. Further, to promote tolerance of the difference, the therapist acknowledged the positive aspects of this difference in emotionality and how it originally attracted them to each other. In addition, the therapist acknowledged the probability that each partner would slip up and become very demanding or withdrawing, despite efforts to change the behavior. This expectation allowed them to be more tolerant of the slip-ups when they occurred. Moreover, Ron and Leslie were encouraged to role-play instances of demanding or withdrawing when they were not actually wanting to seek or avoid closeness so that they could each see the hurtful reactions of their partner to their behavior. Since the partners in the activity of role playing were not actually emotionally engaged in the behavior, they were able to focus on each other's reactions and typically began to understand why their partner reacted as they did. Finally, the therapist explored ways Ron and Leslie could focus on caring for themselves when their partner's demanding or withdrawing behavior was upsetting.

Feedback and Formulation

The first three to four sessions with a couple are considered the assessment phase of therapy. During this time, the therapist collects questionnaires from the couple, meets with the couple together, and meets with each partner individually at least once. The primary purpose of this assessment is for the therapist to develop the case formulation and treatment plan. The first real intervention in ICT occurs after the assessment, during the feedback session, when the therapist presents the case formulation to the couple. The following excerpts are from the feedback session with Ron and Leslie and demonstrate the presentation of the formulation to the couple.

Therapist: Today is the feedback session, and I've been looking forward to it because it's a very challenging time to bring together all the material that each of you have shared with me. I have a number of topics to go over, so in some ways I'll be talking more this session than I will in any other session. On the other hand, even though I try to take good notes and I've videotaped and thought about the sessions, I still don't get everything. And I don't fine-tune it until I meet with you and I get your feedback in addition to what I'm saying. So I want to encourage you to feel free to refine what I'm saying today because those refinements will be very helpful in terms of therapy. So it's really a collaborative session where the three of us try to bring it all together and make a plan for the additional treatment sessions together. So what I'm going to talk about today is basically six topic areas. I'll be talking about the level of distress that the two of you reported on your questionnaires, and then the commitment that you reported, what you identified as issues and problems, our understanding of those issues and problems, the strengths that we see in the relationship, and what we can do in the therapy.

The therapist introduces the feedback session in this manner and covers the six areas listed, focusing primarily on the fourth area (the therapist's understanding of their issues), which is the formulation. It is important to stress that the case formulation is modifiable and to encourage partners to help refine it. Throughout the session, the therapist reiterates this point and continually seeks feedback from the partners.

The first step in presenting the formulation is summarizing the basic difference between partners that creates conflict and explaining the basis for that difference. Frequently, the basis is divergent family backgrounds, as demonstrated in the following.

Therapist to Leslie: Your parents were very outspoken with their negative emotions. Both your mom and your father were quite up front with criticism, judgment, and anger. And you grew up with what you would consider a normal amount of anger, rejection, criticism. A pretty high level by perhaps other people's standards. But that was just normal in your household, there was quite a bit of that going on all the time. . . . And it seems like if there was one theme that you might have taken from your family background, it is perhaps a special sensitivity to being rejected and criticized by others. But certainly a sensitivity to rejection.

The therapist first summarizes Leslie's family background, focusing specifically on the role of emotion in her upbringing and the special sensitivity it may have created. Afterward, the therapist summarizes Ron's family experience, again with a special emphasis on emotionality and the special sensitivity he may have developed around emotionality. After summarizing their family backgrounds, the therapist attempts to bring the backgrounds together by emphasizing the basic difference between the partners that results from their divergent family backgrounds. This is the theme of the formulation. For Ron and Leslie, this difference was in expression of emotion, a primary source of conflict between them.

Therapist to Ron: So you had two parents who were modeling suppression of emotion, but there's all this tension and people know there's all this tension and you were feeling it. But you were the one trying to modulate the emotion and trying to keep things stable, keep it smooth and keep things in check and under control and from getting worse. So that's kind of your role in the family. And so it may have left you with a special sensitivity or vulnerability to not knowing how to deal with strong, intense emotion that's coming full-on at you. And the first thing you do is try to be rational and do the old pattern, and when that didn't work, it would just build up and then you don't know quite what to do when there's this intensity of affect being shared. So that's the difference from your background.

Now you met each other and at first there was a lot of appeal and attraction with this difference, [to Ron] because you saw the intensity and you saw the very positive parts of it that she has—[to Leslie] you're energetic and creative; you're really a go-getter. You talk about how you get an idea and then you go for it. [to Ron] So you found that intensity, energy, and drive attractive and appealing. [to Leslie] And you find his steadiness and his rationality—you've used that word a number of times—the stability, very attractive. So you saw those differences, and both of you talked about how you felt there could be a synergy between the two of you; that you could really complement each other with these differences you have; bring out other parts of yourselves and grow. So the two of you are different, but at times you do have a very positive balance and you each bring strengths to the relationship.

The therapist attempts to highlight the positive side of the difference and can usually find in the dating history some evidence of how the difference was initially attractive to them. However, the therapist must also acknowledge the negative side of the difference and how it creates a cycle of conflict between the partners. This polarization process is part of the formulation and is presented in the following excerpt.

Therapist: Our challenge is the negative side to the connection the two of you have. The positive side is your [Leslie's] emotionality and energy and spontaneity and your [Ron's] stability and steadiness. But what's hard for him is that with that intensity is this intensity of anger and criticism that he's just not used to. [to Ron] And it's not like you have years of training and a comfortable range of skills for dealing with it. So when it comes at you, there's a tendency more to withdraw than to go forward and try to take it on in some way. [to Leslie] And for you, you like his stability and steadiness, but at times you would want him to be more energetic, more spontaneous, and more approaching of you with positive affection. At times, you've said you appreciate that when he's critical he's more indirect than your family was, and you like that. [to Ron] And so some of the indirectness you've learned is helpful. But when you get more withdrawn, more shut down, less spontaneous, and less approaching, then that's a problem; she would like more of you. But it's too intense a demand for you to somehow come forward in a way that's different from what you're used to. So what happens is those differences trigger each other's vulnerabilities. [to Leslie] You end up feeling rejected when he's not as initiating in sex or as validating with affection. . . . What we'll be working on is understanding these situations that end up feeling rejecting to her and how that can trigger feelings of hurt, anger, and resentment. Then that resentment comes out. Then when that strong negative emotion comes out, [to Ron] that triggers your sensitivity to not knowing really how to handle that intense, straight-on criticism, that demanding negativity. And when that comes toward you, your tendency is to withdraw and avoid, which triggers more of her rejection sensitivity. And the cycle gets triggered more and more and more. And so . . . our challenge is to help each of you understand and be more compassionate and sensitive to your partner's areas of sensitivity. And as you do that, it's easier for each of you to approach each other on a middle ground that's more comfortable and more safe and sensitive for both of you.

It is important that the polarization process is presented in such a way as not to place blame on either partner. The therapist uses nonblaming language and emphasizes the interaction between partners instead of the contribution of just one partner to the conflict. Using nonblaming language serves two purposes: It prevents a defensive reaction in partners, and it models a detached and accepting way of discussing and viewing the difference between partners. Finally, in the feedback session, the therapist explains the goals of therapy. In ICT, these goals are acceptance and change.

Therapist: So our goals will be both acceptance of this difference—because we need to understand that you are different, you come from very different backgrounds, you have different personalities, you have different styles, that's what attracted you to each other—so we'll work on understanding, identifying, and accepting those differences; but at the same time, we'll be working on changing those. Realizing that people don't metamorphose into something completely different than what they are, but as they feel more secure and accepted, it's easier to try new behaviors and show more feelings, more spontaneity.

Following this general explanation, the therapist described specifically the things Leslie and Ron would be working on accepting and changing. For Leslie, she would need to work on changing the way she expresses anger and seeks affection and accepting the way Ron expresses his emotions. Ron would need to work on expressing more intimacy and affection and accepting Leslie's anger and demands.

The therapist first presents the formulation in the feedback session but continues to describe conflicts in terms of the formulation throughout treatment. During treatment sessions, the therapist elicits partners' emotional and behavioral responses to conflicts and describes them as understandable reactions to their differences and to the resulting interaction. For Ron and Leslie, the therapist frequently reformulated conflicts as deriving from their difference in emotionality. Eventually, Ron and Leslie learn and adopt the reformulation, which reduces their inclinations to blame each other for the conflicts and increases their ability to change either their own behavior or their reaction to their partner's behavior.

Emotional Acceptance Interventions

Emotional acceptance interventions in ICT can be broken down into two major categories: those that promote intimacy and those that promote tolerance. Ideally, the differences between partners in a relationship can be vehicles for greater intimacy. Some of the emotional acceptance interventions attempt to use the differences between partners to foster intimacy between them. Realistically, differences between partners often cause conflict and are too hurtful to create intimacy. ICT acknowledges that intimacy cannot always be obtained and also includes emotional acceptance interventions that strive for tolerance of differences if intimacy is not possible.

Emotional acceptance interventions designed to foster intimacy include empathic joining around the problem and unified detachment from the problem. These interventions to promote intimacy are illustrated with excerpts from Ron and Leslie's treatment sessions.

Empathic joining through soft disclosures.   One empathic joining intervention consists of the therapist encouraging partners to describe their sad and vulnerable ("soft") emotional responses to conflicts instead of their angry and blaming ("hard") emotional responses. This enables partners to hear about the hurt, not the anger, caused by conflict. Whereas hearing the blame and anger elicits defensiveness, hearing about hurt feelings elicits compassion and empathy, which increases intimacy between partners.

Soft disclosures are illustrated in a session in which Ron and Leslie are very distressed and talking about separating. As Leslie discusses her need for more intimacy from Ron, their polarization process begins to occur. As Leslie's anger escalates, Ron withdraws, consistent with the formulation. The therapist then encourages Leslie to disclose her soft feelings.

Ron: [becoming defensive] I've told you that, I've communicated that to you. The thing that makes it hard is that I've told you that I'm afraid of you and shy sexually.

Leslie: Yes, I know. You start it for a one-week period, and then all of a sudden it stops.

Ron: Right. Because I need your help to continue also.

Leslie: [angrier] I thought I'd been doing that. But see, you have to take the initiative to tell me, "This is what I need, and this is what I need more." I told you I'm willing to help you, to be your partner in what ever you need to do. But it's your initiative for you to do it because I don't know your routine.

Ron: I know that. And then something will happen and I'll get angry at you.

Leslie: [ranting] Right, and then it just blows the whole thing. And then you don't have the capacity to think, "OK, I got off track and now I need to go back." It's like you stop and then there's nothing else, there's nothing in you that pulls it back. I don't see that at all, and that's what pisses me off more than anything else.

Ron: [withdrawn] I don't have that yet. That's true, I don't.

Therapist: What's really positive about this is that you're able to communicate and express how this rage comes out. Remember last time I was asking you to show me what it's like—now you are really showing this rage that comes out. . . . So, we know that there's this volcanic rage that comes out. What other feelings are you feeling inside? If you try to look behind the rage, what kinds of feelings do you discover inside yourself?

Leslie: Behind the rage? I mean, just to focus in on what's—?

Therapist: If you just tuned into yourself, if you said "OK, I know I'm really just raging volcanically mad at him," and you've told him that and you've expressed it with a lot of genuine feeling. So we all know that Leslie's just raging mad at Ron. But if you were to just kind of sit within yourself and just kind of tune in to "OK, besides feeling angry towards Ron, what other feelings do I have?" And could you try to tell him?

Leslie: Well, I've told him whenever I get angry there's other emotions into it. Basically, there's a sense of sadness.

Therapist: OK, tell him about the sadness. Try to really tune into it if you could and try to tell him as close to your heart and as tuned into that part of you that also feels sad besides rageful about the sadness.

Leslie: Well, one, I feel sad that we're always arguing. The other thing is feeling like you don't love me enough. The other thing from the past is that I've worked hard with other relationships too, but this is the first time that I've had to feel like I have to beg for someone to be with me or to make love to me. And so I'm sitting here trying to understand that. . . . There's frustrations from the day and thinking that if we didn't have children maybe the relationship would have been better. Feeling inadequate as far as I'm not doing a career, not doing the things I used to. Feeling shut down, just feeling like I'm in a box. That's about it. [begins to tear]

Therapist to Ron: Can you tell her the feelings that you heard that she's going through besides the anger, just try to feed back to her what you've heard.

Ron: Well, I hear that you're hurt because you feel like I'm not putting enough energy into it. Compared to past relationships, you feel like I'm either withholding or don't love you enough. Or whatever the motivation is, the actions aren't there and so that hurts . . .

Leslie: The other biggest thing is that . . . [crying, pause]

Therapist: Go ahead, just whatever way you can spill it out, it's OK; try to get that out so he'll hear it.

Leslie: [crying] The frustrating part is that I feel guilty because you're a good man and I should be happy and lucky that I have you because of the things you do and the things you put up with. And I feel that I'm asking too much, so maybe I should just be happy with what I have, you know? And I just feel like maybe I'm asking for too much. Because I do want to be with you.

Ron: I don't think you're asking for too much . . . it's the interaction. . . . It's not what you're asking for. It's that whatever you feel that's negative, whether it's frustration, anger, or loneliness, or whatever the base motivation is, you express it in terms of anger and that's the way it comes out.

Leslie: Yes. [crying]

Ron: That's exactly the emotion that I shy away from. . . . I thought I could handle it, but it's not easy.

Leslie: And there's a part of me that feels like [crying harder] maybe I shouldn't be in a relationship. Because I don't think I'm going to find anybody I'm compatible with.

Ron: I'm willing to work through that.

Leslie: I know, but I hurt you in the meantime.

Ron: All these things can be dealt with . . .

This excerpt is an example of how hard emotions can be turned into soft ones, which elicits compassion from the partner. Consistent with their formulation, Leslie's anger toward Ron for not changing his behavior elicits defensiveness and then withdrawal from Ron. The therapist intervenes after this withdrawal and very carefully addresses Leslie's angry outburst. In fact, the therapist comments on the positivity of the outburst to reinforce Leslie for expressing her emotions in the safety of the session and to prevent her from becoming defensive about her anger. The therapist then asks Leslie to talk about any other feelings she might be experiencing besides the anger. In response, Leslie acknowledges feeling sadness but doesn't really express her soft feelings fully until the therapist encourages her to elaborate on the sadness and then asks Ron to paraphrase her feelings back to her. Once Leslie knows that Ron is going to respond compassionately, she feels freer to express the most hurtful feelings of guilt, love, and insecurity. She becomes as intensely sad as she was angry, and the therapist prompts her to continue to express the sadness however she can. In turn, Ron explains that he does not see the problem as her fault but as a combination of her style of expressing emotion and his inability to cope with that style. When she continues to express soft emotions, Ron is compelled to restate his commitment to Leslie and his optimism that they can work through their problems. In contrast to his defensive response to her anger, he is compassionate in response to her hurt. His compassion further softens Leslie, which elicits more compassion. Another cycle is perpetuated that increases the empathy and intimacy between them. This intimacy creates both acceptance and change in behavior.

In encouraging soft disclosures, therapists may need to use other types of interventions than the one demonstrated here. The therapist encouraged Leslie to express her soft emotions, which worked for this couple. However, it may have backfired with another couple by sending the partner into a deeper rage or expression of more hard feelings. The therapist needs to be familiar with the styles of partners and to be aware of their typical response to therapist probes. If the therapist finds that prompts for soft disclosures do not work with a particular couple, other interventions can be utilized. For example, the therapist may need to suggest soft feelings the partner may be experiencing and see if the partner responds to the prompt and elaborates on the soft emotions that were suggested. Although it is most powerful if partners express soft emotions on their own, in reality that does not always happen. The intervention used is not as important as the overall goal of exposing the soft feelings so that the partner can respond compassionately and increase the intimacy and empathy in the relationship.

Unified detachment from the problem.   Another ICT intervention to promote intimacy is unified detachment, which promotes a detached view of the problem in both partners. The therapist describes conflicts in a descriptive, nonblaming way to model this interpretation of conflicts for the couple. In addition, the therapist encourages partners to become observers of their reactions to conflicts, to allow them to step back from engaging in the problem and see the interaction in a detached way. Eventually, the couple begins to describe their own conflicts in this detached and descriptive manner, which enables them to view the problem as something they share as a couple, not something that is the partner's fault.

In this excerpt, Ron and Leslie were discussing a conflictual incident that occurred in the week before the session. Leslie had been at home with the kids all day and wasn't feeling well. She wanted Ron to get home from work and take the kids off her hands for awhile. Since they were not distressed during the session, the therapist attempts an intervention demonstrated later, role playing negative behavior. Leslie is resistant to the role play, and the therapist shifts to a unified detachment intervention.

Leslie: I'm not usually saying it, I'm usually yelling it. I'm much more vicious when I'm "on."

Therapist: Can you say it here with that voice? Can you try that?

Leslie: That's a part of me that I really don't like. It's the face that I keep at home. Because I know what it looks like. If I were in public, people would say I need a straitjacket. I know what it looks like when it's happening inside, and it's vicious. It's real scary, and most people would really cringe at that.

Therapist: So it was hard for you when we had the exercise before when I was asking you to show the anger towards him, even when you weren't feeling it.

Leslie: That was only a quarter of what I can do.

Therapist: This time, was this three-quarters of what you can do, when it was really coming out, or a full 100%? [to Ron] And I'd like to ask your opinion of that too, because you've seen it. How much of it was coming out?

Leslie: Well, vocally, I would say it was close to 100%, but as far as physically, I was holding back. Because to me they are two separate things. And if I were to go full-out like I've done in the past, I'd be whaling on someone and screaming. That would be the fullest thing I would do. But as far as vocally, it's softened. Intent was close to 100%. I don't know.

Therapist: I know this is a hard question, but you've done a good job. You've separated the physical from the verbal.

The therapist shifts from the role-play intervention to asking Leslie to rate her emotionality during the incident they have recounted. Although this focuses on emotion, it encourages an intellectual, observational analysis of the incident, thereby detaching Leslie from the emotions and allowing her to become an observer of the interaction. Then the therapist turns to Ron and enables him to analyze the incident from a detached and observational perspective.

Therapist to Ron: You never saw the 100% physical and 100% verbal, but maybe some of what you've experienced felt that way to you or felt it could get really close. What has your experience of it been, especially during this last incident?

Ron: Well, I think there's been times where I would probably agree that the intensity was 100%. You could see it.

Therapist: You could tell she was feeling it inside?

Ron: Yeah, that she was right on the edge of really losing it. But she was restraining herself. Verbally, other than some of the comments about "I don't want you to come home," I don't think we were quite as biting this time around. . . . I knew she'd been feeling bad, so I think I was able to handle it better and didn't perceive it as extremely biting. Where I think in the past if she'd said that to me, I just would have said "Fine" and hung up the phone and thought, "I'm not coming back."

Therapist: So she'd threaten and then you'd threaten withdrawal.

Ron: Yeah, I'd take it real personally. And this time for whatever reason I didn't take it real personally. That doesn't mean the next time I won't take it real personally [laughs], but this time I didn't.

Therapist: And so you could just stay centered and approach.

Ron: Yeah, but I don't even know if I was really approaching. At that point, it just wasn't a negotiation situation. I just told her "This is what I'm gonna do."

Therapist: Right, and so you came and got the kids. It took you longer than you wanted, you would have wanted to get the kids out before the hour and a half, but you ultimately got the kids and you out of the scene.

Ron: Right, right.

Leslie: And I was appreciative that he stayed for awhile because then I would have nothing to feed on.

Therapist: So if he would have left right away, you would have been stewing and feeling abandoned?

Leslie: No, I didn't feel that way, I was glad they left. I felt like, "Good, he took control because I couldn't do it."

Therapist: Oh, you were just frozen and immobilized and just ready to go completely out of control. And he took control.

Leslie: Right. I always felt like it had to be me that was in control and so it was fine. He stayed centered, and he didn't give me anything to go off on.

The therapist continues to encourage both partners to analyze the incident without engaging in the emotions of the conflict. They begin to talk about and see the incident as an interaction around a common dilemma that they shared, not a problem that their partner was to blame for. Instead of blaming Leslie for being out of control and rejecting, Ron recounts his thought process during the incident, including his awareness that Leslie wasn't feeling well and simply needed a break from the kids. Leslie refrains from blaming Ron for not taking the kids immediately upon returning home and instead thinks about how it was actually better for her that he stayed for awhile and then relieved her of the kids. They both stop engaging in the problem and observe their own and their partner's reactions from a detached perspective. This allows them to unify against the common dilemma of being parents and having stressful caretaking responsibilities. They can share the distress of the problem instead of blaming each other for that distress. This enables them to empathize, provide support, and become closer.

Tolerance Interventions

Sometimes increased intimacy cannot be reached via the three interventions just illustrated, so therapists work to promote tolerance of differences. Four interventions to promote tolerance are typical in ICT. These tolerance interventions are illustrated with transcripts from Ron and Leslie's treatment.

Tolerance through acknowledging positive features of behavior.   In one tolerance intervention, therapists acknowledge the positive features of the difference between partners. Typically, this intervention occurs first in the feedback session, as demonstrated earlier. Therapists point out how the difference once attracted them to each other or how the difference creates a good balance in the relationship. This enables couples to see more clearly the possible advantages to having a difference between them, instead of viewing it as completely problematic for the relationship.

In addition, throughout treatment, therapists point out positive features of behavior that is perceived negatively by partners. In the following excerpt, the therapist attempts to point out that Ron's tendency to hesitate and not respond immediately to Leslie's urgency to do things around the house can be the result of good intentions on his part.

Therapist to Leslie: So there was this barking, chastising meanness [that Leslie grew up with] that was normal for you. And so now you're the mom and you're trying to run a household. And it's a complicated time; the kids are at these hard ages . . . and so part of you just tries to get all of this uncertainty together by doing the pattern that you grew up with. And then assuming he grew up like that too.

Leslie: . . . I know mentally that's it's unfair to him, and it's different, and I didn't like it growing up. And logically I can see all that, but it just automatically kind of happens.

Ron: Right. And I think the other part of it is that I tend to be deliberate in the way I do things, and she wants stuff done now.

Therapist: So by deliberate you mean slow and thoughtful before you act. Methodical?

Ron: Yeah, methodical. Because I've found that for myself I make more mistakes when I do things in a hurry. I can do things quickly, but it's more of a hit or miss whether I get it done right the first time or not. And so, for me, I've learned it's better to do things methodically and look before you leap, before you take the next action. And for me it just saves time.

Therapist: And so part of you doesn't want to disappoint her or screw up, so your wheels are moving as fast as they can to figure out what is the problem and what is the solution. And you're trying to come forward for her, but it might not be as fast as you [Leslie] would like it because he is slower, sort of mentally, verbally, and actionwise so his latency to respond is different.

In this last statement, the therapist takes what Ron said about being methodical because he doesn't want to make mistakes and reformulates it to focus on the positive aspect of his style in interacting with Leslie. The therapist describes the unobservable but positive aspect to Ron's slow response style—his fear of disappointing Leslie and his attempt to prevent that from happening by working to figure out the correct reaction before responding. In essence, the therapist points out how the negative behavior (Ron's delayed response) has a positive element in it (trying not to upset Leslie). This enables Leslie to see that his hesitation to respond, although perceived as a lack of effort, actually results from increased effort to respond correctly. In the future, Leslie can tolerate his delayed reaction more because she can understand how it might benefit her in the long run. Thus, her negative reaction to his hesitation is diminished, the conflict does not escalate, and recovery from the argument is quicker.

Tolerance through role-playing aversive behavior.   Another tolerance intervention is role-playing negative behavior. Although this sounds counterintuitive, partners who exhibit negative behavior at the therapist's instruction, even though they are not really inclined to do so and are not emotionally involved in the interaction, are able to observe and understand their own negative behavior and their partner's emotional response to that negative behavior. In future "real" arguments, partners can better understand and tolerate the reactions of their partner to their negative behavior, reducing the escalation of the conflict.

Therapist: So, do you understand what she's saying? Do you know the experience of her saying something really mean, just almost so it will register hurt?

Ron: Um hmm. Yup, I know the feeling . . .

Therapist to Leslie: Can you role-play here some version of it? Can you do something like what you would do at home?

Leslie: I don't know if I can create that. Like, do you mean what would I say?

Therapist: And some of the tone. [to Ron] Can you suggest a line? Something she's said to you?

Ron: Well, in the past, one thing she would do is [pause] well, when she was pregnant with our first child, I was really unsure about being a father. And so I was really unsure about it, and so I wasn't very supportive. And, so I hurt her. And she really did not let me forget that for awhile, so that would be a weapon, essentially, when we got in a fight. And sometimes that would come out even if it had nothing to do with why we originally started fighting.

Therapist: So was there any particular line that she said? Any phrasing?

Leslie: What I said was [pause] see, because the incident was basically, we were in the doctor's office and I thought I had an ulcer. And she sat us down, and it was an anxious moment and she said you're pregnant. And at that moment I was excited and smiling, but he had a stern look and I could see it from my peripheral view and I thought, you asshole. You weren't supportive of me.

Therapist: That's it; just say it to him. Try to do it right now. Try to get in touch with it, even though you don't have the volcano right now.

Leslie: I think what's hard is that he's asked me not to do it and I've promised and worked on it real hard not to use it. But basically, the things I said were that "you rejected your first child." And that's a thing I would never, never forgive him for when I tell him that. It's something that's going to hang over his head. And "when she's old enough to know, I'm going to let her know that you did not want her the first time the doctor said it."

Therapist: OK, thank you. Is that what it's like?

Leslie: No, it's much more severe, and I'm real sneering.

Therapist: OK, could you do it really severe and really sneering? Just the most dramatic version of it. Really try to get him.

Leslie: I'm trying to work on trying not to do it!

Therapist: I know, I'm asking you to do a really hard thing. What you just did was great, you just have to do it with more volcanic vigor.

Leslie: Sometimes it varies. I know that I'm always spouting so then I'll do it real calm and direct. I change it every time just to throw him off balance. He knows I spout—"You never really wanted your daughter, and you never wanted to be a father to your kids." I can do it real smiling or real matter-of-fact with a real coldness to it.

Therapist: So you really go for the jugular.

Ron: The style is always different depending on the situation but the message is the same.

Therapist: And what was it like for you as she said those words?

Ron: I go ballistic.

Therapist: Did you feel yourself starting to go ballistic here?

Ron: Oh yeah, absolutely.

Therapist: Like on a scale of 1 to 10 when she said "when she grows up as soon as she's old enough to understand, I'm going to tell her that when we first found out I was pregnant you didn't want her"?

Ron: I go to a 10.

Leslie: I've always told him that if he ever divorces me or screws around on me that I would take the kids to another country and he'd never find them. And that's a constant threat.

Therapist: OK, just then on a scale from 1 to 10?

Ron: That's another one, I'd go ballistic. Because she knows how I feel about the kids. Despite what happened when she first got pregnant, she knows deep down what I feel for those kids.

Leslie: I say it just as a way for me to keep safe in case you never really loved me. But I know he loves me and I know he wouldn't do that. He proves himself each time. I believe he does love his daughter.

Ron and Leslie had experienced a good week with very little conflict. They had arrived at the session smiling and refreshed. When this occurs, it is a good opportunity to work on tolerance, especially through role plays. In the preceding interaction, the therapist is attempting to increase Ron's tolerance of Leslie's angry outbursts and to increase Leslie's tolerance of Ron's reactions to those outbursts. To do this, when Leslie is not feeling angry, the therapist asks her to role-play being angry and yelling at Ron. Typically, this allows the role-playing partner (Leslie) to observe the effect of the hurtful behavior on the other partner (Ron) and to see the reaction to the behavior as understandable, given its aversiveness. This observation becomes possible because the role-playing partner is not caught up in his or her own emotions. In fact, Leslie voices some resistance to exhibiting this behavior, recognizing that it will be hurtful to Ron. But the therapist continues to encourage her, and she eventually expresses her anger in a way she thinks is hurtful. In response, the therapist asks Ron to rate his emotions, and Leslie learns that he is as upset as possible when she says those things. Leslie responds to him compassionately, explaining that she does not really mean the things she says and only says them to protect herself from rejection. In essence, she reassures him that she knows what she says is not true and acknowledges his positive feelings toward her and their daughter.

In the future, when Leslie is driven to say similar hurtful things in her angry outburst, Ron will be more tolerant and less reactive to them because he now knows they stem from her own insecurities and do not represent the truth about him. In addition, Leslie will be more tolerant of Ron's reaction to her outburst, knowing that her behavior is aversive and that he is understandably irritated and hurt by her accusations.

Tolerance through preparing for slip-ups and lapses.   A third tolerance intervention consists of acknowledging that slip-ups and lapses into old behavior patterns are expected, even though both partners are attempting to change those patterns. Doing so prevents despair in the face of lapses and enables partners to accept and tolerate these slip-ups as normal and inevitable.

Ron: Leslie kept saying that she was really worried that we were going to, or I was going to, slide into the old stuff, and that didn't help. That angers me or worries me or frustrates me. On the other hand, it never got me so frustrated that I got extremely explosive. I mean, I got mad and I got frustrated, but it didn't escalate into a big thing. But those are the kind of things that, for me, don't help. And I know she needs to express that as she's thinking it, but those are the kind of statements that make me feel like withdrawing.

Therapist: So you're in a quandary in that you want her to voice her negative feelings as sort of a way to get them out and not stew about them.

Ron: Yeah, even if I don't like it. And I may react negatively at that point, but ultimately she has to be able to get them out.

Therapist: Right. At the same time, it makes you feel hopeless and frustrated, so you kind of take them in.

Ron: Right. And so, I suppose that if I'm trying to look at the glass as half full, on one hand I didn't like it but on the other hand I didn't get explosive, so that's a step in the right direction. Even though neither of us was particularly happy about it.

Therapist: So part of you can say, "OK, she's being negative and it's upsetting to hear all these negatives about our future, and it's starting to make me feel hopeless, but maybe it will help her and free her up to get it out and maybe I won't have to take it in like a sponge and have it inside of me." It's hard to do, but there's some exploration of that.

Ron: Um hmm.

Therapist: So every relationship has its ongoing irritants that people live around, they tolerate, they understand, they accept, even if they don't like them. So part of it is realizing that you will have those differences to struggle with. But when this crabbiness is coming on when she is premenstrual, everything is going to escalate and she's going to think about every single one of them, and anything you do gets her going. And you both need to know that and be aware of it. So you can be compassionate of yourself and each other.

Throughout treatment, and especially when there has been a slip-up or when there is an upcoming situation that might produce a slip-up, ICT therapists acknowledge that lapses are likely to occur and should be expected. In this excerpt, the therapist explains that Ron and Leslie's differences are bound to surface on occasion. This prepares them for slip-ups, especially during Leslie's premenstrual days. The preparation then decreases their negative reaction to the slip-ups. In the future when lapses occur, Ron and Leslie will see the lapse as a natural and inevitable slip-up that is an isolated incident, instead of a sign that they are headed back to their old patterns and have not made any progress. This perspective then decreases the amount of conflict over the slip-up and the time spent recovering from it. Further, during Leslie's premenstrual days, both partners will be aware that conflict is more likely, and this awareness reduces the escalation and intensity of the conflict. Again, this means that recovery is shorter and Ron and Leslie can return to their normal functioning sooner.

Tolerance through self-care.   Finally, therapists promote tolerance of negative behavior by exploring with partners how they can care for themselves when they are hurt by their partner. Encouraging self-reliance reduces the need to rely on the partner when negative behaviors occur so that the behavior is experienced as less aversive.

Therapist: Well, we need to anticipate that there will be blow-ups. That things are going better now, but it's inevitable that one or the other of you will get upset and go back to old behaviors. So I'd like you to imagine he's just not initiating things and he's not doing what you want and you're starting to accumulate resentment. Or she's picking on you and angry at you and telling you what you're not doing and what you should be doing more of. And you're just wanting to get away from her or withdraw. So both of you imagine having your buttons pushed and try to get in touch with what it's like when you're in that old state. What can each of you do to take care of yourself at that time? To keep it from escalating, so that the recovery will be quicker?

Leslie: Well, for me it's a little hard, I'm always telling him to go away. Because I can't do it because I have the kids. Then I get stuck being at home, then I become kind of a mole and I just can't get out the door.

Therapist: What if you're feeling rejected by him? He's not making sexual overtures, he's not holding your hand.

Leslie: Oh, I know what I did different. I started an art project, and I hadn't been doing any artwork. And just doing the decoupage I felt more calm, I felt more exuberant doing something. And I did it until about 12:30; he had to come get me to stop. So I did that. I got a quarter way through and I didn't want to stop. And I felt a sense of calmness doing it. I don't think I've been doing anything, as far as any outlet.

Therapist: So, you're a real doer; like you were saying, it's so hard to take a time-out because you want to do something. And so you found something that you can do that you really get lost in and you really feel expresses your creativity. And so one coping skill that you're rediscovering is that if you're feeling rejected, rather than just stewing on it and getting angry, you can go and get out some of that tension in a creative way and take care of yourself. That's so different than being a mole at home.

Leslie: That's something I realized, that all the things I used to do before I was married I'm not doing. I was dancing, acting, I was out and about, and now I'm just home.

Therapist: Right. So this is something that you can reconnect with that's very expressive. So, just remembering what you used to do and doing some of those so that you don't urgently need him to do what you want him to do and stay mad at him for not doing it.

Leslie: Right. I actually felt like "leave me alone," which I never used to want to be alone before. So I actually did some artwork and I couldn't put it down. And I remembered what it felt like.

Therapist: So part of it is realizing that you left a lot of old coping skills behind. Now your needs have changed, and you don't know which of those fit now, but you brought out this old one and said, "Oh, this one fits really well. This really meets my needs now. It helps me take care of myself when he's not available in the way I want him to be available." Great. That's even more than I was expecting. This is a hard one; [to Ron] what can you do when the old pattern is being triggered and things aren't going well? What can you do to protect yourself and tap into your own resiliency? Any ideas for you?

Ron: Sports. It's always been sports, and sleep.

Leslie: Forget the sleep part. [laughs]

Ron: Well, for me, I always do fun things with sports. I mean, I don't run, I don't jog, I don't lift weights, I don't do any of that stuff. Because it doesn't allow me to turn off my head. Because you're just doing the same thing and it's very repetitive. And so I play team sports or ski or that kind of stuff where, when you're doing it, all you can do is think about what you're doing, and everything else doesn't matter because it creates that kind of demand.

Therapist: Now, how do you do a team sport with your busy schedule?

Ron: Well, I have a basketball league I'm part of, so I do that once a week.

Therapist: And then you can shoot hoops on your own . . .

The therapist starts this intervention by utilizing the previous intervention: acknowledging that slip-ups and lapses are inevitable and should be expected. But this intervention goes a step further. The therapist helps partners find ways to care for themselves when slip-ups and lapses occur. What is important in this intervention is that the self-care strategies partners use are not hurtful to their partner. For instance, in this excerpt, the therapist helps Leslie explore using artwork as a way to cope with hurt feelings. This strategy seems helpful in calming Leslie and is easily available to her. Further, it is not hurtful to Ron when she engages in artwork. However, if Ron and Leslie often fought over the amount of time she spends working on artwork, or if her artwork turned into a large expense and Ron and Leslie often fought over finances, then this would not be an appropriate coping strategy for her to use. The therapist would work to help Leslie find a more innocuous coping strategy. In addition, it is necessary that the strategy be readily available. For instance, Ron feels that engaging in sports is a good strategy for him. However, the therapist probes him about the availability of team sports with his busy schedule and tries to suggest sports that he can engage in individually and right at his home. This makes the strategy more practical and more likely to be utilized when needed.

When partners have a coping strategy, they are less insistent that their partner change the behavior, and they give up the fight to change the behavior earlier. Consequently, encouraging partners to care for themselves in the face of aversive situations reduces the escalation of conflict and the amount of recovery time after a conflict.

Conclusions

Our empirical evaluations of ICT to date demonstrate promise in improving the effectiveness of couples therapy for couples such as Ron and Leslie who seek treatment hoping for a less distressed, more satisfying relationship with their partner. When introducing Ron and Leslie, we indicated that, before treatment, Ron was more distressed and less satisfied than Leslie but that both demonstrated clinically significant marital distress. This difference between their scores remained at the termination of treatment and at six-month and one-year follow-ups. However, their scores indicated reduced distress and increased satisfaction after treatment. Specifically, Leslie's MSI scores (higher scores indicate greater distress) were 58 before treatment, 54 after treatment, 53 six months after termination of treatment, and 48 one year after termination. On the DAS (higher scores indicate greater satisfaction), Leslie's scores went from 91 at pretreatment to 111 at posttreatment, 105 at six-month follow-up, and 120 at one-year follow-up. These scores indicate a general decline in marital distress and an increase in marital satisfaction. It appears that Leslie did not experience improvement in the time period from posttreatment to six-month follow-up and, in fact may have become less satisfied with the relationship during this time. Overall, however, she experienced significant relationship improvement and scored in the normal range of marital satisfaction by one-year follow-up. Ron's MSI scores were 71 at pretreatment, 64 at posttreatment, 67 at six-month follow-up, and 73 at one-year follow-up. Ron's DAS scores at these same times went from 88 to 96, 101, and 98. These scores demonstrate that Ron experienced less distress and more satisfaction from pretreatment to six-month follow-up but may have lost some of that improvement from six-month to one-year follow-up, placing him higher in relationship satisfaction than before treatment but still in the distressed range.

The ACAQ indicated some interesting results. Before treatment, it appeared that Ron exhibited positive behaviors more often than Leslie (9.4 per month for Ron's frequency of positive behaviors versus 5.9 per month for Leslie's) but that Leslie felt the frequency of positive behaviors was less acceptable (on a 10-point scale, 5.7 for Leslie's acceptance versus 7.5 for Ron's). After treatment, Ron reported that Leslie exhibited positive behaviors more frequently than before treatment (5.9 per month before and 9.2 per month after), but his acceptance of the frequency was slightly lower than his acceptance of the frequency before treatment (7.5 before and 6.0 after). For Leslie, the frequency with which Ron exhibited positive behaviors remained relatively constant (9.4 per month before and 9.1 per month after), but her acceptance of the frequency substantially increased (5.7 before and 10.0 after treatment). It appears that ICT created positive behavior changes and increased acceptance of the partner for Leslie but not for Ron. Interestingly, although Ron's positive behaviors remained relatively constant, Leslie's acceptance of those behaviors increased. Conversely, although Leslie's positive behavior increased substantially, Ron's acceptance of those behaviors decreased slightly. This may explain why Ron's level of satisfaction increased over treatment but remained lower than Leslie's. These results demonstrate that acceptance may be a powerful factor in improving relationship satisfaction in distressed couples.

Christensen and Jacobson have completed a pilot study designed to compare the effectiveness of TBCT and ICT (Jacobson, Christensen, Prince, Cordova, and Eldridge, in preparation). They recruited 21 distressed couples who were randomly assigned to either ICT or TBCT, and they found favorable results with ICT. Specifically, they found that ICT couples showed significantly more acceptance of negative behaviors than TBCT couples after completing therapy and significantly greater increases in marital satisfaction. Six months after termination of treatment, these differences between ICT and TBCT were increased; ICT couples maintained the improvements made in therapy whereas TBCT couples experienced some relapse. In fact, one year after treatment terminated, all ICT couples were still together, but 27% of TBCT couples had separated. These findings support the prediction that acceptance techniques may decrease distress in couples both immediately following treatment and in the future. Although promising, these findings are preliminary due to the small size of the sample. Recently, Christensen and Jacobson began a major five-year clinical trial of these two treatments.

Study Questions

1. What are the limitations of TBCT, and how does ICT attempt to account for those limitations?
2. What are the components of a case formulation? How is the formulation derived and presented to the couple? What is the purpose of the case formulation?

3. What are the interventions utilized in ICT to promote intimacy and toler-ance? How do these interventions create intimacy and tolerance?

References

Alexander, J. F., Holtzworth-Munroe, A., & Jameson, P. (1994). The process and outcome of marital and family therapy: Research review and evaluation. In A. E. Bergin & S. L. Garfield (Eds.), *Handbook of psychotherapy and behavior change* (pp. 595–630). New York: Wiley.

Baucom, D. H., & Hoffman, J. A. (1986). The effectiveness of marital therapy: Current status and application to the clinical setting. In N. S. Jacobson & A. S. Gurman (Eds.), *Clinical handbook of marital therapy* (pp. 597–620). New York: Guilford Press.

Brown, M., & Auerback, A. (1981). Communication patterns in initiation of marital sex. *Medical Aspects of Human Sexuality, 15,* 105–117.

Christensen, A. (1987). Detection of conflict patterns in couples. In K. Hahlweg & M. J. Goldstein (Eds.), *Understanding major mental disorders: The contribution of family interaction research* (pp. 250–265). New York: Family Process Press.

Christensen, A. (1988). Dysfunctional interaction patterns in couples. In P. Noller & M. A. Fitzpatrick (Eds.), *Perspectives on marital interaction* (pp. 31–52). Clevedon, England: Multilingual Matters.

Christensen, A., & Heavey, C. L. (in press). Interventions for couples. *Annual Review of Psychology.*

Christensen, A., Jacobson, N. S., & Babcock, J. C. (1995). Integrative behavioral couples therapy. In N. S. Jacobson & A. S. Gurman (Eds.), *Clinical handbook of marital therapy* (2nd ed.). New York: Guilford Press.

Crits-Christoph, P., Frank, E., Chambless, D. L., Brody, C., & Karp, J. F. (1995). Training in empirically validated treatments: What are clinical psychology students learning? *Professional Psychology: Research and Practice, 26,* 514–522.

Greenberg, L. S., & Johnson, S. M. (1986). Emotionally focused couples therapy. In N. S. Jacobson & A. S. Gurman (Eds.), *Clinical handbook of marital therapy* (pp. 253–276). New York: Guilford Press.

Hahlweg, K., & Markman, H. J. (1988). The effectiveness of behavioral marital therapy: Empirical status of behavioral techniques in preventing and alleviating marital distress. *Journal of Consulting and Clinical Psychology, 56,* 440–447.

Hahlweg, K., Schindler, L., Revenstorf, D., & Brengelmann, J. C. (1984). The Munich marital therapy study. In K. Hahlweg & N. S. Jacobson (Eds.), *Marital interaction: Analysis and modification* (pp. 3–26). New York: Guilford Press.

Hatfield, E., Sprecher, S., Pillemer, J. T., Greenberger, D., & Wexler, P. (1988). Gender differences in what is desired in the sexual relationship. *Journal of Psychology and Human Sexuality, 1,* 39–52.

Hendrick, S. S. (1997). Digit, change it, suck it up, or split. *Contemporary Psychology, 42,* 1097–1098.

Iverson, A., & Baucom, D. H. (1990). Behavioral marital therapy outcomes: Alternate interpretations of the data. *Behavior Therapy, 21,* 129–138.

Jacobson, N. S. (1989). The politics of intimacy. *The Behavior Therapist, 12,* 29–32.

Jacobson, N. S. (1992). Behavioral couple therapy: A new beginning. *Behavior Therapy, 23,* 493–506.

Jacobson, N. S., & Addis, M. E. (1993). Research on couples and couple therapy: What do we know? Where are we going? *Journal of Consulting and Clinical Psychology, 61,* 85–93.

Jacobson, N. S., & Christensen, A. (1996). *Integrative couple therapy: Promoting acceptance and change.* New York: Norton.

Jacobson, N. S., Christensen, A., Prince, S. E., Cordova, J., & Eldridge, K. A. (in preparation). Integrative behavioral couple therapy: An acceptance-based, promising new treatment for couple discord. University of Washington.

Jacobson, N. S., & Follette, W. C. (1985). Clinical significance of improvement resulting from two behavioral marital therapy components. *Behavior Therapy, 16,* 249–262.

Jacobson, N. S., Follette, W. C., & Pagel, M. (1986). Predicting who will benefit from behavioral marital therapy. *Journal of Consulting and Clinical Psychology, 54,* 518–522.

Jacobson, N. S., & Margolin, G. (1979). *Marital therapy: Strategies based on social learning and behavior exchange principles.* New York: Brunner/Mazel.

Jacobson, N. S., Schmaling, K. B., & Holtzworth-Munroe, A. (1987). A component analysis of behavioral marital therapy: Two-year follow-up and prediction of relapse. *Journal of Marital and Family Therapy, 13,* 187–195.

Lebow, J. L., & Gurman, A. S. (1995). Research assessing couple and family therapy. *Annual Review of Psychology, 46,* 27–57.

O'Leary, K. D., Vivian, D., & Malone, J. (1992). Assessment of physical aggression in marriages: The need for multimodal assessment. *Behavioral Assessment, 14,* 5–14.

Peplau, L. A., Rubin, Z., & Hill, C. T. (1977). Sexual intimacy in dating relationships. *Journal of Social Issues, 33,* 86–109.

Skinner, B. F. (1966). *The behavior of organisms: An experimental analysis.* Englewood Cliffs, NJ: Prentice Hall.

Snyder, D. K. (1979). Multidimensional assessment of marital satisfaction. *Journal of Marriage and the Family, 41,* 813–823.

Spanier, G. B. (1976). Measuring dyadic adjustment: New scales for assessing the quality of marriage and similar dyads. *Journal of Marriage and the Family, 38,* 15–28.

Stets, J. E., & Straus, M. A. (1990). Gender differences in reporting marital violence and its medical and psychological consequences. In M. A. Straus and R. J. Gelles (Eds.), *Physical violence in American families: Risk factors and adaptations to violence in 8,145 families* (pp. 151–166). New Brunswick, NJ: Transaction.

Straus, M. A. (1979). Measuring intrafamily conflict and violence: The conflict tactics (CT) scales. *Journal of Marriage and the Family, 41,* 75–88.

Straus, M. A., & Gelles, R. J. (1990). How violent are American families? Estimates from the national family violence resurvey and other studies. In M. A. Straus and R. J. Gelles (Eds.), *Physical violence in American families: Risk factors and adaptations to violence in 8,145 families* (pp. 95–112). New Brunswick, NJ: Transaction.

Sullaway, M., & Christensen, A. (1983). Assessment of dysfunctional interaction patterns in couples. *Journal of Marriage and the Family, 45,* 653–660.

Weiss, R. L., & Birchler, G. R. (1975). Areas of Change Questionnaire. Unpublished manuscript. University of Oregon, Marital Studies Program, Eugene.

Chapter Four

Pragmatic Couple Therapy: An Informed Pluralistic Approach

Douglas K. Snyder

Clinical interventions, including couple and family therapy, should be guided by comprehensive assessment across multiple domains and levels of system functioning, linkage of assessment observations to relevant theoretical frameworks, and empirical findings regarding the efficacy of interventions derived from competing treatment models (Snyder, Cavell, Heffer, and Mangrum, 1995). Each couple or family presents with unique, diverse patterns of factors contributing to distress, many of which are addressed at varying levels of success by different theoretical approaches. Tailoring clinical interventions to the specific needs of a couple or family in a systematic, theoretically coherent, and competent manner comprises one of the major challenges of effective therapy.

In this chapter, I present both the empirical and theoretical rationale for an informed pluralistic approach to couple therapy. I articulate a sequential model for interventions, ranging from crisis containment to exploration of developmental experiences contributing to current relationship distress. I argue that particularly complex or difficult cases may benefit most from a pluralistic strategy drawing from both conceptual and technical innovations from diverse theoretical models relevant to different components of a couple's struggles. The

Correspondence concerning this chapter should be sent to Douglas K. Snyder, Department of Psychology, Texas A&M University, College Station, TX 77843-4235.

case presented here reflects the level of complexity often requiring a flexible, pluralistic treatment approach.

Theoretical Underpinnings
Effectiveness of Couple Therapy

What do we know about the efficacy of couple therapy? From a meta-analysis by Shadish and colleagues (1993), we know that couple therapy demonstrates moderate, statistically significant, and often clinically significant effects. The average couple receiving therapy is better off at the end of treatment than 75% of couples not receiving therapy. At termination, approximately 65% of couples show significant improvement based on partners' averaged "satisfaction" scores.

However, research on couple therapy also indicates that approximately 35% of couples fail to show significant improvement. In only 50% of treated couples do both partners show significant improvement in marital satisfaction at termination. Moreover, in only 40% of treated couples does the level of marital satisfaction at termination approach the average level of marital satisfaction among community couples. Finally, long-term follow-up studies of couple therapy show significant deterioration among 30–60% of treated couples following termination (Jacobson, Schmaling, and Holtzworth-Munroe, 1987; Snyder, Wills, and Grady-Fletcher, 1991a).

Given the variability in couples' responses to treatment, some investigators have examined moderators of treatment outcome in an effort to answer the question, "For whom does marital therapy work?" Although inconsistent findings and methodological limitations plague much of the research in this area (Whisman and Snyder, 1997), there is growing evidence that various aspects of both individual and relationship functioning predict treatment outcome (Snyder, Cozzi, and Mangrum, in press; Snyder, Mangrum, and Wills, 1993). For example, depression in one or both partners appears to be a negative prognostic indicator in the majority of studies examining this variable. By contrast, higher levels of emotional expressiveness and interpersonal sensitivity denote greater probability of positive outcome. The quality of affection, intimacy, and commitment to the relationship also predict couples' responses to therapy; the more distressed the couple is at intake, the more difficult is the challenge of producing significant, lasting change. However, even these generalizations sometimes obscure complex relations between couples' functioning and treatment response. For example, Gottman and Krokoff (1989) showed that some forms of conflict engagement predict improved marital accord longitudinally, despite a concurrent association with relationship distress.

Mechanisms of Change

How does couple therapy work? Does changing a couple's patterns of interaction produce a change in their marital cognitions and affect? Does changing a couple's relationship beliefs produce a change in their marital affect and patterns of interaction? Or does changing a couple's affect—how they feel toward each other—change their patterns of interaction and their marital cognitions? Do different treatment approaches each achieve their efficacy through their own respective, unique mediators? Or do different approaches all achieve their efficacy through a common set of mediators?

These questions are hotly debated (Jacobson, 1991; Snyder and Wills, 1991; Snyder, Wills, and Faitler, 1988; Snyder, Wills, and Grady-Fletcher, 1991b). Competing models of marital therapy emphasize intervening primarily in one modality with the intent of producing secondary changes in the others. Which models of change have the greatest empirical support? More than 20 years of research indicate that teaching couples more effective communication techniques and increasing the ratio of positive reinforcement to negative reinforcement and punishment in partners' behavior exchanges result in increased relationship satisfaction (Jacobson and Addis, 1993; Shadish et al., 1993). However, there also is growing evidence that couples treated with behavioral techniques alone remain at significant deterioration in relationship satisfaction following treatment (Jacobson et al., 1987; Snyder et al., 1991a). In addition, several studies have found that communication skill acquisition during the course of therapy is not necessarily associated with increased marital satisfaction (Halford, Sanders, and Behrens, 1993; Iverson and Baucom, 1990). Investigators in this area have come to distinguish between behavioral potential and behavioral enactment—that is, between the acquisition of positive communication and behavior change skills and the performance or use of those skills.

Does change in marital cognitions (beliefs, expectancies, and attributions) lead to positive changes in couples' behavior and relationship satisfaction? Thus far, research indicates that the addition of cognitive restructuring and emotional expressiveness training to traditional behavioral marital therapy techniques does not appear to enhance overall treatment effectiveness in promoting marital satisfaction, although it does produce improvements on variables specifically targeted by these components (Emmelkamp, vanLinden van den Heuvell, Sanderman, and Scholing, 1988; Halford et al., 1993).

Does change in marital affect lead to constructive changes in couples' patterns of interaction and relationship cognitions? Some evidence has been obtained indicating that marital therapy approaches that address covert affective components to marital conflicts may provide longer-lasting improvements in marital satisfaction (Johnson and Greenberg, 1985; Snyder et al., 1991a). However, the number of studies in this area is small and replication is needed.

The Basis for Informed Pluralism

Couple therapists confront a tremendous diversity of presenting issues, marital and family structure, individual dynamics and psychopathology, and psychosocial stressors characterizing couples in distress. The causes of relationship distress vary, as do appropriate criteria for defining treatment success. For some couples, strengthening the affective relationship may be a primary goal, whereas for others, negotiating constructive dissolution to a dysfunctional marriage may be more appropriate. Because the functional sources of couples' distress vary so dramatically, the critical mediators or mechanisms of change also should be expected to vary—as should the therapeutic strategies intended to facilitate positive change.

Given the diversity in couples' needs, effective treatment is most likely to be rendered when the couple therapist has a solid grounding across diverse theoretical approaches, has acquired a rich repertoire of intervention techniques linked to theory, engages in comprehensive assessment of the marital and family system, and selectively draws on intervention strategies across the theoretical spectrum in a manner consistent with an explicit case formulation. By this definition, theoretical and technical pluralism does *not* equate to sloppy thinking, trial-and-error interventions, or simply "doing what feels right." Theoretical and technical pluralism, when expressed in a conceptually coherent and well-planned manner, provides both the comprehensiveness and the flexibility essential to tailoring clinical interventions to the unique characteristics and needs of our clients.

A Sequential Model for Organizing Interventions

A pluralistic approach to couple therapy may be facilitated by conceptualizing the therapeutic tasks as progressing sequentially along a continuum reflecting the couple's overall level of functioning—from the most chaotic relationship rooted in significant behavioral dyscontrol in one or both partners to the relatively benign but unfulfilled relationship in which conflicts involving such issues as autonomy or trust compromise emotional intimacy. Couples enter treatment at varying levels of functioning and require different initial interventions. Couples also proceed along the continuum of overall functioning during treatment, both requiring and enabling interventions of increasing depth and emotional challenge. Therapeutic movement is rarely linear, and an ability to recycle through more fundamental interventions to facilitate the couple's preparedness for conceptually more challenging work is the hallmark of effective treatment.

I have found it useful to conceptualize the therapeutic tasks of couple therapy as comprising six levels of intervention (see Figure 1). The model proposes a progression from the most fundamental interventions promoting a collaborative alliance to more challenging interventions addressing developmental sources of relationship distress. Consistent with our belief that couple therapy often proceeds in nonlinear fashion, the model depicts flexibility of returning to earlier therapeutic tasks as dictated by individual or relationship difficulties.

The most fundamental step in couple therapy involves developing a collaborative alliance between partners and between each partner and the therapist. The collaborative alliance begins with establishing an atmosphere of therapist competence through engaging in relevant assessment of both rela-

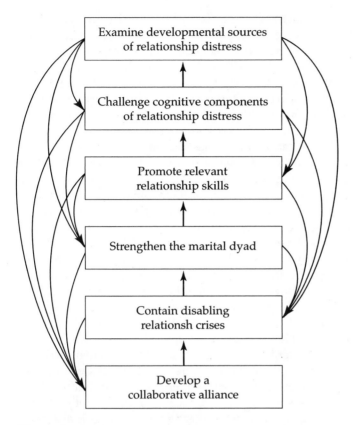

Figure 1
A sequential model for pragmatic couple therapy.

tionship and individual strengths and deficits and through modeling appropriate communication behaviors (Jacobson and Margolin, 1979). The collaborative alliance also requires establishing an atmosphere of safety in which the therapist sets limits on partners' negative exchanges within the session and provides an empathic response to both overt and covert expressions of partners' distress. Another vital component of the collaborative alliance is therapeutic trust, fostered by identifying the "relationship" as the client and articulating therapy ground rules around such issues as verbal and physical aggression, confidentiality, or handling of individual communications outside of sessions. Finally, the collaborative alliance is strengthened by offering a clear formulation of the couple's difficulties, outlining treatment objectives and basic strategies, and defining all participants' respective roles.

Couples sometimes present with disabling relationship crises that, until resolved, preclude development of communication skills and progress toward emotional intimacy. Occasionally, such crises emerge in otherwise healthy couples who return to a high level of functioning with minimal intervention emphasizing crisis resolution; such crises may be precipitated by unexpected job loss or financial hardship, illness or death of a family member, an unplanned or terminated pregnancy, and similar events (McDaniel, Hepworth, and Doherty, 1995; Mikesell and Stohner, 1995). With such crises, couples can be assisted in developing more adaptive attributions regarding their distress by distinguishing external stressors from relationship characteristics and by the therapist's actively promoting intermediate solutions (Shoham, Rohrbaugh, and Patterson, 1995).

More often, relationship crises among couples presenting for therapy occur against a backdrop of communication difficulties and an impoverished or insecure emotional context. A common crisis involves physical aggression by one or both partners against the other. Interventions to contain aggression must precede other efforts to strengthen the relationship and may include nonaggression pacts specifying guidelines for time-out, withdrawal to separate safe places, nonpursuit by each partner of the other, and availability of the therapist or other agent for crisis mediation between sessions (Heyman and Neidig, 1997). Another domain of crises requiring immediate attention involves major psychopathology and substance abuse disorders. Although such disorders nearly always contribute to and are frequently exacerbated by relationship difficulties, separate treatment for individual partners or other family members is often warranted—including medical, legal, financial, or other psychosocial intervention (Gotlib and McCabe, 1990; Halford and Bouma, 1997).

Couples in distress often describe an erosion of positive exchanges that has developed in response to internal discord and external stressors but that also leaves the relationship more vulnerable to subsequent challenges and conflicts of marriage and family life. For such couples, reducing conflict is not sufficient for restoring a healthy relationship; increasing positive interactions is also vital. With only a modicum of direction from the therapist, relatively well-functioning couples can sometimes mobilize dormant communication skills in constructing positive change agreements on their own, promoting a stronger "friendship" quality to the relationship (Bornstein and Bornstein, 1986).

However, other couples often lack communication skills essential to promoting positive change or are so burdened with negative affect as to preclude effective use of those skills. Such couples often require direct interventions by the therapist aimed at strengthening the relationship and securing a foundation of goodwill so that the couple can pursue the more difficult task of developing communication skills sufficient for constructing future agreements on their own. Strengthening the marriage sometimes requires little more than clearly identifying the marital dyad as the primary family unit and promoting an organization of the family system that honors parents' needs separate from those of their children, defines the parents' rights and responsibilities of leadership in the home, and establishes appropriate boundaries with respect to both families of origin (Todd, 1986). More often, couples displaying impoverished communication skills or overwhelming negativity require specific positive exchange agreements developed to a large degree by the therapist in consultation with both partners. That is, at this earlier developmental stage of couple therapy, the therapist may function more as a mediator and instigator of behavior change than as a communication skills trainer. A wide range of interventions for promoting reciprocity of positive interactions have been described in the literature, including methods of expanding companionship activities, restructuring habitual stressors, and contracting for mutual exchange of desired behaviors (Jacobson and Margolin, 1979; Stuart, 1980).

Sustaining a satisfying marriage requires a broad range of relationship skills. Primary among these are communication skills, long the hallmark of behavioral and related theoretical approaches to couple therapy. I find it useful to distinguish between *process-focused* and *problem-focused* communication skills. The former include (1) identifying feelings and beliefs, (2) conveying these feelings and beliefs to one's partner, (3) paraphrasing (mirroring) feelings and beliefs expressed by one's partner, (4) checking out assumptions, (5) giving behavior-effect feedback, and (6) acknowledging differences in perspective. Process-focused communication fosters intimacy through sharing of the private self not ordinarily disclosed in nonintimate relationships, particularly in discourse divorced from disagreements. Couples frequently identify such communication as a primary source of attraction early in their relationship.

By contrast, problem-focused communication has as its primary objective the resolution of interpersonal conflict. Promoting conflict resolution skills typically emphasizes such behaviors as (1) identifying or defining the problem, (2) generating and evaluating potential solutions, (3) selecting and implementing solutions, and (4) evaluating the solution's impact on the conflict and relationship. Problem-focused communication does not emphasize intimacy, although the impact of reduced conflict may facilitate other positive, intimate exchanges. Moreover, problem-focused communication may be hindered by deficits in process-focused communication skills. Partners may find it difficult to collaborate or compromise when either one feels misunderstood or unappreciated by the other. Thus, in most applications, training couples in both types of communication skills typically proceeds concurrently (Christensen, Jacobson, and Babcock, 1995).

However, the essential skills for a satisfying relationship extend beyond communication. In many areas, effective communication presumes a prerequisite knowledge base—something partners often lack and must be provided by the therapist or through adjunct resources identified by the therapist. For example, in addition to affective intimacy promoted through emotional expressiveness training, couples may benefit from interventions aimed at behavioral and physical intimacy. Behavioral intimacy may be enhanced by such behaviors as shared leisure activities that have declined through habituation, failure to develop new mutual interests, or deficits in protecting relationship time from external demands of career or child rearing. Sexual intimacy may suffer from the same processes or may stem from more basic information deficits regarding sexual anatomy and physiology. In both domains, the therapist serves to provide information, to direct the couple to outside sources of learning, and to promote new patterns of interaction (Spence, 1997).

In addition to intimacy skills, effective marital and family functioning typically requires a broad range of skills related to such challenges as parenting (Sanders, Markie-Dadds, and Nicholson, 1997), financial management (Aniol and Snyder, 1997), and negotiating competing demands on time (Thompson, 1997). As with more basic communication skills, the effective couple therapist functions to provide expertise concerning common strategies for mastering such tasks, assists the couple in exploring their own attitudes in these domains and in developing relevant new skills, and directs the couple to additional sources of information and support outside of therapy.

A common impediment to behavior change involves misconceptions and other interpretive errors that individuals may have regarding both their own and their partner's behavior (Epstein, Baucom, and Daiuto, 1997). Not only do such cognitive mediators contribute to negative affect, but they also result in behavioral strategies that frequently maintain or exacerbate relationship distress. A couple's resistance to interventions aimed directly at strengthening the marital dyad or promoting relevant relationship skills can often be diminished by examining and restructuring cognitive processes interfering with behavior change efforts. A considerable body of literature has emerged regarding both the nature of cognitive components contributing to relationship distress and strategies for intervention (Baucom and Epstein, 1990; Bradbury and Fincham, 1990; Dattilio and Padesky, 1990). For example, Baucom, Epstein, Sayers, and Sher (1989) have proposed a conceptual model for classifying cognitive factors into categories reflecting assumptions and standards, selective attention, expectancies, and attributions regarding the causes for relationship events. Interventions targeting each of these components of relationship distress have also been described; for example, couples can be taught to explore alternative explanations for negative exchanges that reduce a tendency to ascribe global, negative motives to their partner.

An important source of beliefs and expectancies regarding intimate relationships involves partners' developmental experiences within their family of origin and other intimate relationships in late adolescence or adulthood predating their current one. Relationship expectancies operate at multiple levels of awareness and contribute to both affective and behavioral predispositions that drive interpersonal exchanges in a distorted or exaggerated manner (Sager, 1981). It is my contention that an important source of current marital difficulties includes previous relationship injuries, resulting in sustained interpersonal vulnerabilities and related defensive strategies interfering with emotional intimacy. As such, interpretation of maladaptive relationship patterns evolving from developmental processes often comprises a critical element of effective couple therapy; it is to this treatment component that I give special attention.

Affective Reconstruction
of Relationship Dispositions
Theoretical Foundations

Relational models of psychodynamic therapy developed in the past 20 years for work with individuals offer important perspectives for approaching developmental sources of relationship distress with couples. As examined by Messer and Warren (1995), these relational models have their origins in the interpersonal constructs of Sullivan (1953) and other post-Freudian theorists, in revisions by object relations theorists such as Klein (1950) and Kernberg (1976), and in more recent conceptualizations of attachment theory (Bowlby, 1969; Kobak, Ruckde-schel, and Hazan, 1994) and interpersonal schemas (Horowitz, 1988). Adaptations of this work to brief psychodynamic therapy with individuals by Luborsky and colleagues (for example, Luborsky, 1984) and by Strupp and colleagues (for example, Strupp and Binder, 1984) have particular relevance to couple therapy.

In contrast to earlier psychoanalytic models emphasizing drives and personality structure serving drive containment, relational models emphasize recurrent maladaptive patterns of relationship behavior based in early interpersonal experiences—particularly in the family of origin but extending to significant attachments in adolescence and early adulthood. Sustained maladaptive patterns of relating to others in adulthood are viewed as defensive strategies aimed at controlling relationships in such a way as to minimize expected traumatic or painful outcomes (Messer and Warren, 1995). Common themes underlying previous relationship injuries may be experienced as persistent anxiety related to self (for example, enduring feelings of inadequacy, guilt, and shame) or persistent anxiety related to others (for example, fears of disapproval or abandonment). Common interpersonal strategies for containing such anxiety include exaggerated efforts at controlling oneself or others (particularly a partner in an intimate relationship), exaggerated attachment aimed at protecting against abandonment, or exaggerated autonomy intended to reduce personal vulnerability to anticipated loss. Contemporary relational models of therapy emphasize the cyclical and self-fulfilling nature of maladaptive interpersonal patterns

> in which feared and anticipated relational events tend to be elicited and enacted by the individual in his or her interactions with others, who, in turn, will tend to respond in ways complementary to the interpersonal actions of that individual. (Messer and Warren, 1995, p. 120)

Therapeutic Techniques

Developmental origins to interpersonal themes and their manifestation in a couple's relationship are explored in a process referred to as "affective reconstruction" (Snyder and Wills, 1989; Wills, Faitler, and Snyder, 1987)—roughly akin to traditional interpretive strategies promoting insight but emphasizing interpersonal schemas and relationship dispositions rather than instinctual impulses or drive derivatives. Previous relationships, their affective components, and strategies for emotional gratification and anxiety containment are reconstructed, with a focus on identifying for each partner similarities in their interpersonal conflicts and coping styles across relationships. In addition, ways in which previous coping strategies vital to prior relationships represent distortions or inappropriate solutions for emotional intimacy and satisfaction in the current relationship are articulated.

Obviously, an essential prerequisite to affective reconstruction of relational themes is a thorough knowledge of each partner's relational history. Construction of a genogram (Aylmer, 1986) often facilitates understanding not only of the individual's relationships within the family of origin but also relational themes in the family extending to prior generations. Beyond the family, intimate relationships with same-sex as well as opposite-sex peers from adolescence through the current time offer key information regarding such issues as perceived acceptance and valuation by others, trust and disappointment, stability and resilience of relationships to interpersonal injury, levels of attachment and respect for autonomy, and similar relational themes.

Initially, previous relationships are explored without explicit linkage to current relational difficulties in order to reduce anxiety and resistance during this exploration phase. Often individuals are readily able to formulate connections between prior relationships and current interpersonal struggles; when this occurs, it is typically useful for the therapist to listen empathically, encouraging the individual to remain "intently curious" about their own relational history but to refrain from premature interpretations that may be either incorrect, incomplete, or excessively self-critical. Just as important is for the individual's partner to adopt an accepting, empathic tone during the other's developmental exploration, encouraging self-disclosure in a supportive but noninterpretive manner.

Provided with relevant developmental history, the therapist encourages each partner to identify significant relational themes, particularly with respect to previous relationship disappointments and injuries. Gradually, as the couple continues to explore tensions and unsatisfying patterns in their own relationship, both partners can be encouraged to examine ways in which exaggerated emotional responses to current situations have at least partial basis in affective dispositions and related coping styles acquired in the developmental context. Both individuals can be helped to understand that, whereas certain relational coping strategies may have been adaptive or even essential in previous relationships, the same interpersonal strategies interfere with emotional intimacy and satisfaction in the present relationship.

Cognitive linkage of relational themes from the developmental to the current context frequently is insufficient for reconstructing or modifying these interpersonal patterns. Often the individual must be encouraged to work through previous relationship injuries—grieving losses and unmet needs, expressing ambivalence or anger toward previous critical others in the safety of the conjoint therapy, and acquiring increased differentiation of prior relationships from the present one. Understanding both the nature and the origins of cyclical maladaptive patterns paves the way for the therapist to promote alternative, healthier coping strategies to enhance relationship functioning. Similar to individual therapy adopting a relational model, the therapist serves as an "auxiliary processor" helping to "detoxify, manage, and digest" the client's relationship themes in a manner that promotes interpersonal growth (Messer and Warren, 1995, p. 141).

Specific therapeutic techniques relevant to examining relationship themes in individual therapy (compare Luborsky, 1984) apply to affective reconstruction from a relational model in couple therapy as well. For example, it is essential that the therapist recognize each partner's core relationship themes, that developmental interpretations link relational themes to a current relationship conflict, and that therapy focus on a few select relationship themes until some degree of resolution and alternative interpersonal strategies are enabled. It is also important that the extent and complexity of interpretations take into account the following:

1. The affective functioning of the individual and his or her ability to make constructive use of the interpretation
2. The level of insight and how near the individual is to being aware of the content of the proposed interpretation
3. The level of relationship functioning and the extent to which developmental interpretations can be incorporated in a mutually supportive manner

Therapeutic Benefits

Exploring relationship themes in the context of couple therapy provides clear advantages but also some potential risks relative to similar work in individual therapy. With regard to benefits, as in individual therapy, examining their own developmental components to current relationship distress offers each partner

- anxiety relief secondary to reduced confusion regarding their own emotional reactivity
- restored hope for greater emotional fulfillment in the relationship by resolving previous relationship injuries and developing new patterns of relating
- resolution of persistent conflicts and cyclical maladaptive patterns through redirected cognitive and behavioral interpersonal strategies

Moreover, in couple therapy, the "corrective emotional experience" (Alexander, 1956) of disrupting previous pathogenic interpersonal coping strategies and promoting new, more satisfying relational patterns has an opportunity to emerge not only between the individual and therapist but between the individual and his or her partner. As a participant-observer in their partner's work on developmental themes, the individual frequently comes to understand their partner's behaviors in a more accepting or benign manner—attributing damaging exchanges to the culmination of acquired interpersonal dispositions rather than to explicit motives to be hurtful. Oftentimes, this new understanding enables the partner to depersonalize the noxious effects of the other's behavior, to be less wounded and consequently less reactive in a reciprocally negative manner, and, instead, to provide emotional and strategic support for change.

The risks of examining developmental components of relationship distress in couple therapy relate primarily to the levels of trust that each partner experiences from and promotes in the other. Unless an atmosphere of safety can be established that extends beyond therapy sessions to the couple's interactions outside of therapy, each individual may be reluctant to disclose the intimate and emotionally difficult material from previous relationships essential to the process of affective reconstruction of relationship themes. Consequently, it behooves the therapist to discriminate carefully for which couples and at which point in therapy examining developmental components of relationship distress is likely to be beneficial (compare Strupp and Binder, 1984). Both individuals must be open to examining current relational difficulties from a developmental perspective. Both should exhibit some capacity for introspection, be open to examining feelings, and be able to resurrect salient affective experiences from previous relationships on a conscious level. Each partner needs to have established a basic level of trust with the therapist, experiencing the exploration of cyclical maladaptive patterns as promoting the individual's own relationship fulfillment. Moreover, both individuals need to exhibit a level of personal maturity and relationship commitment that enables them to respond to their partner's intimate disclosures with empathy and support, rather than seizing details of previous relationships as new and more potent ammunition in a mutual blaming process.

The case that follows exemplifies the application of a pluralistic approach to marital therapy with a couple presenting with extensive individual and relationship difficulties within both their own marriage and their respective families of origin. The therapy proceeded over a period of two years, generally following the sequential model outlined previously. In discussing this case, special attention is given to therapeutic work addressing developmental sources of relationship distress for both partners.

The Case: A Couple with Sexual and Financial Difficulties

Tom and Nancy, ages 45 and 44, had been married 24 years and had two sons, 15 and 18, when they were referred for couple therapy by a previous therapist. The couple reported extensive marital difficulties throughout their marriage, including conflict regarding their sexual relationship and financial stressors. The husband demanded that the wife act out sexual fantasies in which she would pretend to seduce him and engage in a variety of sexual roles and behaviors that she found degrading; if she refused, he would become enraged and threaten to leave her, at which point she experienced panic and typically complied with his requests but subsequently would become acutely depressed with suicidal ideation. In addition to their own difficulties, the couple's sons had dropped out of school, and the older one had begun to experiment with illicit drugs. The couple described a pattern of confusing daily oscillations between episodes of intense anger and displays of profound affection.

The couple met the year before Tom completed college and Nancy completed her associate's degree; they dated for a year before marrying. Tom stated that he was initially attracted to Nancy's warm and cheerful disposition; she offered that she had been drawn to his apparent confidence and sense of purpose. Since Tom's graduation, they had initiated several small businesses together in retail clothing, but the first three of these had failed. Both partners indicated that they had difficulty separating stresses of home life from stresses at work.

Ten years into their marriage they sought couple therapy for the first time, reporting that their therapist had helped both partners to "recognize individual rights as well as responsibilities." Five years later, living in a different community, the couple again sought therapy with the intent of developing better communication skills, reporting that this had been modestly successful. Several years later, after Tom became involved sexually with a woman he had met through work, the couple sought sex therapy; Nancy reported that their therapist had helped to demagnify sexual conflicts between them and had supported her in "working less hard" to please Tom and refraining from sexual activities with which she was uncomfortable. They had also previously sought family therapy related to their sons' school difficulties and rebelliousness at home. They acknowledged that, although each of the previous therapy experiences had provided them with important insights and improved communication skills, they often found if difficult to draw on these resources once they had entered into an argument. A month earlier, Tom had grown particularly frustrated with continuing sexual and financial disagreements with Nancy. He announced that he was "tired of hitting [his] head against a wall" and asked Nancy for a separation. At the time of this assessment, both partners professed a mix of bitter resentment as well as sadness concerning the potential end of their marriage.

As part of the initial assessment, both partners completed the Marital Satisfaction Inventory-Revised (MSI-R) (Snyder, 1979, 1997), a multidimensional self-report measure identifying sources and levels of relationship distress across 13 scales (see Figure 2). The couple's MSI-R profiles confirmed moderate levels of overall distress for both partners, with extensive conflict involving finances, their sexual relationship, and relationships with their sons. Both partners also reported substantial difficulties in problem solving or conflict resolution, although each expressed relatively greater satisfaction with expressions of affection. Nancy's profile indicated concerns regarding Tom's potential for aggression, although she subsequently clarified that this involved primarily emotional and verbal abuse. Relative relationship strengths included shared interests and a basic enjoyment of each other during lapses of overt conflict, as well as shared values concerning child rearing. Both partners' MSI-R profiles also indicated extensive distress in their respective families of origin.

Developmental Histories

Nancy was the third of eight children. Her father, deceased for ten years, abused alcohol and had been physically and emotionally abusive toward his wife and children. Her mother was still living at age 65 and suffered from

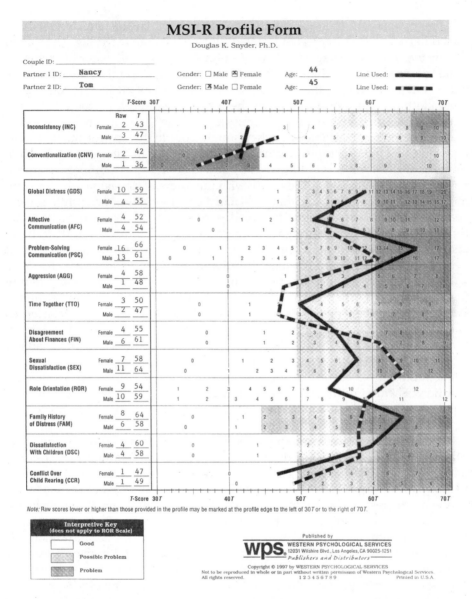

Figure 2
Couple profiles on the Marital Satisfaction Inventory-Revised (MSI-R) at initial assessment. Reprinted by permission.

manic-depressive illness with a history of suicidal behavior over the past 20 years. Her grandparents had also exhibited alcohol abuse or major psychiatric disorders. Nancy's older brother and sister and two younger sisters all suffered from psychotic disorders and had been hospitalized repeatedly; two other siblings had extensive histories of substance abuse and incarceration. Nancy had one younger sister who, like herself, had been spared major psychopathology but had experienced chronic relationship difficulties.

A major stress for the couple was the constant intrusion of Nancy's mother and several of her siblings. Members of her family frequently came to the couple's home while they were at work and stole food and clothing; the mother's manic depression often went uncontrolled because she refused medication, while demanding at the same time that Nancy and Tom provide for her physical and financial well-being. Nancy had been the major caretaker in her family of origin since early in adolescence and found it extremely difficult to establish any boundaries to protect the emotional well-being of her marriage and children. She felt responsible to provide for her siblings' children, who suffered considerable neglect, but also recognized that many of her own rescuing efforts sustained her sibings' dysfunctional behavior.

Tom's parents were both living and in retirement, but his father had been seriously ill for several years. Tom was the second of five children, with a younger sister and three brothers. Although neither parent demonstrated substance abuse or major psychopathology, it became apparent that there had been considerable dysfunction in his family of origin and that sexual conflicts pervaded his siblings' lives. An older brother revered in the family for his outstanding intellect had an extensive history of soliciting sexual partners for his wife so that he could observe them in intercourse. A younger brother had committed suicide as a young adult after determining that he was gay. Tom's third brother had been able to maintain a stable marriage but was generally withdrawn from the family and obviously anxious about sexual matters. His younger sister had been married to a sexually abusive man and, after experiencing divorce and other failed abusive relationships, had determined to remain single.

Tom denied that there had been any sexual or physical abuse in his family but reported that his father was frequently overseas for extended periods due to military service. Tom had always struggled in school, and his academic difficulties were exacerbated by his family's frequent moves. He tearfully recalled being taunted by his older brother for being "stupid" and with equally distressed affect described vague memories of standing outside school alone and crying. Tom's own sexual development had been conflicted. He recalled as an 11-year-old being pronounced as "the man in charge" at home but feeling inadequate to the challenge while his father served abroad and his older brother had left for college. He was acutely aware of his sexuality, recalled observing a neighbor woman who often undressed at night with her shades up, and acknowledged sexual arousal when occasionally sleeping with his mother when she became frightened at night by outdoor noises.

A critical incident occurred at age 12 when, growing increasingly preoccupied with sexual thoughts and curiosity, he approached his younger sister, then 8, on several occasions to examine and fondle her genitals. On one of these occasions he was discovered by his mother, and his parents' furious response and their branding Tom as a "pervert" continued to haunt him. Until the present therapy, Tom had never discussed this incident with anyone. One of his greatest fears continued to be that someone would determine that Tom was "perverted" and that, if he agreed to examine the nature and basis of sexual conflicts he and Nancy experienced, Tom would be required to relinquish his sexuality entirely.

Overview of Therapy

Initial interventions.   The couple entered treatment in crisis, still struggling with Tom's threat to leave Nancy if "she won't meet my needs." The couple agreed to an initial eight-week moratorium on any decisions to dissolve the marriage and to work during the interim on confronting immediate stressors and restoring at least a modest flow of positive exchanges. The initial phase of therapy lasted about four months and emphasized three components: (1) reducing escalation of negative exchanges, (2) containing external stressors, and (3) promoting positive exchanges.

With respect to negative exchanges, the couple reported that minor incidents frequently triggered negative exchanges that quickly escalated into major confrontations, which might last for days. Even within therapy sessions, once affect intensified, both partners' responses became increasingly hostile, threatening, and distorted—driven more by their own anxiety and misinterpretation of the other's comments or intentions than by the actual content of each other's statements. The couple's negative affect clearly had to be contained and allowed to dissipate before constructive communication skills could be mobilized. Toward this end, both partners agreed to de-escalation procedures, emphasizing renewable 30-minute time-outs with a commitment to resume productive discussion of issues once negative affect had dissipated.

Additional work during this initial phase of therapy emphasized containment of stressors related to work and Nancy's family. Tom had consistently been devoting at least 80 hours per week to their retail clothing business; he expected Nancy to do the same and his sons to work each afternoon and on weekends. He focused on their collective "need to do this for the family" and had little insight into his own fear of failing in another business or the reactivation of deep shame and feelings of inadequacy he had harbored since his youth. Tom felt unappreciated and exploited by his wife and sons, as they did by him. His need for control also caused him to interfere in his wife's and sons' efforts in the business, reducing their effectiveness and the business's profitability. Couple therapy during this initial phase emphasized negotiating domains of respective responsibility and authority for Tom and Nancy both at home and at their business, without interpreting underlying pressures that had contributed to their exaggerated roles.

During the second month of therapy, Nancy's mother insisted on moving to the couple's community from out of state, where she had alternated living with her children or on the streets. Her mother was acutely manic, but Nancy initially felt obligated to have her move in with them, moving their two sons into one room. Predictably, her mother's illness (including prolonged sleeplessness, unpredictable rage episodes, and stealing of money) severely disrupted their family life and further eroded family members' ability to function effectively during the day at the business. Nancy began to recognize her own helplessness in managing her mother's behavior and gradually became receptive to exploring alternative community mental health and social services. With direction from the therapist and encouragement from Tom, she established boundaries on the family's and her own response to her mother's demands when her mother refused treatment. Alternative living was identified for her mother, and modest stabilization of her mother's illness was achieved.

As crises at home diminished and the couple was able to establish a more functional distribution and balance of efforts at work, Tom and Nancy became somewhat more effective in restoring positive interactions in their relationship. However, progress in increasing positive exchanges was constrained by a history of impoverished relationship rewards outside their business and their sexual relationship and by both partners' initial reluctance to discuss specific content of their sexual conflicts in therapy. An avenue of increasing satisfaction that proved fruitful was promoting the couple's collaboration in pursuing a family vacation and other nonwork-related activities with their sons.

Midtreatment interventions.   Reduction in the frequency and intensity of negative exchanges and a gradual increase in Tom and Nancy's positive exchanges permitted greater emphasis in therapy on developing the couple's communication skills. Although both individuals made efforts to exercise active listening, in fact, their efforts to paraphrase were consistently riddled with distortions, inaccurate attributions about their partner's underlying emotions or intentions, and projections of their own feelings and beliefs. Moreover, as the affective intensity of their discussions mounted, the couple's efforts at problem solving frequently became increasingly disorganized. The content of their verbal exchanges became progressively tangential to the identified problem, generativity of alternative solutions stalled, and each partner's respective attachment to their own favored proposals became increasingly inflexible. Handouts on effective communication behaviors, modeling and intensive shaping of more effective communication, and identifying early indicators of less constructive exchanges in order to implement corrective strategies all gradually combined to produce more consistently positive discourse during and between sessions.

Over the ensuing year, Tom and Nancy began to use therapy sessions to collaborate on goals extending beyond their own immediate relationship, aimed at enhancing the overall functioning of the nuclear family and at differentiating from pathogenic stressors in the extended family system. For example, several sessions were used to discuss ways of granting additional autonomy to their sons, appropriate to their respective ages, while establishing clear guidelines and consequences for illicit drug use. The couple continued to define the limits of their responsibilities with respect to Nancy's mother and siblings. They also collaborated in supporting each other's efforts to increase their own individual sources of self-esteem; for example, Tom offered greater support for Nancy's involvement in the church, and Nancy provided greater opportunity for Tom's pursuit of physical exercise.

In addition, both partners were encouraged to build on family strengths. For example, Nancy was encouraged to fortify the relationship with the sister who shared Nancy's relative resilience to her family's pathology, to visit the sister for a week, and to explore with her their respective roles in the family and the strategies they had used to survive their father's abuse and their mother's emotional instability. The sister helped Nancy to discern her caretaker role in the family of origin as well as ways in which she had generalized this in an unhealthy manner to her husband and sons. Similarly, Tom was encouraged to visit his dying father and was able to affirm his parents' pride in his accomplishments, to distance himself from his older brother's inappropriate sexual solicitations, and to establish a leadership role in helping the family cope with his father's subsequent death; he also began to move beyond residual shame in reuniting with his sister and providing her with encouragement and emotional support in her own relationship struggles.

During this middle phase of therapy, both individuals also became more receptive to exploring cognitive components of their relationship distress. Several sessions were devoted to beliefs each held regarding appropriate roles in their marriage—particularly Tom's exaggerated reliance on his role as financial provider for feelings of worth in the family and Nancy's excessive emphasis on her role as emotional provider and her deep disappointment when her efforts failed to yield the reciprocity of attachment she sought. Tom also began to acquire greater recognition of ways in which he interpreted Nancy's rejection of specific sexual behaviors as an indictment of his sexuality. Although both Tom and Nancy had modest levels of insight into their respective interpersonal patterns, their previous level of relationship distress and the frequency of conflict had heretofore precluded exploration of these dynamics and their developmental origins on an affective level. Only after trust deepened in their marriage and in their own emotional resources could this couple pursue a more penetrating examination of early relationship experiences and subsequent effects on their own relationship.

Concluding phase of therapy.   During the final six months of therapy, Tom and Nancy began to consolidate important insight into developmental sources of their relationship distress. Although Nancy had achieved substantial gains in setting appropriate boundaries with members of her family, she continued to struggle with feelings of guilt and inadequacy when her mother or siblings challenged these limits.

Late in the therapy when her mother faced removal of a diseased kidney, Nancy began the session in a state of heightened anxiety.

Nancy: I don't know what to do. After her surgery, Mom's going to need someone to look after her. If I don't do it, who's going to? She's talking about coming to our place, and it's going to be hell all over again.
Tom: We can do it if we have to. Besides, there may be some other options.
Nancy: I don't want to go through what we did a year ago. It's not just that she'll have to stay in bed and I'll have to tend to her full-time . . . she *won't* stay in bed. She'll be up all to time, won't listen, probably break her stitches open, and I'll feel to blame. And who's going to help at the store?

Just now when we're starting to get on our feet financially and Dave and Mike [their sons] are getting squared away.

Therapist: It feels like a threat to what you and Tom have accomplished?

Nancy: It feels like a threat and it feels hopeless . . . a no-winner. Maybe it's not, but that's the way it feels right now. We're not just talking about Mom's feelings here; her health and maybe her life are at stake, and I feel responsible.

Tom: You're not responsible, and you're not alone. We're all in this together, okay?

Therapist: Nancy, I know this is a hard one and I hear your frustration. But it also seems to me that these feelings are similar to ones we've worked on before.

Nancy: Yeah, I guess so, just stronger.

Therapist: Would you be willing to look at those feelings some more today and see if you can figure anything out that might help them seem a bit less overwhelming?

Nancy: It just feels like it used to . . . that I've got to be the one to hold things together. I know we've talked about that before . . . about being the caretaker.

Therapist: How does it feel to be the caretaker?

Nancy: Lousy, but maybe sometimes not so lousy.

Therapist: Tell me more about that.

Nancy: Well, at least I know where I belong. I have a place. My family depends on me, they look up to me. Even if they use me half the time, at least they know that I'm there for them.

Therapist: It feels good to be looked up to.

Nancy: Yeah, and it feels good to me to know that I'm taking care of someone, that they can count on me. And besides, I'm her daughter. That's supposed to count for something, right?

Therapist: Sure.

Nancy: So at least I have something to count on.

Therapist: What are you counting on?

Nancy: A place for me, I guess. I may not be that smart, or that pretty . . .

Tom: Sure you are.

Nancy: . . . but I know I can help take care of someone, at least if they'll let me.

Therapist: And that's the part that feels good?

Nancy: Mostly, I guess.

Therapist: Having a place for you?

Nancy: Yeah.

Therapist: What would you have if you gave that place up?

Nancy: Gave it up?

Therapist: Who would you be if you weren't the caretaker?

Nancy: I don't know. [pause]

Therapist: Who would you have?

Nancy: I don't know that, either.

Tom: You'd have me.

Nancy: Bullshit! What do you think I face with you? [starts to cry] It's the same old thing all over. You tell me that you need me . . . need me sexually . . . but it's got to be your way or it's no good, or I'm rejecting and hurting you, and I'm just a selfish bitch . . . [continues to sob]

Tom: I'm sorry . . . [pause]

Therapist: The "selfish" part . . . Is that familiar, too?

Nancy: They both used to say it, all the time. I looked out for everyone else when Dad was drunk, even Mom. I'd keep them out of his way. He usually wouldn't hit me. But he'd call me a whore and a selfish bitch if I didn't get him whatever he wanted.

Therapist: What did he want?

Nancy: Nothing sexual, if that's what you're wondering. Mostly more booze, or his slippers, or his boots. Whatever it was I brought him, he wanted something else instead. Except when he was sober.

Therapist: What was it like then?

Nancy: Then I was special. He counted on me . . . 'cause half the time when Dad was sober, Mom was in one of her manic rages. And when she wasn't in a rage, he was usually drunk. I never really had either one of them.

Therapist: That was the lousy part?

Nancy: Yeah, whatever I did, it wasn't enough. So I'd try harder, whatever they wanted, whatever worked. But it never did.

Therapist: What would have happened if you had stopped trying?

Nancy: Stop? I don't know. I think the whole family would have fallen apart.

Therapist: Fallen apart?

Nancy: I just don't know.

Therapist: What would have happened then, if the family had fallen apart?

Nancy: I don't know. [long pause] I had to hold things together.

Therapst: Is that the panic you feel with Tom?

Nancy: Yes, exactly. I have to hold us together, whatever it takes. It used to be I just couldn't stand it when he'd get angry. I'd do anything. But then I'd feel resentful and depressed afterwards. Because it's never enough, and I don't get what I'm supposed to.

Therapist: What's that?

Nancy: I'm supposed to be held, too.

Therapist: Like the child?

Nancy: Like the child. Cuddled and loved. But I feel unlovable, even after we have sex, because its not like he's really attracted to me; he's just trying to deal with his own needs.

Tom: Nancy, that's not the way I mean it to be. [pause] I do find you attractive, and you are intelligent. I love the way you're sensitive to everyone else's feelings, but it can't be at the cost of how you feel about yourself because that ends up not being good for us anyway. When you dislike yourself, you end up disliking me.

Therapist: Nancy, its pretty scary as a youngster to feel like you're responsible for holding the entire family together, and even scarier to imagine your own vulnerability if the family falls apart around you.

Nancy: Yeah, it is.

Therapist: But you're not as exposed or without resources as you were as a youngster. And Tom's a lot healthier than either your mom or dad were, and he's not going to fall apart on you if you don't provide him everything he wants.

Tom: I won't fall apart . . . [pause]

Therapist: And at this point in your marriage, I don't think he's about to leave you either.

Tom: I'm not about to leave. I still get frustrated and angry sometimes, and that's my own issue, and I've got to get better about that. But we can make it through.

Nancy: You don't get nearly as angry as you used to. You withdraw, but I can give you the space. You don't come after me and call me names anymore. You've gotten a lot better.

Therapist: Nancy, I want to help you with the feelings you're struggling with today concerning your mom. Is there a way you could give up some of the caretaker role and still retain the identity of faithful daughter that you value?

For the remainder of this and the next session, Nancy and Tom explored ways of dealing with her mother's impending surgery. Together they identified resources in the community to provide limited nursing and supervision of her mother at her own home during the day for the first month following surgery. They added temporary help at the store so Nancy could spend more time with her mother, and Tom relieved her most nights so she could get respite and spend time with their sons. In addition, Nancy's sister came from out of state to care for their mother for two weeks. Nancy developed an enhanced sense of efficacy not only for dealing with her mother and siblings but also for collaborating with Tom and developing more constructive solutions to long-term struggles in their marriage.

Nancy was also able to generalize her heightened sense of identity and capacity for limit setting to the couple's sexual relationship. Although they engaged in intercourse several times weekly and Nancy generally enjoyed these times, she found an increased ability to decline participation in specific sexual behaviors she experienced as emotionally uncomfortable. She became stronger in tolerating her anxiety induced by Tom's displeasure with her, anticipated and weathered the initial escalation of his anger, distanced herself from his criticism, but remained available to him once he approached her in a collaborative and nonaggressive manner.

Tom also made progress in examining developmental sources of anxiety contributing to current struggles, although his gains were slower and more labored. During the initial phase of therapy, he was openly resistant to such work, acknowledging that early experiences likely exerted a major influence on his conflicts with Nancy, but also asserting that the prospects of examining these experiences were so threatening that he found himself blocking out discussion of those events, becoming confused, and subsequently feeling more agitated during the week. The therapist's tact was to accept Tom's resistance, welcoming his acknowledgment of these feelings and offering reassurance that Tom could proceed at his own pace and explore these issues as he felt comfortable and inclined to do so.

Initially, Tom's successes involved his attaining greater insight into nonsexual components of his feelings of inadequacy. He spent considerable time examining his position in the family growing up and his enduring feelings of intellectual inferiority. His feelings of inadequacy were compounded by both brothers' professional and financial success as adults. The apparent confidence that Nancy had been drawn to during their courtship had been in part a facade, and Tom had felt increasingly compelled to affirm his worth to her in the face of their financial difficulties and business failures. He tearfully recalled repeated events throughout his childhood and adolescence when he had felt woefully inadequate at school, socially isolated and inept, and with few attachments other than the caring he experienced from his mother.

As Tom disclosed these hurtful experiences, Nancy provided a remarkable level of empathy and reassurance. She disclosed her own perception of ways Tom continued to be minimized by his older brother but also noted ways in which both Tom's parents and sister looked to him to provide leadership in their family around issues of his parents' care. Nancy also affirmed Tom's success in their current business, noted external factors that had contributed to their shared failures in the past, and expressed her wish that Tom would share more of the business challenges with her so that he wouldn't experience the unfair burden of singular responsibility for its success or demise. Gradually, Tom began to experience Nancy's efforts to share in administration of their business as a source of support rather than as a threat, a cognitive shift that generalized to their sons' contributions as well.

Tom's insight into the sources and pattern of his sexual conflicts with Nancy came more slowly and with considerable struggle. With time, he became aware of his heightened sexual exposure during his latency years. For example, he had vivid recollections of listening at night to his parents' lovemaking, his older brother's explicit discussion of sexual topics, and their shared experience of perusing sexually-oriented magazines and being aroused by descriptions of unconventional sexual practices. He also recalled the implicit prohibition against discussing sexual matters in his family and the tremendous guilt and shame that accompanied his sexual fantasies. Tom had almost no dating experiences during adolescence and few male friends. Early in his relationship with Nancy, the conflict between his sexual preoccupation and guilt found expression in his efforts to have Nancy assume the initiative in acting out sexual fantasies he found particularly arousing, providing him with a heightened sexual experience but partially absolving him of responsibility for the sexual exchange. Typically, this proceeded by Tom's scripting sexual scenarios for the couple in which Nancy was to assume the role of sexual aggressor. Although

Nancy was comfortable with some of the roles Tom scripted for her, she found others degrading or incongruent with her values. When she resisted these roles, Tom typically experienced a flood of anxiety, perceived Nancy's protest as an indictment of his own sexuality, and retaliated by verbally attacking Nancy or threatening to leave their relationship.

The goals of therapy related to this destructive cycle were to help Tom

1. understand the sources of both his sexual arousal pattern and the anxiety and shame linked to these
2. distinguish between the acceptability of sexual fantasies versus the challenges of enacting these fantasies in a relationship with someone having different sexual values or arousal patterns
3. distinguish between Nancy's resistance to specific sexual behaviors and a generalized rejection of either their sexual relationship or Tom's sexuality

Therapeutic progress toward these goals required alternating exploration of early experiences with interventions aimed at strengthening the marriage and Tom's confidence in himself, due to the tremendous anxiety he experienced in recalling the profound feelings of inadequacy and shame that had pervaded his youth.

Toward the latter part of therapy, having explored many of these dynamics on previous occasions, Tom introduced this topic at the beginning of a session once again following conflict he and Nancy had experienced in their sexual relationship earlier in the week:

Therapist: Where would it be helpful to begin today?

Tom: Well, I think I'd like to work on an incident that occurred this week between Nancy and me in our sexual relationship.

Therapist: Nancy?

Nancy: That's fine with me. I think we need to take another look at this.

Tom: I know we've been through this before, but I'm still having trouble with it . . . [pause]

Therapist: With . . .

Tom: With Nancy's saying no to things I want sexually.

Nancy: Not everything, not even most things.

Tom: No, I know that. But that's not how I experience it then. I can usually see that later but not at the moment. I still feel this panic . . . scared . . . like I'm not going to be able to have sex with you at all, that you find me disgusting.

Nancy: Tom, that's not how I feel. I wish you could see that.

Tom: No, I know. but when it happens, I still panic.

Therapist: Tom, can you talk about the panic?

Tom: Well, it's like we've discussed before . . . like that post-traumatic stress thing we've talked about.

Therapist: Uh-huh.

Tom: Well, I know that I'm vulnerable in this way. I used to feel like such shit all the time. I tried to hide it, I guess even from me. But it was still there.

Especially around sex. I was always horny . . . guess I still am . . . I know that's sometimes how I try to feel good about myself. I really need Nancy to want me sexually.

Nancy: Tom, I do.

Tom: But there are some things you think are perverted.

Nancy: I don't know that they're perverted, but I don't always like them. Besides, sometimes when we're acting out scenarios I feel like you're having sex with someone other than me. That's okay sometimes, but sometimes I just want you to make love with the real me.

Tom: See, I really have trouble with that. Because I know you're right and I can see that now, but the other night I couldn't see that at all . . . [long pause]

Therapist: Tom, you've been working a long time to develop a better understanding of what goes on with you during these exchanges with Nancy around your sexual relationship.

Tom: Yeah, I have.

Therapist: My sense is that you've actually acquired a lot of insight into this pattern and that you can gain perspective on these exchanges much more quickly now—usually by the next day, sometimes even an hour or so later.

Tom: Usually, I can.

Nancy: That's really true, Tom. I know you still really struggle with this, and I don't like these times when we get into conflict any more than you do. But it's a lot better than it used to be.

Tom: Well, I think that's because you've really gotten healthier. I just wish I didn't still have this panic and then blow up.

Nancy: Well, I think I have gotten better. I don't have the same panic myself when you get angry with me. I can give you some space, and I don't feel like I have to rush in there and make sure we're okay so much. But it really isn't just me, Tom. You reconnect with me a whole lot sooner than you used to. And you don't make threats about leaving anymore . . . [long pause]

Therapist: Tom, it sounds like you're having trouble taking the insight you've gained from your work here and drawing on that insight during these moments of conflict with Nancy.

Tom: Well, that's right. It's hard to use what I know rationally when that panic jumps out again and makes me irrational.

Therapist: Is there some way you could preserve those insights and make them more accessible to you when you feel panicked?

Tom: I don't know. I know I'm not able to hear anything constructive from Nancy at those times. [long pause]

Therapist: What would it be like if you were to write down your understanding of this pattern in your own words, when you're not feeling panicked?

Tom: You mean like today? Because I really think I can see clearly that Nancy wasn't rejecting me or my sexuality. She just didn't want to act out that particular scenario at that particular time.

Therapist: Uh-huh, like today. Talk with me about how that could work, how you could make use of that.

At this point, the therapist chose not to do additional exploratory work but, instead, to explore ways of strengthening the insight and making it more accessible using more cognitive strategies.

Tom: Well, I guess I could write it down and then review it when I'm feeling really anxious about Nancy's and my sexual relationship.

Therapist: Do you think you could direct yourself to review what you had written in those "irrational" moments when you feel overwhelmed?

Tom: I think so. Sometimes, just taking time-out from Nancy helps. But other times when I do that, I start cycling through all those negative thoughts in my head, and they just get worse. So being able to read what I've written myself when I'm more rational might help to interrupt that.

Therapist: Good for you. So what kinds of things do you think it might be important for you to write down in a preparatory kind of way to help you when you're feeling so anxious?

Tom: Well, I think I could remind myself that just because Nancy doesn't want to do something sexually at that time doesn't mean she won't possibly be open to it some other time. And even if she's not, that doesn't mean that she doesn't like having sex with me or that she finds me disgusting.

Therapist: Would that be helpful to you?

Tom: I think so. At least I'd like to try it. Because lots of times I can really see it now, what's going on between us, and what's going on with me that makes me get crazy. Used to be I could never see that . . . but now I can. I just need to figure out a way of holding on to that better.

Conclusions

In introducing a pluralistic approach to pragmatic couple therapy, I asserted that complex or difficult cases often require conceptual and technical innovation from diverse theoretical models relevant to different components of a couple's struggles. Not all couples require each of the treatment components outlined in the sequential model proposed here. Nor do most couples require the extended duration of therapy that this couple required. With relatively higher functioning couples, I have been able to implement the complete model in as few as eight to ten sessions.

Which aspects of assessment findings for this couple suggested the need for a broad pluralistic approach? One obvious element was the diversity of individual and relationship deficits across behavioral, cognitive, and affective domains. Although Tom and Nancy had received couple and family therapy previously and had acquired some understanding of fundamental communication skills, they consistently had difficulty implementing these skills effectively in emotional exchanges. Expectations they held for themselves and their partner interfered with negotiating more successful patterns of relating at home and at work. Moreover, it became apparent early in treatment that exploration of relationship beliefs and patterns of negative exchange rapidly evoked immense anxiety and defensive strategies for both partners, interfering with a more narrowly cognitive approach. The extent of psychopathology in both families of origin and its continuing intrusion into the couple's relationship also indicated the need for broad, systems-focused interventions. Finally, the lifelong history of relationship struggles and emotional lability of both partners suggested underlying characterological deficits that would likely undermine cognitive-behavioral strategies restricted to current interaction patterns.

Initial assessment findings also suggested the potential benefit of a relational approach incorporating affective reconstruction of developmental relationship experiences. Both Tom and Nancy recognized the pervasiveness of relationship disturbances in their families of origin and had a vague but incomplete appreciation that their developmental experiences likely contributed to their own marital struggles. Each of them felt generally positive about their previous therapeutic experiences and generalized this confidence and trust to the present therapist. Moreover, both partners were able to offer each other considerable support and empathy in exploring their respective family dynamics and their relevance to current difficulties. Their capacity for emotional support and fundamental commitment to the marriage were reflected in their initial MSI-R profiles: While reflecting extensive deficits in problem-solving skills and considerable conflict in selected domains, test findings suggested only moderate levels of overall relationship discontent or distress regarding nonsexual affective or behavioral closeness. Had either partner not been able to provide support to the other during sessions emphasizing affective reconstruction, additional preparatory interventions targeting reduction of relationship animosity and empathy training would have been necessary.

Finally, the nonlinear progression of couple therapy from a pluralistic approach should again be noted. Although the sequence of interventions generally advances from crisis containment to promoting relevant skills and examining developmental sources of relationship distress, both external stressors as well as regressive responses to internal anxiety frequently require a return to interventions operating at a more fundamental level in the strategic hierarchy. Integration of technically and theoretically diverse interventions, applied flexibly in a manner guided by a comprehensive conceptual model of the couple and extended social system, maximizes the potential for offering treatment relevant to a couple's unique needs at any time during the therapeutic process.

Study Questions

1. The author asserts that couple therapy is most effective when the therapist draws on conceptual and technical innovations from diverse theoretical perspectives. What findings regarding the efficacy of couple

therapy and moderators and mediators of treatment outcome support this assertion?

2. Do different treatment approaches each achieve their efficacy through their own respective mechanisms, or do different approaches all work through a common set of mediators? Support your own position on this debate.

3. The author describes a sequential model for organizing treatment interventions with difficult or complex cases. What are the major components of this model, and what rationale is provided for their sequence? What couple characteristics might argue for a different organization to treatment?

4. How do relational models of psychodynamic therapy differ from traditional psychoanalytic approaches? How does the author generalize relational models of treatment to couple therapy? Describe both the rationale and techniques of affective reconstruction.

5. Describe individual and relationship characteristics that would influence you to use or not use techniques of affective reconstruction with a couple.

References

Alexander, F. (1956). *Psychoanalysis and psychotherapy.* New York: Norton.

Aniol, J. C., & Snyder, D. K. (1997). Differential assessment of financial and relationship distress: Implications for couples therapy. *Journal of Marital and Family Therapy, 23,* 347–352.

Aylmer, R. C. (1986). Bowen family systems marital therapy. In N. S. Jacobson & A. S. Gurman (Eds.), *Clinical handbook of marital therapy* (pp. 107–148). New York: Guilford Press.

Baucom, D. H., & Epstein, N. (1990). *Cognitive-behavioral marital therapy.* New York: Brunner/Mazel.

Baucom, D. H., Epstein, N., Sayers S., & Sher, T. G. (1989). The role of cognitions in marital relationships: Definitional, methodological, and conceptual issues. *Journal of Consulting and Clinical Psychology, 57,* 31–38.

Bornstein, P. H., & Bornstein, M. T. (1986). *Marital therapy: A behavioral-communications approach.* New York: Pergamon Press.

Bowlby, J. (1969). *Attachment and loss: Vol. 1. Attachment.* New York: Basic Books.

Bradbury, T. N., & Fincham, F. D. (1990). Attributions in marriage: Review and critique. *Psychological Bulletin, 107,* 3–33.

Christensen, A, Jacobson, N. S., & Babcock, J. C. (1995). Integrative behavioral couple therapy. In N. S. Jacobson & A. S. Gurman (Eds.), *Clinical handbook of couple therapy* (pp. 31–64).

Dattilio, F. M., & Padesky, C. A. (1990). *Cognitive therapy with couples.* Sarasota, FL: Professional Resource Exchange.

Emmelkamp, P. M. G., van Linden van den Heuvell, C., Sanderman, R., & Scholing, A. (1988). Cognitive marital therapy: The process of change. *Journal of Family Psychology, 1,* 385–389.

Epstein, N. B., Baucom, D. H., & Daiuto, A. (1997). Cognitive-behavioural couples therapy. In W. K. Halford and H. J. Markman (Eds.), *Clinical handbook of marriage and couples interventions* (pp. 415–449). New York: Wiley.

Gotlib, I. H., & McCabe, S. B. (1990). Marriage and psychopathology. In F. D. Fincham & T. N. Bradbury (Eds.), *The psychology of marriage: Basic issues and applications.* New York: Guilford Press.

Gottman, J. M., & Krokoff, L. J. (1989). Marital interaction and satisfaction: A longitudinal view. *Journal of Consulting and Clinical Psychology, 57,* 47–52.

Halford, W. K., & Bouma, R. (1997). Individual psychopathology and marital distress. In W. K. Halford and H. J. Markman (Eds.), *Clinical handbook of marriage and couples interventions* (pp. 291–321). New York: Wiley.

Halford, W. K., Sanders, M. R., & Behrens, B. C. (1993). A comparison of the generalization of behavioral marital therapy and enhanced behavioral marital therapy. *Journal of Consulting and Clinical Psychology, 61,* 51–60.

Heyman, R. E., & Neidig, P. H. (1997). Physical aggression couples treatment. In W. K. Halford and H. J. Markman (Eds.), *Clinical handbook of marriage and couples interventions* (pp. 589–617). New York: Wiley.

Horowitz, M. (1988). *Introduction to psychodynamics: A new synthesis.* New York: Basic Books.

Iverson, A., & Baucom, D. H. (1990). Behavioral marital therapy outcomes: Alternative interpretations of the data. *Behavior Therapy, 21,* 129–138.

Jacobson, N. S. (1991). Behavioral versus insight-oriented marital therapy: Labels can be misleading. *Journal of Consulting and Clinical Psychology, 59,* 142–145.

Jacobson, N. S., & Addis, M. E. (1993). Research on couples and couple therapy: What do we know? Where are we going? *Journal of Consulting and Clinical Psychology, 61,* 85–93.

Jacobson, N. S., & Margolin, G. (1979). *Marital therapy: Strategies based on social learning and behavior exchange principles.* New York: Brunner/Mazel.

Jacobson, N. S., Schmaling, K. B., & Holtzworth-Munroe, A. (1987). Component analysis of behavioral marital therapy: Two-year follow-up and prediction of relapse. *Journal of Marital and Family Therapy, 13,* 187–195.

Johnson, S. M., & Greenberg, L. S. (1985). Differential effects of experiential and problem-solving interventions in resolving marital conflict. *Journal of Consulting and Clinical Psychology, 53,* 175–184.

Kernberg, O. F. (1976). *Object relations theory and clinical psychoanalysis.* Northvale, NJ: Aronson.

Klein, M. (1950). *Contributions to psychoanalysis.* London: Hogarth.

Kobak, R., Ruckdeschel, K., & Hazan, C. (1994). From symptom to signal: An attachment view of emotion in marital therapy. In S. M. Johnson & L. S. Greenberg (Eds.), *The heart of the matter: Perspectives on emotion in marital therapy* (pp. 46–71).

Luborsky, L. (1984). *Principles of psychoanalytic psychotherapy: A manual for supportive-expressive treatment.* New York: Basic Books.

McDaniel, S. H., Hepworth, J., & Doherty, W. (1995). Medical family therapy with somatizing patients: The co-creation of therapeutic stories. In R. H. Mikesell, D. D. Lusterman, & S. H. McDaniel (Eds.), *Integrating family therapy: Handbook of family psychology and systems theory* (pp. 377–388). Washington, DC: American Psychological Association.

Messer, S. B., & Warren, C. S. (1995). *Models of brief psychodynamic therapy: A comparative approach.* New York: Guilford Press.

Mikesell, S. G., & Stohner, M. (1995). Infertility and pregnancy loss: The role of the family consultant. In R. H. Mikesell, D. D. Lusterman, & S. H. McDaniel (Eds.), *Integrating family therapy: Handbook of family psychology and systems theory* (pp. 421–436). Washington, DC: American Psychological Association.

Sager, C. J. (1981). Couples therapy and marriage contracts. In A. S. Gurman & D. P. Kniskern (Eds.), *Handbook of family therapy* (pp. 85–130). New York: Brunner/Mazel.

Sanders, M. R., Markie-Dadds, C., & Nicholson, J. M. (1997). Concurrent interventions for marital and children's problems. In W. K. Halford and H. J. Markman (Eds.), *Clinical handbook of marriage and couples interventions* (pp. 509–535). New York: Wiley.

Shadish, W. R., Montgomery, L. M., Wilson P., Wilson, M. R., Bright, I., & Okwumabua, T. (1993). Effects of family and marital psychotherapies: A meta-analysis. *Journal of Consulting and Clinical Psychology, 61,* 992–1002.

Shoham, V., Rohrbaugh, M., & Patterson, J. (1995). Problem- and solution-focused couple therapies: The MRI and Milwaukee models. In N. S. Jacobson & A. S. Gurman (Eds.), *Clinical handbook of couple therapy* (pp. 142–163). New York: Guilford Press.

Snyder, D. K. (1979). *Marital Satisfaction Inventory.* Los Angeles: Western Psychological Services.

Snyder, D. K. (1997). *Manual for the Marital Satisfaction Inventory-Revised.* Los Angeles: Western Psychological Services.

Snyder, D. K., Cavell, T. A., Heffer, R. W., & Mangrum, L. F. (1995). Marital and family assessment: A multifaceted, multilevel approach. In R. H. Mikesell, D. D. Lusterman, & S. H. McDaniel (Eds.), *Integrating family therapy: Handbook of family psychology and systems theory* (pp. 163–182). Washington, DC: American Psychological Association.

Snyder, D. K., Cozzi, J. J., & Mangrum, L. F. (in press). Conceptual issues in assessing couples and families. In H. Liddle, R. Levant, J. Bray, & G. Diamond (Eds.), *Family psychology intervention science.* Washington, DC: American Psychological Association.

Snyder, D. K., Mangrum, L. F., & Wills, R. M. (1993). Predicting couples' response to marital therapy: A comparison of short- and long-term predictors. *Journal of Consulting and Clinical Psychology, 61,* 61–69.

Snyder, D. K., & Wills, R. M. (1989). Behavioral versus insight-oriented marital therapy: Effects on individual and interspousal functioning. *Journal of Consulting and Clinical Psychology, 57,* 39–46.

Snyder, D. K., & Wills, R. M. (1991). Facilitating change in marital therapy and research. *Journal of Family Psychology, 4,* 426–435.

Snyder, D. K., Wills, R. M., & Faitler, S. L. (1988). Distinguishing specific from nonspecific interventions in comparative outcome studies: Reply to Collins and Thompson. *Journal of Consulting and Clinical Psychology, 56,* 934–935.

Snyder, D. K., Wills, R. M., & Grady-Fletcher, A. (1991a). Long-term effectiveness of behavioral versus insight-oriented marital therapy: A four-year follow-up study. *Journal of Consulting and Clinical Psychology, 59,* 138–141.

Snyder, D. K., Wills, R. M., & Grady-Fletcher, A. (1991b). Risks and challenges of long-term psychotherapy outcome research: Reply to Jacobson. *Journal of Consulting and Clinical Psychology, 59,* 146–149.

Spence, S. H. (1997). Sex and relationships. In W. K. Halford and H. J. Markman (Eds.), *Clinical handbook of marriage and couples interventions* (pp. 73–105). New York: Wiley.

Strupp, H. H., & Binder, J. L. (1984). *Psychotherapy in a new key: A guide to time-limited dynamic psychotherapy.* New York: Basic Books.

Stuart, R. B. (1980). *Helping couples change: A social learning approach to marital therapy.* New York: Guilford Press.

Sullivan, H. S. (1953). *Interpersonal theory of psychiatry.* New York: Norton.

Thompson, B. M. (1997). Couples and the work-family interface. In W. K. Halford and H. J. Markman (Eds.), *Clinical handbook of marriage and couples interventions* (pp. 273–290). New York: Wiley.

Todd, T. C. (1986). Structural-strategic marital therapy. In N. S. Jacobson & A. S. Gurman (Eds.), *Clinical handbook of marital therapy* (pp. 71–105). New York: Guilford Press.

Whisman, M. A., & Snyder, D. K. (1997). Evaluating and improving the efficacy of conjoint couple therapy. In W. K. Halford and H. J. Markman (Eds.), *Clinical handbook of marriage and couples interventions* (pp. 679–693). New York: Wiley.

Wills, R. M., Faitler, S. M., & Snyder, D. K. (1987). Distinctiveness of behavioral versus insight-oriented marital therapy: An empirical analysis. *Journal of Consulting and Clinical Psychology, 55,* 685–690.

Chapter Five

Structural Family Therapy

Sylvia Kemenoff, Jolanta Jachimczyk, and Andrew Fussner

Structural family therapy is a systemic treatment approach associated with Salvador Minuchin and his colleagues, first at the Wiltwyck school for delinquent adolescents and then at Philadelphia Child Guidance Center. This model was conceptualized and further developed throughout the 1960s. As in all systemic models of treatment, the identified patient's symptomatic behavior is seen as representative of a dysfunctional family system and must always be understood in terms of the context in which it occurs. Within the context of the family, the identified patient (IP) is perceived as a symptom bearer who expresses the family's disequilibrium or dysfunction (Goldenberg and Goldenberg, 1996; Hazelrigg, Cooper, and Borduin, 1987). Given this conceptualization of psychopathology, the goal of all systemic therapies is to assist the family in changing their system, with the focus of therapeutic intervention being upon family relationships and processes as opposed to the individual identified as having the problem. Ultimately, changing the familial interaction patterns is expected to result in the resolution of the IP's original problem(s) (Goldenberg and Goldenberg, 1991; Hazelrigg et al., 1987).

Theoretical Underpinnings

The structural family therapy approach is unique from other systemic models in its use of spatial and organizational metaphors, both in describing problems and in identifying avenues for solutions, and in the active role assigned to the therapist as an instrument of change (Colapinto, 1991). According to the structural model, as families evolve, they develop their own specific patterns of interactions that, in time, are solidified and become rules for future interactions. These rules ultimately limit the range of the individual family members' behavioral repertoire within the family context. These invisible rules, which determine the family's transactions (for example, how, when, and to whom to relate), make up the internal organization—the structure—of the family (Minuchin, 1974). According to Minuchin and Fishman (1981), the essential task of the family is to support the individuation and growth of the individual family members while maintaining their sense of belonging. How well a family achieves said function depends on the family structure and on its adaptability (Colapinto, 1991).

Family Structure

Structuralists contend that all families need some form of structure, some degree of differentiation between subsystems, and some kind of hierarchy (Minuchin, 1974). With regard to structure, all families consist of several coexisting *subsystems*. The various subsystems have different functions. There could be several subsystems based on gender, generation, common interests, or function (Goldenberg and Goldenberg, 1996). However, the most prevalent subsystems are the spousal, parental, and sibling subsystems. The primary functions of the spousal subsystem are the continuation and enhancement of the marital bond, the protection of the spouses from the intrusion of in-laws, children, and others as they negotiate the demands of their relationship, and the creation of a nuclear environment in which children are nurtured and protected. The parental subsystem's function is the rearing and socialization of children. The primary role of the sibling subsystem is to assist the children within the family develop the skills of cooperation, competition, and negotiation, which they can, in turn, utilize outside of the family context (for example, with peers).

Subsystems are protected by *boundaries*, which are rules that govern which family members can have contact with other family members around different functions or tasks (Colapinto, 1991). Examples of boundaries are that children should not participate in disputes between spouses, parents should not overly intervene in conflicts between siblings, and grandparents should not interfere with rearing children. As noted by Goldenberg and Goldenberg (1996), the composition of any subsystem is not nearly as important as the clarity of boundaries. The boundaries between the subsystems (1) ensure that the different functions of the family are carried out, (2) develop the components of each family member's self as they carry out their respective functions in the different subsystems to which they belong, and (3) maintain each member's separateness while emphasizing their belongingness to the family system. The permeability of boundaries falls along a continuum. Enmeshed families have boundaries that are diffuse and therefore easily intruded upon by family members. On the other hand, disengaged families have rigid boundaries, thus making contact between the subsystems difficult. Well-functioning families are characterized by clearly defined boundaries that maintain separateness while allowing contact between the subsystems.

Another aspect of family structure is *complementarity*. As families develop and organize, a mutual accommodation occurs between family members, such that there is a process of correlated differentiation. For example, for one of the family members to act like a parent, another member must act like a child. Similarly, for one spouse to be active in one area of decision making, the other must be passive. As a result of this process of mutual accommodation, family members develop reciprocity—with each family member's behavior being the context for another's actions.

Another component of the family's structure is its *hierarchy*, which is defined as the rules that dictate the distribution of decision-making power among family members and subsystems. In well-functioning families, parents have more power than their children. They have the authority required to perform the tasks of rearing, teaching, and protecting the children as well as making decisions involving the well-being of the entire family, such as where to live and where the children go to school (Colapinto, 1991). In dysfunctional families, the hierarchy is unclear, and parents either do not have or do not exercise the power and authority required to carry out their parental and executive functions.

Within the family structure, family members align with one another in their performance of a family activity. *Alignments* refer to the emotional or psychological connections family members make with one another (Goldenberg and Goldenberg, 1991). A *coalition* is a form of alignment in which two or more family members join together against a third. Coalitions that are cross-generational (such as triangulation or a detouring triad) are considered dysfunctional by structuralists.

Although each aspect of family structure—subsystems, boundaries, complementarity, hierarchy, alignments, and coalitions—has been separately delineated for purposes of clarity, they are, in fact, strongly interrelated. For example, if there is a diffuse boundary around the spousal subsystem, a cross-generational coalition may develop between one parent and a child. This weakens the alignment between the spouses, in turn reducing their parental power (Goldenberg and Goldenberg, 1991).

Adaptability

Aside from its structure, adaptability also determines how well a family achieves its primary function of nurturing the growth of its members while maintaining their sense of belonging. Adaptability is the family's ability to reorganize its structure in response to its changing needs, which emerge as it evolves (for example, as children grow older and/or leave the home) (Colapinto, 1991). According to Minuchin, pathological families are unable to adapt to their changing needs and instead respond to the associated stress by increasing the rigidity of their historical patterns of transaction (Minuchin, 1974, as cited by Goldenberg and Goldenberg, 1991). Most commonly, families who cannot adapt respond to the stress created by the pull for change by locating a problem within one family member. They narrowly and rigidly apply transactions to "fixing" the identified patient, leaving other alternative transactions unexplored.

Structural Family Therapy

Based upon the structural theory of family functioning, the structural family therapist has two interrelated goals: (1) to change the family's definition of the problem from being the IP (and his or her symptomatic behavior) to being their dysfunctional family structure (patterns of transacting) and (2) to reorganize the dysfunctional structure so that the family can use alternative transactions— transactions that no longer require the symptomatic behavior of the IP and that nurture the growth of its individual members.

Assessment

In assessing the family to identify areas of dysfunction as well as possible avenues for change, a structuralist concentrates on the following areas:

1. Composition of the family's subsystems and their ability to carry out their respective functions
2. Permeability of current boundaries
3. Hierarchy
4. Existence and function of alignments as well as coalitions
5. Adaptability

Assessment occurs throughout the process of treatment. Even before the family begins their participation in the therapy, structuralists start to form a conceptualization of the structure of the family, the areas of dysfunction and, in turn, hypotheses about possible areas of therapeutic intervention (for example, restructuring) from the earliest available data (referral materials, phone contacts, and intake). This process is called preplanning. Another assessment device associated with structural family therapy is family mapping, which is a visual diagram of the family's current structure (transactional patterns). The concrete visual depiction provides a basic schema for conceptualizing the complex transactional patterns of the family, which can be invaluable in planning therapeutic interventions.

Joining

The hypotheses generated during preplanning are only initial conceptualizations of the family structure. These hypotheses are refined as the therapist experiences the family structure through the process of joining. According to Minuchin and Fishman (1981), "joining is more of an attitude than a technique and it is the umbrella under which all therapeutic transactions occur. Joining is letting the family know that the therapist understands them and is working with and for them. Only under his protection can the family have the security to explore alternatives, try the unusual and change" (pp. 31–32). Specific techniques of joining include accommodation, affiliation and confirmation, and tracking. *Accommodation* is adjusting to the family's style of interacting and their current rules of transaction (for example, speaking first to the family member who the family allocates as the leader). The therapist employs mimesis in this process; specifically, the therapist proceeds according to the family's tempo, uses their language, and assumes their postural stance. *Affiliation and confirmation* involve connecting with family members, recognizing their strengths, and validating their reality (for example, their thoughts and feelings). *Tracking* involves following the content and process of the family interaction. While doing so, the therapist becomes familiar with the structure that governs the behavior of its members.

Techniques of joining, although more heavily emphasized during the beginning phases of therapy, are used throughout the process of treatment and are continually interwoven with restructuring techniques. For example, while joining with a family, the therapist may implement a restructuring technique if the family presents a spontaneous transaction that is consistent with the goal of restructuring. Similarly, when implementing a restructuring technique, if the stress among the family members becomes too intense (that is, beyond what the therapist perceives as therapeutic), the therapist may retrieve or refocus the intervention (for example, on another restructuring technique or on joining) to reduce stress. Lastly, as Minuchin (1974) notes, even the process of restructuring is a joining maneuver because it provides the family with hope that alternatives are possible.

Reframing and Restructuring Techniques

There are a variety of techniques that a therapist employs to achieve the interactive goals of redefining the problem and restructuring. These include focusing, enactment, teaching complementarity, boundary making, unbalancing, achieving intensity, and challenging cognitive constructs.

Focusing is the selection of elements of information that seem relevant to therapeutic change. For example, the family attempts to focus upon the IP's symptoms, while the therapist focuses on information related to transactions (such as data related to hierarchical arrangements, boundaries, and coalitions).

Enactment is the essence of structural family therapy (Simon, 1995). It is the actualization of transactional patterns under the control of the therapist (Colapinto, 1991). The therapist directs the family to interact with each other in an area that is related to the defined problem or the structural goal. Once the interaction is under way, the therapist observes and studies the sequence of processes that occur among the participants so that they can intervene to create alternatives. Particular areas attended to by the therapist are the degree of permeability of the family's boundaries (that is, the proximity of members); the hierarchical arrangement of members (that is, who controls whom); and the existence of alignments or coalitions. If the dysfunctional structure is considered to be related to issues of control, the therapist may direct the parent to assert control over the child and intervenes in such a manner to create that outcome. It should be noted that relevant transactions may also occur spontaneously by the family and are immediately utilized by the therapist for restructuring.

Teaching complementarity is the process of pointing out to family members the mutuality and reciprocity of their interactions (that is, how the behavior of one member is the context for another's behavior). The therapist challenges the symptom as being within an individual, suggesting that it may be related to transactions. For example, a therapist might ask, "Is Pat depressing you?" (Minuchin and Fishman, 1981, p. 195). This question reframes depression from being an intrapsychic phenomenon to one that is maintained by transactions. The therapist can also challenge the idea of linear control and introduce reciprocity by describing the behavior of one member and assigning responsibility for that behavior to another. For example, the therapist might say to a child, "You are acting like a 4-year-old" and then turn to the parents and ask, "How do you manage to keep him that young?" (Minuchin and Fishman, 1981, p. 197). Lastly, during enactments the therapist can use punctuation to show the family a transactional version of their behavior.

Boundary-making techniques are interventions employed by the therapist to change subsystem membership or distance between subsystems in order to modify patterns of over- or underinvolvement. Specific boundary-making techniques include introducing rules (for example, only the person holding the wand can speak); assigning tasks (for example, requesting a grandparent to observe the transactions between a parent and child without intruding, telling a teenager to go out with friends at least once a week); use of space (for example, requesting a child who is overinvolved with his parents to sit apart from them); and use of self (for example, the therapist using his own body to separate an overinvolved dyad and/or making comments regarding intrusive or disengaged processes) (see Minuchin and Fishman, 1991, pp. 149–150 for details).

Unbalancing techniques include a group of techniques employed to challenge and modify a rigid family hierarchy. Specific unbalancing techniques are: affiliating with family members, ignoring of family members, and entering coalitions against family members (see Minuchin and Fishman, 1991, pp. 163–190 for an elaboration of these techniques).

Techniques that increase intensity are those that increase the level of challenge to the current family structure. The level of intensity creates different levels of stress among family members. The level selected depends upon the rigidity of the pattern being challenged. Specific techniques include: repetition of the same message; repetition of transactions that highlight a pattern (for example, a problem of control); reducing or extending the length of interactions beyond what is generally permitted by the current family rules; changing the level of proximity between family members from that which is prescribed by the current family organization; and resisting the family's invitation to focus upon content and process that is not considered therapeutically relevant.

Challenging cognitive constructs. It should be noted that structural family therapy is action oriented. The therapist actively intervenes (via the techniques previously described) to change the actual behavioral transactions that occur among family members in order to reorganize the family structure. However, as recognized by structuralists, a family not only has a structure but also a belief system. The structure and belief system legitimize and validate each other in an interactive fashion; therefore, each can be a point of therapeutic entry (Minuchin and Fishman, 1981). The structuralist employs the following techniques to challenge the family's belief structure: (1) the use of cognitive constructs, which includes emphasizing universal truths, expanding the family's current truth, and offering expert advice; (2) the use of paradox; and (3) highlighting strengths in opposition to the family's emphasis on deficits (Minuchin and Fishman, 1981). However, as emphasized by Colapinto (1991), even when challenging belief systems, "the therapist uses actual transactions in the room as referents. Changes in clients' experiences are brought about not by the therapist's long explanations, but by his or her brief punctuation and reframing of enacted transactions" (p. 441).

The Cases: Four Examples of Dysfunctional Family Structures

The goal of this section is to illustrate the application of the structural model. Four cases are presented, each depicting a different dysfunctional structure and, therefore, a different structural goal. The techniques employed to achieve the respective therapeutic goals are highlighted. Prior to the presentation of the cases, we give a brief description of the authors and the general population with whom the authors work.

The Authors and Their Setting

The first two authors are a psychologist and a social worker, respectively, employed at a residential setting for boys who are 5–12 years old. The third author has been a consultant to the clinical staff at the residential center for several years, providing training and supervision in structural family therapy. He is a social worker, a former associate director of the Family Therapy Training Center at the Philadelphia Child Guidance Center, and currently an international trainer in family therapy.

The first and second authors work as a cotherapy team in the provision of family therapy for the children within their unit. The children who reside in this facility arrive with a variety of psychiatric diagnoses and/or emotional/ behavioral problems. Many also have serious histories of abuse and/or neglect. Regardless of their individual disorder(s), their condition has been considered serious enough (by either the family, state authority, school, or psychiatrist) to require placement in a residential setting.

The process of placing a child in residential care—separating that child from his or her family—explicitly underscores the perception held by the family and the involved professionals that the problem is located only within the child. Therefore, the task of reframing the problem as one that is maintained by a dysfunctional family structure is particularly challenging within this setting and is addressed immediately from the initial contact. For example, during the intake procedure the family members are asked, "What needs to change for the IP to return home?" The family generally responds by stating that the behavior of the IP needs to change (locating the problem within the IP). The therapists respond by asking what else in the family needs to change for the IP to return home, thereby immediately expanding the definition of the problem to include the family. At this time, the family is also informed that their participation in treatment is crucial, thus further reinforcing their contribution to the problem and its resolution.

Another challenging task for the authors is achieving the process of joining with parents because of the extensive and often negative experiences they have had with the "system." An agencywide "family-friendly" approach is used in an attempt to engage and join with parents and includes such activities as

- accommodating schedules to meet the needs of the parent(s)
- acknowledging and accommodating the family's religious affiliation
- soliciting and respecting parents' wishes regarding certain aspects of their child's physical care (for example, the style of their hair, food to serve on their birthday)
- seeking parents' input regarding the emotional/behavioral functioning of their children

All of this is done prior to commencing formal "family therapy."

Case 1: A Detouring Triad and the Use of Preplanning

The Smith family consists of a mother (Jane), a stepfather (Jeff), and three boys, Brian (age 8), Michael (age 9), and Robert (age 10). Michael is the IP, with presenting problems of severe impulsivity, aggression, and explosiveness in response to adult authority and structure. During intake, a history of domestic violence and use of excessive corporal punishment by the parents were confirmed. It was reported that Michael, the IP, began to exhibit his severe behavioral problems upon the entrance of the stepfather into the family system and that he subsequently required three psychiatric hospitalizations during the two years prior to his placement at the residence. Additionally, each time Michael returned home, his functioning rapidly and severely deteriorated. Immediately upon his entrance into the unit, Michael's preoccupation with strength and power was noticed.

Based upon this preliminary data, a hypothesis was developed that the dysfunctional structure in this family was a detouring triad; more specifically, that the spousal conflict (which historically escalated to violence without any adaptive resolution) was detoured through Michael. Michael's behavior, therefore, played an important role for maintaining the safety of the family unit (that is, it is generally less dangerous when a child becomes aggressive than when adults do). Based upon this conceptualization, the planned structural goal was to assist the spouses in developing adaptive conflict resolution skills while blocking Michael's participation. The dysfunctional structure and the consequential structural goal can be mapped as shown in Figure 3.

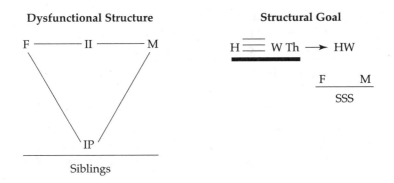

Figure 3
Removing identified patient from mother father dyad.

The following excerpts are from the first session with the Smith family; they illustrate how the initial hypothesis regarding the family was further assessed and depict how the process of joining is continuously interwoven with reframing and restructuring. The first intervention by the therapy team is to invite the family to sit down (without providing any further instruction). Notably, the family members sit as indicated in Figure 4. The Xs depict the seats that are left vacant by the family and are subsequently taken by the therapists. Therefore, via this first intervention, the hypothesis of an existing triangle involving Michael and his parents is supported. After some casual discussion regarding the weather, the drive up, a recent visit to the family's home by the social worker, the family's evolution (for example, when the stepfather entered the family), and an exploration of the relative sizes of the boys (initiated by Brian and tracked by the therapists), all in the pursuit of joining, the therapists begin to assert a leading role. One of the therapists proceeds to obtain a wand, simultaneously outlining a rule that only the holder of the wand can speak. The topic to be discussed is then presented to the family.

Therapist 1:   All right, while you have the wand, share what you think needs to change for Michael to come home. [holding the wand in the direction of the parents] Who'll start?

The role of the task involving the wand is to provide a means of assessing the family structure (for example, hierarchy by observing who reaches for the wand, alignments by observing who passes it to whom, boundaries by noting whether they can follow the prescribed rule). However, the pointing of the wand

Mom	Brian

Michael		Robert

Dad	X	X

Figure 4
Family seating arrangement.

in the direction of the parents is an example of joining through maintenance—respecting the universal rule that parents are in charge of their children.

Mom: [reaches for the wand] I will. Michael needs to take his time-outs. He needs to learn how to deal with his anger without outbursts. [hands the wand to Dad]

Dad: [handing the wand to Robert] Boys first. If I share what I think, they won't share their own ideas.

In this brief segment, Mom immediately locates the problem within Michael. Dad's refusal to take the wand, as wished by Mom, suggests a weakness in the spousal system.

Robert: [remains silent and appears confused]

Therapist 1:   Maybe you can tell us what you wish for when Michael comes home.

Robert: That he stops his tantrums. [hands wand to Brian]

Brian: [pushes the wand away]

Mom: You have to take it.

Therapist 2:   Good, Jane. You tell the boys what you would like to see happen.

Brian: [still hesitates and appears anxious and says nothing]

At the beginning of this segment, the therapist restates the task in more child-friendly terms. This is an action employed to join with the sibling subsystem (that is, by employing language that they can understand) but is also a boundary-making maneuver because it implies that different language is used with parents versus children. The fact that Robert also perceives Michael as the problem indicates that this perception is the family's "truth."

Mom: You want Michael to stop hitting you.

Brian: You read my mind!

Therapist 1 to mom: Don't steal his voice. Instead, help him to find his own voice.

Mom: [with a supportive tone] What is it, Brian?

Brian: [almost in a whisper] When Michael hits me, and— [prolonged silence]

Dad: Come on, Brian!

Mom: I'm not going to talk for you. [still silence]

Therapist 2:   Good job, Jane. You're really helping him speak for himself.

Mom: Brian, say what's on your mind. Keeping it in is a heavy burden to carry. [still silence]

Therapist 1 to Brian: Can you tell Michael? [still silence]

Mom: [following the therapist's lead] Maybe you can tell either Jolanta or Sylvia after we're gone.

Therapist 2:   Well, actually if he told us instead of telling you, we'd be worried because that would suggest he trusts us more than you, and we're not his parents.

Brian: I forgot the question.

Therapist 1 to parents: Do you buy that?

Mom and Dad: [simultaneously] No.

Mom: I'm still not going to talk for you. [still silence]

Therapist 2:   Okay. [to parents] Maybe it would be better for you to help Brian find his voice at home in your own way.

Mom: [nods in agreement and reaches for the wand]

Brian: [clutches the wand]

Therapist 1:   It seems like he is trying to find his voice.

Brian: [rolls his eyes and sighs in frustration, still holding onto the wand]

Therapist 1:   Oh, it's so hard when part of you wants to do something, but another part doesn't.

Brian: [gets out of his seat and turns his back to the family and speaks almost in a whisper] When I tell that Michael hits me, he gets in trouble and goes to the hospital. [crouches to the floor and bursts into tears]

Mom: [joins Brian and holds him] You feel it's your fault? [prolonged silence] [Michael spontaneously gets out of his seat and joins Brian and mom, gently touching Brian on the shoulder.]

Mom: Michael, do you blame Brian?

Michael: [without hesitation] No, I blame myself.

Dad: Michael, sit down.

Therapist 1:   I'm impressed. You were able to help Brian find his voice. You helped him to find the courage to express himself. I wonder if he is the voice of the family's pain—about Michael not being at home—about who is to blame?

In this segment, Brian's comment that his mother "read his mind" is a red flag for the therapists, suggesting that there is a lack of psychological separation and that within this family children do not directly speak about difficult areas. The parents take on the voice of their children when the stress associated with the topic becomes too intense and, in turn, prevent the discussion of topics that would overwhelm the family, thus maintaining the family homeostasis. The therapists' interventions throughout this segment (for example, setting up the enactment in which the parents are asked to help Brian speak for himself, during which the intensity is increased by repeating the direction, allowing silence, and, in turn, extending the length of their usual interactions; providing expert advice regarding ambivalence) challenge the family's current patterns of transaction. This challenge and its resulting stress enabled the family to experience an alternative transaction if even for a brief moment. Specifically, Brian shares that there is more to the problem than just Michael. His telling on Michael and, in turn, the parents' actions of sending Michael to the hospital are also part of the problem. However, the family system quickly regains its equilibrium. Michael quickly resumes the role of being the sole problem, stating "I blame myself." The therapist counters with a different reality, punctuating Brian's comments, which suggest that others are also to "blame" for the problem, while also highlighting complementarity (that is, that it was the parents' actions that helped Brian to speak up).

Therapist 1:   [takes the wand and hands it to Michael] All right, if it's okay with your parents, it's your turn.

Dad to Michael: What do you wish for . . . you know, to make it all better?

Michael: To stop hitting my brothers.

Dad: Both of them? When you hit them, do they hit you back?

Michael: Sometimes.

Brian: He hits me because he knows I won't hit him back.

Mom: [to Brian] But you give him that power. You can take it away by telling us so that we can give him a time-out. Do you understand that?

Therapist 1:   Jeff, ask Michael if there is anything else.

Dad to Michael: Do you wish for anything else? You know, to fix Mom and Dad or anybody else in the family?

Michael: You and Mom to stop fighting.

Dad: Have we been fighting a lot lately? [Michael does not respond]

Robert: It's close to one o'clock!

Dad: Okay, so we used to fight. But what about now? [no response from Michael]

Therapist 1 to dad: I'm not sure Michael thinks it's okay for him to talk about this. Convince him that he can tell you anything that's on his mind.

Dad to Michael: So what about the fighting? You need to let me know what's broke so that I can fix it. The fighting used to be bad. It's gotten better. Do you still think that it needs to get better, or are we where we need to be?

Michael: Yelling.

Dad: Is it bad to fight just with words?

Mom: Is it the tone? [Michael does not respond and looks down]

Michael has apparently received the message that his parents' physical fighting is off-grounds and takes on his prescribed role of the detourer of conflict by focusing on himself.

Mom: Michael, why are you so upset? Are you mad?

Michael: No.

Mom: Sad?

Michael: Yes.

Mom: Why?

Michael: Because I wanted to stay home.

Mom: [leans closer to Michael and rubs his shoulder] You wanted to stay home.

Michael: I wanted to stay home. [Dad also leans over and together with mom comforts Michael]

At this point, the positions of Michael, his mother, and his stepfather form a physical triangle.

Dad: Do you think you're ready to come home?

Michael: [nods]

Dad: You are?

Mom: You think you've changed?

Michael: Yes.

Dad: Michael, Michael . . . [stated in a tone that suggests Michael needs to reassess what he's said]

Mom: Do you think we've done what we need to do as a family?

Michael: Yes. [excusing the family from any responsibility for the problem, most notably, removing the focus yet again from the fighting between the spouses and bringing it back upon himself; Michael cries]

Therapist 1:   Jane and Jeff, you have somehow given your sons the courage to talk about some difficult issues. To talk about what else in the family needs to change besides Michael's behavior, like your fighting. You have helped your children to express themselves honestly.

The session continues with the father taking his turn at the assigned task, during which he describes Michael's behavioral difficulties that need to change for him to come home.

At the beginning of the preceding segment, the family truth that Michael is the problem is once again confirmed by Michael's statement. However, the therapist, knowing that the system was shaken by the stress of the interactions described in the previous section, takes the opportunity to challenge this family truth by setting up an enactment. The father is simply asked to encourage his son to talk more about what else needs to change, thereby indicating that there is in fact more to the problem. Michael responds by highlighting the spousal fighting as a problem and, in so doing, is no longer functioning as the detourer of conflict. The system quickly reacts in a protective manner to regain its homeostasis. First, Robert attempts to divert the discussion, taking on Michael's usual role of detouring. The parents, as the gatekeepers of permissible topics, make comments that subtly indicate that their fighting is not a topic to be discussed directly. Michael responds to their maneuvers by taking on his habitual role of detourer. The focus of the family interactions once again surrounds Michael (for example, his emotions, his problems) and the exploration regarding spousal fighting is once again detoured. Especially striking in this regard is that the physical triangle, which emerges between Michael and his parents at the juncture noted previously, parallels their psychological triangle. Thus, the hypothesis that the dysfunctional structure within this family is a detouring triad was confirmed. Therefore, the structural goal of assisting the spouses in dealing directly with their conflicts without the involvement of the IP (or the other children) was pursued. Jeff and Jane were referred for marital therapy. This intervention set up an impermissible boundary between the spousal and sibling subsystems—providing the couple an arena to deal with their conflicts without the involvement of the children. The marital therapist also worked with the couple to develop a safety plan, given their history of domestic violence. It is important to note that a referral to a spousal batterers' group should be considered, depending upon the dynamics of the violence.

The authors continued to work with the entire family system in the areas of reframing (that is, the identification of family problems) and restructuring (that is, strengthening the boundaries between the subsystems), with the ultimate goal of helping the family develop alternative transactions that would allow Michael to return home and, more importantly, to stay at home.

Case 2: An Overinvolved Dyad and Boundary-Making Techniques

The Jones family consists of a mother (Mary), a father (John), and three children, Susan (age 11), Ray (age 9), and Cathy (age 7). Ray is the IP who, prior to arriving at the authors' unit, already had been in residential placement for two years. Presenting difficulties that resulted in his initial placement included sexual acting-out (that is, with his siblings) and severe aggression. There was known physical abuse of the children by the father (as well as domestic violence) and an allegation of sexual abuse of the IP by an extended family member. The father was removed from the home and disallowed contact with the family by the legal system during the majority of the time that the authors were involved in the case. During the first two years of his placement, the focus of treatment was upon Ray's sexual acting-out (for example, assisting him to process his abuse trauma, closely monitoring him in the milieu for any sexual behaviors, and processing his sexual acting-out with the family members). When the authors acquired the case, they modified their conceptualization of the case according to the structural model. The dysfunctional structure within this family consisted of the diffuse boundaries and lack of differentiation among family members. Therefore, the structural goal was to establish clearer boundaries among the family members, in turn increasing each member's sense of individuality. This dysfunctional structure and the consequential structural goal can be mapped as illustrated in Figure 5.

Some sessions were held with all of the family members (later including the father), while others included only the IP and the mother, as they were considered to be particularly overinvolved. The following excerpts are from a session that occurred several months into the family's treatment with the authors. This session, which included only the IP and his mother, was selected for presentation because of the clarity with which it illustrates boundary-making tech-

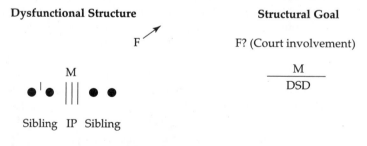

Figure 5
Clarification of diffuse boundaries.

X

Ray   Mom

Th1   Th2

Figure 6
Family seating arrangement.

niques. It should also be noted that during prior sessions, much of the focus was upon setting up spatial boundaries between Ray and his mother (for example, having them sit in their own chairs, not touching each other) and in helping them to verbally define their separateness (for example, reminding the mother to refer to herself as "I" and to call her son by his first name rather than referring to him as "baby" or "babe"). The second author, in individual work with Mary, also encouraged and assisted her to become involved in extrafamilial activities. Ray was able to expand his individuality by participating in peer group activities during his stay at the residence. The seating arrangement throughout this session was generally as depicted in Figure 6.

During the beginning of the session, the discussion centers on the reason Ray was unable to go home for a visit during the upcoming weekend as previously planned. According to the mother, this visit was cancelled by the governing social service agency because of the behavior of the children who were at home. Notably, the lack of differentiation among the children within the family system was paralleled by the larger social system.

Therapist 1:   Aside from that— [turns to therapist 2] because I think we do
   have to acknowledge Mary's feelings that others are punishing her and
   also her pain with regards to how [names the social service agency in-
   volved] has kept the family apart— [turning back to mom] but what are
   the issues within the family?—aside from everything else, which does
   have to be acknowledged. It must be frustrating that the girls act up and
   Ray can't come home. But what do you think the family needs to do for
   Ray to come home safely? What do you need to do? What does Ray need
   to do? What about each of the girls?
Mom to therapist 1:   The number one factor was the sexual acting-out. Since
   I've stopped harboring on it like you told me to, he has stopped. [Ray
   gets out of his seat and hugs his mother] The girls have also stopped.
   [Ray stops hugging his mother but still stands right beside her]
Therapist 1 to mom: How do you feel about this change?
Mom: Ecstatic.
Ray: She must be super, super, super happy!
Therapist 2 to Ray: How about you? How do you feel?
Ray: Super, super, super happy!
Therapist 2 to mom: Ask him to explain what he's so happy about.
Mom: So, Ray what makes you so happy?

Ray: [hides his face and sits on his mother's lap] Because I've stopped doing S-E-X.

Mom and therapist 1 at the same time: Yeah.

Therapist 1:   So even though we don't want to focus on the sexual acting-out, because Ray is not only that—he's not only Mr. Sexual Acting-Out—that was a big step for the family.

Therapist 2:   Mary, could you ask him to not sit on your lap, given that he is a big boy?

The preceding segment commences with the therapist refocusing the dyad to explore the problems within the family structure, while confirming the mother's pain about the impact that the larger social system has had upon her family's life. This intervention is a joining and a reframing maneuver—that is, although there are larger systemic issues, there are also problems within the family that need to be addressed for change to occur. By asking what each family member needs to do, the therapist is punctuating the individuality of each member. It is notable that the mother responds by stating that the sexual acting-out was the biggest factor. This response indicates that the family's definition of itself continues to be narrowly linked to sexual acting-out. The therapists track this content area but with a focus on clarifying the dyad's boundaries, which has been identified as the structural goal. Our structural hypothesis that the actual problem in this family is the diffuse boundaries among family members is supported by the fact that when the dyad discusses the issue of sexual acting-out, they become fused both emotionally (they are both super, super, super happy) and physically (Ray sits on his mother's lap). In response, the therapists employ two techniques. First, they set up an enactment (mother is directed to ask Ray about what makes him happy) in an attempt to place a boundary around their individual feelings. Second, they employ space (asking Mary to direct Ray to sit apart from her) to highlight their physical separateness. In accordance with the structural concept that a family's constructions support their structure, the therapists proceed to expand the family's definition of themselves from being more than a sexually acting-out organism.

Therapist 1:   Okay, so the sexual acting-out is better. What else? What else needs to change within the family for Ray to go home? [no response from Ray or his mother] Well, what about what you were talking about last time—you know, about Dad coming back home. Is that another step for Ray to go home? [At the mention of his father, Ray quickly assumes a fetal position, hiding his face in his lap.]

This segment is significant because it indicates how difficult it is for the family to go beyond their constrained definition of themselves. Therefore, the therapist introduces the new content area to be explored.

Ray: [briefly looks up and responds very quickly and emphatically] Uh-huh. Uh-huh. [looks back down]

Therapist 2:   Good, Ray. [to mom] He's able to tell you and show you how he feels about talking about his father.

The therapist punctuates Ray's ability to speak up for himself.

Mom: It's a confusing topic.

Ray: I tell you if Daddy . . . if Daddy—if he was working for Grandpa, he would be so, so, so scared to tell him to— [he, in turn, sits up with his feet on the table] Why is everybody looking at me? I want to go and play. [he gets out of his seat]

Ray's preceding comment nicely illustrates his poor differentiation. He fuses his relationship with his father with the relationship between his father and grandfather. In addition, although the topic appears stressful to both Ray (he wants to go play) and his mother (she reports the topic is confusing), the therapist refocuses the dyad onto the topic at hand to assist them in going beyond their usual pattern of avoiding difficult content.

Therapist 2 to mom: Tell him to come and sit back down—talking about his father is important.

Therapist 1:   He said "yes" pretty quick, so it must be important.

Mom: Ray! [points to his chair, gesturing that he sit down; he complies] Yeah . . . you see, this is—this is where it's hard for me to talk about it—

Ray: No! This is where I get harder. [sits briefly in a plane crash position and then sits up]

Mom: I have so many mixed feelings about this. [ignoring Ray's struggles/feelings]

Ray: Daddy! Daddy! Forget about Daddy! [curling up in a fetal position with his behind facing his mother, in essence mimicking his mother's inability to handle this topic]

Therapist 1:   What's he telling you? [points to Ray] What is his behavior telling you?

Mom: That he doesn't like his dad too much. That I already knew.

Therapist 1:   [mimics Ray's physical posture] What is this?

Mom: Scared.

Therapist 1:   Tell him to talk to you about that. He had a lot of courage and trust in you, Mary, to be able to say, "Yes, I want to talk about daddy."

Ray: [maintaining the same position] I don't even dare to talk about Daddy!

Therapist 2 to mom: Use your own words to help him.

Ray: I don't even dare to talk about Daddy!

Mom: Why? Sit up so that Mommy can hear you.

Ray: He scares me! [maintains same position] I don't ever want him to come home.

Mom: I know he scares you, baby, 'cause at times he scares Mommy too.

This statement by the mother illustrates the complete lack of boundaries between the dyad with respect to their emotions. She is able to reflect back his feelings not because he told her but because she also experiences the same emotions, indicating their lack of psychological boundaries. The therapist responds by setting up an enactment that focuses on Ray's individual feelings.

Therapist 2 to mom: Talk to Ray about whether or not his father is going to be there and his feelings about that.

Ray: I hope Daddy doesn't come back to the house. That's one thing I'm sure about!

Mom: Babe, see that's the thing. He's really changed. I've seen it and so have your sisters. He really wants to come home. And I think I want him to come home too.

Ray: All right!

Therapist 1:   Hold on! Before we go any further, I want to help your mom with something. [gets up] Let me come over here [simultaneously moving to the chair between Mary and Ray, facing Mary] I want to come over here and tell you that we know you have a real tough job here [touches Mary's arm in a supportive manner] and I'm interrupting you— [Ray gets up from his seat and stands in between his mother and therapist 1 but closer to his mother] No, Ray, please sit back down while I talk to your mom.

Mom: [gesturing to Ray to reoccupy his chair] Nu-uh, Ray. [Ray responds by sitting on the floor between therapist 1 and his mother.]

Therapist 1 to Ray: I need to help your mom with something, and then she'll talk again with you.

Mom: [gesturing to Ray to sit in his chair] Over there! [Ray sits back in his chair.]

Therapist 1 to mom: You see, we know that it's difficult for you to talk to your son about his own feelings about his dad because you are a wife . . . and you have your very own feelings . . . but he is a son—who has his own feelings about his father. And what we're asking you to do is very tough because we're asking you to focus just on his feelings even though you have your own stuff. [mom nods] Ask him what scares him about his father.

Mom: Okay, Ray, sit up 'cause Mommy has something really important to say.

Mary proceeds to tell Ray that his sisters have directly told their father, during his visits to the family's home (supervised by an extended family member) that he scares them and that they are angry with him. She, in turn, suggests that this is what Ray needs to do to resolve his fear. Ray responds to this suggestion by softly stating, "No, No" and curls into a fetal position with his buttocks in the air.

The mother does not follow the directions provided by the therapist at the beginning of this segment. Instead, she proceeds to talk about who wants the father to come home. In response, the child remains loyal to the family organism and denies his own feelings with regard to his father. Because of the rigidity of the dyad's interactions, the therapist increases the challenge to the family—increases intensity—by using several specific boundary-making techniques. One, the therapist uses herself to physically separate Ray and his mother, while providing expert advice to the mother about the different feelings that she and Ray are likely to have because of their different roles in the family (that is, their different relationships with the husband/father). Because of the intensity of this challenge, the therapist simultaneously confirms the mother's probable struggle with the task. Notably, during this therapeutic maneuver, the family's homeostatic mechanism emerges. Ray intensifies his proximity to his mother. The therapist, in turn, uses space (directing him to sit back in his chair) to challenge their fusion. Despite the intensity of the challenge, however, the mother continues to be unable to focus on Ray's feelings and, instead, merges him again with his sisters.

Therapist 1 to mom: We don't want you to think that we don't recognize the progress that has been made between the other children and their father. But the bottom line is that your son is hiding when he talks about his father. So no matter how much talking you do, something else needs to happen. You need to ask him what he needs to feel safe around his father.

Therapist 2 to mom: So ask him.

Mom: Okay. [to Ray] What do you need to feel safe around your father? [Ray remains in a fetal position and does not respond.]

Mom: Come on, Ray. Tell me. What do you think? Look at me. [Ray looks up.] Ray, I can't help you if you don't tell me.

Ray gets up and whispers something to therapist 2 who, in turn, gently tells him to share what he said to her with his mother.

Ray: I want him to come here—to these meetings. Yeah, we could have him come here so he doesn't try to hurt me.

Mom: Okay. So I'll see if Daddy can do that. Okay?

Ray: And I want my friend next door [referring to the staff crisis worker whose office is next to the therapy room and who is a large male] to come here too.

Therapist 1 to mom: So, see how when you ask him directly about what he needs, he got the courage to tell you?

In the preceding excerpt, the therapists continue to raise the intensity and prescribe another enactment. Finally, a psychological boundary is established between the dyad, and Ray explores his own feelings with his mother. In summary, although the content changed throughout the session (that is, from sexual acting-out to the discussion about the father), the dyad's diffuse boundaries continued to dominate their transactions. The therapists, in turn, employed a variety of boundary-making techniques (for example, setting up enactments around issues of individuation, use of space, and use of self). A variety of other structural techniques, including refocusing, confirmation, punctuating interactions in which the dyad was able to maintain an appropriate boundary, and the use of expert advice, were also employed to achieve the structural goal of clarifying boundaries. This resulted in the mother being able to provide the context in which Ray was able to identify his own needs with regard to his father (that is, without the intrusion of his mother's needs/feelings), thereby allowing each to experience their own individuality, if only for a moment.

Case 3: Unequal Spousal Power and the Use of Alignment and Blocking

The Taylor family consists of a father (David), a stepmother (Sharon), and one boy, Bobby (age 9). Bobby, the IP, was referred for residential placement due to severe aggression (toward other children and his stepmother), cruelty to animals, self-harmful behaviors, and fire setting, which were not ameliorated by four psychiatric hospitalizations. The stepmother joined the family four years ago. From the age of 0–3 years, Bobby resided with his biological mother, who physically abused him severely. Mr. Taylor was uninvolved during this time, but when he learned about the physical abuse of his son, he sued for and obtained custody of Bobby. Since then, Bobby's biological mother has been absent from his life. Bobby's relationship with his stepmother was reported to be particularly conflictual. During the intake and admission process, Sharon was observed to make all the decisions (for example, about who would come to visit Bobby, who would participate in his treatment team meetings, and under what circumstances Bobby could return home). If David disagreed, he was either immediately undercut or he ended up eventually concurring with Sharon. Based upon the preceding data, the dysfunctional structure within this family was the unequal power between the spouses (and, in turn, as parents). Therefore, the structural goal was to equalize the spouses' relative power within the family by enhancing the father's status as a father and as a husband. This dysfunctional structure and the consequential structural goal can be mapped as shown in Figure 7.

The first intervention employed by the therapists was to exclude the stepmother from the first session by simply not inviting her. This is the most obvious blocking maneuver employed to decrease a family member's power within the family system. During that session, the therapists aligned with the father in order to increase his status. The important role that Mr. Taylor played as a model and mentor to Bobby was emphasized. Several enactments were set up in which the dyad explored their mutual ways of dealing with anger. During these enactments, Mr. Taylor's expertise and experience were repeatedly highlighted by the therapists. As well, Bobby's keen interest in the information being provided by his father (evident in his verbalizations as well as his facial expressions) was punctuated.

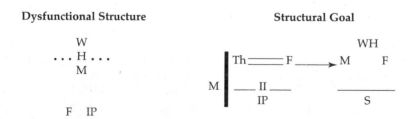

Dysfunctional Structure   **Structural Goal**

Figure 7
Enhancement of husband's spousal power.

```
        Bobby

Mom          Dad

   Th1  Th2   X
```

Figure 8
Family seating arrangement.

This basic strategy to increase the father's status in the family was re-peated during the second session. Enactments were once again set up in which the father and son dyad explored the same content. However, this time, the stepmother was invited to the session but was blocked from taking over the familial interactions via a variety of techniques (use of space, use of self, and a continued alignment with the father). These techniques are illus-trated in the following excerpt. The family came in and sat as indicated in Figure 8.

Therapist 1:   What we want to do today is to continue the work, David, that you did with your son last week. David, fill Sharon in about what hap-pened last time.

Dad: Umm . . . It was basically Bobby and I discussing how we can deal with our anger. Dealing with it—without hurting other people.

Immediately, the therapists align with the father and ask him to explain to his wife what happened last week, thereby increasing his status.

Therapist 1 to dad: Exactly. You did an excellent job helping your son. [to mom] And so, because David, as a father, can help his son to deal with his anger, we want them to continue with what they started last week. David did such an excellent job last week helping his son. So we want you to join us and come over here. [points to the seat beside the father] Come and watch with us.

In the preceding segment, the technique employed by the therapist is use of space. Specifically, by requesting the mother to reposition herself as de-scribed creates a seating arrangement in which the mother is physically ex-cluded from the father-son dialogue.

Mom: Okay. [Mom moves over to chair that is beside the father. At this point, the father is facing his son ready to begin a conversation with him. His back is toward the stepmother.]

In response, David immediately jumps into the task at hand and discusses with his son a variety of topics related to anger and anger control (for example, how Bobby has been dealing with his anger in the residence, stories of how he has dealt with his anger in the past, and, lastly, Bobby's recollection of his early physical abuse). Throughout this process, Sharon generally remains silent.

There is only one occasion when she attempts to intervene, to which the therapists respond with a blocking maneuver as follows:

Dad: You don't remember any stories that may have been told to you when you were younger?
Bobby: Yeah.
Dad: Well, what?
Bobby: What kind of stories?
Dad: Violent stories.
Bobby: Uh . . . I don't know anything about violent stories.
Mom: I'm gonna help you.
Therapist 1:   [to mom, hand gesturing to stop] No. No. Let them continue.

In response, David continues the discussion with his son. As the conversation between the dyad proceeds, the therapists repeatedly punctuate David's effectiveness in helping his son —again, increasing the father's status within the family. In his exploration of anger control, David gives an example of how he deals with his anger toward his boss. The therapists, after tracking this content, employ the concept of "boss" to explore and assess the spousal relationship.

Therapist 2:   What about at home? Who's the boss?
Bobby: Mom and Dad are boss. I'm only a little bit the boss.
Dad: [laughing] Mom is more the boss.
Therapist 1 to mom: Do you agree? Do you think you're the boss?
Mom: Yeah, probably.
Dad: She keeps me in line.
Mom: Yeah.
Therapist 2 to parents: Do you ever disagree about Bobby?
Mom and dad: [jointly] Never!

As the conversation begins to focus on the marital relationship, the therapists dismiss the child by instructing him to play, thereby achieving a boundary around the spousal subsystem. The comments of the parents confirm the therapists' hypothesis about the hierarchy in the family. Their statement that they "never" disagree about Bobby is particularly striking and supports the therapists' observation of David's tendency to defer to his wife when there is any initial disagreement. When asked about this, the dyad explains that they resolve their parenting disagreements via discussion. Therefore, the therapists shift the discussion back to having the couple explore their previous statements.

Therapist 2:   So, what then did you mean about her being the boss?
Dad: She keeps me in line.
Therapist 1:   Yeah, let's hear more about that.
Dad: Umm . . . [crosses his arms]
Mom: I can think of 20 examples. [Therapists ignore her comment and look toward David to continue.]

Dad: I'm laid off right now. I'm in the house a lot right now, and she keeps me on track with the house stuff. I make dinner sometimes.

Mom: Really? How many times did you actually make dinner?

Dad: [laughs] I help. [both David and Sharon laugh]

Therapist 2 to dad: So what else do you do?

Dad: Well, I don't know. She also takes care of the money.

Therapist 1:   But what else are you the boss of?

Dad: [crossing his arms] The cat. The dog. [again, both David and Sharon laugh]

Therapist 2 to mom: So, is there any area in which David is the boss?

The addition of "any area" to the preceding question is the first punctuation of the dyad's complementarity.

Mom: Yes! David is the boss. He—we do discuss things. Umm. David has a very lazy streak.

Dad: That's not true. I do do stuff around the house.

Mom: You do fix things. The vehicles and stuff. But as far as picking up after yourself. No way. No way.

Dad: That's not true.

Mom: I always pick up after you.

Therapist 1:   So, is there anywhere where you help her out?

Dad: I do the laundry.

Therapist 1:   No, not the house stuff. Where do you help her out?

Dad: I push her . . . I push her. She'll come home with problems at work and I'll say, "You gotta lay your foot down."

Therapist 2:   So, you help her with work stuff.

At the beginning of this segment, the family rule that Sharon is the boss and, in turn, David's perception of himself as not having any status within the family become poignantly clear. The therapists first attempt to challenge this family rule through David (that is, asking him to define in what area he is the boss). When these attempts fail, they work through Sharon. They ask her to define the areas in which David is the boss. She, however, quickly returns to the status quo, highlighting how she takes care of him (for example, picks up after him). The therapists, therefore, challenge the family rule once again by repeating the stated question to David. It is this repetition that increases the stress upon the family system—the stress that, at this point, is necessary for restructuring this very rigid family structure. This more intense challenge is met with David identifying his assistance to Sharon with regard to her work. An alternative to the traditional family rule has emerged—one in which David has some status. This alternative is quickly punctuated by the therapists. During the next phase of this session, the dyad proceeds to further discuss how David assists Sharon with her problems at work and Sharon herself acknowledges David's assistance. The following segment commences with the therapists directly punctuating the dyad's complementarity.

Therapist 2:   So look how you help each other. Do you guys see that? [to dad] You say she's the boss, but you help her out with work. You help her figure things out. [mom nods]

Therapist 1 to mom: So you agree.

Mom: Yes, when I first met David and I got to know him, he didn't realize how helpful he really was to me. He doesn't see it.

Therapist 1:   Stop right there! [turns Sharon's chair so that she faces David] Tell him right now.

Mom: Umm . . . [to David] You are very helpful to me in a lot of ways. Like you said, in situations outside of the house, like stuff at work. I want to run and hide and you push me. You say, "You're a big girl. You can do this." You really build me up so I do it. [David looks at her with apparent disbelief and surprise.]

Therapist 2 to dad: Did you know that?

Dad: No. [simultaneously shaking his head]

Therapist 1 to dad: Tell her what it's like to hear that. She seems very touched when she talks about you helping her. [David begins to talk to the therapists.]

Therapist 1 to dad: No. Tell her. Tell your wife.

Dad to mom: Your sister, she really pushes you to do things the way they should be done and so I usually step aside.

Mom to dad: No, you don't realize that you're there with your comments. You're really quiet. At first, you don't say anything. There are long pauses. Then you come up with a comment that's the right thing. And it blows me away. It makes so much sense, and it's the right thing to do. You don't realize how much I listen to you. You don't give yourself enough credit. Now, don't go on and get a big head.

Therapist 1 to dad: Tell her how you felt when you heard what she said.

Dad to mom: Surprised. I was shocked because I don't see myself as an adviser. [crosses his arms]

Mom to dad: You don't? But you really are to me. [silence]

Therapist 1 to mom: I wonder if that's all he felt. Do you think there was more?

Mom: Yes.

Therapist 1:   So find out.

Mom to dad: So, did you appreciate . . . I mean, did you like hearing what I said?

Dad to mom: Yes. But I was surprised because I never used to see myself as an adviser.

Therapist 2:   So it was a very nice moment. Very touching. Together you were able to find an area in which David helps you out.

In the preceding segment, Sharon responds to the therapists' punctuation of the dyad's complementarity by further expanding upon David's role as her adviser—thereby challenging the family rule that delineates David as having no power. David, however, responds in such a manner that reestablishes the family's homeostatic functioning. He discounts his role as adviser to his wife (and, in turn, his power in the family) and assigns the role to someone else (Sharon's sister). However, the reorganization of the family structure (to one in which there is more equal status and, in turn, more equal power between the spouses), first emerging in David's ability to identify his assistance to Sharon with her work, has begun. Sharon, responding to the shift in the family system, challenges David herself (and, in turn, the old family rule), affirming David's role as adviser, ultimately highlighting his status in the spousal subsystem and further contributing to the restructuring of the family organization. The therapists create enactments in which the dyad explores David's associated reactions to his wife's comments to underscore the change that has occurred in the family structure. Ultimately, the change in the spouses' transactions that occurred during this session (and, in turn, changed their positions via one another) created a change in David's context, ultimately allowing him to expand his definition of himself to include one of being an "adviser" to his wife—a role that clearly allocates him with power in the relationship. Overall, then, in pursuit of the structural goal of equalizing the power between the spouses (and, in turn, as parents), David's status first as a father and then as a spouse was enhanced throughout this session. Subsequent sessions continued according to the same therapeutic strategy.

Case 4: A Weak Parental Hierarchy and the Use of Unbalancing Techniques

The Johnson family consists of a mother (Sonya) and two boys, Jim (age 9) and Jack (age 7). The boys' biological father has been uninvolved with the family since Jack's birth. Jim is the IP who was referred for residential care due to severe aggression toward his brother and peers, cruelty to animals, oppositional behaviors both at home and in school, and severe hyperactivity, none of which improved with two psychiatric hospitalizations. Additionally, during several intake interviews and the admission process, it was discovered that Sonya relied heavily upon her mother in the care of the boys. The weak parental hierarchy was also immediately observable. The mother and grandmother were involved in a pattern of transactions that culminated in keeping the mother an ineffective parent. Specifically, Sonya's own ineffectiveness in controlling the boys was exacerbated by her mother either undercutting her or ultimately stepping in and achieving effective control, thereby further substantiating Sonya's role as an ineffective parent. The dysfunctional structure in this family was the weak parental subsystem contributed to by the grandmother's intrusion into the parental subsystem. Therefore, the structural goal was to clarify the hierarchy within the family structure, such that the mother gained the control of the executive subsystem with regard to her sons. The dysfunctional structure and the consequential structural goal can be mapped as illustrated in Figure 9.

In pursuit of the structural goal, a primary task was to block the grandmother from the parental subsystem. This could have been done in two ways. First, the grandmother could have been excluded from the sessions. This

Dysfunctional Structure   **Structural Goal**

MGM

M	IP Sib

MGM
M ======Th

IP   Sib

MGM
M

B   B

Figure 9
Strengthening of mother's potential power by blocking grandmother.

intervention would have set up an impermeable boundary around the parental subsystem and would have allowed Sonya to parent her sons without intervention from the grandmother. The other option would have been to invite the grandmother to the sessions but to block her participation in the mother-children transactions (for example, via use of self and space). Sonya elected not to have the grandmother participate in the sessions and, consequently, the former method of blocking occurred. The therapists felt comfortable in respecting Sonya's choice in this matter because the grandmother was a very competent woman who was employed full-time in her chosen career and was involved in many community organizations.

With the grandmother's interference blocked, the task of unbalancing the hierarchy of the mother-children subsystem could begin. A variety of unbalancing techniques were used, including affiliating with the mother as an adult to increase her status within the family, ignoring the sons to demote them, setting up enactments around the issue of control, and punctuating interactions such that the mother's effectiveness in controlling her children was highlighted. The overall task of unbalancing the hierarchy within the family and the techniques employed to achieve said task are nicely illustrated in the very first session with this family. Participants in this session were Sonya and Jim. The seating arrangement throughout the session is depicted in Figure 10.

Therapist 1 to mom: Nice to see you again. Please get your son to come and sit down. [Jim is currently playing apart from the adults]

Mom   Jim

X   X

Th1   Th2

Figure 10
Family seating arrangement.

Mom: [walks over to where Jim is playing] Let's go sit down.

Jim: [argues with his mother] No! No!

Mom: [to Jim as she points to a chair] You are going to sit right down there! [Jim sits in the chair]

Therapist 1 to mom: Good for you!

In this brief excerpt, several interventions have already occurred. The very first comment by the therapist is an affiliation with the mother. The subsequent request made of the mother sets up an enactment around the issue of control. The final comment made by the therapist is the first punctuation of any effective control by the mother.

Mom to Jim: Do not get up! Do not get up! [Jim looks as if he is ignoring his mother.]

Therapist 1:   Do you often have this problem with Jim not seeming to hear you?

Mom: [nodding] I had his hearing checked twice because I thought that there was something wrong with it. But it's fine. If I promise to give him something, like money—ten dollars—or if I disconnect everything in his room, like his computer or nintendo, he will just sit there. He'll be good for a little while. But as soon as he gets out of his room, he'll usually go hit my other son or my nephews if they're visiting.

Jim: [with a belligerent tone of voice] You don't have no nephews!

Therapist 1:   Do you appreciate him talking to you like that when you are talking to other adults?

The first comment made by the therapist in the preceding segment defines the problem as being one that occurs between Jim and his mother, not a problem within Jim. In response to Jim's belligerent comment, the therapist affiliates with the mother, addressing Jim's intrusion into her adult conversation.

Mom: He plays with me like that, but he knows how far to go.

Therapist 1:   So that was okay?

Mom: No. Jim will do things to bother me. Like right now, he's going to talk between us to bother me. When he wants something, he'll just keep bothering me. Like he kept asking me why I always send him away but not my other son.

Therapist 1:   That's a good question. Tell him what he did to make you decide to send him away. That's a good question.

Mom to therapists: They are always fighting.

Therapist 1:   Tell him. This is very important.

Mom to therapists: Jim is different than his brother, though.

Jim to therapists: [making fists and moving about in his chair] I'm gonna fight you!

Jim's comment could be viewed as the voice of the system, claiming that it would fight any change (that is, to its structure or homeostatic functioning).

Mom to Jim: [while putting her arm across him so he remains in the chair] Do not move! [to therapists] He does things to really get on my nerves. [to Jim] You know something. I am taking this radio away! You know that.

Jim: [pleadingly to mom] No!

Mom: You ain't keeping that because you can't listen.

Sonya then proceeds to tell of several incidents in which Jim hits his younger brother, Jack, with the last incident resulting in Jack crying.

Jim: No! I told you that Jack started it.

Mom: No! You did. I—

Jim: [interrupting mom] I did not!

Therapist 2 to mom: Let me ask you something. Do you mind that Jim is interrupting you when you are talking with other adults?

Mom: See, he thinks that because I'm talking with someone else I'm not going to do anything about what he's doing.

Therapist 2:   Okay. So what are you going to do about it right now? [Jim, at this point, attempts to get out of his chair.]

Mom: [again places her arm across Jim's chair so that he can't get up] No! You sit here when I am talking. I've come a long way to be here. You are going to sit here and you are going to listen. Because if you don't, you won't be coming home next week. I'll take everything back that I brought for you. Do you think that I can't take back everything that is here? I'm going to prove my point! [reaches for the items on the table]

Jim: [grabbing for the items] No, no, no. Why? Why?

Sonya, in turn, proceeds to tell the therapists of more incidents in which Jim hits his younger brother.

Therapist 1 to mom: So, what you are saying— [Jim interrupts] I'm not going to listen to your son right now because you are an adult and I am talking to you. So, what you are saying is that Jim's hitting is a big problem. Do you think that he understands that this is a big problem?

Sonya then proceeds to tell more stories of Jim's fights both with his younger brother and at school.

In the preceding segment, several techniques were employed. First, an enactment was set up around the issue of Jim's placement. Even with a repetition of the request to "tell" Jim why he was placed, Sonya does not follow through. Instead, she tells "stories," which locate the problem in Jim, moving away from the therapists' emphasis on interaction. Jim interrupts his mother's stories, and they soon begin to argue as equals. Therefore, to increase the mother's status, the therapists again affiliate with her as an adult by underscoring Jim's intrusion into her adult conversation. This pattern of interaction (that is, Jim's interruption of his mother) was the focus of the next enactment set up by the therapists. Although the mother briefly establishes effective control via her threat to take away the radio, she quickly retreats into stories about Jim—this time about his fighting. When the therapist is talking directly with Sonya, summarizing that fighting between the boys is what really bothers her, Jim interrupts the therapist. The therapist responds by directly ignoring him, while making statements of adult affiliation to the mother, thereby increasing the mother's status and demoting Jim. The next segment begins with the therapists setting up an enactment, which is the focus of the remainder of the session. Specifically, Sonya is asked to "tell" Jim what he needs to change to return home.

Therapist 1:   Stop right there! Tell Jim, in your own words, that it's the fighting that has to stop.

Mom: [begins to cry and states to Jim] You have to stop hitting Jack and your cousins. You are bigger than all of them. Every time you hit them, I'll bring you back here. [to therapists] But then he'll come back here and be good. And then after awhile, I'll finally let him come home and it'll all start again.

Therapist 1 to mom: So you don't want to let him go home for good only because he is doing well here. You want him to do well at home. I understand because what I am seeing today is a very different child than what I see in the living group. He is very different. He is not listening. He is not taking you seriously.

Therapist 2 to mom: You are upset and he is still ignoring you. He seems to, in fact, know how to hurt you. His behavior seems to hurt you.

Therapist 1 to mom: How do you feel about his behavior? [Jim again interrupts] I'm not going to talk to him, and before you go today, I want you to tell him what behaviors you want to see before he can go home for good.

Mom to Jim: Are you ready to go home? Do you want to go home?

Jim: Yeah . . . Yeah.

Therapist 1:   Sonya. This is very important. You are his mom. Children sometimes have trouble understanding these kinds of questions. So, instead of asking him, tell him what you want him to do.

Therapist 2:   It's not important what he wants but what you want. He is a little boy and you're the adult. [Jim begins to sing, giggle, and move about in his chair.] You see what he's doing right now.

Therapist 1 to therapist 2:   I don't like it.

Therapist 2 to therapist 1:   I don't like it either.

Therapist 1 to mom: What about you?

Mom: Jim. Stop it!

Therapist 1 to mom: And if he's behaving like this at home, I wonder how that will affect your decision as to whether he is ready to come home? And you know, Sonya, he is very good at getting us off track. How many times have we tried to get you to tell him what needs to change for him to come home? [Jim again starts to laugh, clap, and move about in his seat.] He's had a lot of control over what's been happening during this session versus you and the adults. Is this behavior going to get him home?

Mom: No.

Therapist 1 to mom: Tell him what he needs to do to get home.

Mom to Jim: You need to listen to me and to other adults, like your teachers. You don't listen—

Jim: I listen.

Mom: Yeah, because you are here, right?

Therapist 1:   Do not ask him. Just keep telling him what you want. Keep going.

Mom to Jim: When you come home, you are still going to have to go to school and you're gonna listen!

Jim: Yeah. If it's a better school.

Mom: It ain't got to be a better school; it could be the same school.

Jim: But if it's the same school, I will not do it.

Therapist 2 to mom: Are you going to allow him to argue with you? Tell him what you want. [to therapist 1] I care about what she wants.

Therapist 1 to therapist 2:   Me too. [to mom] Keep going.

Mom: You argue with Jack or beat him up. You aren't going to beat on him. When I tell you to put your toys up, when I tell you to turn the games off, you're gonna do it. It ain't gonna be "oh, man." [Jim smirks at his mother.]

Therapist 1 to mom: Do you like that face? His face seems to be telling you that he's not taking you seriously.

Mom: Jim likes to play this macho person—like he can't be hurt—

Jim: I beat up kids outside.

Therapist 1 to mom: [ignoring Jim's comment] Do you want Jim to look at you that way when you talk to him—

Jim: [interrupting] They were trying to beat me up and do karate on me, so—

Therapist 1 to mom: We are not listening to him. We are talking to you, Sonya.

Jim to therapist 1:   So what, punk?

Therapist 1 to mom: Did you like that face, Sonya?

Mom to Jim: Sit back!

Therapist 1 to mom: We expect something better and different for you and your son, Sonya. [Jim again tries to interrupt.]

Mom: Jim. Be quiet! [silence]

Therapist 1 to mom: Tell him if you liked the way he looked at you.

Mom: [to therapists, crying] Jim don't care.

Therapist 2 to mom: You are frustrated and hurt about his not listening to you. He's counting on you becoming upset. You see, because he has learned that if he gets to you, you'll eventually give in.

Jim: [angrily] I don't want to talk about it!

Therapist 2 to mom: You see, he does not want me to tell you about what's happening between the two of you.

Jim: I don't want to talk about it.

Therapist 2 to mom: I don't care what he wants. We're here to help you manage his behavior.

Therapist 1 to mom: Now we can see the struggle you two have at home.

Jim: I don't have no problem at home.

Therapist 1 to mom: It's happening right here.

Therapist 2 to mom: That's right. So turn him around and continue to tell him what you expect. Don't ask him, just tell him.

Therapist 1 to mom: And if at any time, he does something you don't like— like make a face at you—tell him what you want to see instead. And there is another thing that we want to let you know. Because we are going to make changes, it is going to get worse before it gets better.

Jim: [with a smirk] We will not make changes!

Mom: [turns Jim's seat so he faces her] Sit down! Be quiet! Put your feet down! Sit back!

Therapist 1 to mom: Keep going, Sonya. Keep telling him what you want. Don't give up now. What else? Keep going.

Mom to Jim: Bottom line. When I tell you to do something, you're gonna do it.

Jim to mom: I'll kick you!

Mom: No, you ain't!

Therapist 2 to mom: He is challenging you, Sonya. What are you going to do about that? What are you going to say to him?

Mom: [to Jim] Sit back! [to therapists, pointing at a radio on the table] Is there a way that I can take it back?

Jim: [pleadingly] No! Don't take it!

Therapist 1:   You decide as a parent what you want to do and we will support you.

Jim: No! Don't take it! I don't want it gone. Don't take it!

Therapist 2 to mom: Keep going.

Therapist 1 to therapist 2:   I think she will show him she really means business.

Mom to Jim: If you can't listen, you ain't getting nothing.

Therapist 1:   Good, Sonya. [to Therapist 2] She let him know she meant it.

Mom to Jim: I'm taking away your computer too. [Jim turns his back to his mother and starts to get up.] Sit back down! I'm talking to you.

Therapist 2 to mom: Tell him what you want him to remember from today's session.

Mom: [turns Jim to face her] If you don't listen, everything will go, one by one. You ain't getting nothing from me.

Therapist 2 to mom: Make sure he heard you.

Mom to Jim: You understand what I said?

Jim to mom: I don't feel good.

Mom: [gently] You don't feel good?

Jim to mom: My stomach hurts. I'm gonna throw up.

Therapist 2 to therapist 1:   Did you hear what he said? I won't be bothered if he did. Would you?

Therapist 1 to therapist 2:   Me neither. [to mom] Would you, Sonya? I don't think you would change your mind even if he did.

Mom to Jim: You are still not getting this computer.

Therapist 2 to mom: Tell him again what you expect from him.

Mom: [turns Jim to face her again] You will stop fighting, arguing, talking back. Did you hear what I said? When you come back down to the house, the minute you move out of line, you will be right back here and you will learn to listen.

Therapist 2:   I think we should stop. [to mom] Good job, Sonya.

Therapist 1:   Very good job, Sonya.

In the preceding segment, while the dyad participates in the enactment around the issue of what Jim needs to do to return home, the therapists intervene in their interactions to achieve their structural goal of unbalancing the hierarchy. The therapists employed several techniques. They achieved intensity by expanding the length of the interactions (for example, telling the mother several times to "keep going") and by repeating their message (for example, instructing the mother to "tell" Jim what she wants again and again). The resulting level of intensity was deemed necessary to adequately stress the family system so that restructuring could occur. The therapists also employed the technique of refocusing. Specifically, they were not diverted from their goal of unbalancing the hierarchy by Jim's verbal or nonverbal threats, insults, or claims that he would be sick. The ignoring of Jim's comments and behaviors was also a specific unbalancing technique because doing so reduced Jim's overly powerful position in the family. The therapists also employed the technique of teaching complementarity. Specifically, they provided an interactive explanation of Jim's apparent misbehavior and, in turn, lack of empathy for his mother when she cried in response, outlining that Jim behaved in such a way because he had learned that if he did so his mother would give in to him. Lastly, and most importantly, the therapists employed punctuation. They ended the enactment immediately after Sonya (with appropriate parental authority) told Jim (who was appropriately listening) what he needed to do to return home, while praising the mother for her good work. As a result, the mother was able to experience herself as an effective parent, with Jim concurrently experiencing himself as an obedient child. Hence, the hierarchy was unbalanced—at least for that moment.

Treatment with this family lasted approximately one year. All sessions followed the same basic strategy (and techniques) used in the first session. In addition, the therapists worked with Sonya's constructions. Several sessions occurred involving only the mother, during which the therapists provided expert advice about a variety of issues, including the extinction process (for example, the idea that her son's behavior would become worse before it became better because she was changing the rules), the difference between the children's needs and their desires, the benefit of prioritizing behaviors to be targeted, and the importance of threatening only with consequences that could be followed through on.

Additionally, given (1) the long history and continuation of conflicts between Jim and Jack, (2) the fact that as Jim's behavior improved, Jack's behavior worsened to such a degree that Sonya was considering the idea of seeking assistance to have him hospitalized, and (3) Jim's statement during a previous session that it was his brother who kept him "acting like a monster at home," the therapists did some work with the sibling subsystem. Most notably, a session was held in which two therapists (therapist 1 and Jim's individual therapist) assisted the boys in talking with one another about a variety of issues while their mother watched behind a one-way mirror with therapist 2. It became evident from the boys' discussion that they believed that their mother could not love them equally and that she could not manage them both at the same time; they therefore concluded that they could not live at home together for any period of time. The mother's response to the boys, presented in the following, nicely illustrates how the hierarchy had been effectively unbalanced such that Sonya had regained her executive position within the family.

Therapist 1:   I think we need Mom to come back and talk to the boys about what they talked about. [to therapist 2 and mom] Come on back, you guys. [mom and therapist 2 return from observation room]

Therapist 1 to mom: Your boys did wonderful work.

Therapist 2 to therapist 1 and boys: Sonya and I were talking back there and I think she has some ideas of what to say to the boys.

Therapist 1:   Very good. I think you should be very proud of your sons.

Mom: [sits down in between the boys, pulling their chairs closer to her] Okay. [points at and states to Jim] You're getting ready to come home. [points at and states to Jack] And you're not going nowhere. I love both of you the same. You're gonna be treated the same. It is going to be different this time. 'Cause I'm going according to what you need and not what you want. You understand? [Jim and Jack nodding] You're gonna be in the same house until you move out and go away. But, until then, I love you both, and I'm so happy now that both of you are gonna be home. [pointing to Jack] It ain't gonna be just you. Jim's coming home. But you're not going anywhere.

Therapist 1 to mom: [pointing to Jack] Did you see that smile?

Mom: [nodding] [to both boys] I believe I can handle both of you. I did it before and I can do it again. But this time, it will be different. Either you listen or there will be consequences. Got it? [both boys nod]

Therapists 1 and 2:   [applauding] Yes! Yes! Great!

Therapist 2 to mom: Well, they sure know who the boss is now.

Overall, after approximately a year of treatment, the structure of this family system was reorganized. The mother became an effective parent and, in turn, Jim became a little boy—no longer a despot. Not surprisingly, Jim was discharged home and Jack went "nowhere."

Conclusions

Structural family therapy is a systemic model. As in all systemic therapies, a dysfunctional family system is hypothesized to underlie the identified patient's symptomatic behavior. Given this conceptualization of psychopathology, the goal of any systemic therapy is to assist the family to change their interaction patterns. As a result of these changes in the family, the IP's original problem is expected to resolve. As noted by Colapinto (1991), the uniqueness of structural family therapy lies in two factors. One, this model conceptualizes problems and change processes in terms of family organization and spatial relations. As families evolve, they develop solidified patterns of interaction that become rules for future interactions. These rules make up the internal organization—the structure—of the family. According to Minuchin (1974), pathological families are unable to adapt (that is, change their structure) to their changing needs. Instead, such families increase the rigidity of their historical patterns of transaction and maintain their prior structure. Therefore, the goal of the structural family therapist is to actively change the family's transactional patterns and, in turn, their structure. It is, in fact, the active role of the therapist that is the second unique factor of the structural model. The structural therapist joins the family system and then, either by observing spontaneous familial interactions or by creating them, begins to *experience* the family's preferred patterns of transaction. By doing so, the structuralist also begins to feel what alternatives, currently submerged, might become accessible to the family (Minuchin, Lee, and Simon, 1996). In this model, the therapist uses a variety of specific techniques to help the family make small changes in their current transactions. These small changes, in turn, enable the family to tap into alternative transactions that previously had been latent. Therefore, as noted by Minuchin and his colleagues (1996), although it is the structuralist who is the catalyst for change, it is the family who is the healer. Given this conceptualization of the healing process, it is not surprising that structural family therapy can be used with many cultures and/or diverse familial arrangements (for example, single-parent families, gay and lesbian couples, multiracial families). This is simply because each family, regardless of its culture or specific arrangement, has a structure, which, when dysfunctional, needs reorganization. Historically, structural family therapy has employed live supervision in the training of structuralists at all levels of expertise. The supervisor actively experiences the therapeutic context and, in turn, assists the therapist to differentially respond (that is, to access his or her submerged ways of interacting in therapy) according to the needs of the client family (Minuchin et al., 1996). If live supervision is not available, viewing and discussion of videotaped sessions is often utilized.

Study Questions

1. In the Smith family, if Michael were out of the home, and if the spouses were not assisted in dealing with their conflicts adaptively with one another, what would be the hypothesized effect on the different family members?
2. In the Jones family, a direct method of working on the enmeshment between Mary and Ray (reported to be used in previous sessions) was not used in the presented transcript. Specifically, the therapists did not directly address the mother's use of language in describing herself ("Mommy") and

her son ("baby") when she was talking with Ray. Develop an intervention that directly targets this interaction.

3. In the Taylor family, why was it so important to block Sharon from intervening in the father-son interactions in the beginning of therapy? Generate some of the possible responses of different family members and therapeutic interventions to address said reactions.

4. In the Johnson family, what would have been the impact on the family structure if the therapists directly corrected Jim's behavior during the sessions?

References

Colapinto, J. (1991). Structural family therapy. In A. S. Gurman & D. P. Kniskern (Eds.), *Handbook of family therapy, Volume II* (pp. 417–443). New York: Brunner/Mazel.

Goldenberg, I., & Goldenberg, H. (1996). *Family therapy: An overview* (4th ed.). Pacific Grove, CA: Brooks/Cole.

Hazelrigg, M. D., Cooper, H. M., & Borduin, C. M. (1987). Evaluating the effectiveness of family therapies: An integrative review and analysis. *Psychological Bulletin, 101*(3), 428–442.

Minuchin, S. (1974). *Families and family therapy.* Cambridge, MA: Harvard University Press.

Minuchin, S., & Fishman, H. C. (1981). *Family therapy techniques.* Cambridge, MA: Harvard University Press.

Minuchin, S., Lee, W. Y., & Simon, G. (1996). *Mastering family therapy.* New York: Wiley.

Simon, G. M. (1995). A revisionist rendering of structural family therapy. *Journal of Marital and Family Therapy, 21,* 17–26.

Chapter Six

The Brief Therapy Approach of the Palo Alto Group

Karin Schlanger and Barbara Anger-Díaz

The Palo Alto Group, as it is known internationally, was a central contributor to the paradigm shift that occurred in the field of psychotherapy in the late 1950s and 1960s. It was the time when family therapy began in the United States and therapists realized that the emotional problems their clients had were often related to family interactions. The Palo Alto Group, under the lasting influence of the anthropologist Gregory Bateson, and constituted by notable therapists and researchers such as Don D. Jackson, John Weakland, Jay Haley, and, later, Paul Watzlawick and Richard Fisch, embraced Ludwig von Bertalanffy's systems thinking. This model was closely aligned with their already espoused beliefs in communication theory. The family therapy they created was the result of

- their own research into the nature of communication
- von Bertalanffy's general systems theory
- cybernetic thinking
- constructivism
- hypnotherapy as practiced by Milton Erickson

Gregory Bateson's approach to behavior, one of always seeking to find the context that makes odd patterns meaningful, left its distinctive mark. It contributed heavily to the group's nonnormative, nonpathologizing view of their clients. Earlier, under a Rockefeller Foundation grant to study the different levels and channels of human communication, Bateson and his research group had settled into the Palo Alto Veterans Administration to study the patterns of communication of schizophrenics and their families. Group members John Weakland and Jay Haley interviewed families as part of this research and were soon giving requested advice to the family members. This led to their formulating and practicing family therapy. Don Jackson, while working in his Palo Alto practice, had already been including some of the client's family members in his therapies. He began collaborating with the Bateson group in their work with schizophrenics, which led to their now famous interactional view of schizophrenia (Bateson, Jackson, Haley, and Weakland, 1956). Jackson was later able to get sizable donations toward the creation of an institute, where family interaction could continue to be studied and where family therapy would have a home. The Mental Research Institute (MRI) was founded by Jackson in 1959 and became the place where the Palo Alto Group operated. Gregory Bateson, although intellectual author of much of the thinking that went into the early therapeutic practice at the institute, never joined it but remained associated with it.

In light of communication and systems theory, the origins of problems were no longer sought intrapsychically but in the interaction between people. Solutions were now looked for in the communications arena. In fact, the Palo Alto Group began to focus on presenting problems rather than concluding that symptoms reported by clients were part of a greater underlying pathology: There was a problem to be solved and not a pathology to go looking for. This was the beginning of making therapeutic work briefer.

Theoretical Underpinnings

Systems thinking and communication theory soon began to dominate the relatively new field of family therapy. Nevertheless, understandings of these theories, therapeutic techniques used, and interpretations of problems in the family varied extensively. For example, for Virginia Satir (who had been invited by Jackson to join him in founding the MRI), "communication" was the expression of feelings and content. She encouraged family members to improve their communications and to strive for congruence between direct expression and metacommunicational levels of the same. Satir believed this would improve self-esteem in individuals and, ultimately, family functioning. Jackson, on the other hand, was interested in the cognitive aspects of communication and strongly believed that what one thinks influences what one does. This concept of "reframing" became part of the evolving therapeutic model of the Palo Alto Group at MRI, and the relational aspect of communication became essential.

Family therapy, as developed by the Palo Alto Group, was a direct result of the shift to systems thinking and was also strongly informed by a constructivist epistemology, according to which we construct our own world view, our reality, in the interaction between ourselves and the world around us. What we know depends on what we come in contact with and on the signs we learn to decipher in the interaction. From birth on, we "construct" a world inside us (a structure created by neuronal networking), with which we approach the world outside, interpret it, react to it, and let ourselves be transformed by it. Without these inner constructions, we would be incapable of perceiving our environment. We "learn" to see, hear, feel, smell, and taste the world. We also participate in the constructions of others. In our interactions, in the mutual adaptation of our behaviors, we build those aspects of our world that we share with one another. This is the essence of communication: building a world in common through interaction and continual mutual adaptation. We might actually say that our world view is "coconstructed" with others and depends on communicative exchanges.

Furthermore, our own existence is determined by the contexts of basic interactions with others, which is why we experience ourselves differently depending on who we are interacting with. Our identity is not something static but a process in itself: It is in the interaction that we exist in any given way. Because of our interactional nature, therapeutic change is possible.

The Palo Alto Group has evolved its therapy by closely studying the interactions surrounding a problem situation and determining what in the interaction needs to be changed to obtain a different outcome. Countless therapeutic cases have provided evidence that changed behavior changes the interaction, which changes perception and outcome. As Heinz von Foerster said: "If you want to learn how to see, learn how to act." Central to this therapy is the belief that, as Popper (1984) states, the truly creative aspect of human beings is that we create and allow ourselves to be re-created by our creation. Therapy can facilitate this re-creative process when certain perceptions make our constructed reality no longer viable. If we have created an interactive vicious circle because of actions that do not work, we can create a new situation by acting differently, re-creating ourselves in the process. Just as a change in perception (belief) leads to a change in behavior (actions), changed behavior leads to changed perception and, therefore, experience. If who we become at a given moment is shaped by the interaction, so are the difficulties that we encounter.

Consistent with systemic and constructivist thinking, then, when everyday difficulties turn into a lingering problem, it makes sense *not* to concentrate on the individual but to focus instead on the relational context of the problem. The reality created in a certain interaction can be changed with a change in the interactive pattern. All members of the system will change in response to changed behavior. From a constructivist view, all interactions are acceptable. They are not labeled or judged by any outside context or frame of reference. There is no predetermined notion as to what relationships should or should not be. The approach is thus nonnormative because no guiding principle informs us as to how people should behave with each other. Within this theoretical framework, therapy singles out and concentrates on changing only those interactions that have become problematic for the client, who defines them as such. This way of respecting the client is what makes the work of the Palo Alto Brief Therapy Group distinct from other family therapy approaches.

What the Palo Alto Brief Therapy Group at MRI does today, 30 years later, continues to be different in practice from what has become mainstream family therapy. Furthermore, its own methodology has evolved in the years since the beginning of the Brief Therapy Center. In 1967, the team worked together and observed each other's sessions from behind the one-way mirror. After viewing many sessions and still working together every Wednesday afternoon, the work revolves around the hypothesis that if clients change what they are doing to solve the problem, a change in the presented problem can be achieved. It is in fact the clients' attempted solutions that are feeding the problem, ergo perpetuating it. The focus of therapy is on these solutions, and the central job of therapy becomes

1. to get a concrete, clear description (in behavioral terms) of the presenting problem (as defined by the client)
2. to find the common denominator or main thrust of all the attempted solutions
3. to use the therapist's influence to get the client to do something completely different (in words and/or action)

In fact, Richard Fisch today says that since the problem *is* the attempted solution, the main focus of therapy is on the cessation of that attempted solution. "We don't treat problems, we treat solutions," he says.

Follow-ups at three months and one year after the last session confirm that getting clients to depart from their attempted solution and to try a totally different venue solves the problem in an effective way. Because it is the client who determines what the problem is, it is also the client who decides that, when the problem is no longer a problem, it is time to terminate therapy.

For many family therapists, the family, now seen as a system, evokes a notion of "deep and multi-layered" relationships to be explored and redirected (Goldenberg and Goldenberg, 1996, p. 3). The underlying premise is that individual symptoms reflect family system dysfunction and that these symptoms persist only if they are maintained by that family system. From this point of view, the family *needs* the symptom in order for its members to function, thus the symptom is maintained at whatever the cost. Not surprisingly, this perception leads to attempts on the part of therapists to "fix" the dysfunction by many means, often resulting in drawn-out therapies, whether in an attempt to reshape the family members or their interrelationships. The group at the Brief Therapy Center came to the conclusion that, while indeed present behaviors maintained the problem (symptom), these behaviors did not necessarily have another function (for example, that of keeping the family going). They concluded that the attempted solutions (behaviors maintaining the problem) were mostly commonsense reactions (often culturally determined) on the part of the participants that were simply not working. That is not to say that when a problem is solved (that is, the nature of the interaction has changed), new difficulties may not arise as people adjust to the changes. Difficulties arise with changing life. As John Weakland often said, when a client resolves a problem, he exchanges the same damn thing over and over again for one damn thing after another.

While we certainly acknowledge that people are the sum total of their experience, past history is not the focus of therapy. Taking the family's *complaint* as the problem, the therapy shifts the focus from why they are doing what they are doing to what they are doing that keeps them stuck in a situation that is painful to at least one of its members. This way of looking at people's troubles has an implicit positive message: Clients actively contribute to their own misery, and, by the same token, they can stop doing so by doing something different. Not only does this shift implicitly give hope by focusing on what can be changed, but it allows us to proceed with a work methodology that is more expeditious. In other words, we stay away from delving into the historical or genetic reasons for a given difficulty. We believe people are unable to cope with some of life's difficulties because of the way they manage them in their attempt to resolve them.

In our view, every question asked potentially widens the scope of therapy and therefore lengthens treatment. This is why, in order to shorten it, we very consciously limit our questions to those that provide pieces of information vital to our therapy: questions that lead us to a clear description of the presenting problem, the interactions involved, and the client's position and attempted solutions. Another way of making therapy briefer is to work with the main complainant, that is, the "customer." Going on the assumption that the person most afflicted by the problem is likely to be the one most willing to do something to change the situation, we check for "customership" and concentrate our work on getting that person to make a change. From our perspective, it does not matter at what point the system is intercepted. The changed behavior of one member will force changed responses from the others.

In speaking about our client's "position," we are referring to the frame of reference the client is using to evaluate the situation of the problem. A parent complaining about his son can view the very same objectionable behaviors as stemming from emotional weakness (child is "mad") or from rebelliousness or meanness (child is "bad"). We respect our client's frame of reference, and it is not our intention to change it. We have found the assessment of a client's position useful, for it permits us to sell our interventions in a language consistent with that frame. In order to get our client to do something different, we often spend considerable effort in developing a rationale as to why the client would do well to engage in what will be new behaviors, ensuring that those behaviors are consistent with the client's position. We speak of "salesmanship" as a prerequisite for a therapist trying to influence a client's behavior. If the parent's position is that his son's behavior is caused by emotional weakness, we are unlikely to get him to deal with the son differently if we frame our rationale for doing so in a context suggesting the son's rebelliousness. We will more likely be successful if we label the suggested new and different behavior as a way of fortifying the son emotionally.

As this chapter deals with the *practical* application of therapy, the case presentation illustrates the following aspects of the Palo Alto Brief Therapy Group's approach:

- Making the initial phone call
- Defining the problem
- Identifying the attempted solutions

- Identifying the main thrust of the attempted solutions
- Determining the position of the client
- Designing an intervention
- Selling an intervention
- Homework
- Homework follow-up
- Termination

The Case: An Adult Son Remains at Home
Background

The García family, seen in the Latino Brief Therapy Center, was self-referred for brief therapy because the parents were concerned about their son Pablo (age 20) staying at home too much. The father had called and made the initial appointment. The family consisted of a mother (Dolores), who was a homemaker and who volunteered at an Overeaters Anonymous group; a father (Juan Ramón), who was a manager at a local company, and two older brothers (Julián and Saúl), ages 25 and 28, who had their own families and were working. The therapist whose turn it was to see this family has been with the Brief Therapy project for many years. There was a team behind the one-way mirror, communicating by phone or in person, at all times.

As we have already mentioned, with this approach to therapy it is important to determine early on who the client is. Therefore, in the first telephone conversation with the parent, the therapist taking the call (who may or may not end up being the therapist working with the family) tries to find out who is most concerned with the current state of affairs. This is particularly important to do with cases in which the person complained about (known in other models as the identified patient) is an offspring. In such a case, most often the parent calling will want the therapist to work with the child and "fix it." This, of course, is one thing that a therapist looking for the problem in the interaction will not set out to do, and it is important to start therapy on track.

One useful way to begin working with the person who is most concerned and therefore most motivated to change the situation (usually *not* the child) is to ask the parent on the phone whether the child is eager to come in for therapy. This is an example of the therapist's use of language early on as a tool of influence because the following is a likely scenario: This problem has been kept alive for some time now, and the parents have been talking with their son about getting some help for it. The young person does not want to see a psychotherapist and has come up with all kinds of excuses. Finally, something has happened in the last week or so that prompts another talk with the son, during which the parents convince him that therapy is necessary. Triumphantly, they now call the therapist and say that their son has finally agreed to see her. However, when asked whether the son is eager to see the therapist, the parent has to admit that no, he is not eager. This provides the opportunity for the therapist, who from the beginning suspects that it is the parent who is most motivated to change and has therefore made the initial contact, to say that since the parent knows the son much better than the therapist ever could, the therapist would like to meet with him first to get an idea of what is happening. At the same time, the therapist usually asks how much of a problem this situation is for the child's other parent. If it is stated that it is a problem for the other parent as well, the parents are invited to come to the first session together for the therapist to get information.

In the Palo Alto approach to brief therapy, the therapist starts the session by asking what the problem is. It is one way of conveying to the clients that their complaint will be taken seriously and that the therapist is going to tackle things immediately.

Case Transcript

Therapist: What is the problem, what is the concern that brings you here today? Do you want to start?

Father: Well, since it was my idea . . . we have a 20-year-old who has dropped out of school. Actually, his grades were such that he couldn't go back. He's sitting at home. He, for whatever reason of his own, is unable to get his act together, go out and get a job, or go back to school. Now this is not new. This is something that's been going on for a long, long time. I think the roots are in his own personality and revolve around issues with self-worth, self-esteem. And he has been, at various times, with counseling of different types, different levels, and none of it's ever really worked too well. So this is a strategy that I'm proposing. It may be half-baked, it may have some merit. He has shown great skill in absorbing all kinds of counseling and disappearing. In other words, nothing really gets accomplished. So . . . excuse me, let me . . . what I said, "Okay, fine." Probably Dolores and I are the two people who . . . we really have great influence with him, and I think he would dearly love to do what we ask [from him]. What I want to do is help the guy, and I think I need professional skills, to help the guy, or I need somebody to tell me, "This is a bum approach, and let's try something else."

Therapist: Okay, okay.

Father: Did I cover it?

Mother: Yes, you did. He's full of rage, which he's turned inward, on himself. He hates himself, and it literally paralyzes him, I think. He knows he should be getting his act together and going out and looking . . . just looking for a job. But I think he feels absolutely paralyzed, as he's told me; he said, "I just can't cope with that idea."

Therapist: With the idea of getting a job?

Mother: Yes. And he knows, he knows the world expects this of him. He knows his friends are . . . well, at least he feels they're all scoffing at him behind his back.

Therapist: Has he said that?

Mother: Yes, to me. I mean, he talks quite openly to his father and I, but we're the only ones he does talk to, and this therapy, that Juan Ramón mentioned . . . he has admitted he would answer their questions. And I said, "Oh," because, you know, how would they know what to ask unless he comes out with some of his ideas? He wasn't telling them what he was feeling.

In this segment, the therapist has chosen to start by hearing what the father has to say. This is done in a casual manner, but it is intentional since in this case it was the father who made the initial phone contact. The therapist is particularly interested in hearing his version, because she is assuming that he is the main client. In this first session, foremost in the mind of the therapist is the need to focus on what is a problem that can be narrowed down to something workable. Because there is a tendency on the part of clients to want to explain rather than describe ("the roots of the problem are in his lack of self-worth, self-esteem"), the therapist in contrast uses very concrete language and elicits examples. She comes back to the issue at hand, which is Pablo's lack of interest in finding work for himself.

Therapist: Since June, he's been, you said, the couch potato, is it?
Father: No, he was employed during the summer, by relatives. I'll let Dolores explain that, because she put the deal together and . . .
Mother: Well, it was a deal. I don't think they need to know all the background. The upshot is that he went up to the mountains, where I have relatives, and I think the first evening he was there, they sat around the table and thought, "What'll we do with Pablo?" So, my niece's husband, who is a contractor, employed him, and he worked there, let's see, through July, August, September, and half of October. He felt he was doing dreadfully because it was all new to him. But his boss was quite pleased, and they actually want him to come back this year if he's not doing something else in between.
Therapist: So he did hang on to a job for that many months, though, okay?
Mother: He did an adequate job, certainly, otherwise they wouldn't want him back. He's very conscientious. He's very prompt. You see, if you can once get him working for someone, he is the ideal employee. He's never absent.
Therapist: What happened with that job, then?
Father: It was seasonal. You know, when it gets cold in the mountains, it's outside, so they can't do any outside work.
Therapist: He didn't quit, he didn't get fired. The job ended.
Father: Yeah. It was on the understanding as soon as the weather turned poor.
Therapist: I am curious, has he tried to get a job, at all?
Father: No, not at all.
Mother: He says this is what he can't cope with.
Therapist: Does he . . . I'm curious if he does anything, like read the newspaper, or make a phone call, or just . . .
Father: No, not that I am aware of.

The therapist needs to narrow down a complaint so that it can be worked on efficiently. It is important to check whether for these parents it would be acceptable for Pablo to go back to school as a way of doing something different from what he has been doing up until now. In this model, hypotheses that the therapist might develop are always checked. In other words, it is important not to start working on a problem that is then going to be changed by the clients. Therefore, the therapist needs to check whether it is work or school that is most important for these parents. This continues to be a focusing of the problem.

Therapist: Let me check with you: If he can go back to school, or he can go back to work, either one's fine, or do you have a preference for which way you're . . .

Father: No, I have no preference, as long as what he is doing does not happen anymore.

Therapist: Okay. And let me check: You were saying, he's not going to school, he isn't going to work. I think I heard you say, and let me check with you, too, that it doesn't matter what direction he takes, it's just, take a direction . . .

Mother: No. You know, I think he wants to have a goal before he tries any school again, and he does not have a goal.

Dolores has now stated that it is more important that Pablo get work because he does not have a goal to go back to school. From now on, the therapist will focus on what this family is doing in order for Pablo to get a job. She continues the session, trying to get concrete information by asking for examples, dialogue, and action with Pablo both from the mother and the father.

Father: Let me comment first, and then you can go after it. I've asked him a couple of times. In other words, "What is the problem?" In the past he's said, "You know, I don't have any problem filling out the application or going through the interview process; I just don't want to start work because I'm afraid I'll fail. Not I'm afraid, I know I'll fail."

Therapist: He says, "I know I'll fail?" Is that what he says?

Father: Yeah. Now I wanted to clarify this fine point before coming in here, and I talked to him about a week ago about it, and now he says he's afraid to even fill out an application. He just says, in other words, he can't bring himself to do it, and that's the way he explains it to me.

Therapist: You said (turning to mother) that he has a lot of rage turned "inward," I think, were your words. How does he convey that rage turned inward?

Mother: Well . . .

Father: You sense it.

It is very common for clients to be vague and not descriptive. In the brief therapy approach, the therapist cannot work unless she gets the information from the client, so this is an example of how she tries in different ways to get to the concrete information she needs in order to progress and move forward. In asking questions, she uses the client's language literally. It is also important to keep in mind that clients can utter words in response to the therapist's question but that these words often are not really an answer to the question posed. The therapist must listen very carefully to what the client is saying to make sure she gets an answer to her question. The therapist *needs* to get an answer to the question posed, and so she gets back to it.

Therapist: What does he say, what does he do?

Mother: Sometimes, I mean, if he's really angry, he'll go . . . and really hit something, or . . . I mean, I've got some dents on the refrigerator from that, and we've got holes in the wall.

Therapist: So that rage turned outward.

Mother: Well, that's outward, but mostly I feel that it's inward. It doesn't come out against us. Don't you think all this hate, this hatred of himself . . .

Therapist: So he doesn't get mad at you.

Father: No. It's literally boiling inside. For example, I'll come home and I'll say hello to him, and I'll know . . .

Mother: Yeah, you can tell.

Father: That he's boiling inside.

Therapist: Which is . . . how can you tell? What does he do, or say, or look like?

Father: In other words, it isn't anything that I could detect in his manner, or his voice, or his behavior, but the signal is there.

Therapist: Well, he doesn't look at you, or he doesn't catch your eye, or he doesn't talk to you, or he . . .

Father: Yeah, I think probably he's at a distance. Maybe that's a good way to put it.

At this point, Dolores and Juan Ramón disagree on the way they see his distance affecting their relationship with him. In other models of family therapy, the therapist could capitalize on the way the parents deal with one another around this difference and make this a couple's problem, which would in turn be affecting the performance of the son. In other words, this couple could be seen as needing the son to be acting the way he is so that they do not have to face the "real" issue, which is that their relationship is failing in some way. From the brief therapy point of view, the therapist will listen to both points of view and come back to the problem that they brought in: Pablo is having trouble finding a job.

Mother: But sometimes, when he is like that, he *does* want to talk to us, and this is where we need the help because we can't relate to it. We can't relate to anything he's going through.

Father: That's fine, but let's get back on how . . . we talked about boiling inside. Let's see, the only way I can tell you is, when he's in a mood, and we use the word "mood," we sense it almost immediately, and I really can't tell you how, except that he is remote, and . . .

Mother: Well, he's distant.

Father: Kind of withdrawn.

Mother: He goes into the bedroom and sleeps, sure.

Father: I don't see that as often as I see him sitting in the living room and . . . maybe that's it. He withdraws.

Mother: But then, many times . . .

Therapist: I'm curious what you do . . .

Mother: I mean, we're saying almost opposite things here, though, because often, when he's in one of those moods, he wants to talk, and he'll go on and on, and he'll repeat the same things, and he keeps asking, "What should I do about this? Why do I feel this way?" And I have no answers. So this is what makes me feel so helpless.

Therapist: So when he gets into one of these "moods," as you're calling it, sometimes he's withdrawn and quiet, and sometimes he's saying, "Mom, what should I do about it?" or . . .

Father: I suspect, in this area, he talks to you more than he talks to me. Quite often, he will come in and sit down and say, "How come I'm such a shit-head?" This is the signal he wants to talk. And you stop what you're doing and pay attention. And sometimes it's very difficult because it becomes a dialogue consisting entirely of questions. [phone rings]

Therapist: They just want to double-check. Is that how he actually starts the conversation? He'll just walk into the room, flop down, and say, "Why am I such a shithead?"

Mother: Yes.

Therapist: That's where it starts?

Father: Well, not always, but quite often.

Therapist: You'll be reading the paper, and he'll come in and flop down and say this.

Father: Precisely, precisely.

At this point, the therapist begins to focus on the attempted solutions. What have Dolores and Juan Ramón been trying to do, in their best effort to change this painful situation, that has not worked or has not worked well enough? To start out, the clients describe different things that they have done. What people have usually tried are a variety of "commonsense" solutions, which have actually worked in the past but are no longer working. Clients often describe solutions that seem different because they involve different actions but are, in fact, of the same kind. It is the task of the therapist to find the common denominator or main thrust of the attempted solutions and then to check with the parents for accuracy.

Therapist: What do you do in response to that? Let's say he's just come in, he's flopped down and says, "Why am I such a shithead?" What do you say next?

Father: Just, the first thing to do is, just get him talking.

Therapist: How do you do that? What do you say? Make me a picture.

Father: Okay, well, the picture is generally, "Okay, fine," and I just go, "All right, tell me about it, why do you feel the way you do?" Sometimes it's productive, sometimes it's just a repetition of clichés: "I'm no good, why don't you kick me out, why can't I change?" In other words, that's what I'm talking about. It's a whole dialogue of questions.

The therapist now has an idea that what the father has been trying to do is draw Pablo out to talk about what is going on in his head in the hope that he will see the error of his ways and change. She now wants to know in more detail what Dolores has been trying.

Therapist: Let me tell you what I'm up to, Juan Ramón. It saves us time if we know what doesn't work.

Mother: What definitely doesn't work is to tell him he isn't a shithead and he's a very lovable young man, which I have tried, and of course, that's of no use at all.

Therapist: It rarely works. To reassure him . . .

Mother: Yeah, I try to reassure him and tell him that nobody feels he's that at all, except himself, and . . .

Therapist: What does he do in response, when you try to reassure him by saying, "You know, you're not really *that*."

Mother: He throws his hands up or turns away in disgust or something. He doesn't accept it.

The mother's attempted solutions are more in the direction of reassuring him. Both parents are very intimidated by Pablo's lack of initiative in looking for work.

Therapist: What does Pablo do with his time? If he's not working and he's not going to school, what does he actually do all day?

Mother: Well, he sleeps very late, as you can imagine. Two or three times a week, he will go out walking. He'll take the dog for an eight- or ten-mile walk.

Father: Yeah, that's one healthy dog. [laughter] The thing is not going to resolve itself. Past approaches have not been very fruitful, and under those circumstances, I always try to strike out in a new direction. That's the way I operate.

Therapist: Okay. And I'm making a mental assumption, so let me check it out loud . . . is that you're supporting him? Is that accurate, or is he paying his way at home?

Father: He's not.

Therapist: Does Pablo know that you've come to talk to someone?

Father: No. Dolores asked me not . . . the answer is, "No."

Mother: The first thing he said to me when I even suggested that we might like to do something like this, get some guidance, in order to help him, was, "If you do anything like that, I'll leave." That was his immediate reaction. "I'm out the door." Now, of course, we didn't call his bluff, but . . .

Therapist: This is for him to go to, right?

Mother: No, for us!

Therapist: Oh.

Mother: See, it's guilt. I think he feels terrible that we are driven to have to go out and get help to deal with him. I think he feels terribly guilty about this.

Therapist: So how are you keeping it from him, then, that you're here? . . . because he said that? Is that . . .

Mother: Well, yes. I was not about to burst out . . . isn't that silly? I mean, it's obviously going to come out anyway, eventually. And he's in Santa Cruz for a few days right now, so he isn't even home to say, "Where were you?" when I come in.

The therapist ended the first session telling the parents that they were to think about telling Pablo that they had come to therapy but that they were to do nothing different that week, until they all met again. This is a common homework assignment given after the first session, particularly when parents are indicating that change will be hard. While asked not to change anything yet, it gives them something different to focus on, which might result in a decrease in the attempted solutions with the son. This intervention contains a note of hope: The implicit message is given that things *will* change. It might take some time.

Session number two starts with the therapist inquiring whether anything different has occurred vis-à-vis the problem during the week that just passed. Both parents say no, and so the therapist continues with where they had left off the previous session. It will take some time to lay the groundwork so that these parents will be able to consider doing something other than reassuring and trying to draw out the son. This work on the part of the therapist is what is needed before she is able to "sell" an intervention. The father tells the therapist that he has thought about telling Pablo that they are coming to therapy:

Father: He knows what I'm doing in general, but he doesn't know what I'm doing in specifics. Because what I have told him is, and I've told him this way: "I am frustrated because I don't know how to help you, and if I have to get help to get the skills, I will get them." So this, to me, was an indication of priority, and we went back . . . I took him back to a couple of areas where he had some talents and aptitudes, and that was in drawing and writing. I think, when he was a youngster, he showed good aptitudes there. His attitude towards both of those interests was essentially the same, and he said, "Well, it's been too long," and he's now too far behind to catch up, as far as developing these talents or interests.

Therapist: To catch up to what? Do you know?

Mother: He must have some standard in his mind that he can't catch up to.

Father: It's too late. It's all gone. It's bad, it's gone, it's cast in concrete. Let's not talk about it—in other words, it's final.

It is clear from the parents' description that trying to draw him out to talk about what is going on or to reassure him is what, according to this model, is keeping the problem alive. These are the very attempted solutions that will have to change in order for the presented problem—Pablo not being able to look for work—to be resolved. In order to be sure that these are the attempted solutions that are not working, the therapist double-checks with them once more. This is also useful in that it gives the message that, if therapy is to help, the parents will have to do something different.

Therapist: Is this a usual response of his? When you're trying to say, "Look, you can do it. Here's . . . look at these other things that you were pretty good at," and then he kind of goes . . . [pushes hands outwardly]. It sounds like it doesn't really matter too much, but as long as you're saying, "Gee, why don't you try this," or "You can do that," or, you know, when you're reassuring him about his abilities and possibilities, is that . . .

Father: Yeah, we're tossing ideas or suggestions to see if he'll grab them, and it's rejected out of hand.

Therapist: Would it be safe to say that when you are, just in general, when you're offering him ideas, so the ideas are coming from *you*, either one of you, to him, that he tends to reject them?

Mother: I would think so.

Therapist: On the topic, if you're saying to him, "Look, gee, why don't you try this, or why don't you try that," or "You're good at this, you could go do that," and then it's like . . .

Father: Yeah, this is an area of frustration because he tends to reject them out of hand.

Therapist: Yeah, okay. So that, in terms of . . . what I'm looking at is what works and what doesn't work. So in terms of we're working together to come up with what's going to work for you: You don't need more skills in giving him ideas. He needs to come up with them himself.

Mother and father: Yeah. Okay.

In going over the tape, the team and the therapist decided to use the success story of when Pablo had been employed during the summer in the mountains. Because it is easier to build on success, the therapist proceeds to find out more of how that success happened and what, if anything, the parents had done differently to make it take place. This would again be a way of conveying implicitly that they already know what it is they have to do: They just have to do more of it.

Therapist: Well, so that it's not Mom and Dad doing it for him. You mentioned last week about the job at Tahoe and that he . . . how did that happen? How did he . . . I think your words were you cut a deal or something, but how did you succeed at getting him into a job up in the mountains?

Mother: Well, it all started out . . . my sister's mother-in-law has a cabin and she's well up into her 80s. She wanted to go up last time, only she didn't want to be there alone, and so she wanted a companion in the house. Someone who could help, take her shopping, things like that, and I guess my sister and I kind of looked at each other and said, "Well, maybe Pablo would be willing to do it. He's not doing anything else." And so he went back and forth. At first he said, "Yeah," and then he said, "No, no." He did go back and forth a number of times.

Therapist: So you suggested it to him, that he go up?

Mother: Yeah. And we tried to tell him pretty much what it would entail, and he finally agreed to go, so he packed up the car and took off. And I'm not sure how exactly he started working except that, as I say, I think the relatives sat around the dinner table and thought, "Well, this isn't going to be enough to keep Pablo busy." So that's when they talked him into working there.

Therapist: So you didn't have anything to do with him actually working up there. You just had to do with getting him there. When you spoke to him about what the job would entail, when he was going up there, what did you tell him?

Mother: Well, that he should be there at night, not gallivanting around, and that he would probably be taking her shopping or on any errands she wanted to do. That was pretty much it.

Therapist: And when he was going back and forth about, "Oh, yes I'll do it," or "No, I won't." When he was saying like, "No, I'm not going to do it," what did you say to him? What did you do or say?

Mother: Well, I really did leave it up to him. I said, "You'll have to be the one to decide," and then I said, "Why don't you write down the advantages and the disadvantages? It's a nice spot to be," and "You'll be on the lake, there's family up there." What he was afraid of was that he would be bored.

Therapist: Is that what he told you?

Mother: Yes.

Therapist: And what did you say, when he said, "I think I'll be bored"?

Mother: I said, "It's true you won't have any friends around, but there are lots of . . . well, I wasn't very reassuring probably. I said, "There's lots of solitary pleasures."

Therapist: *But you weren't very reassuring,* and he went.

The therapist does not make a huge deal about this but just underlines, by repeating it, that when the mother does something other than to reassure him, it has positive consequences. The therapist continues trying to find out more about what the parents' attempted solutions are, particularly around Pablo finding a job now. It is of greatest importance to devote as much time as needed to explore the attempted solutions because this direction has become the mine-field on which the therapist does not want to step. Anything that is suggested in therapy has to be different than that which has already been tried by the parents or anybody else in the client's immediate circle.

Therapist: I am curious, with regards to finding a job: Do you do anything, like take a newspaper and sort of put it under his door? I mean, that's too much, but do you do things like that, that try to get him interested in something, or get him to take a first step?

Father: Yeah, I have. I've actually clipped advertisements out of the paper and showed them to him.

Therapist: You clipped it and handed it to him?

Father: I said, "Here. This looks like a good one. We can even show you . . . we'll walk you through it. We'll tell you where to go, to fill out the application."

Therapist: What'd he say in response to that?

Father: He really didn't say. He said, "Well, all right." He'd peter out conversations. That's the problem. He just kind of strolls off.

Therapist: So, he just looks you in the eye and then walks away?

Father: Yeah.

At the end of session 2, the parents were told that the team would like to meet with Pablo as the next step. This is something that is routinely done because having met with the son gives the therapist more credibility when telling the parents what they need to do differently. Another routine procedure that takes place when the brief therapist is working with different family members is that the therapist will personally call the other person (in this case, Pablo). Sending a message to another person runs too high a risk of getting distorted. So the therapist talked with Pablo directly and asked him if he would be willing to come in at least once to help us figure out what his parents were complaining about. It is very unusual that a person will not agree to come in once to help the therapist out. What follows are abstracts of session number three with the son alone.

Therapist: One of the things your parents mentioned as they were talking about the issues is that they seem to have some concern about you.

Son: Yeah.

Therapist: Now, I don't know if they're making a mountain out of a molehill, so before I get into any other things, I wanted to ask you whether you think there's any need for them to be concerned about you.

Son: I'm not really motivated to do a lot. But it seems like just one of those things that eventually works itself out . . . in my case.

Therapist: You are saying there's no need to be worried.

Son: Yeah, it's hard to explain, actually. I guess, just that I do express a lot of concern about myself. I do have trouble, going out and looking for a job, right?

Therapist: What kind of trouble?

Son: Just, I don't know. It's as if part of me wants to, but then another part of me just won't do anything about it. It's really weird. So I usually never get around to even looking.

Therapist: Okay. Well, I can understand that. Looking for a job is a real drag.

Son: Yeah, I don't know. I'm kind of a perfectionist . . . and also lazy.

Therapist: A lazy perfectionist, huh?

Son: It's kind of a tug-of-war kind of thing.

Therapist: Push-pull kind of thing, yeah.

Son: Yeah, so if somebody comes up to me and offers me a job, I'll take it. But I won't go out and look.

Pablo is obviously not concerned with his situation. He is well groomed and engages pleasantly in conversation with the therapist. He is there to help the therapist figure out what it is that he needs to do to calm his parents down.

[Phone rings.]

Therapist: They're saying, haven't you ever heard that saying about "somebody needs something to worry about," and you're supplying them with that. So they don't have to worry about how well they like each other, or what they are going to do when they're retired and have to deal with each other 24 hours a day. I mean, if you're there, then they don't have to. So I'm thinking, you may be doing them quite a favor by not getting a job, not going to school, not moving to Santa Cruz. You may be really helping them out by saving them from looking at the next steps in their lives. That may be something that they would have to face if you started making moves towards getting a job. What are your concerns about them? Every kid has concerns about their parents, I guess.

Son: Just that I would wonder if they would be able to get along, just the two of them. They have things that they do together. They go to plays every once in a while and stuff like that, but they don't really talk a lot anymore. And it seems like it's really hard for the two of them to relate.

Therapist: The team back there wanted to say they're very much in agreement with the most important sacrifice you're making. That many kids just grow up and they move on, and they figure parents, that's a phase every parent has to go through, but for you to take on that sacrifice, a little bit of pride, a little bit of dealing with other people's judgments . . . but you're saving them. I know it sounds strange, but some people at an unconscious level really care enough that they're going to do that kind of a sacrifice to save their parents from facing what their relationship has come to, and what they might have to work on, after you've moved on.

The session ends with the therapist thanking Pablo for having come in and lets him know that if anything comes up that he wants to talk about, he should give her a call. The next session is with Dolores and Juan Ramón again. The therapist and the team met after the last session and have an intervention that they want to deliver for the parents to try. However, in order to deliver it successfully, the therapist spends most of this session selling them on the idea that they will have to do something different. This is the stage at which the influence of hypnosis (Milton Erickson) is most evident in this approach to solving problems. The therapist uses language with extreme care and closely watches the responses given by both parents before she continues. Nothing other than a "yes" response or a nod is acceptable in order to continue along the planned lines. The therapist opens the session by focusing on the success story they had worked on during the previous session.

Therapist: The success you had, I'm looking at her, because you were the one that got him to go to the mountains . . . I was just thinking, if you had had any more solid ideas about your success in getting Pablo up there, when instead of encouraging him and urging him and reassuring him, you had, in effect, kind of discouraged him, saying, "Yeah, it's going to be boring." Have you had any more solid thoughts around how that worked, paradoxically, and got him up there? Any more solid thoughts on that?

Mother: Well, not any more, really. Except apparently the reassuring and the encouraging doesn't work, I mean, that has hit.

Therapist: The only thing we really know, is that when you, if anything, were a little discouraging, which was the only thing that you were really doing differently, he started to move. Encouragement, and support, and then the urging, don't work.

Mother: Yes.

Therapist: In our meeting with Pablo, after we met with him, the team . . . we all sat down and went over the tapes and what you'd said you're here for and what you want and things you've tried and so on . . . and after consulting, you know, at great length on it, it seems to us that, if there's going to be any beneficial change in Pablo—and talking with him confirmed our suspicions before we met him—if there's going to be any beneficial change, you're going to need to be the ones to help him.

Father: We were hoping that we were the best bet.

Therapist: Yes. And, as a matter of fact, you're unavoidably in the only spot to help him. So, in your words, "It's not a bum approach." It's the right approach that you two are the ones to help him.

Father: Well, that's very reassuring. Can you equip us with the tools?

Therapist: We can do our best. They're going to be different tools from the ones that you came in here, hoping that we'd make you better at. And that's often the case. It's often the case with problems that we work so hard at a particular solution, that we figure if we just get better at it, that'll be it. So, for example, we could help you urge and encourage and support even better than you ever did before, and it will not work, even more than it ever did before.

Mother: So, we ditch that.

Therapist: Yeah, in exchange for another set of skills; because you are in a spot that, if there's going to be change, you're in a spot to really help him. It's also going to be different from the other skill that I think you came in to get, which was how better to draw out from him what the problem *really* is so that you can really help him even better.

Father: No, that's fine, that's fine. Keep going.

In the following segment, the therapist makes use of the very words that the parents used to describe their son when they first came in. This is a very useful way of using words to influence the course of therapy in a direction that the therapist believes can be helpful. Since it is important to get "yes" responses from the parents at this time, it would be very unlikely that they would say no to something they themselves said when they first came in and described the problem situation. Neither the therapist nor the team really believes that Pablo is experiencing low self-esteem. The term in itself is a label that is not used in this approach.

Therapist: But we want to give you a different set of skills, and as I think we talked about in session 2, they're going to be more subtle. I'll tell you why. In talking with him, first of all, all of us felt that he has very low self-esteem.

Father: You got it.

Therapist: And here's where we needed to do some reading between the lines . . . and underneath at a deeper level, what contributes greatly to the low self-esteem is he's got a fear that he's being a great bother to the two of you and that he really troubles the two of you.

Mother: Yes. He even said that to us.

Therapist: Okay.

Father: Which is true.

Therapist: Right.

Mother: Yeah, he does trouble us.

Therapist: And it's one of those vicious circles, in that he has low self-esteem, he's afraid that he's bothering the two of you and that it's troubling the two of you and it's causing you grief. And so, it's one of those odd things, that the more you try and help him, in a straightforward way . . .

Mother: Oh, the more bother he feels he's being.

Therapist: Exactly. And so that is what I mean by the vicious cycle. In helping him in that fashion, it lowers his self-esteem even more because it confirms his fear that he's really being a bother to you, and then he feels less about himself. And of course, he needs his self-esteem to rise a bit so that he can have enough self-esteem. It doesn't take, you know, gobs, but he needs enough self-esteem to be able to go out and . . . school, job . . . am I making sense?

Father: Um-hum, you're making sense.

Therapist: Okay. So what we want to do is get *you* out of that vicious cycle. Plus, at this point in time, I'm not sure if he could talk about what it is that is the problem. Since he . . .

Father: Is it possible he doesn't know what the problem is?

Since the father presents this as a possibility, the therapist hurries to agree with him, again, not because she believes this to be true or false but because, if the father thinks that this is the case, he will stop asking the son to talk about what is really the problem. In a way, it provides a block for the father to stop urging the son to talk about what is wrong, thus freeing them both to engage in a different kind of dialogue.

Therapist: It's likely. What I was thinking about is, in people's development, as they grow and mature, we get better able to introspect and understand ourselves.

Mother and father: Um-hum.

Therapist: Does that fit with . . .

Mother: I'm sure it does. I had not thought of it, but it makes sense.

Father: I think I agree with that. I think he feels very uncomfortable, and I think this is why he wants us to push him out and get rid of him.

Therapist: Again, it's another element of really trying to support him and urge him and encourage him. Let me make clear that those are important skills. One of the things I was thinking about is you . . . the two of you have been working very hard at that and working hard at getting even better at it. Two thoughts on it: One is, there's nothing wrong with those skills. They're important skills, up to a certain stage, and then there's a shift that needs to happen. And so, I think you've laid all the ground-work, using those skills with him. And I think that, well, he has low self-esteem, and we need to give you the skills to help him up that enough that he can go out and get a job. I think that at an unconscious level he knows that you care about him, in the work that you've been doing with him, and it's just time now to make a shift.

Father: Back off?

Therapist: Yeah. Back off in a different way from what you may be expecting, but to give him the space to fumble around in the privacy of his own be-ginnings, without the worry that, "God, Dad can do this so well, I may as well not try." You know that . . . and he's being troubled by bothering the two of you, so he can't figure out how come he can't get out. And his es-teem gets lower and lower, at which point things appear as if, to him, there's nothing he can do about them. I mean, it isn't true obviously, but it seems that way to him. And so the more we pay attention to it, the worse it seems to him, and the lower his self-esteem goes. It's just the vi-cious cycle, which is why you're unavoidably in this spot, and luckily in this spot to help him. We can start changing the cycle from your side.

Father: Okay, I don't know how I can conceal the concern because it's too easy to show.

Therapist: Yeah. And that's why we thought long and hard on it. And we went back and forth saying, "You know, we're going to be asking them to do some of the more difficult things that the parents have to do." And I'm not sure. We went back and forth with you, we finally decided that if you can do all you've been doing, there's a chance that— Imagine that the three of you live in a house on a lake, and you've got a rowboat down at your dock. And across that lake is work. And what you've been doing is, you've been sitting on the dock with him, putting your feet in the water, talking to him about how come he doesn't get in the rowboat and row across.

Mother: Um-hum.

Therapist: And, "Gee, you really ought to get in the rowboat and row across, and you know, it's all right." He'll say things like, "I'm scared," or "I can't," or "I don't know how," or "I don't know why I don't get in the rowboat." I think what you've been doing is, you got in the rowboat and showed him how to row, so you made sure he knew how to row a boat, and then you got in the rowboat and you went across the lake, checked out things, and brought him back some applications and told him how great it was over there, and it was just fine and, "No big deal, calm weather, you can do it, you can do it." And then he's sitting on the shore watching you row that boat so beautifully, straight line all the way across, okay? And he's getting more and more and more ashamed of himself for not getting in the rowboat and afraid to do it.

Father: What do I do next, drain the lake?

Therapist: Yeah. [laughter; looking to the mirror where the team is] Should they drain the lake? [to mother and father] No, see, and that's where the shift is, which is the more now that you pay attention to that rowboat and try to get him into that rowboat, the lower his self-esteem is about doing it and the farther it is across that lake to those things that he needs to do. He needs to get into thinking about it differently. Since he's operating on this idea, wherever he got it, that it's distressing to the two of you, that he's not moving, he's therefore not moving. To talk about *why* with him only adds to the distress because it conveys you're bothered; to encourage and urge and cheerlead, or support or listen for hours until your heart breaks, it just doesn't work at this stage. But also, we realize that for you to just keep quiet about it and not say anything more about it, that won't work either, because he'll remember what's been going on, and he'll then assume that your silence is just . . .

Mother: Resignation, yeah.

Therapist: Fear, and suffering, and that you've just gone underground with your suffering. I mean, that would be easy for someone with low self-esteem to do.

Father: Yeah.

Therapist: So it would be much better for you to say something, and this is where the shift of skills comes in, and it's going to be very different and real hard for you to do. When he gets into, for example . . . and I'm thinking about, for example, he comes in and sits down and says, "Why am I such a shithead?"

Mother: Yeah, and he's all ready to launch into . . .

Therapist: So, as the kids say in the vernacular, "Lighten up a little on it." And so you might say something to him that is different. And the point, which you would be up to, is not making him feel like this is great trouble to you—minimize that, and it would be something like, and you could pick your own, these are ours, we're not very good at it. But it would be something like . . . he comes in, flops down, and says, "Why am I such a shithead?" And you, Dolores, say, looking at Juan Ramón, "Well, I think it came from his side of the family." [laughter]

The session finishes with the therapist asking the parents to think about this and to look for potential problems if they were to say something like that to him. They come back the next session reporting that they have tried it and that it had gone very well: the three of them had had a good laugh. "Things seem to be lighter around the house," says the mother. The father still seems rather reluctant to implement the other part of the intervention, which is to encourage Pablo by discouraging him. So, when Pablo starts wondering why he cannot get a job, the parents are to tell him that he should take his time and that maybe he is not quite ready to do so. Dolores is delighted with the idea "because that is different than reassuring him, which has not worked," she says. Just as earlier during the treatment, they have different ways of looking at the situation, so the therapist leaves them with different homework: If they think it is time to accelerate change, the mother will be in charge of "encouraging by discouraging." But since the team is concerned with change occurring too fast, the father will put on the brakes by going back to the old attempted solutions of pushing his son to talk about why he cannot find a job and get on with life. They both agree that they will give this a try.

When they come back after three weeks, they have tried it out and the father has had no chance to put on the brakes because he has been too busy. He reports that it is unusual for him not to have time to explore this subject with his son, but he is pleased with the way Pablo looks: he has not seen "the mood" in a long time. The therapist underscores the fact that they must have been doing something different in their interaction with Pablo by asking: "Are you aware of what you have been doing differently so that your son began to act better?" It is the clients who get all the credit for doing something different.

At this point, both parents say that they would feel more comfortable not setting another appointment because they have to give this new direction a fair try and they would rather keep the remaining sessions "in the bank" in case they need anything in the future. The therapist and team agree and warn them about the disadvantages of changing too fast. She reminds them that they know what it is they have to do if progress starts getting out of hand. Treatment ends with the therapist reminding the parents that they will be getting calls from a member of the team to conduct follow-ups.

If these parents had failed to carry out their assignment (the checking of which is always the first point on the next session's agenda), the therapist would have taken the blame ("We have failed to consider the difficulties in carrying it out" or "It is clearly premature for us to be asking you to change this problem").

At the time of the three-month follow-up, Pablo had a part-time job, and at the time of the one-year follow-up, he had full-time employment and had a girlfriend. He was still living at home, and this was not a concern for either parent.

Conclusions

The Palo Alto Brief Therapy Group, located at the Mental Research Institute, has developed an approach that is more than therapy—it is a problem-resolution approach being applied in very different settings, such as schools, large organizations, businesses and the political arena. The work of family therapy is made brief by concentrating on *one problem*, which is presented by the client. The assumption is that problems are to be found in the interactions that occur among individuals. To have a different outcome, change must occur in that interaction. Changes in thought and/or action produce this change in interaction. Since it is held that the client's nonworking attempts at solving the problem have actually been maintaining it, the crux of the therapy rests on successfully influencing the "customer" to depart from his or her attempted solution and do something different. The therapy benefits from the therapist's speaking the client's language and from generally letting the client take the lead, thereby being very respectful of the client as a person. Historical incursions are avoided since historical data does not contribute to making the changes in the interaction needed in the here and now. The model is nonpathologizing and nonnormative. Through our case presentation and our running commentary, we have attempted to illustrate how what we have stated theoretically translates into practice.

Study Questions

1. Can you think of a way in which this case could have been handled differently, say, if the parents had not been available?
2. Given the attempted solutions these parents had tried, the team and therapist came up with one possible intervention. What other interventions can you think of that would have been equally effective in getting these parents to depart from what was keeping the problem alive?
3. We have pointed out differences with other family therapy approaches. Can you think of how different models of family therapy would have dealt with the same family in different ways (for example, structural, strategic, narrative, or solution focused)?

References

Bateson, G., Jackson, D. D., Haley, J., & Weakland, J. (1956). Toward a theory of schizophrenia. *Behavioral Science, 1*(4): 251–264.

Goldenberg, I., & Goldenberg, H. (1996). *Family therapy: An overview* (4th ed.). Pacific Grove, CA: Brooks/Cole.

Popper, K. R. (1984). *Auf der Suche nach einer besseren Welt. Vorträge und Aufsätze aus dreissig Jahren.* Munich: Piper.

Chapter Seven

The Humanistic Approach of Virginia Satir

Edith C. Lawrence

Virginia Satir is often referred to as "the Columbus of family therapy" because of her keen interest in exploring new ways to promote, support, and celebrate human potential. A more apt way to capture her lasting contributions, however, may be to understand that she was, first and foremost, our Mother Teresa. As one of the early visionaries of family therapy, Satir brought great compassion and clarity of purpose to her conviction that people are inherently capable of healthful growth and connection with one another.

Conceptualized as offering a humanistic approach, Satir was a believer in "the healing power of love" but not as a simplistic, Pollyannaish process (Satir and Baldwin, 1983). Rather, the "love" she practiced in therapy and postulated as a necessary condition for actualizing an individual's capabilities was based on her assumptions about people, problem formation, and what facilitates change. Collectively, these beliefs served as her theory of therapy and provided her, and those influenced by her, with a map for helping people achieve their potential. This chapter highlights the relevant components of Satir's theory that have informed my own work (Waters and Lawrence, 1993a, 1993b), followed by segments of a therapy consultation that illustrates these elements.

Theoretical Underpinnings
Assumptions about Human Nature

Virginia Satir had great faith in humankind, individually and collectively. She was always interested in helping people expand their ability to manage their lives from a sense of strength and self-valuing. This faith in people stemmed from her conviction that a health rather than a pathology orientation better captured people's potential:

> In a pathology-oriented approach, one starts with emphasis on pathology or symptom, the hub, making it the center of one's attention. Thus, one selects out in an individual only that which is destructive and symptom-related. In a health-oriented approach, I see the hub as the potential health of the individual— present but untapped, covered over, and therefore out of reach to that person. In this framework the symptom is an attempt to express that health even though the individual, by beliefs and rules, blocks the manifestation of that health. (Satir, 1986, p. 283)

Satir assumed that people want to be whole, to grow in authenticity, sensitivity, and the ability to be genuine with one another (Satir and Baldwin, 1983). Thus, she looked for and found in people signs of their healthy intentions, even when these were deeply embedded in unhealthy behavior. This process of searching for positive intentions does not mean minimizing problems or avoiding them entirely; rather, it means taking symptoms seriously, but as "adaptive attempts gone awry," not as complete and fixed descriptors of a person (Waters and Lawrence, 1993a).

By establishing a safe context within which people could look at and accept all their feelings more fully, Satir was able to help them recognize and make better use of their inherent capabilities. She was interested in helping people discover and lead with their richer, more self-congruent parts rather than with their conflict-driven, reactive parts. For example, with an adolescent caught in a pattern of blaming his parents for untold injustices, Satir would try to help him rechannel the embedded useful energy in these protests toward a more genuine and self-responsible declaration of wanting to be valued by them.

There are two obvious clinical advantages to adopting a view of people as inherently healthy and growth oriented. First, the assumption of a healthy core invites the therapist to move closer to people, even when they lead with their dysfunction. The therapeutic context becomes a process of unearthing the underlying health rather than cautiously waiting for the "real" pathology to emerge. The closer the therapist gets, the clearer the client's health and growth potential becomes. Second, the assumption of and focus in therapy on positive intentions, in and of itself, creates space for people to begin to see for themselves the possibility of healthier alternative outcomes (O'Hanlon and Weiner-Davis, 1989; Satir, 1988; Waters and Lawrence, 1993a). When an adolescent feels his tantruming is also being recognized as an attempt to be taken more seriously, not just as a sign of continued immaturity, it opens up possibilities for him to feel free to choose different

ways he might convey his seriousness. This view of people makes unhealthy behavior seem less fixed and static; growth and change seem possible.

Assumptions About Problem Formation

Virginia Satir assumed that family dysfunction stems from blockages in personal growth, which, in turn, are the result of individual members' low self-
esteem (Satir and Baldwin, 1983). Children develop low self-esteem when they
deny, project, or distort what they feel because expressing these feelings means
risking the loss of parental love and approval. Children comply with rules such
as "big boys don't cry" or "girls should be quiet" even when they are feeling
something different. While this process of denying unacceptable feelings safe-
guards children's connection to their parents, it also disconnects them from
themselves by forcing them to devalue the legitimacy of their feelings. According to Satir (1967), denying the validity of our emotional experience leads to low
self-esteem; and, in a cyclical process, low self-esteem leads to more hiding,
which leads to lower self-esteem.

Satir maintained that the way the family communicates with one another
mirrors each members' feelings of self-worth. Additionally, she postulated that
how an individual communicates "is the largest single factor determining what
kinds of relationships she or he makes with others, and what happens to each
in the world" (Satir, 1988, p. 51). Thus, assessing a family's communication patterns and intervening at this level was a major focus of her work. Satir identified four universal patterns that she believed people use to hide their unwanted
feelings: placating, blaming, computing, and distracting (Satir, 1988).

When using a *placating* pattern of communicating, a person presents solely
as self-effacing, weak, and in need of someone else's approval. Other feelings
of independence and assertiveness are unacceptable and too risky. When stuck
in the *blaming* pose, a person acts all knowing, powerful, and accusatory, attempting to mask feelings of emptiness, unworthiness, and unlovableness. In a
computing stance, the person acts intellectual, removed, and rigid and is afraid
to feel vulnerable, especially in relation to desires for connection and intimacy.
Finally, in the *distracting* position, a person responds irrelevantly to whatever is
said, presenting as if becoming emotionally involved is an impossibility. This
pose masks the unacceptable feeling of having no place in the family if the individual were to seriously share feelings with other family members.

According to Satir, a person using one of these poses not only communicates incongruently but also has difficulty listening nondefensively to what others are feeling (Satir, 1988). When unable to tolerate our own internal feelings
of shame, for example, it is difficult to hear others talk about their experiences
of shame and nearly impossible to tolerate a suggestion that we might be feeling shame, too. Satir discovered that people use more than one pose, although
she concluded that most tend to have a favorite.

Significantly, Satir saw as a goal of therapy not to label and attack these dysfunctional communication patterns but to help people understand that they are
using poses *and* to make it safe for them to accept and share the real feelings

hiding behind the pose (Satir, 1988). She saw problems as indications that people were "starving for something" because they were not fully authentic; she sought ways to help them nourish themselves by being more accepting of their unacceptable feelings (Satir and Baldwin, 1983). So, for example, she looked for ways to make it safe for a woman in a placating pose to also acknowledge her desire to act independently or for a man assuming a blaming pose to make friends with his feelings of unworthiness. When people are able to communicate more congruently about what they are feeling, both their sense of self-worth and their sense of self-determination grow. Satir was always interested in helping people make conscious, informed choices based on healthy intentions, not unconscious conflicts.

Assumptions About the Therapist's Role

Throughout her life, Virginia Satir taught that therapy should be oriented toward "reshaping and transforming into useful purposes the energy bottled up in a person's or a family's demonstrated pathology" (Satir, 1986, p. 282). In order to do this, a therapist must be active, intimate, and sensory focused (Satir, 1967, 1988; Satir and Baldwin, 1983). She viewed the therapist's role as that of teacher, coach, supporter, and, when needed, gentle challenger; she utilized many techniques to facilitate this process. In conjunction with two colleagues (Bandler, Grinder, and Satir, 1976), Satir identified the following as critical elements in her therapeutic approach: "challenging the built-in expectations in the family's existing communication patterns, helping the family members work together to understand what they want in terms of change; preparing the family for a new growth experience; helping the members learn a new family process for coping; and providing the tools they will need to continue the change process after therapy" (Goldenberg and Goldenberg, 1996).

Andreas (1989, 1991) translated these general descriptions of Satir's therapeutic focus into specifics. He identified seven essential elements in her work:

1. a solution-oriented focus on the present and future rather than a problem-oriented focus on the past
2. an assumption of positive intentions; adopting a nonblaming attitude
3. a focus on developing positive ways of interacting among family members rather than punishing dysfunctional behavior
4. an assumption of equality with clients, not domination; therapist suggests directions but tentatively, not insistently
5. an emphasis on verbal patterns as the key to understanding and the venue for changing family dysfunction
6. a premium on action in therapy; helping family members actually try out new ways of communication
7. the use of touch in therapy as a way of communicating; "I know that one touch with energy passing back and forth—a real feeling of one human being really touching another in a literal sense—is probably worth hours and hours of something that doesn't contain that" (Satir quoted in Andreas, 1989, p. 80)

While several of these elements can be found in the clinical illustration that follows, it is important to note that the session with this family was most influenced by two aspects of Satir's legacy: (1) the balance she struck between a non-blaming attitude while simultaneously challenging and inviting people to lead with their healthier parts and (2) the value she placed on connections.

In the early days of family therapy, challenging and confronting often came out of a context of power; therapists were to be more powerful than clients, parents more powerful than children. The emphasis was on hierarchy, control, and authority (Goldenberg and Goldenberg, 1996; Nichols and Schwartz, 1995). While Satir clearly saw the value of hierarchy and discipline in families, she helped families establish these by emphasizing nurturance, compassion, and a nonblaming attitude in her work with them as well as in their interactions with each other. She accepted each person's "dark side" and was interested in understanding and unraveling the context in which those patterns had been learned. She knew facing unwanted feelings could be a scary process and viewed resistance as "mainly the fear of going somewhere you have not been" (Satir quoted in Simon, 1989, p. 39). Viewing resistance in this way enables the therapist to lend acceptance, courage, and hope to clients who have doubts about their worth and worthiness (Waters and Lawrence, 1993a).

Connection was viewed by Satir as a critical component of human growth—genuine connection with oneself, first, and then with others. She believed that "every individual is geared to survival, growth and getting close to others and that all behavior expresses these aims, no matter how distorted it may look" (Satir, 1967, p. 96). Problems occur when people disconnect from their feelings because they believe these feelings are unacceptable.

Part of valuing ourselves is accepting that we are all different, have different feelings, and are each unique. She sought to help families deal with this conflict and differentness between family members by employing exploration, negotiation, and connection rather than by using power and disconnection (Satir, 1988). From this nurturing and sensitive base, Satir helped people accept and understand all parts of themselves, not just the "nice" parts. When individual family members learn to accept the denied, "different" parts of themselves, the family as a whole is better able to tolerate and be respectful of one another's differences; tolerance begets tolerance. Just as importantly, reclaiming and accepting the parts of themselves that have been denied and then sharing those parts with one another opens the way for a new level of connection.

The Case: Rebuilding Connections in a Family Coping with Incest

The case that follows illustrates several components of Satir's humanistic approach to clinical work. It is an emergency consultation by a seasoned psychologist who was asked to the therapy session by a doctoral student who felt overwhelmed by the family's escalating crisis. Several things that the consultant does exemplify Satir's influence: (1) taking a health-oriented approach with the family, (2) focusing on helping each member communicate more congruently, and (3) adopting a nonblaming attitude while simultaneously challenging the family members to lead with their healthier parts. The goal of the consultation is to help mother and daughter begin to move from a dysfunctional connection with one another following disclosure of incest to a functional, growth-promoting connection.

Amy, age 15, had been sexually abused by her paternal grandfather, Melvin, for ten years. She told her mother, Belle, a year ago, but Belle did not believe her because Amy had a habit of lying, even about important things, and Melvin was a "good man"; he had provided critical emotional and financial support to Belle when she was leaving her abusive marriage. About a month ago, Amy told her teacher at school about the abuse, and Belle again questioned the veracity of Amy's story until Amy's two younger siblings meekishly confessed that they, too, had recently been sexually abused by this man; turmoil followed. Melvin denied the allegations and his wife sided with him. Social services intervened: They filed charges against Melvin, mandated no contact between Melvin and any of Belle's children, and ordered Belle to take Amy to individual therapy.

Several other stressful transitions were occurring in Belle's and Amy's lives at the same time. Divorced for several years from Amy's father, Belle began dating Dwayne about ten months ago. Soon after, she became pregnant and, two months ago, Dwayne and Belle married; the baby is due in the next few weeks. Additionally, Amy has been "discovered" by boys at school, and Belle worries that these boys do not respect Amy.

What follows are segments from Amy's fourth therapy session. Amy begins the session very upset about how "rocky" her relationship is with her mother.

Therapist: How are you doing?
Amy: [shakes hand in a way that means "so-so"]
Therapist: [repeats the gesture] Okay? What's going on?
Amy: [clears throat and looks down at her feet] I'm just [shakes head].
I don't know. Me and my mom are kind of on a rocky area again
[pauses], and . . . I told her I was going to live with my dad and she said,
"I'd like to see how far you'd get when you live with him." Because
my mom and dad had problems with my dad being selfish; but it's not
that way anymore. And I asked my dad twice if I could move in with
him and he said that's fine and [clears throat] he's giving it until the 26th
for it to become better and if it doesn't, I'll tell him and he's gonna talk
to my mom.

Of note, living with her father is an unrealistic option for Amy. He has been inconsistently involved in her life up until now and, while he tells Amy living with him is a possibility, he tells Social Services that it is not.

Therapist: Uh huh. How do you feel about that?
Amy: I'm surviving.

Therapist: Yeah? What's been rocky between you and your mom?

Amy: They would . . . my stepdad and mom would falsely accuse me of something, and I would always get in trouble for it. And they wouldn't believe me. I guess because of my history of lying.

Therapist: Like what kinds of things have happened recently that they've accused you of?

Amy: This is stupid. Okay, my stepdad has Brut shaving cream. Honestly, think about it. Would I take [smiles and giggles and points to herself] Brut shaving cream? I don't think so. And my brother sat there and said he didn't take it; and my little sister sat there and said she didn't take it; and come to find out, my brother took it and didn't return it and didn't come forward with it; and me and my little sister had to suffer the consequences because of my brother. And they, the thing that ticks me off about them is, they never apologize when they're wrong. They always have to be right. They can't be wrong about anything.

Amy talks further about the consequences for her when her brother gets in trouble: Mom and Dwayne get in bad moods and start lecturing them about all the past, present, and future problems each of the children have caused or will cause them. The whole house becomes a tense battlefield with Mom and Dwayne on one side and the children on the other. Since Amy has the reputation in the family for "messing up" the most, she feels they come looking for her mistakes first. Amy goes on to talk about all the pressures she feels right now. In addition to the tension between her and her mother, she is deciding with whom she wants to live, her mother is about to have a baby, and the abuse trial is in two months.

Therapist: That's a lot to think about, isn't it?

Amy: [nods yes]

Therapist: Do you think about all those things?

Amy: [nods yes]

Therapist: Yeah?

Therpist: What's on your mind most right now?

Amy: My mom.

Therapist: Your mom. Your relationship with your mom?

Amy: [nods yes]

Therapist: I noticed before we came down here, you—when you were leaving the waiting room, you put your hand onto your mom's shoulder.

Amy: I teased her, I blipped at her cheek. [flicks finger playfully at her cheek]

Therapist: Yeah? It looked, it looked pretty playful. Do you guys, uh, play around a lot like that?

Amy: [long pause] Can I ask you a question?

Therapist: Uh huh.

Amy: Is it possible if I can talk to my mom?

Therapist: Now?

Amy: [nods yes]

Therapist: Sure. You want to talk to her now?

Amy: [nods yes]
Therapist: [gets up; looks at Amy] Do you want me to wait here? Or do you want me to have her come in here?
Amy: You can come in here. It doesn't matter.
Therapist: Do you—you want me to have her come back down here?
Amy: [nods yes]
Therapist: Do you want to talk before she comes down? Do you want to tell me what you want to tell her?
Amy: Um, I just want to tell her my feelings.
Therapist: [pauses] OK. Do you want to talk about it with me first or just [pause] have her come right down?
Amy: Have her come down.
Therapist: Okay. [pauses, then opens door and walks out]

While it probably would have been more beneficial for Amy if the therapist had spent additional time finding out about her concerns with her mother and what Amy hoped to accomplish in a meeting with Belle before bringing them together, he didn't. This was early in the therapist's training and he felt compelled, both by the urgency of Amy's request and by the depth and genuineness of Amy's sadness about her deteriorating relationship with her mother, to act quickly. Although Amy's feelings are important to validate, it would have been better therapeutically for Amy to experience how to sit with her sadness in a way that would allow her to make a thoughtful, well-reasoned plan for herself rather than responding reactively. Over the years, she has developed a crisis mentality and, thus, needs guidance in developing alternative ways of managing her stress and anxiety.

Belle agrees to come into the session but appears very guarded as she sits beside Amy on the couch. The issue Amy begins with is how she felt unsupported that Belle did not go with her to the preliminary court hearing in which Melvin was charged with sexual abuse.

Belle: [sitting down] OK.
Amy: [speaks in a high, childlike voice and shrinks back a bit] OK, what?
Belle: You want to speak to me.
Amy: [still in a childlike voice] Yeah, I do.
Belle: [crosses arms and looks guarded] About?
Amy: About our relationship.
Belle: Yeah?
Amy: It's not going too well.
Belle: [tensely] Well, it's not worse than it has been. It's gonna take some time, Amy.
Amy: [voice gets small] I know, Mom, but I don't feel like I'm getting any support from you.
Belle: Like how?
Amy: Just, [pause] you weren't here for [pause] the hearing.
Belle: [slightly interrupting in a sharp voice] I know that and we discussed that, and it was agreed by you that it was okay. Neither of us had any clue what that hearing really was about. [pauses as she continues to look

at Amy, whose head is down as if being punished] We discussed that at
length before we ever left. [pause] Isn't that right? And what did you say?

Amy: I don't remember.

Belle: Tsk.

Amy: I don't.

Belle: You said that it was perfectly all right for H and T [a couple from
church] to . . .

Amy: I know, but that's . . .

Belle: [starts to finish her sentence but stops]

Amy: . . . because you all planned to go on vacation.

Belle: [sharply] Amy, we were perfectly willing to stay if we needed to.

Amy: But y'all needed to get away.

Belle: Well, that's true, too. [pause] But we still discussed it with you, and
you said, "no," that it was fine for them to take you. [long pause]

Amy: Just— [pause] I feel neglected by you.

Belle: How?

Amy: [voice gets smaller and words become hard to understand, mumbles]
You don't show you love me.

Belle: [sounds impatient] Like how am I supposed to?

Amy: [shoulders hunched, head down, starts to cry] When I do good in
school, you don't tell me I do a good job.

Belle: [slightly raises voice] Amy, that is not true.

Amy: Yes, it is.

Belle: It is not.

Amy: When I come home and tell you I have 95s [pause] on papers, I don't
hear "Good job."

Belle: That is not true. I have commented on every single good paper that
you have brought. [Amy shakes her head no and looks at Belle.]

This argument continues for several minutes; neither listens to the other nor
concedes any ground. It begins to become clearer how hard it is for Amy to
communicate congruently with her feelings when she is with Belle. She is anxious about her ability to successfully connect with Belle but masks this by assuming a blaming pose even from the beginning; "OK, what?" is her opening
remark to Belle, yet she invited Belle to come into the session. She blames Belle
for not being at the hearing but had agreed earlier that Belle should go on vacation instead. It is a clear example of the cyclical process that Satir identified
as the basis of problem formation in a family: Amy has low self-esteem, so she
communicates incongruently with what she is feeling; the communication is
not successful, which adds to her low self-esteem. Both people feel unheard and
angry.

This next segment shows more clearly Belle's role in their communication
impasse. Unable to hear any criticism from Amy, she assumes a blaming pose
as well.

Amy: [small voice] And another thing is [pause] when I'm trying to tell the
truth and [pause] Dwayne doesn't believe me, you go along with what he
says. [starts to cry]

Belle: [sternly] Well, Amy, unfortunately, when you—when you're in a habit of not telling the truth, we have a very difficult time trying to decide when you're telling the truth and when you're not.

Amy: [cries] But that isn't my fault.

Belle: I'm not saying it is.

Amy: Can't you understand that?

Belle: I'm not saying it is. But that's not our fault either that we don't know when you're telling the truth and when you're, when you aren't. And all we have is evidence to look at.

Amy: Do you honestly think—why would I use a man's Brut shaving cream?

Belle: Well, okay, that happened.

Amy: And the thing that bothers me is when you guys are wrong you don't admit it, and you don't come back and you guys don't ever apologize—

Belle: [interrupts] We did admit it for the Brut cologne.

Amy: [shakes head no]

Belle: Yes, we did. Yes, we did, both of us did, and Dwayne even said he was sorry. And that wasn't me. And besides that, this is what I'm telling you, Amy; when you tell lies, Amy, you do automatically get [pause] accused of things.

Amy spends the next ten minutes trying to convince Belle that she is not at fault for misbehaving during the past month. She blames her brother for angering her mom and thereby getting her in trouble; Belle for marrying too quickly and adding to both their stress levels; and both Belle and Dwayne for not letting her do anything "reasonable" (like hanging with boys at the mall), thus "forcing" her to have to act unreasonable as well. Belle is unmoved. She counters each incident with examples of Amy's deceit and manipulation: Amy is not to be trusted as evidenced by her long history of lying. They remain at loggerheads, each decreasingly capable of speaking civilly to the other. The therapist excuses himself at this point and seeks an emergency consultation before a huge meltdown occurs.

In the consultation, the therapist shares his frustration about Belle. While he can see that Amy tends to blame others for her problems, he views this as a likely consequence of her having lived with abuse for so long. What he cannot understand is how Belle can be so cold and unempathetic to Amy, given all Amy has been through. In fact, that is also the perception all the professionals involved in this case hold of Belle; she did not believe Amy initially and, worse, is still ambivalent about believing Amy despite the overwhelming evidence. When professionals interact with Belle, they report that she is compliant but in an aloof, defensive, and cool way. Her continued focus on Amy's misbehaviors rather than Amy's pain is interpreted as further evidence that Belle does not really care about Amy. Not knowing how to resolve this, the professionals have ignored Belle for the most part and have focused their energy on providing Amy with the support she deserves. The therapist knows that neither ignoring Belle nor accusing her of indifference would be useful, but those are the only alternatives he can think of.

This treatment impasse is not an uncommon dilemma for those working with families in which intrafamilial sexual abuse has occurred. Such families typically need attention on many fronts. Decisions must be made as to court intervention, who should receive treatment (child, offender, nonoffending family members), in what format (individual, dyadic, family, group), and in what order (Silovsky and Hembree-Kigin, 1994; Trepper and Barrett, 1989). Most models suggest individual and group treatment first, followed by family treatment only when (1) the offender is willing to apologize for the abuse and (2) the mother accepts responsibility for not believing and protecting the child, if this occurred. (See Silovsky and Hembree-Kigin, 1994, for a further delineation of a model for making these treatment decisions.) With few exceptions (for example, Laing and Kamsler, 1990; Sheinberg, True, and Fraenkel, 1994), the proclivity toward individual and group intervention may delay the mother-daughter component of treatment for some time, especially if the mother remains ambivalent about the veracity of the abuse. In this case, Belle was not only equivocal in her support of Amy around the abuse but was also unwilling to be in therapy herself. Add to that Belle's absorption in her new marriage and the baby soon to arrive, and it becomes clear why the treatment team was working around her.

The perception of mother-as-villain in intrafamilial abuse cases is also not unusual (Elbow and Mayfield, 1991; Strand, 1990). The mother has been viewed as "responsible" in a number of ways. Research has shown that an important component of long-term recovery for incest abuse victims is whether they are heard and believed by their mother upon disclosure (Finklehor and Browne, 1985). More significantly, that abuse occurred at all has been conceptualized as a result of the mother's collusion with the offender, her passive-dependent personality, and/or her "psychological absence" as both a mother and a wife (see Laing and Kamsler, 1990, for further elaboration). While this perception of the mother has been challenged, primarily by those adopting a feministic lens (Laing and Kamsler, 1990; Salt, Meyer, Coleman, and Sauzier, 1990), old habits die hard.

When adopting this kind of pathology-oriented focus, it is easy to overlook the protective and healthy things Belle does for Amy. Although the initiation was not hers, she does cut off contact with Melvin (despite the pain this causes her), brings Amy to therapy sessions (despite questioning its usefulness), and comes into Amy's session when asked (despite knowing she will be blamed for something). Satir's template for looking at the healthy potential now embedded in unhealthy behavior holds out far more possibility for discovering Belle's potential growth with Amy. Could Belle's resistance to connection with Amy be more usefully conceptualized as her fear of entering a scary place? What unacceptable feelings may be blocking Belle's growth and potential as Amy's mother? Could her aloof and defensive stance take on new meanings for her and for those working around her? Placating to the numerous requests made by experts and her new husband perhaps masks Belle's fear of acting independently. Having been exposed as a mother lacking in good judgment—she trusted an abuser with her children—Belle has relinquished her nurturing and protecting role to others. Perhaps her blaming pose, especially with Amy around issues of trust and responsibility, is an attempt to hide from herself the depth and painfulness of her own guilt and shame for feeling untrustworthy and irresponsible with Amy; perhaps it is she who cannot accept that she did not protect Amy.

Based on this frame, the consultant encourages the therapist to make it safe for Belle to express her full range of feelings about what happened to Amy: her sadness, guilt, and anger; her fears of having failed as a mother. By helping Belle tolerate these unacceptable feelings, perhaps Belle could begin to connect more genuinely with her daughter. The consultant also agrees to join the therapist in the session if he feels overwhelmed; he says he already does, so she promises to join him soon.

When the therapist reenters, Belle and Amy continue to talk about their disconnection until he finds an opportunity to ask Belle, noncritically, about her frustrations with Amy.

Belle: Well, I do get frustrated when—when Amy— [sighs] she makes excuses for [pause] whatever happens. And I get very frustrated and I feel like, you know unless I, I can't read her mind, and there are things that she feels like I'm responsible for that I don't know how I could have known about, and, it does, it frustrates me, and I don't know how to deal with it. I don't know how I can, you know like, when she told me a year ago. I had no way of knowing and even when she—when she told me in August, I didn't believe her. I—because this person has been a part of our lives for 20-some years, and never has there been a question. My, all my children have been with him on weekends. They've, they've done things; he's done things for us. I have no, I have no reason whatsoever to believe otherwise. And yet she feels like I'm responsible because I didn't—I didn't believe her. And yet she's told so many lies and done so many things that I don't know how I should . . . I don't know how—you can't—it's hard to distinguish when she's telling a lie and when she's not.

Amy: Mom, my whole life was a lie.

Belle: [defensively again] Well, then how am I supposed to have known?

Amy: I mean, he told me I'd regret it if I told. I mean honestly, Mom, when somebody threatens you, you think you're gonna tell?

Belle: I didn't say they did, but that still doesn't change the fact that I have no way of knowing that.

Amy: I was five. I didn't know what he was doing. I didn't know if it was right.

One of the clues Satir advocates using to assess how authentically and fully people are communicating their feelings with one another is their tone of voice and body language (Satir and Baldwin, 1983). Belle's tone is cold and defensive, her posture blaming and distant. The consultant joins the session with the goal of trying to make it safe for Belle to acknowledge and share the defended-against, unacceptable feelings that are adding to her low self-esteem. This involves blocking the repetitive, incongruent sequence and supporting Belle's moving closer to feeling her unacceptable feelings. After introducing herself and shaking hands with Belle and Amy, the consultant pulls up a chair near Belle's side of the couch.

Consultant: I understand this is the first time for a family session, so I thought I might join because I know that you guys [looking at Amy and the therapist] have been working together. And I thought that I might, uh, [looks at Belle, faces her, leans forward, and speaks gently] just as mother to mother, talk to you for a minute.

Belle: Sure.

Consultant: [almost whispering] Do you believe her now?

Belle: Yes. [nods]

Consultant: You think it happened?

Belle: Uh huh.

Consultant: Okay, 'cause you know [pause] your voice is still the old voice.

Belle: [pause] I mean, I don't have a choice to believe her. I—there are too many things that—that have been consistent that, there isn't a choice. But, there, still in the back of my mind . . .

Consultant: [nods in agreement] Okay, have you cried with her about it yet?

Belle: [shakes head] No. Because she hasn't been able to share it with me, for one thing.

Consultant: How about inside you?

Belle: [begins to get teary] I've cried. I've cried many a night with my husband.

Consultant: About it?

Belle: Yeah.

Consultant: Yeah. [pause] Because it just is, awful, to think that, this would happen to your daughter.

Belle: Yeah, to all my children.

Consultant: By somebody that you trust and, and that is . . . just awful. Have you [pause] let her see your tears? [Amy shakes her head to indicate no.]

Belle: Well, [looks at Amy] I think I've, I think I've cried a couple of times when H and T [couple from church] were there and [pause] I don't know. I don't remember, to tell you the truth.

By beginning with a self-disclosure ("mother to mother"), the consultant is able to effect joining quickly. Satir believed that self-disclosure is appropriate if used as a way to facilitate a genuine connection with people. The consultant's soft tone conveys respect and a "we're in this together" stance. Next, she helps Belle share what she feels when she allows herself to believe Amy was abused: her pain as evidenced by her tears.

In the next segment, the consultant continues to invite Belle to feel more fully her pain about Amy's having been sexually abused by someone Belle trusted. Somewhat prematurely, the consultant also invites Belle to enact a protective connection with Amy. It is not yet safe enough between them to do this, so the consultant returns to helping Belle feel more clearly and congruently her pain about and connection to Amy. Notice how the consultant turns a potential distractor (the baby moving in Belle's stomach) into a way for Belle to connect more fully with her maternal feelings. Satir often attended to clients' physical states as well as their emotional states in her efforts to connect fully and genuinely.

Consultant: Is this your oldest?

Belle: No.

Consultant: This is where?

Belle: Second.

Consultant: Second, okay. [pause] And to think of something like that happening to her must hurt terribly.

Belle: Yeah.

Consultant: And to think that [pause] it happened [pause] with somebody that you trusted [pause] must hurt terribly. [pause] My guess is that there's a part of you that wants to defend against that hurt, and there's another part of you that [pause] when you feel it, you feel overwhelmed by it.

Belle: [begins to get teary again] Yeah, and plus there's another part of me that, that—it's very hard to—to hold, uh, the hatred that I'm sure she feels [pause] against him because of all the things that he's done for our family.

Consultant: [nods in agreement] Okay.

Belle: And not—not just for my family. I've seen very good things that he's done for other people. He's a very good-hearted person. He's not an all-bad person.

Consultant: [nods head in agreement with her, pauses, and then whispers] But he did a bad thing to her.

Belle: Yes. [nods head and begins to tear up again] I know that. [wipes her eye] And it's, you know, that bothers me a lot.

Consultant: How much?

Belle: A lot.

Consultant: [gestures with hands first close together then spread apart] How much?

Belle: I don't know. [laughs and looks at Amy] But, I mean, it does.

Consultant: [softly] It makes you cry sometimes?

Belle: Yes, and it makes me feel guilty because she's my daughter.

Consultant: Yes. [nodding] Does it make you want to scoop her up and [pause] protect her?

Belle: Sometimes. [wipes eye]

Consultant: And make sure that nothing like that ever happens to her again?

Belle: Yeah [tears up more], and that's one of the reasons why I'm very fearful of letting my children do things that ordinarily I wouldn't have thought twice about before.

Consultant: [nods in agreement] Have you scooped her up and told her that?

Belle: No. [looks at Amy] Probably not. [Amy shakes head slightly.]

Consultant: [whispers] Try that first. [pause; both look very hesitant]

Consultant: [gently] Do you want to try that now?

Belle: I asked her before and she didn't want to get close to me.

Consultant: Maybe she would be open . . . [Belle reaches her arm toward Amy and Amy responds by hugging Belle back, both somewhat stiffly.]

Belle: She knows I love her. I do love her. [pats Amy on the back]

Consultant: She knows at one level, but both of you . . . [Amy pulls back from the hug.] Is that it? That's it for scoopin'? [looks at Amy] How old are you?

Amy: Fifteen.

Consultant: [looks at Amy] Fifteen-year-olds need much more scooping than that. [whispers to Belle] It's hard for them, though! [Belle and Amy laugh.]

Consultant: That's it? [pause]

Belle: [becomes teary again] She gets hugs at home and hugs me at home.

Consultant: [nodding yes] You two need to cry about this *together*. [to Belle] You need to cry with the little girl part of her. . . . It's the little girl part [pause] that needs to hear, "God dammit, that's not fair. You're a little girl and you can't understand [pause] all how to do this; and know how to say 'no' to somebody completely. You can't know how to do that, and it's not fair that he took advantage of you. It's just not fair." That's probably part of what you cry with your husband about.

Belle: [nods head and begins to tear up again] Yeah.

Consultant: She needs to see that. She needs to hear your—hear your indignation about it. And I understand the dilemma for you about him [Melvin], but she needs to know absolutely that you're holding her hand on this. Even when she wiggles away at times. [Belle's stomach noticeably moves. She rubs it.] When is this one due?

Belle: Very shortly. [laughs and wipes eyes]

Consultant: Yeah. And you want to make sure it stays safe too, don't you?

Belle: [nods yes tearfully]

Consultant: And what a dilemma for a mom [pause] when your kid gets hurt by someone you trusted. [long pause] Maybe you're spending too much time trying to [pause] defend yourself from the pain and guilt. It's okay. You need to feel it . . . but feel it with her. [Belle lets herself cry.]

During the segment, Belle has begun to feel her pain for Amy more fully and openly. With the consultant's help, she slowly allows herself to cry and feel vulnerable in front of Amy. The consultant also introduces the possibility that Belle could share the indignation she feels about the abuse ("that bothers me a lot") with Amy.

As Belle lets herself cry more, the consultant notices that Amy looks increasingly anxious. Again, following Satir's map that resistance is the normal fear of going into an unfamiliar place, the consultant moves toward Amy and helps her tolerate and accept her mother's vulnerability as a first step in learning to accept her own.

Consultant: [gently to Amy] What's it like when you see Mom's tears about it?

Amy: [little voice] It makes me feel [mumbles].

Consultant: Makes you what?

Amy: [takes hand away from mouth] Feel sad.

Consultant: Sad.

Amy: And makes me feel guilty.

Consultant: [quiet voice] Yeah.

Belle: [through her tears] Well, a lot of it, too, I have a, a [sob] a problem with sharing [sob] a lot of my emotions because I feel like they have enough [sob] to deal with without having to deal with whatever I'm going through.

Consultant: [nodding] Yeah.

Belle: And so I've—I've tried [sob] to really hold it back as much as I can except for [sob] with my husband.

Consultant: Yes, I understand. And I think that, that dis- [pause] connection between the two of you [looking at both Belle and Amy] is what she's really pushing against but in a wrong way, okay? But she doesn't know how to connect. [to Amy] I mean, I think it makes you feel guilty [to see Mom's tears]. I think it also maybe makes you feel safe with Mom when you see her cry because you know how bad she hurts for you then. And I think it—if you can see her tears then you can understand maybe when she says, "You can't go to the mall because I want you safe. I want to make sure that everything's okay with you. I want to make sure that you're getting healed. I don't want anything terrible like this to happen to you again." [to Belle] You know it's from your heart that she needs to hear it, but to do that you're gonna have to let her see the tears, too. Because once you touch that heart, right, they're right there.

Belle: [nods through her tears]

Consultant: [pats Belle on the knee] It's okay. They're supposed to be there. And she's supposed to see them. [to Amy] Can you, would be willing to see some of Mom's tears [pause] about it? [Amy begins to tear, nods cautiously.] [to Belle] Would you be willing to do that?

Belle: [nods yes]

Consultant: To really talk about this. To really tell her how awful you feel about it and how it [pause] "tears" you up.

In this last segment, Belle and Amy are both experiencing more self-congruent communication with each other. They are more willing to tolerate their own and the other's tears and pain. In addition to supporting and encouraging the expression of this pain nonanxiously, the consultant also hints at the possible healthy intentions in Amy's misbehaviors. Perhaps this is her way of protesting the disconnection from her mother. Perhaps she is attempting to be noticed and attended to by Belle but in a way that generates negative, not positive, attention.

In the last five minutes of the session, several things occur. The consultant invites Belle to be confident that she can be of help to Amy, reminding her that she is older, wiser, and capable of giving Amy needed guidance. She also encourages Belle to understand some of Amy's manipulations as "confusion about how to connect" because of the distortions she learned over the years of abuse with Melvin. Belle reaches for and "scoops up" Amy near the end of the session, and they have a gentle discussion of finding "girl time" with each other to continue talking about the abuse, their guilt and shame, and their caring for each other.

Over the next week, they had two "girl times" before the baby arrived. Belle initiated the first by taking Amy out alone for a soda. For the first time, Belle was able to listen quietly and supportively while Amy talked in detail about the sexual abuse she had experienced. They also talked about the impact the baby might have on their relationship, and Belle invited Amy to be her chief helper when the baby arrived. Their second "girl time," initiated by Amy, involved painting each other's fingernails and discussing how complicated it was being a girl these days!

Conclusions

Belle, Amy, and the family continued to receive therapy in different configurations (individual, dyadic, family, and group) on and off for the next two years. Significant progress was made, especially by Belle and Amy, in increasing self-esteem, decreasing denial as a defense mechanism, and developing close interpersonal relationships. In a follow-up meeting with the consultant two years later, Belle identified this session and the resulting "girl times" as an important beginning to the changes she and Amy had made in their relationship. Although not able to articulate exactly what had helped, Belle said she remembered feeling a release of pressure following the session. She mentioned feeling accepted by the consultant and having more confidence in herself and her ability to help Amy (and her other children) heal from the abuse. She was surprised by how much easier it was to listen to Amy talk about the abuse during their "girl time"; she said they used lots of Kleenex. Belle and Amy's therapist reported that Belle had become a stronger supporter of Amy's following the session.[1]

The sexual victimization of children can create a significant amount of emotionality and reactivity within and between the offended, the nonoffending family members, and the system of helpers working with them (Sheinberg, 1992). All of those involved experience, to some degree, a sense of violation and powerlessness. All are faced with multiple decisions. It is easy to fall prey to pretending that these decisions can be conceptualized as black or white, good or bad; usually they are more complicated than that, and it is necessary to unpack these complications if people are to feel fully congruent with their decisions. It is important to "transform 'either/or' impasses into 'both/and' possibilities, which are not a simple combination but, rather a new order of meaning" (Sheinberg, 1992, p. 203).

Virginia Satir was interested in helping family members arrive at a new meaning of themselves and each other that offered more possibility for growth and connection. She did this, in part, by helping families see, hear, and feel more fully and congruently. Her compassion for and nonblaming attitude toward people's unhealthy patterns enabled her to invite people to see that they have many more choices about how to connect with themselves and with one another than they were aware. As she noted, "It is in honoring all parts

---

[1]Although the abuse case was settled out of court for technical reasons, Belle challenged Melvin and his wife to admit the truth; when neither would, she stopped contact with them.

of ourselves and being free to accept those parts that we lay the groundwork for high self-esteem" (Satir quoted in Simon, 1989, p. 34). Satir advocated an approach to therapy that transformed impasses such as those presented in this case by lending people acceptance for what has been, vision for something different, and courage to make that change.

Study Questions

1. Given that Belle later evidenced a less defensive and distant relationship with Amy following this session, what do you think were the curative influences of this consultation?
2. Find further examples of when Belle and Amy communicated incongruently. What poses did each adopt? How might a psychodynamic family therapist conceptualize their exchanges with one another?
3. How many specific elements of Satir's therapeutic approach, as delineated by Andreas, can you locate in this consultation? List each with a short example.
4. If this was ongoing therapy with mother and daughter rather than a consultation, what other techniques might a Satir-influenced therapist use to help them understand and change their problematic interactions?
5. Pick another therapeutic approach (for example, structural, strategic, behavioral) and delineate how similar or dissimilar the consultation would be in terms of the theme(s) selected and technique(s) used.

References

Andreas, S. (1989). The true genius of Virginia Satir. *The Family Therapy Networker, 13*(1), 46, 51–54, 78–80.

Andreas, S. (1991). *Virginia Satir: The patterns of her magic.* Palo Alto, CA: Science & Behavior Books.

Bandler, R., Grinder, J., & Satir, V. (1976). *Changing with families.* Palo Alto, CA: Science & Behavior Books.

Elbow, M., & Mayfield, J. (1991). Mothers of incest victims: Villians, victims, or protectors? *Families in Society: The Journal of Contemporary Human Sciences, 72,* 78–86.

Finkelhor, D., & Browne, A. (1985). The traumatic impact of child sexual abuse: A conceptualization. *American Journal of Orthopsychiatry, 55*(4), 530–541.

Goldenberg, I., & Goldenberg, H. (1996). *Family therapy: An overview* (4th ed.). Pacific Grove, CA: Brooks/Cole.

Laing, L., & Kamsler, A. (1990). Putting an end to secrecy: Therapy with mothers and children following disclosure of child sexual assault (pp. 151–181). In M. Durrant & C. White (Eds.), *Ideas for therapy with sexual abuse.* Adelaide, Australia: Dulwich Centre.

Nichols, M. P., & Schwartz, R. C. (1995). *Family therapy: Concepts and methods* (3rd ed.). Boston: Allyn and Bacon.

O'Hanlon, W., & Weiner-Davis, M. (1989). *In search of solutions: A new direction in psychotherapy.* New York: Norton.

Salt, P., Meyer, M., Coleman, L., & Sauzier, M. (1990). The myth of the mother as accomplice to child sexual abuse. In B. Gomes-Schwartz, J. M. Horowitz, & A. Cardarelli (Eds.), *Child sexual abuse: The initial effects* (pp. 109–131). Newbury Park, CA: Sage.

Satir, V. M. (1967). *Conjoint family therapy* (rev. ed.). Palo Alto, CA: Science & Behavior Books.

Satir, V. M. (1986). A partial portrait of a family therapist in process. In H. C. Fishman & B. Rosman, *Evolving models for family change* (pp. 278–293). New York: Guilford.

Satir, V. M. (1988). *The new peoplemaking.* Palo Alto, CA: Science & Behavior Books.

Satir, V. M., & Baldwin, M. (1983). *Satir step by step: A guide to creating change in families.* Palo Alto, CA: Science & Behavior Books.

Sheinberg, M. (1992). Navigating treatment impasses at the disclosure of incest: Combining ideas from feminism and social constructionism. *Family Process, 31*(3), 201–216.

Sheinberg, M., True, F., & Fraenkel, P. (1994). Treating the sexually abused child: A recursive, multimodel program. *Family Process, 33,* 263–276.

Silovsky, J., & Hembree-Kigin, T. (1994). Family and group treatment for sexually abused children: A review. *Journal of Child Sexual Abuse, 3*(3), 1–20.

Simon, R. (1989). Reaching out to life: An interview with Virginia Satir. *The Family Therapy Networker, 13*(1), 36–43.

Strand, V. (1990). Treatment of the mother in the incest family: The beginning phase. *Clinical Social Work Journal, 18*(4), 353–366.

Trepper, T., & Barrett, M. J. (1989). *Systemic treatment of incest: A therapeutic handbook.* New York: Brunner/Mazel.

Waters, D., & Lawrence, E. (1993a). *Competence, courage and change: An approach to family therapy.* New York: Norton.

Waters, D., & Lawrence, E. (1993b). Creating a therapeutic vision. *Family Therapy Networker, (17),* 53–58.

Chapter Eight

Milan Systemic Therapy

Frances F. Prevatt

The Milan systemic approach to therapy is a model of interviewing based on communication theory (Goldenberg and Goldenberg, 1996). Because it has evolved substantially over the past 25 years, a brief history of the approach to be used in this chapter may be helpful. The Milan group originated with four Italian therapists: Luigi Boscolo, Gianfranco Cecchin, Mara Selvini-Palazzoli, and Giuliana Prata, who split off from a larger group and formed the Center for Family Studies in Milan in 1971. Their early work was heavily influenced by the work of the Mental Research Institute group in Palo Alto, California, in particular by the book *Pragmatics of Human Communication* (Watzlawick, Jackson, and Beavin, 1967) and by the writings of Gregory Bateson.

Theoretical Underpinnings

One of the Milan group's first major publications, *Paradox and Counterparadox* (Selvini-Palazzoli, Boscolo, Cecchin, and Prata, 1978) focused on the "games" played by families, particularly families with a schizophrenic member. Several strategically oriented techniques were incorporated into their theory. For example, the MRI concept of therapeutic double bind became the *counterparadox*. A common counterparadoxical intervention might be to suggest that the family was performing in a manner necessary to maintain their functioning and that no change should be considered. Reframing became *positive connotation:* Symptomatic behavior was stated as a positive event that helped to maintain the family's balance and homeostasis, thus allowing the family to function in a cohesive fashion (Goldenberg and Goldenberg, 1996). Clients were seen as exhibiting a great deal of resistance, which had to be overcome in a strategic manner.

During the next stage of their development, the Milan group was heavily influenced by Gregory Bateson's *Steps to an Ecology of Mind* (1972). At this point, their thinking became less strategic and more systemic. They developed and refined a therapeutic approach with three major tenets: *hypothesizing, neutrality,* and *circular questions* (Selvini-Palazzoli, Boscolo, Cecchin, and Prata, 1980). Hypothesizing is an assessment technique, neutrality is a basic therapeutic stance, and circular questioning is an interviewing technique.

Hypothesizing is the process by which the therapist and team formulate ideas as to what is happening in the family, the patterns that sustain the behaviors, the purpose of the behaviors, and the contributions of each system member to family functioning (Boscolo, Cecchin, Hoffman, and Penn, 1987). It usually begins at the first intake phone call or meeting and is done conjointly with the family. Hypothesizing is a continual, interactive process. The therapist begins to develop a working hypothesis, which is then continually modified based on the answers provided by the system members. Hypotheses guide the types of questions asked, which in turn further modify the hypotheses. It is not necessary that the resulting interpretation be "true"; it merely represents the family and the therapists' jointly created world view. (Many readers may realize that this is very similar to social constructivists' notion of a constructed reality.) This world view then becomes useful in that it helps the family to consider alternate possibilities, which then may lead to different ways of functioning as a family. Hypothesis formation may begin by asking the family what the current problem is and then inquiring who noticed the problem first. This accomplishes two things: one, it gives an interpersonal definition to the problem since the problem cannot exist without a noticer, and two, it defines the problem as an event outside any one person.

The second key concept in the Milan triad—neutrality—is often misunderstood, as it is erroneously believed that the therapists do not take a stance, never make value judgments, and never side with any family member at any time during the sessions. In fact, neutrality is closer to multipositional than nonpositional (Boscolo et al., 1987). This means that the therapist does not remain sided with a particular position and that, at the end of a session, the family cannot state what the position of the therapist might be. The therapist accepts, without judgment, the perceptions of all family members as legitimate. It is important to realize that accepting the members' perceptions of the problem is different from accepting the problem itself. A therapist practicing neutrality would refrain from presenting his own personal goals for the family. Rather, the therapist would assume that the family has the capacity to both discover its problems and to develop a range of alternative solutions. This allows the therapist to move throughout the system as needed, without becoming trapped within the family's dysfunctional system.

The concept of circular questioning provides the basis of a technique for interviewing a family. The technique rests on the belief that systems are characterized by loop formations rather than by linear sequences of cause and effect.

Circular questions, therefore, are ones utilized by the therapist to highlight and/or reveal patterns that connect persons, events, behaviors, thoughts, and feelings in recurrent circuits. These questions tend to be neutral, nonjudgmental, and accepting of current functioning. It is believed that circular questions, in and of themselves, have the potential to trigger major changes in the client's patterns of thought by allowing the individual and family members to hear each other's perceptions (and therefore their individual realities) of any given event or behavior. Therefore, no distinction is made between assessment and therapy. The process of asking for information is seen as therapeutic in and of itself.

The Milan group characterizes circular questions as highlighting differences. Four major areas of difference are explored: relationships, degree, now/then, and hypothetical/future. The Milan notion of circular questions has been expanded by Tomm (1987a, 1987b, 1988) to include *interventive interviewing,* in which the assumption is made that, while a particular question may carry a certain importance for the therapist, the real effect of any particular question is determined by each person's individual perception of reality. The questions asked by the therapist are geared more to trigger a response than to determine specific information.

Tomm's characterization of *reflexive* questions is very similar to the Milan group's description of circular questions. Tomm describes questions as being of the following eight types (1987b): future oriented, observer-perspective, unexpected context change, embedded suggestion, normative-comparison, distinction clarifying, hypothesis introducing, and process interruption.

Because circular questions are so critical to Milan systemic therapy, they merit a detailed description. The original Milan categories are combined here with a subset of the Tomm categories (many of these are overlapping). Henceforth, the term *circular questions* will refer to these combined categories. Table 1 (based on the work of Boscolo et al., 1987; Prevatt and Worchel, 1993; Tomm, 1987a, 1987b) gives an overview of the types of questions utilized, their rationale, and examples of each.

Another technique utilized by the Milan group includes an *end-of-session intervention.* This might be in the form of a letter that is read to the family, describing the therapist's views as to what is occurring within the family. This statement to the family often contains either a counterparadoxical instruction or a positive connotation.

The Milan approach is generally considered short term, typically about ten sessions. In the beginning, families were often seen only once a month due to the great distances many families had to travel to Milan. It was believed that the extended length of time between sessions would facilitate the family's ability to process the new way of thinking engendered by the previous session. A team approach was always utilized, with a male and female therapist conducting a session and a minimum of two team members behind the mirror. It was believed that the cotherapists would model appropriate gender-specific couple behavior. This view was later amended, and therapists were more likely to work singly in front of the mirror so that different interpretations or hypotheses were not being

Table 8.1
Circular Questions

Category	Definition/Function	Examples
Differences in relationship	Establishes interpersonal relationships, subsystems, and alliances.	Who are you closest to in the family? Who do you confide in the most?
Differences in degree	If a problem can be more or less, then it also has the potential to cease.	Who worries more about your son? Is the fighting worse or is the running away worse? On a scale of 1 to 5, how much does that worry you?
Differences in time	If a problem has a beginning, then it can have an end.	Does she cry more now that you are separated, or did she cry more when you were together? Who noticed first? Who was cooperative before he became cooperative? Are you closer now than you used to be?
Hypothetical/ future	Establishes a sense of control over actions.	If you were to leave, what would he do? When daughter leaves for college, how will your husband react?
Observer-perspective	Help individuals to recognize how their own reactions, behaviors, and feelings may serve as links in the family interactions.	Who agrees that this is a problem? How does your father express love? Who is your mother likely to get support from? How would your daughter describe your discipline style?
Normative-comparison	Promote healthy functioning by establishing a healthy frame of reference. Allow individuals identified as the problem to feel less abnormal.	Does your family fight more or less than other families? Is your family more or less tight knit than other families? Is your son more rowdy than the other boys his age? Do you and your husband argue more than other couples you know?
Hypothesis introducing	Help move the family toward new insights or solutions by imbedding a working hypothesis into a question.	If you get angry to cover up your vulnerability, does your family interpret that as your being hostile? Do you see your shyness as a way of not getting close to others or as a way of being selective about who you want to be friends with?
Linear	Noncircular questions used when history or specific information is desired.	Where are you employed? How long have you been married? What other problems do you see? How long has he been gone? How do you punish him when he misbehaves?

pursued simultaneously. Additionally, it was believed that modeling tacitly implied that the family's way of doing things was wrong and that the therapist's way of doing things was correct. The team behind the mirror continued to be an important component of the therapy. Generally, the therapist would take a break midway through the session to discuss process with the team and to contemplate an end-of-session intervention. In addition, the team would have an extended postsession discussion to analyze the case.

In 1980, Boscolo and Cecchin split off from Selvini-Palazzoli and Prata, the former focusing more on training and the latter on research. One major difference between the two groups involved the goals of systemic therapy. Selvini-Palazzoli developed a more strategic approach, the goal of which was to disrupt and expose games played by family members. Alternately, Boscolo and Cecchin moved away from strategic manipulation of families into a more collaborative approach, in which they worked directly with families to form systemic hypotheses about their interactions and relationships (Nichols and Schwartz, 1995). They believed that curiosity about a family's interactions would allow the family to examine their own behaviors and would lead to a systemic change if the family believed such a change was necessary. Thus, interventions by the therapist were downplayed in lieu of helping the family with self-discovery. As this chapter deals with the practical application of therapy, the case presented here focuses on the later work of Boscolo and Cecchin. The case presentation illustrates the following aspects of the Milan approach:

- Constructing a working hypothesis
- Exhibiting a therapeutic stance of neutrality
- Using circular questioning as both an assessment and a therapeutic technique
- Working with a team to monitor process
- Identifying labels that are used by the family
- Identifying openings or themes to be explored
- Using positive connotation of problematic behaviors
- Using an end-of-session intervention

The Case: Acting-Out Children Provide a Shield for Marital Difficulties
Background

The Parker family was self-referred for family therapy at the suggestion of the school guidance counselor after a son had been suspended for eight days for fighting at an after-school basketball practice. The mother had called and made the initial appointment. The family consisted of a mother (Leslie), who was a homemaker; a father (Jerry), who sold retirement plans to state employees; twin boys (Andrew and Alex), age 16, and a daughter (Barbara), age 20, who lived in another city with her boyfriend. All family members except the daughter came to the initial session.

The therapy was conducted by a doctoral-level therapist working in a university-affiliated training clinic, with a team of three graduate students observing from behind a one-way mirror. The team had been together for about six months and had established a good working relationship. With each case, team members rotated turns conducting the therapy and serving behind the mirror. Generally, the therapist either took a self-imposed break or received a knock on the door at least once during a session. The team always held lengthy discussions after each session to analyze the case, discuss and revise hypotheses, and plan for future sessions.

Case Transcript

Therapist: Tell me what brings you here today.

Mom: Well, it's just the straw that broke the camel's back, you know. Alex is the one who got in trouble this time, but they have both been problems and it's just getting out of hand.

Therapist: So Alex and Andrew got you here equally.

Mom: Well, they didn't get us here. I got us here. I had to threaten to get them here.

Therapist: And they went along with your threats?

Mom: Well, yes.

Therapist: What about you, Dad? Did you have to be threatened, or did you come on your own?

Dad: [laughs] Oh, she threatens me all the time. But I know I have to do what she says.

Therapist: So do you agree with Mom that Alex and Andrew got you here, or did you come because Mom threatened?

Dad: [mumbles and laughs] Well, I don't really know. I just . . . I don't know.

Therapist: Don't quite know why you are here?

Dad: Well, yes they are problems, but you know that's just how kids are, and they are 16 and very active guys. They both play basketball and . . . [shrugs and throws up his hands]

Therapist: So Mom is pretty sure of herself and takes strong steps to get things done. Dad is not so sure but is willing to go along with Mom.

Mom: Well, I wouldn't say he always goes along with me. He gets upset all on his own. He just gets mad at different things, and then he gets out of control and hollers.

Therapist: Oh? What kinds of things upset Dad?

Mom: Well, little things, like if the papers are left on the floor and not put up immediately.

Therapist: So Mom and Dad both get upset but over different things. What about you, Alex; what upsets you?

Alex: Mom is crazy.

Therapist: Oh? What kind of crazy things does Mom do?

Alex: She's always upset over any little thing. Always nagging us.

Therapist: So Mom gets upset more than Dad?

Alex: Oh, yeah.

Therapist: Who tends to notice first when Mom gets upset?

Alex: Well, it depends on what she does. If I come home and she's going nuts because I screwed up, then I notice. But I ignore it if I can.

Therapist: How does she get you to notice when you are trying to ignore her?

Alex: Well, sometimes it works. I just say yeah, man, and go on and say I gotta go practice or like that.

Therapist: So you do that pretty well. What about Dad? Is he better than Mom at getting upset?

Alex: Well, he's harder to ignore for sure.

Therapist: And what about Andrew? How often does he get upset? Less than Mom? Less than Dad?

Alex: Andrew?

Therapist: Yes, that guy right there.

Alex: Well . . . never, really.

Therapist: Andrew, is that right?

Andrew: I get upset some.

Therapist: At who? Who do you get upset with the most?

Andrew: Dad and Mom. Mom more because she's around. Its hard to get mad at Dad because he's never there. But when Dad blows, he blows and, oh man, watch out.

Therapist: Sounds like you agree with Alex. Dad can be a volcano when he wants to and you have to sit up and take notice.

In this segment, the therapist has avoided a content discussion of the problem. These discussions are generally nonproductive and only serve to increase tension and place blame. Thus, in the beginning, she refrains from asking such questions as how the boys get in trouble, the circumstances of their getting in trouble, or the parents' reactions to their getting in trouble. Rather, she has immediately set the stage for a systemic view of the family by identifying a theme (getting upset) and asking questions about behaviors that everyone participates in. The family has presented a label (Mom is crazy), which the therapist will monitor but avoids reinforcing by instead focusing on behaviors. A positive connotation is offered when the therapist suggests that Mom is pretty sure of herself and takes strong steps to get things done and Dad is not so sure but is willing to go along with Mom (as opposed to Mom is upset and Dad is uninvolved). The therapist solicits everyone's opinion regarding how people get upset, using circular questions, such as who notices first and who gets more or less upset. An initial determination of relationships and roles reveals Mom as the spokesperson, Dad as more distant, and the boys as a single unit. An initial hypothesis at this point is that Mom has taken over the parenting function for the family, with Dad being less involved. Dad may be using humor as a way of deflecting emotion, with perhaps a passive resistant style ("I do whatever Mom says, but I get my way by refusing to be involved").

The therapist continues to explore this hypothesis, asking about the different ways in which the mother and father perceive the family, their emotional connectedness, as well as their involvement in the family.

Therapist: Dad, do you agree with Mom about her concerns for the family? [long pause]

Mom: I'm going to wait for him to say something, I usually . . .

Dad: Just straighten the boys out.

Therapist: So you also see the boys as a problem?

Dad: No, they're not a problem; they're just normal kids, you know, get out of hand once in a while. So, you know, you get mad at them sometimes when you say you gotta do something and they just walk away.

Therapist: So how do you get their attention?

Dad: Just holler.

Therapist: So you use a verbal two-by-four. Does it work?

Dad: Yeah.

Therapist: Alex and Andrew seemed to think you get their attention better than Mom. Do you agree?

Dad: Oh, yeah, she doesn't holler; she's real nice . . . except to me. She gets mad at me.

Therapist: So you holler and Mom is nice, yet the boys think she is the one who acts crazy. Is anyone else in the family nice and crazy?

Andrew: Barbara, definitely Barbara.

Therapist: And how long has Barbara been doing crazy things?

Andrew: Well, not so much now because she's not around, but you know, when she was our age and in high school too and being the first one and a girl, it was even harder for her.

Therapist: So now that she's on her own, she doesn't have to do crazy things anymore. Do you think she grew out of it or was it more not being around you all?

Andrew: Probably just being away. When you're on your own, you make your own rules and do your own thing.

Therapist: So, Mom, maybe if you got to make more rules you would enjoy that?

Mom: Oh, definitely.

Therapist: What rules would be different?

Mom: Well, everyone would have consideration and respect for each other, and I think that's the main thing I see that upsets me so much.

Therapist: So if all of a sudden they started respecting everyone and being nice . . .

Mom: What would I worry or fuss about then? [laughs] I'm the kind of person I think I've figured out myself, that I like to worry about something all the time.

Therapist: So you're the family worrywart. If you're the worrier, who's the happy-go-lucky person? [Dad raises his hand.]

Mom: He acts like he's happy-go-lucky, but . . .

Therapist: So she doesn't totally agree with you, Dad.

Dad: Well, maybe she doesn't see it.

Therapist: Who sees that side of you?

Dad: I think all of them sometimes. [Mom, Alex, and Andrew are all shaking their heads no.]

Therapist: Looks like they're overruling you.

In this segment, the therapist explores the family's views and labels for one another. Can being crazy be owned by everyone, or can it be replaced with other perceptions, such as the family worrywart? How might the disappearance of these symptoms change the family? The label that Mom is crazy is also confronted as the therapist asks how long others have acted crazy: If Barbara can stop and start being crazy, then being crazy is controllable. Some marital issues begin to emerge (Dad's comment that Mom is only mean to him), yet this is not followed up at this early stage. Mom's and Dad's different perceptions about the boys and each other's reactions add credence to the hypothesis of some difficulties in the parenting subsystem. An early hypothetical/future question hints at Mom's need to maintain the boys' symptomatic behaviors. This is not probed thoroughly at this early point, but this issue will be addressed again in the second session.

As the session continues, Mom continues to be very involved and animated, with Dad remaining relatively distant. In an effort to learn more about the father's role in the family, the therapist asks some background information of him, primarily using linear questions. This focus on background or history is not routinely part of an initial session but is used here to gain a better understanding of the father. It should be noted that, from a strategically oriented therapy, asking the father these questions would be done with the intent of changing his behaviors in the sessions so that he becomes more active. From a Milan approach, however, his lack of involvement is seen as neither good nor bad. This questioning is solely for the purpose of gathering information.

Therapist: Dad, tell me a little about yourself.

Dad: Well, uh, what do you want to know?

Therapist: The part that's most important.

Dad: OK, I work mostly at the university. I handle employee retirement accounts. It's pretty hectic; I work a lot. Long hours.

Therapist: Enjoyable work?

Dad: Well, it's a good job.

Therapist: How long have you been doing that?

Dad: Well, actually, I lost my job three years ago. That was a pretty rough time. I was what you would probably call an alcoholic, but I quit.

Therapist: Oh? Tell me about that.

Dad: Well, there's not much to tell. It just happened. I just decided I needed to stop drinking, so I quit.

Therapist: How was that for the rest of the family?

Dad: Oh, not too big a deal.

Therapist: Mom?

Mom: Well, I had gone to visit my brother in Alabama, and when I called home he had gotten notice that day about his job.

Therapist: What about the drinking?

Mom: Well, yes, that's always been there. But not any longer. Like he said, he just quit.

In this segment, the father continues his somewhat reserved style, with a brief yet intense revelation of some dramatic information. Attempts to query this reveal little further information. Again, the intent here is not to discuss content but to evaluate family style, so very little probing is done of this issue.

In the ensuing conversation, the mother returns to her concerns regarding Alex and Andrew, including their refusal to go to church, their disrespect for her, and their argumentativeness. She mentions an incident in which Alex threw a knife at Andrew. Shortly after this, the team knocks on the door to discuss the case. Together, the team and the therapist form a hypothesis that it is extremely difficult to get noticed in this family. The therapist continues the session by probing this idea.

Therapist: I am curious about something. We were discussing how concerned you were [to Mom] to come in here, and it took an awful lot to get everyone here. But then we started talking about how Dad stopped drinking and nobody noticed. I was wondering what it takes to make an impact in this family. What about when you [Alex] threw the knife at him? Who noticed? Who did something?

Mom: We weren't there. I had gone to the store and Jerry was at work.

Dad: Uh huh.

Mom: And they [points to the boys] came walking up to the house. I think he was dragging Andrew.

Alex: I carried him.

Mom: Well, I didn't see him carry him, but when I got home Andrew was dripping blood all over. I thought he might need stitches or something.

Therapist: Did anyone panic?

Dad: No.

Mom: No, I just said, "well, wait till your father gets home."

Dad: I got home and Leslie says, "Andrew's got a knife in his leg." I say, "Is he hurt real bad?" "No, I don't think so." [laughs] Oh, boy, like the last basketball game of the season, he gets walloped under the basket and the other guy goes down, and that poor kid gets six stitches in his chin.

Therapist: Oh?

Dad: Yeah, what a way to end the season!

Therapist: So I think it seems that this family doesn't get real upset over what many people would say are pretty major events . . . [Everyone laughs.]

Mom: I guess we're desensitized.

Therapist: Except maybe Mom who the boys think is crazy because she does get upset? [No one responds.]

Therapist: Dad, tell me more about when you gave up drinking. Who noticed that?

Dad: Well, you know, you don't really know if you're an alcoholic. I only drank beer, so I just quit.

Therapist: Did you just come home one day and say, "Gee, I quit today"?

Dad: I didn't say anything to anybody.

Therapist: Really?

Dad: I just quit.

Mom: No, he didn't say anything.

Dad: Like smoking. I just quit. I was smoking two and a half packs a day and so I just quit.

Therapist: That's a pretty big deal. You didn't tell anybody you were doing it?

Dad: Why make a big deal of it? It's gotta be you that has to do it. No one else is going to do it for you.

Therapist: Who was most concerned about your drinking and smoking?

Dad: Probably Leslie.

Therapist: Did you notice when he quit? Did you comment on it?

Mother: Well, I probably didn't say much. I'd lived with it for 25 years.

Therapist: Did it bring you closer together when you noticed he'd quit?

Mom: Not really.

Therapist: So it didn't really change anything. Did the kids notice?

Dad: No. [Throws hands up in air]

Therapist: Alex? Did you notice?

Alex: No ma'am. I think maybe we were too little to notice that kind of stuff.

Andrew: I don't know if we were little or not. I don't know when it was.

Dad: I quit for myself.

Therapist: What have you done that's had the most impact on them?

Dad: Nothing . . . my next project is to lose 50 pounds.

Therapist: Who would care the most if you did?

Dad: No one. It's mine for me to do. Ninety years old, slim, sharp, and driving a Corvette! Well, maybe Leslie would appreciate that . . .

Therapist: Mom, is that something you would notice?

Mom: Yes, well, but I'm not going to hold my breath on that one. Let's see . . . how many times have I heard that?

Therapist: So you don't really expect drastic changes. So maybe when something drastic happens, everyone forgets to notice.

In this segment, the therapist explores the theme of getting noticed in this family. Again, the therapist makes no assumption that this is a pathological response, only that this *is*. Questioning does not attempt to intervene or to change the family's tendency to notice; rather, the questioning inquires about this phenomenon so that the family can come to a collectively generated reality concerning how their family operates. During this questioning, the team is struck by the family's nonchalance over significant events.

There appears to be some ambivalence in the father's responses. On the one hand, he claims to do things for himself, not caring who notices. He cautiously

mentions that if he lost weight his wife might care. She responds with a depre-
cating remark, which might contribute to the father's self-protective stance.

The team remarks on the discrepancy between the boys' appearance and
behavior and the initial statement that the boys are a problem. The boys are
very attractive and neatly groomed. They are attentive and well mannered
throughout the session and always respond politely when questioned. A hypothesis is formulated that the boys' difficulties are covering up underlying
marital difficulties. Some team members recommend bringing back only the
parents the following week. Others suggest that this would be premature and
would frighten the parents, leading to premature termination. It is decided to
bring back the family as a whole to gather more initial impressions and to explore the family's sense of important events. In line with more recent Milan
formulations, no end-of-session intervention is implemented. Rather, the circular questioning itself serves the purpose of changing the family's world
view.

The mother calls to cancel two weeks in a row, leaving messages that the
boys are too busy with basketball and that the father cannot get off from work.
On the third attempt to meet, the family shows up. The boys walk in, smirking,
sit down with arms folded, as far away from the therapist as possible. Mom is
laughing.

Therapist: How did you manage to get these guys in this time?

Dad: I don't know. She just picked me up from work.

Mom: And says you're going? So she kidnapped you? [Dad laughs.] How
about the boys?

Mom: You know, I just finally said we're going, so be quiet and do it.

Therapist: So you're the heavy. [to Dad] Does she play the heavy more often
than you?

Dad: Well, you know, I work.

Therapist: So you work, and you're the heavy at home. That's kind of surprising to me. [to Mom] Last time you were saying the boys were kind of
out of control and not being able to handle them, yet it's pretty clear that
if you put your foot down, you can get action. Is that right, guys? Is she
better at playing the heavy or is Dad? [Boys stare at the therapist but
don't respond.]

Mom: They're not going to talk.

Dad: They decided this on the way over. They're not going to answer you.

Therapist: So you can get them here but not make them talk. Is that the deal?
They say, we'll show up but not participate?

Mom: Sort of like that, yeah.

Therapist: Well, that's really interesting. Which one decided, Andrew or
Alex?

Mom: I think Andrew. He likes more to be in charge. [Alex waves his arms,
gesturing no. Points to himself.]

Therapist: So they want to communicate, just not with words. So Alex decided? [Alex nods vigorously.]

Therapist: Do they do that a lot at home? Is that one thing that brings them together, rebelling against you? Or are they pretty much independent in terms of rebelling?

Mom: I think it's independent. They're both just very stubborn.

Therapist: Who did they learn that from? Mom or Dad?

Mom: More from their Dad. He can be very stubborn when he wants to.

Therapist: I was wondering which of these two, Alex or Andrew, has more power in the family to get the others to do what they want.

Mom: I think Andrew.

Therapist: Dad? How would you rank them, including Barbara? One, two, three. Who has the most power to get the others to do what they want?

Dad: Well, I'd agree Andrew first, then Alex, then Barbara.

Therapist: So do Alex and Andrew not talk to get power? What will happen when you leave here?

Mom: Well, I already told them before we came not to embarrass us or yourselves. But you're wasting their time.

Therapist: [pointing at Alex] He was really grinning when I asked that question. So is his aim to get back at you by embarrassing you?

Mom: Well, I'm sure this silent treatment is something to that effect in their own little way.

Therapist: Dad, what do you think?

Dad: Well, to a point they are disrespectful to an average family. But I don't know what an average family is.

Therapist: So this will bother Mom more than you?

Dad: Yes, I think she gets more concerned over some minor issues than I get.

Therapist: How will you react when you leave here? What will you say to Alex and Andrew?

Dad: Nothing.

Therapist: So it takes much more than this to get the volcano to blow.

In this segment, the therapist continues to maintain a stance of neutrality by accepting both the family's reluctance to come to therapy and the boys' refusal to talk. The therapist maintains a sense of curiosity about the boys' behavior. Positive connotations are used: First, the therapist suggests that the boys' misbehaviors are "rebelling that brings them together." Later, the therapist asks whether the boys' not talking is a way to be in charge and maintain power; again, a more positive interpretation. The family's behaviors are explored in terms of how the family functions and makes decisions, not as problems. Circular questions are continued, primarily to clarify relationships, and comments are again made on the extremes to which individuals must go to get noticed in this family. This appears to be a recurring theme that may be useful later in the therapy. The therapist continues to gather information related to the hypothesis that the boys' problems are a means of avoiding the parents' relationship difficulties.

Therapist: When did you first notice the boys being stubborn?

Mom: Oh, probably as they got to be teenagers, you know, when they were 8 and 9 they were angels, so sweet and helpful.

Therapist: Who noticed the change from angels?

Mom: Well, I did since I was the one to deal with them all day. Jerry was just starting this job and really not too involved at the time.

Therapist: Is that right, Dad, did Mom see the angels disappear before you did?

Dad: Well, I'm not sure I agree with the angels. Most boys are devils, don't you think? But yes, I guess she saw before me. Usually, I get reports from her like, "well, you won't believe what they did today."

Therapist: Who changed first? Alex or Andrew? [Andrew raises his hand.]

Therapist: Andrew thinks he did. So he and Alex need to figure out who gets to be in charge. [Both boys raise their hands.]

Mom: They would both like to be in charge. Sometimes one is sullen and the other is good and then before I know it, they've flipped. I sometimes wonder if they're playing a trick on me.

Therapist: So they can take turns being the bad guy and the good guy. When Barbara left home, how old were they?

Mom: Well, she's been gone since high school; let's see, OK, they were 14. Two years ago.

Therapist: Is that right Andrew? [Andrew nods in assent.] Have they been more good guys or bad guys since Barbara left home?

Mom: More bad than good.

Therapist: Dad, do you agree, more bad than good since Barbara left?

Dad: Well, maybe more rowdy, I'm not really sure.

In this segment, circular questions are used to probe different family perspectives of roles. It appears to the therapist that fairly normal developmental changes have been described for the two boys. The therapist wonders if the daughter's departure from home and the boys' normal pull away from the family has created a loss for the mother. This idea is explored later.

The team is quite taken with the boys' plan of not talking. Two hypotheses emerge. One is that not talking is a metaphor for this family. Difficult subjects should be avoided. The parents have avoided talking to each other about their relationship. The team wonders why this is: Are the parents equally committed to the relationship? Does one fear that bringing up unpleasant issues will jeopardize the relationship? A second hypothesis is that the boys must go to extreme measures to get attention due to the emotional lack of connection in the family. It is decided at this point to gather more information directly from the parents. It is also suggested that the father has been very remote and uninvolved in the sessions so far. Perhaps it would be useful to explore how this couple handles an expression of emotion. The team calls the therapist out of the room and makes this suggestion.

The therapist returns to the room and explains that she would like to spend the remainder of the session with the parents. The boys go out to the waiting room.

Therapist: The team has some questions that they thought it would be helpful to address with the two of you. It seems to them that perhaps Leslie is
more concerned about the behaviors of the boys and that Jerry doesn't
feel as much of a need to be here.

Mom: Well, I feel almost desperate at times, like I just need to leave everyone.

Therapist: That was the sense I had. You feel desperate and you [turns to
Dad], do you think you feel as desperate as Leslie?

Dad: Oh, sometimes I feel desperate too, like I want to walk out the door,
but you can't just do that.

Therapist: So you both feel this. Do you think you express it in the same way
or in different ways?

Mom: Different. He has the luxury of just leaving every day and maybe
working 14 hours a day, but not me; I am left to deal with everything, so I
get more crazy.

Therapist: So if Dad were around to help out with some of this, you wouldn't
need to be as crazy?

Mom: Maybe.

Therapist: Who was the first in the family to notice when you started acting
crazy?

Mom: Well, my daughter, even though she had to leave and live on her own,
maybe to escape it, you know?

Therapist: How about you, Dad, how do you express your feeling of being
desperate?

Dad: I'm not sure, I'm not even sure what I'm desperate about.

Therapist: No?

Dad: Well, maybe I have this sense that it doesn't matter what I do. It's not
really going to make her happy, you know? So if I work or if I'm home
doesn't really matter, maybe it won't work out anyway.

Therapist: What won't work out?

Dad: [shrugs] You know . . . us.

Therapist: So how does that affect you? What if Leslie were to announce that
it's curtains for the two of you?

Dad: If she says it's curtains?

Therapist: What does that do to you? Anything?

Dad: Yeah. But what am I supposed to do?

Therapist: Well, I'm not sure. What would happen to you and the kids if she
really did leave?

Dad: What would happen to us? We would go on somehow.

Therapist: Who would be more affected? You or the kids?

Dad: Oh, that would hurt me, but I'd get over it. You would have to.

Therapist: What would you do to try and keep her from leaving?

Dad: Ask her, you know. What can I do to get you to stay?

Therapist: Leslie, what about you? If he walked out because he felt so desperate? What would happen?

Mom: Financially, it would be a mess, which would be an emotional stress
on me. Um . . . just another abandonment for me.

Therapist: Another abandonment?

Mom: [tears up a little] Something . . . I can't talk about it.

Therapist: [to Dad] Is this something you understand, or is it a secret to you, too?

Dad: I guess . . . I mean, I don't know.

Mom: It's not a secret. It's just the way I feel.

Therapist: You feel you've been abandoned?

Mom: Sort of. My dad and then the children and him, too. Rejection.

Therapist: Who gives you the most support?

Mom: My daughter.

Therapist: What does she do that you need?

Mom: She's lived through it. Kind of a repeat of me.

Therapist: Does she feel abandoned, too?

Mom: By him [points at Dad] and her brothers.

Therapist: Who else in the family feels abandoned?

Mom: Probably Jerry. I'm not close to him at all.

Therapist: Is he closer to the boys?

Mom: No, he just ignores them.

Therapist: What if he became closer to the children? How would that make things different for you?

Mom: I wouldn't be the same person any longer. I've considered that before. I talked to a friend about it.

Therapist: So the role you're serving in this family would be gone?

Mom: Definitely. But you have to bring the alcohol part into it. I've been kind of a crutch for him, maybe the wrong thing for him.

Therapist: When he stopped drinking, did you think now there will be some changes; you might be closer, or he might get closer to the kids?

Mom: I never thought of it like that. I think he's afraid to get close to us.

Therapist: Jerry, is she on target? From your perspective?

Dad: Probably, yes, sometimes.

Therapist: Is it hard to get close to her?

Dad: It would be difficult. She fights me.

Therapist: She hits you?

Dad: Oh no, I mean she won't let me up to a point. She likes to sit down and talk, and I don't like to sit down and talk.

Therapist: So who's fighting who?

Dad: Well, I mean, we have different interests. She likes to go shopping and I would rather watch TV; you know, that kind of thing.

Therapist: So what would it be like if you took up shopping, really got into it with her?

Dad: Huh?

Therapist: What would it be like to do that together?

Dad: I don't know, I'm not sure I'm up to it.

In this segment, there are several avenues the therapist could have taken. For example, when the mother talks about the daughter being the one to notice when she acts crazy, it would have been logical to follow up on the theme of the mother and daughter's relationship. However, the therapist decided that the purpose of this interchange was to bring the father into the session more fully and to explore the ability of the couple to discuss their relationship. Therefore, at that juncture the therapist continued with the discussion of how each partner felt desperate. A few sentences later, the father alludes to his fear that the relationship might not work out. Although it is fairly early in the therapy, the therapist decides to pursue this emotionally laden issue. Using hypothetical/future circular questions, the therapist explores this possibility with both Jerry and Leslie. This leads to some revealing perceptions from both spouses: Leslie's sense of abandonment and Jerry's fear of being close. A hypothetical/future question in the opposite direction (increased closeness) seems to take Jerry by surprise.

Thus, at the end of two sessions, the team formulates an evolving hypothesis. It appears as though the parents have difficulty with emotional closeness. The father admits to being an alcoholic and states that he quit drinking about three years ago. Shortly after this, the mother began having difficulty with the boys. At about the same time, the daughter, with whom the mother had been very close, moved out of the home. Many times, when one spouse is alcoholic, the other spouse takes on a role of dealing with the effects of the alcoholism: making excuses for employers, protecting the children, taking care of the alcoholic during binges or crises. Perhaps when the drinking stopped and the mother's close involvement with the daughter ended, she was faced with the choice of getting close to her husband or creating a new crisis. The boys' natural developmental changes as adolescents could have provided an excuse for her and her husband not to deal with their marital issues. Granted, some of the boys' behaviors were extreme (throwing a knife). But these may be evidence of a pattern in the family—of vacillating between not wanting closeness yet engaging at times in extreme behaviors in an attempt to be noticed. It was decided to bring the parents back for a third session that would focus on investigating this hypothesis. It was expected that the parents would be ambivalent about this, both fearing the issues that might emerge and at the same time wanting them to come up. It was decided to address this issue with the parents before they left.

Therapist: We feel it would be helpful for you two to come in for a session without the boys to talk some more about some of the things that have come up today. This will probably be something that one or both of you might want to avoid talking about. In the past, it has been useful to avoid noticing things because you were very busy as a family. Jerry had a very stressful job and was trying to stop drinking at the same time he needed to deal with changing jobs. Leslie was very busy raising three children with very active lives. It might have been selfish of Leslie or Jerry to demand that the other devote time to talking about the marriage during that time. So you worked hard at allowing family members to sometimes go overboard and pretending not to notice. But now it may be time to change that, maybe not. Sometimes you are not sure it is the right time to change that, so you don't let it happen yet. It may have been a very good thing to go slow and wait a while between the first and second sessions before proceeding. Perhaps that is still necessary. Leslie, can you tell me how you might know this week that it is not the right time for you and Jerry to come back and begin talking to each other?

Leslie: I don't know that it's ever the right time. I guess at some point you just wake up and get tired of being unhappy with your life and tired of deluding yourself and looking around at everyone else and saying there must be more than this.

Therapist: And so you've felt that way now more than ever before, enough to convince you to take some action?

Leslie: Yes, I guess that's it.

Therapist: Jerry, how about you? What will you watch for this week?

Jerry: Well, I have to admit that this is an eye-opener for me. I think that there were things I was doing to show my love for Leslie and maybe she never knew that! Like you would say, she never noticed . . . I guess I also didn't know how close she was to giving up on us. Maybe I thought if you make it 25 years, nothing will change and you quit worrying. But that's not the case, is it?

Therapist: No, I guess not. So, Jerry, if Leslie gives you a reason not to come back next week, like the boys need her, how will you know if that's legitimate or her trying to say the time is not right?

Jerry: I guess just ask her!

Therapist: And Leslie, if Jerry says on Thursday he can't get off work, how will you know how to respond?

Leslie: I guess like I did today. Just say you're coming and we'll talk about what you are trying to pull when we get here! I'll let you figure it out! [laughs]

Therapist: Fair enough. See you next week.

During this segment, the therapist provides a logical connotation for the previous behaviors of the family. This is very similar to reframing, in that behaviors that might be interpreted as problematic are viewed as necessary or adaptive in a given system. Next, the therapist addresses the issue of not coming back directly. Giving an excuse for not returning is not portrayed as resistance, merely as a possibility. In an earlier stage of development, the Milan therapists might have dealt with this more strategically; for example, prescribing the symptom ("I think that there is a good chance that you won't come back next week") or using paradox ("If the boys truly are in control of this family, they will find a way to keep you two from coming back next week"). However, it is now believed that an end-of-session prescription is not needed, that merely asking questions will be the intervention that will change the family's behaviors.

Jerry and Leslie do return the following week. During this session, the therapist questions them about the effect of Jerry's drinking on the family.

Therapist: Jerry, tell me again how long it has been since you stopped drinking.

Jerry: Oh, two to three years now.

Therapist: And tell me what changes you have seen in the family since that time. What things have gotten better?

Jerry: Better? Well, I spend a lot less money. [laughs] Seriously, I am in control of myself now and I don't wake up after a three-day binge and wonder what hellacious things I've screwed up this time. And I've kept a job for two whole years and am doing pretty well at it.

Therapist: Have there been any changes for the worse?

Jerry: Well, sometimes I think life's not nearly as much fun. And it sure is easier to deal with stress out of a bottle.

Therapist: What about between you and Leslie? What changes have you seen since you stopped drinking?

Jerry: Well, she doesn't yell at me much anymore.

Therapist: What does she do instead of yelling? Does she talk to you more now?

Jerry: Well, not really. Are you trying to say that my drinking was a way of getting her to talk to me?

Therapist: I don't know. Leslie, what do you think about that? Did you communicate with Jerry more when he was drinking?

Leslie: Define communicate . . . yes, I mean no, I mean, yes I get it. I always had something to complain about when he drank. Why don't you mow the yard? Why do you always get drunk when the boys have a game? Why does Barbara avoid you all the time? How are we supposed to live without a paycheck?

Therapist: So what kind of things do you talk to Jerry about now?

Leslie: Not much, really; the boys did this, the boys did that. Well, it doesn't take an idiot to figure out what you're getting at. I don't have anything to yell about, so now I have to find something else to yell about. Guess I must enjoy yelling.

Therapist: Do you think you yell just as much now, only about the boys instead of Jerry's drinking?

Leslie: Not really; I probably don't really talk to him as much now, yelling or otherwise.

Therapist: So for you, would it be a good thing if he started drinking again, so you would have a reason to communicate?

Leslie: Oh, heavens no! I may be crazy but not like that. That was not a good time for us in any way. I can't tell you how close I came to taking the kids and walking out. But I don't believe that would have been the thing to do, so I didn't.

Therapist: Do you ever worry that he will start drinking again?

Leslie: Sometimes, yes, it does have to concern me.

Therapist: What kinds of things do you do to help him not to start drinking again?

Leslie: Well, I sure don't keep beer around the house.

Therapist: Do you try to protect him in other ways? Does it worry you when he is a volcano?

Leslie: I guess I never really thought about protecting him. He is gone so much I think he protects himself. He won't let me protect him.

Therapist: Jerry, is this what Leslie meant when she said you won't let her get close? Is it your turn to do the hard job of protecting yourself?

Jerry: Perhaps. I did put her through an awful lot. Maybe I don't want her to have to take care of me anymore . . . no, maybe I think she doesn't want to take care of me anymore.

Therapist: So you've done a lot of things to try to take care of yourself. Does she still think you need her to help out?

Jerry: I don't know. [to Leslie] Do you?

Leslie: Do you want me to?

Jerry: Do you want me to want you to?

Therapist: Who wants to risk making the first commitment?

Leslie: Guess we're pretty good at this routine.

This segment appears to support the hypothesis that Jerry's drinking has changed Leslie's role in relation to him and that the boys have provided a substitute for that role. The couple shows some insight into this behavior, discussing their lack of communication with one another. They remain hesitant about emotional commitment to one another, yet this is probably adaptive given the length of time they have related in a distant manner and their lack of certainty about the other's intentions. The remainder of the therapy (a total of ten sessions) involves several sessions with the couple, in which they continue to discuss ways of relating to one another. The daughter, Barbara, comes in for a session, and she and her parents discuss her relationship, how that has changed since she has left home, and how she can maintain a close relationship with both parents. Andrew and Alex return for some family sessions, in which developmental changes of adolescents are discussed as well as the impact on the family when the boys leave home. At termination, the family reports increased closeness between Jerry and Leslie, with the boys' behaviors seen as less of an issue.

Conclusions

This is a fairly straightforward case that could be approached from several theoretical perspectives. For example, a Bowenian perspective might look at family-of-origin issues in each of the parents. Is there a history of alcoholism in Jerry's family? Is his lack of involvement in the family similar to his experience as a child? Was anyone "crazy" in Leslie's family? The intergenerational duplication of patterns would be explored, with a focus on interpersonal histories. From a structural approach, as advocated by Minuchin, the therapist would focus more on the subsystems and hierarchies in this family. A family map or diagram would look at possible enmeshment between the mother and Barbara, with the father being more distant from the family. The therapist would likely be more directive, entering the family system to solidify the spousal and parental subsystems. The therapist would likely ask fewer questions and spend more time directing the parents to talk to one another about their perceptions. Alternately, a behavioral family therapy approach would focus more on specific parenting styles of the parents and how these might relate to the boys' misbehaviors. Much more information would be gathered regarding the specific problem behaviors, parental responses, and antecedents and consequences. The therapist would likely choose one or more specific behaviors to address with didactic teaching, homework, review, and feedback.

In the Milan approach, the therapist gives very few direct interpretations or directives. The Milan group believes that very little is accomplished by suggesting specific strategies or solutions and that this rarely results in a change in behaviors. If the therapist's recommendations are implemented, change is often only short term. Instead, questions are used almost exclusively. In this way, an extensive discussion of the family system results in a change in the way the family views their world, allowing them to come to new understandings and, in turn, creating a new filter through which to view behavior. These discussions also allow family members to reflect on their current (typically, linear) perceptions of family interactions and to create numerous possibilities that provide alternatives for solving problems. For example, if Mom is crazy, she is likely to be ignored. If she is merely upset, and other family members also get upset, then her beliefs and actions may garner more respect. As another example, the therapist could have presented her insight that the parents feared closeness, wondered aloud whether this was due to the departure of Barbara, and blamed Dad's overwork on an inability to become emotionally involved with Mom. An alternative to this strategy is to ask questions that allow the parents to create their own view of the situation, not one directly suggested by the therapist. This view then allows the parents to come to their own truth, cocreated with the therapist, thereby reducing resistance.

In other approaches, Andrew and Alex's refusal to speak might have been seen as resistance, with the therapist instructing the parents to solicit cooperation from the boys or engaging in a discussion as to why the boys were being uncooperative and whether this was an example of their "bad" behavior at home. As could be seen here, the boys' silence was met with interest, and the therapist merely inquired as to how it had come about, with no negative connotation presented.

Hypothesizing was continually refined throughout the first two sessions, both by the therapist as she worked and in conjunction with feedback from the team. At times, alternate hypotheses would be developed regarding the same events. If possible, these hypotheses would be explored until additional information served to confirm one or the other or an entirely new hypothesis. Circular questions were developed to expand on these hypotheses; answers to these led to revisions in the hypotheses. The team was critical in monitoring the progress of the therapist. At times when the therapist appeared to be stuck or when a line of questioning was deemed useful, the team would knock on the door so that timely changes in the direction of the therapy could be implemented. Although it is certainly possible to conduct Milan-style therapy without a team, it is quite beneficial to incorporate this approach into the therapy.

Study Questions

1. What is your opinion about the decision to treat the parents separately from the rest of the family? Do you think this case could have been handled strictly as a family case?
2. Using Table 8.1, try to identify several examples in the sessions of each of the eight types of circular questions.
3. An end-of-session intervention is used in session 2. Try to write down a directive or summary that could be utilized at the end of session 1.
4. Therapy sessions generally involve decisions regarding which themes should be followed at any one time, with numerous opportunities for divergence. Find several instances where alternate themes or openings could have been followed.
5. In the "Conclusions," three alternate techniques are mentioned for dealing with this case—Bowenian, structural, and behavioral. Can you think of other theories and ways that might be used to approach this case?

References

Bateson, G. (1972). *Steps to an ecology of mind.* New York: Ballantine.

Boscolo, L., Cecchin, G., Hoffman, L., & Penn, P. (1987). *Milan systemic family therapy: Conversations in therapy and practice.* New York: Basic Books.

Goldenberg, I., & Goldenberg, H. (1996). *Family therapy: An overview* (4th ed.). Pacific Grove, CA: Brooks/Cole.

Nichols, M. P., & Schwartz, R. C. (1995). *Family therapy: Concepts and methods* (3rd ed.). Boston: Allyn & Bacon.

Prevatt, B. C., & Worchel, F. F. (1993). A design for conducting effective assessments: Substance abuse and sexual abuse as models. *Employee Assistance Quarterly, 9*(2), 47–64.

Selvini-Palazzoli, M., Boscolo, L., Cecchin, G., & Prata, G. (1980). Hypothesizing-circularity-neutrality. *Family Process, 19,* 73–85.

Selvini-Palazzoli, M., Boscolo, L., Cecchin, G., & Prata, G. (1978). *Paradox and counterparadox.* New York: Jason Aronosn.

Tomm, K. (1987a). Interventive interviewing: Part I. Strategizing as a fourth guideline for the therapist. *Family Process, 26,* 3–13.

Tomm, K. (1987b). Interventive interviewing: Part II. Reflective questioning as a means to enable self-healing. *Family Process, 26,* 167–183.

Tomm, K. (1988). Interventive interviewing: Part III. Intending to ask lineal, circular, strategic, or reflective questions? *Family Process, 27,* 1–15.

Watzlawick, P., Jackson, D., & Beavin, J. (1967). *Pragmatics of human communication.* New York: Norton.

Chapter Nine
Strategic Therapy

Jim Keim

Psychotherapists have two great teachers—success and failure. Success is the most inspiring, and failure is the most common. This chapter is based on decades of failure and success in working with oppositional behavior at the Family Therapy Institute of Washington, D.C., founded by Jay Haley and Cloe Madanes in 1974. After a review of strategic therapy, a specific intervention for oppositional behavior in children and adolescents will be detailed. In keeping with family therapy and strategic tradition, this problem will be viewed from both behavioral and communication perspectives.

The summary of strategic therapy that follows describes the model as it is currently taught at the Institute. Most textbooks describe the model as it was practiced in the 1970s, but, as with most other schools of brief and family therapy, the approach has undergone appreciable evolution during the intervening years.

At the heart of this intervention is a new way of viewing oppositional behavior; it is an advance in description rather than a new theory, however. Also included in this chapter is a four-step intervention and a transcript of the therapy involving a 10-year-old child.

The reader may recognize contributions from MRI (Weakland, Watzlawick, and Fisch), structural (Minuchin, Montalvo, and Fishman), and other models of therapy. This does not represent an integration of other models with strategic; the strategic approach has always borrowed from and contributed to other approaches. While significant differences exist in practice among the various models, the process of integration of one another's ideas and language continues unabated.

Theoretical Underpinnings

Strategic therapy is intimately tied to the development of the brief and family therapy field. This approach developed in the 1950s out of the intersection of the work of psychiatrist Milton Erickson and the work of the Bateson Project, consisting of Gregory Bateson, Don Jackson, John Weakland, and Jay Haley. In the 1970s, the centers of strategic therapy were the Mental Research Institute in Palo Alto, California (Weakland, Watzlawick, Fisch, and others) and the Family Therapy Institute of Washington, D.C. (Haley and Madanes). This chapter describes an approach developed by the Haley/Madanes group, otherwise known as the *Washington School*.

The Washington School is characterized by a wide range of practice. No one clinician employs all the concepts and interventions of the model. Clinicians employing this model have the following ideas in common:

- a certain perspective by which problems are viewed
- an approach to intervention
- an emphasis on maintaining a cooperative relationship with clients
- a tradition of and dedication to mentorship, training, and collaboration with other schools and disciplines

Clinical Focus

The simplicity of the description of strategic therapy is purposeful: Therapy theories do not attempt to describe the total reality of people and their problems. Instead, psychotherapy models focus therapists on just three or four variables that, when addressed, are most likely to help people with their problems. Although therapists are informed to a lesser degree by many other variables, the four foci employed by Washington School therapists to define and clarify therapy dynamics are the concepts of *protection, units, sequence,* and *hierarchy.* Jay Haley developed the acronym PUSH as a lecture aid, and it has been adopted by Washington School therapists.

Protection.   The concept of protection describes the theory of motivation with which Washington School therapists begin therapy. The Washington School therapist assumes that there is a loving motivation behind the behavior of the child.[1] It may never be clear what the loving motivation is, but a therapist will treat a youth more benevolently when the concept of protection is assumed. When therapists emphasize loving motivation, they tend to foster loving solutions. When therapists emphasize authoritarian motivations, they tend to foster authoritarian solutions. The concept of protection is not applied to abuse or certain other extreme behaviors.

Protection thus involves the therapist's taking a positive view of human potential. Within common reason, clients are viewed as having the competence to

[1]A child is defined in this chapter as anyone under 30 who has not yet left home.

solve their problems if their social structure will allow. The strategic therapist starts from the position that problems between loved ones tend to be "love gone wrong," that problems often represent efforts of loved ones to help each other. This unfortunate helpfulness is called protection. It is similar to the MRI idea that the problem represents an unfortunate attempted solution (Weakland, Fisch, Watzlawick, and Bodin, 1974).

The concept of protection further helps the therapist by encouraging the investigation of pivotal relationships. Looking for protection in a symptom leads the clinician to think in a benevolent and interactional fashion. It is, however, merely a clinical tool and is not assumed to always exist in reality.

Unit.   Unit refers to the number of parties that therapists tend to include in a description of a problem. The Washington School prefers to view problems as involving the interaction of at least three parties (a triangle). The triangle is the minimum unit required to apply coalition theory (a coalition is a minimum of two ganging up for or against at least one other), but units larger than three become unwieldy in the imagination of the clinician. The unit of three, the triangle, is thus the preferred way of describing interaction. A marital problem is thus not just an issue involving two spouses; the importance of the triangle leads the Washington School therapist to look energetically at the effect of in-laws, kids, lovers, work, and so forth on the couple.

Sequence.   In the strategic tradition, problems and their solutions are described in part as sequences of behavior between people. An interactional sequence may be linear (A led to B, which led to C) or it may be circular (A led to B, which led to C, which led to A). Often, clients describe a problem in individual terms, and the therapist must—in his or her own head, at least—move to an interactional description. Thus, a shoplifting incident by a teen would not only be viewed as an individual act but also as a sequence of events involving peers and parents. Strategic therapy focuses on changing the interactional sequence of the problem. The tendency in the Washington School is to replace a problem sequence involving painful or escalating sequences of behavior between loved ones by a preferred sequence that usually involves soothing between loved ones.

Hierarchy.   The Washington School integrates many of Minuchin's concepts of hierarchy (Minuchin, 1974; Haley, 1976). Although both Milton Erickson and Gregory Bateson demonstrated great sensitivity to issues of social hierarchy, it was not until the work of Minuchin and his colleagues that this concept became a clinically practical tool. Hierarchy is one of the most important guiding concepts for the Washington School.

In relation to problems involving children, the Washington School describes hierarchy as the relationship between perceived roles and functioning in a family. In other words, does a child function as a child in the family or as an adult? Does a parent function in a family as a child? The Washington School does not view any family structure as being inherently dysfunctional. Rather, problems are seen as arising when people are not happy with their own role or with the role of others in the social context. Thus, the fact that a child is functioning as an adult in a household is not by itself a problem. The problem is defined only by unhappiness with the child's assuming that role.

Parents want to feel secure in their role as parents, and children want to feel secure in their role as children. But most child-related problems brought to therapy involve complaints from parents and children that the other party is not fulfilling their "job description."

Problems involving oppositional behavior involve children who want parents to be more parental in a certain sense and parents who want their children to be more childlike. Typically, the parents want the child to be more accepting of their authority and affection; the children, on the other hand, want the parents to be more empathic and effective at making them feel secure. This gap between role and perceived functioning is, in the view of the Washington School, best described and best changed through use of the concept of hierarchy. Instead of the word *hierarchy*, though, we could just say "the difference between various significant others' senses of role, the roles implied by how they treat each other, and the comfort or discomfort with that difference." (Most prefer to use the word *hierarchy*.)

A similar concept describing this interactional comfort or discomfort with the degree of recognition of role from others is contained in the term *preferred view*, which is used by the brief narrative therapists Joe Eron and Tom Lund (Eron and Lund, 1996). It is also described in the 19th-century works of Charles H. Cooley and the early 20th-century work of Mead.

The issue then becomes, "How does a therapist help people to become more secure in their roles?" The following chart is a guide to responsibilities that, when carried out by adults and perceived by children, help each to feel more secure in their roles.

The Hard Side of Hierarchy	*The Soft Side of Hierarchy*
Who makes the rules?	Who soothes whom?
Who defines the punishments?	Who provides reassurance to whom?
Who carries out punishments?	Who protects whom?
Who tells whom what to do?	Who has responsibility for expressing love, affection, and empathy?
Who has final responsibility for making major decisions?	Who is the provider of good things and good times?
Who is responsible for making others feel safe and provided for?	Who usually determines the mood of situations?

Hierarchy is divided into "hard" and "soft" responsibilities (Keim, 1993). To the degree that an adult carries out the responsibilities described in the chart, and to the degree to which there is balance between the hard and soft sides of hierarchy, the benevolent authority and influence of an adult is maximized in relation to a child. To the degree that children inappropriately assume these responsibilities or farm out the responsibilities to peers, the ability of adults to benevolently guide children is minimized, and the children feel insecure about their roles in relation to adults. In addition, to the degree that children are denied age-appropriate assumption of the responsibilities, they tend to grow up too slowly; to the degree that children assume the responsibilities too early, they tend to grow up too quickly.

The therapeutic relationship.   Respectful treatment of clients is a hallmark of strategic therapy. Training workshops in the 1970s and early 1980s tended to focus on techniques specific to the strategic approach and tended not to emphasize issues generic to almost all models of psychotherapy. In the mid-1980s, generic issues in therapy began to be emphasized more, and these included emphasizing the power of a good relationship with clients.

The Washington School clinician treats people as courteously and normally as possible, respects and tries to work within the clients' world views and language, and stays within the clinical contract. Strategic therapy recognizes that the quality of the therapeutic relationship is central to the success of therapy. Third-party qualitative research has found that clients of the Washington School find their therapists to be very warm, likable, and genuinely interested in their clients. However, unlike schools that emphasize transference or other issues in the therapist-client relationship, strategic therapy emphasizes politeness and normal responsiveness. Whether written or verbal, the completed contract in strategic therapy emphasizes that the client is hiring the therapist to do the client's bidding (Haley, 1976).

The acronym FACE summarizes the Washington School's sense of the four necessary ingredients for a quality therapeutic relationship, which this school calls "the cooperative relationship":

1. *Familiarity*—clients need to feel that the therapist is familiar with the client's problem and its social context.
2. *Admiration*—clients should feel that the therapist admires their good qualities.
3. *Competence*—clients should feel that the therapist is competent to help them with their particular problem.
4. *Empathy*—clients should feel that the therapist has empathy for some part of their situation.

Clinical Intervention

Strategic therapy employs two general styles of directives to change the presenting problem—therapist inspired and client inspired. A therapist-inspired directive is one in which the therapist urges clients to try an idea or action that the therapist primarily developed. A client-inspired idea is one in which the therapist urges the clients to try an idea or action that they have primarily developed. Strategic therapy uses a mix of client-inspired and therapist-inspired ideas.

The most common therapist-inspired directives are (1) the coaching of negotiation between significant others and (2) advice based on past experience for what helps a specific problem. The intervention described in this chapter uses mainly advice types of directives (for example, a therapist might mention something to try with a child and might say "this has worked for some people and might be worth experimenting with"). It is important for the Washington School clinician to recognize that advice is a type of directive; it communicates the message "try this."

A Tradition of Training and Discourse

The founders of modern strategic therapy, Jay Haley and John Weakland, spent ten years as members of the Bateson project and a greater number of years studying the work of Milton Erickson. Both Erickson's work and the work of the Bateson Project primarily developed out of conversation, and, despite its numerous publications, strategic therapy remains a model that is best taught through oral tradition, mentorship, and training with one-way mirrors. Workshops given by prominent Washington School clinicians do not teach the whole model but offer people ideas that they can integrate into their own frameworks. Washington School therapists usually spend two years in once-a-week training in order to develop an intuitive sense of how to use the approach and to truly develop a good ability to maintain a strong therapeutic relationship with the client.

A Specific Intervention: Oppositional Behavior in Children

The concepts of protection, unit, sequence, and hierarchy are demonstrated in the following intervention for oppositional behavior. Before describing the intervention, however, it would be helpful to review the pros and cons of labels such as "oppositional." For strategic therapists, labels are helpful only to the degree that they lead the clinician to specific therapeutic interventions and to the degree that the labels do not damage clients. Furthermore, labels are viewed in the strategic tradition as pragmatic constructions and not as real entities. "Oppositional behavior" fits the preceding criteria for the following reasons:

- When carefully defined, the term leads the clinician to specific interventions such as the one described in this chapter.
- The label does not disempower clients by mystifying the behavior; the term *oppositional* is clear, everyday English.
- The term does not suggest that the problem is outside the expertise of the average parent and thus passes the "fence test." The fence test suggests that a client should, when talking with a neighbor across the backyard fence, be able to use the term and then receive advice or consolation rather than a confused look.
- The strategic therapist thinks of this term as a pragmatic construction rather than a real entity.

Oppositional behavior.   The term *oppositional* has been used to describe a youth with a strong and unusual tendency to confront, provoke, and challenge authority figures (see APA, 1994). Children and adolescents go through stages characterized by increased resistance to adult authority, but the term is applied to behavior that is outside the norm for the youth's age group.

The definition of oppositional behavior that follows exists primarily for one reason: to inform therapists as to when the following intervention should be used. The definition may or may not be helpful to those whose goal is to achieve a broader understanding of such behavior.

Defining the problem in terms of sequence and unit.   The Washington School therapist uses the term *oppositional* to describe a child who is *process-oriented, win-lose oriented,* and *high-hierarchy.*

Process orientation describes a person who tends to be significantly more focused on the process of confrontation than on the outcome. When a process-oriented person is win-lose oriented (that is, someone who tends to approach difficult conversations with an authority figure with the perception that one party must win and the other must lose), the process-oriented person's sense is that "winning" is accomplished by determining the process of the confrontation. Outcome orientation describes a person who is more focused on the outcome of confrontations. Differences in communication focus are particularly painful when the child is focused on winning by determining the process of the confrontation and the adult is focused on winning by determining the outcome of the confrontation.

The sequence of the oppositional confrontation is as follows. During the confrontation, the child

1. approaches the discussion as a win-lose argument.
2. focuses on winning by determining the process of the confrontation, which is for the child largely a matter of determining the following three issues:
   a. Who determines the timing of the confrontation?
   b. Who determines the topic and direction of the confrontation?
   c. Who determines the mood of the confrontation?

During the confrontation with the oppositional child,

3. the adult tries to win by determining the outcome of the argument.
4. the adult gets his or her "buttons pushed."
5. third parties are often openly triangulated into the arguments.

At the point that third parties are actively triangulated into the confrontation, the emotional pain of the confrontation reaches new heights. Thus, both the adult and the child reach the point in the discussion where it becomes a win-lose conversation. The child tries to win by determining process. The adult tries to win by determining outcome. And both get very frustrated. Process orientation has thus been specifically characterized by a focus on the the three preceding confrontation-related issues of who determines the timing, the topic and direction of discussion, and the mood of the confrontation.

Defining the problem in terms of hierarchy.   In order for a child to be considered oppositional, the youth must be process oriented (the sequence) and must be experiencing role confusion. The role confusion is that the child is inappropriately trying to assume adultlike levels of influence (as defined in the chart describing the hard and soft side of hierarchy). Usually, the parents complain that the child is attempting in inappropriate ways to determine the following hard-side issues:

- Who makes the rules?
- Who defines the punishments?
- Who carries out punishments?
- Who tells whom what to do?
- Who has final responsibility for making major decisions?

It is important to note that these behaviors focus on the hard side of hierarchy. In other words, *oppositional behavior focuses on the hard side of hierarchy. When the adult in the system joins the child in being overfocused on the hard side of hierarchy, the oppositional interaction escalates markedly and becomes particularly painful for all involved.* When the adult buys into the myth that power is mainly about who determines the hard side of hierarchy, we have an example of what Bateson referred to as the danger of the "myth" of power (Haley, 1980).

Expected conversations.   One of the generic aspects of family therapy is the importance placed on helping families talk to each other about important topics. Strategic therapy emphasizes the idea that therapy often involves those conversations that should be happening but that, for one reason or another, are not. From this perspective, we pay attention not only to the escalation in oppositional behavior but also to the conversations that are not taking place. In step 4 of the following intervention, the focus moves beyond avoiding unhelpful arguments to successfully discussing difficult topics.

A four-step intervention.   The steps that follow are designed for the average case involving oppositional behavior that presents at the Family Therapy Institute. The characteristics of such cases are generally as follows:

- Oppositional cases usually arrive at the Institute as chronic problems, not as crises, and the motivation and energy levels of the parents tend to be rather low.
- The parents are prone to be somewhat suspicious of the philosophy of therapists in general, as they tend to view therapy as anti-parent.
- By the time the clients have sought therapy, the parents often state that, though they still love the child, they do not presently like the child very much.

The order of the steps of the intervention may change if the preceding conditions are not present. The steps are as follows:

1. *Creating an empowering definition of the problem with the parents.* A crucial part of this first step is to deal with blame issues. The therapist reviews the concepts of process and outcome orientation with the parents. The clinician helps parents to understand differences in adults' and children's perceptions of what is happening during arguments.

2. *Coaching the parents to employ this new information on the perception of argument by resisting the child's attempts to draw them into confrontations.* During this second step, attempts are made to strengthen the parents' marriage or connections with adult friends. One goal of this stage is to have the parents determine their own mood rather than allowing the child to determine their mood. The second step also begins interventions directed at increasing the amount of parent-inspired intimacy with the child in question.

3. *Creating a new system of positive and negative consequences.* The new system is sensitive to the process orientation of the child. Included in this step are

- emphasizing to parents that parent-inspired intimacy with the child is the most important source of parental authority
- setting limits, rules, and consequences and putting them down on paper for the children to see
- timing of "tagging" and giving consequences
- nonconfrontational punishments
- the two-tier system of consequences
- not pushing parents too hard initially in setting limits
- making sure that there are regular, scheduled times for positive parent-child interaction regardless of the child's behavior
- rewards as shaping tools

4. *Moving the parents from merely focusing on maintaining a loving attitude themselves to actively attempting to change the child's mood from a negative to a positive state.* Whether or not the parent succeeds is not as important as whether the parent *tries* to lovingly soothe the child. The crucial part of this stage is for the parents to show that they can handle having the expected conversations, that is, those discussions that a family expects to have but that never seem to be able to take place. These conversations are frequently about issues that are painful for the family. Severe oppositional behavior is significantly helped by parents' demonstrations that they can handle the most difficult conversations in a soothing way.

The Case: Working with an Oppositional Child and Her Family

This interview is an example of step 4 of the intervention—soothing the child and having an expected conversation. The therapy started two months earlier and is now in the seventh interview. Five years before the start of therapy, the childless parents adopted four siblings simultaneously, and the oldest, Tara, has decided to leave home. Tara is 17, Alice is 10, Sylvester is 9, and Melissa is 7. Before adoption, the children experienced multiple and unstable caretakers, severe abuse, and lived at times on the street. Tara has a different father than the younger three children. Though the adoption is open, there is not much contact with the biologically related relatives.

The family was referred for therapy after Tara was hospitalized for drug abuse. The hospital where Tara was placed referred the family in preparation for Tara's return home. However, Tara decided that she did not want to return to the home of her adopted parents but instead wanted to move to a different state to live with her late stepfather's parents (the parents of the biological father of the younger three children). After Tara announced that she was leaving home, Alice went from being a moderately oppositional child to acting out in severe ways. Alice's issues are further complicated by attachment disorder.

The parents have progressed through the first three steps of this intervention. They are no longer allowing Alice to inappropriately determine the process of confrontations. They have a new and workable system of positive and negative consequences. And they have divided negative consequences into two categories: cooperative and noncooperative. The noncooperative punishments are used only as backup for the cooperative punishments. The first three steps helped the parents regain their self-confidence, and they are ready to move on to the last stage of this intervention.

During step four of this intervention, the adults not only avoid the unhelpful arguments and confrontations that characterize oppositional behavior; their goal is to also soothe the child in part by having the expected conversations. The goal of this session is for the parents to soothe Alice by having an important expected conversation with her about the pain that she is experiencing over her older sister Tara's departure from the home. The parents have been coached for two months, usually without any children present, on how to approach Alice. They have been told that oppositional behavior tends to decrease in this final step when the child can be soothed to the point that she can tell her parents her greatest pains and when the parents can handle the discussion of these painful issues in an empathic and still soothing manner.

The session started with the therapist's meeting alone with the parents. The therapist reviewed the goal of the session, talking about Alice's pain over her sister's departure. Alice is then brought in, and her father states that we would like to talk to Alice about how she feels about Tara's departure. Immediately, Alice explodes.

Therapist: Would you like . . .
Alice: Shut up!!!!
Therapist: . . . to sit down in between your parents?
Alice: No!!! Get off!!! No! I want to see her. I don't want to be with her! I
    don't want to be with you either! 'Cause you ruin my life! Get off of me!
Dad: No, come here. Come here.
Alice: No!

Alice is pained by her sister's decision to leave home. She wants that pain to be soothed. On the other hand, Alice is afraid to accept soothing. She wants to be what in her view is adult, and nothing challenges that adult identity more than being soothed by adults. Alice leaves the room and stays in the hallway, listening to the conversation. The adults begin talking to each other about the therapist's school visit when Alice steps back into the room and immediately interrupts.

Alice: Why do I need to be in here???!!!!
Alice: You're not talking to me!
Therapist: And I also think . . .
Alice: You're talking about me!

When a strategic therapist is conducting an interview with a child, the child is often allowed to determine the topic and direction of communication. In the average family interview, however, normal rules of politeness hold, and the child is not allowed to inappropriately interrupt adults. If the child interrupts in appropriate ways, the interruption is allowed.

Alice: Why do I have to be in here? You're not talking to me, you're talking about me!?
Therapist: 'Cause I explained . . .
Dad: It's about you and . . .
Therapist: Yeah.
Alice: No, I don't!
Therapist: The people I spoke to were, were having to . . .
Alice: No, I don't!
Therapist: . . . speak to the counselor and the principal at the school. So I had to do a second trip.
Mom: Yeah?
Therapist: Well, anyway, let's talk about the, the things that include Alice now.
Mom: Mmmm.
Therapist: That's a really nice outfit. Is that from one of those catalogs? [pause]
Mom: I think it's from somebody who gave us a [pause].
Therapist: It's a pretty outfit.
Mom: I think it was a gift.
Therapist: Um-hm. I love children's clothes.
Mom: Yeah. Yeah. They're really fun.
Dad: So we were talking a bit about [pause] before, but we thought we should talk with you while you're here. And, um, you've told us a number of times, and it's, it's clear from what you've said that you're upset a little bit because Tara's leaving now and she won't be in the family, at least at home. And, um, I thought you might want to say something about how you feel. [pause]
Mom: Alice gave me a wonderful massage last night.
Therapist: Did she?

Mom: Yeah. She wanted me to come into her bed, and I went into her bed, and she's, just a really nice massage. She's very good at that.

Alice: Next time I'll be sure to kill you.

Therapist, Dad, Mom: Mmmm

Mom: I know she's feeling mad.

Dad: I, I think we know that you don't mean those things you say them.

Alice: Phahhhhhhh!

Dad: We know that you're upset.

Therapist: You know, and . . . Tara will always be in the family, but you know, she's at the age where she can, um, you know, where she's going to be making her own decisions and going on with her life and career.

Mom: Yeah, Tara—when Tara first came to us, she'd been with her mom for ten years. Ten long years. And so her mom is, basically, that's her mom. You guys . . .

Dad: In her mind, that's her mom for life . . .

Mom: Even after she's come to us.

Dad: No matter what.

Therapist: Because at that age, especially, when you're 10, the person that you look at as, as your mom is the person you've considered your mom.

Dad: Um-hm.

Alice: Well, I still consider her my mom, my old mom, but you guys just came and adopted us and now you're treating us like we're nothing!

Dad: I hope not. You're very special.

Alice: And you call people selfish!

Therapist: But, but you can understand . . .

Alice: And you lie!!

Therapist: . . . how, when, um, how it's very upsetting for them when Tara's . . .

Dad: Yeah.

Alice: No! Why don't you listen to me?!!

Dad: Well, I think he was, don't you?

Alice: No, no! I am sick of Mom calling me selfish because that is not true.

Mom: You're . . .

Alice: And I'm sick . . . no! I'm sick of you calling me selfish, I'm sick of you lying, 'cause I know when you're lying, 'cause you're cheeks turn bright pink.

Dad: Well, we're pretty concerned about what you read.

Alice: I don't care. I'm sick of reading all the books you want me to read and doing all the stuff you want me to do.

Therapist: Why don't you let her know that, that, you know, just remind her that, that, um . . .

Alice: And every time we go out somewhere . . .

Therapist: . . . that the decision's up to Tara, that you've asked her to come back, but Tara's going to decide . . .

Alice: . . . every time we go out somewhere, if I haven't been behaving how you want me to, you don't let me eat . . .

Therapist: . . . and she'll always, she'll always be around and, um . . .

Alice: . . . starve me or make me eat bad food, so disgusting.

Therapist: . . . and, um . . .

Alice: I'm talking!

Therapist: . . . what, um, and it's okay for her to feel, you know, strange about it.

Mom: Yeah, I think it would be . . .

Dad: Yeah, that's, that's something that might be helpful for you to know, Alice. That sometimes kids do feel bad about something, like you feel bad about Tara leaving, but we all have to accept it; eventually, Tara gets old enough to make those choices for herself, and we know you feel bad . . .

Alice: [sweet singsong voice to therapist] Here, Jim!

>•◀

Therapist: . . . behave?

Alice: Yes!

Therapist: So, she's she's even . . .

Dad: Even without toe shoes, she can stand on the tip of her toes.

Therapist: That's incredible.

Mom: Yeah.

Therapist: That's incredible.

Dad: Very well coordinated. And lately she's learning domestics routines that she can do a back walkover, very gracefully.

Alice: Back walkover, front, front, back flip . . .

Dad: Front flip . . .

Therapist: Um-hm.

Alice: Splits. I can do anything I want to do.

Dad: Cartwheel . . .

Alice: Right now, I don't want to do anything.

Therapist: Um-hm. Did, did you know the dance that they were talking about? Or the . . .

Mom: I think it was a line dance or was it the thing from the western . . .

Therapist: A line dance, that thing . . .

Dad: And we went to sort of a western dinner at the elementary school and they were teaching line dancing.

Mom: Yeah, yeah.

Dad: But Alice went up and volunteered to be the, um, partner for the guy who, who was teaching it.

Therapist: Um-hm.

Dad: And he'd demonstrated the steps . . .

Alice: That's Mom's!!

Dad: They would just, um, she would do it right with him.

Alice: That's Mom's!

Therapist: Um-hm.

Alice: This is Mom's!!!

Mom: And she's very gifted . . .

Alice: Mom's!!!

Mom: Very loving. She can be extremely loving sometimes and real caring.

Therapist: And tell, tell her how much, how, um, how much you like that.

Alice: Say anything and I'll kill you!

Mom: See, it makes me feel really good when she's really loving, 'cause it just shows me that she can, she can . . .

Alice: Hold on, I'm putting down every word of this!

Mom: . . . she can have a good life when she's like that.

Dad: Yeah. And it shows that they have the capacity for very positive feelings.

Mom: Yeah.

Dad: Yeah. I think when somebody has that ability that, even though it gets clouded by bad feelings sometimes, that they can always go back to the good feelings.

Therapist: Um-hm.

Mom: Yeah. And it's, it's . . .

Dad: We're very lucky.

Mom: She's very beautiful when she's like that. When she's, when she's very giving, her whole being is like really radiant, and it's really beautiful.

Therapist: Um-hm.

Mom: And everybody wants to be with her.

Therapist: Um-hm.

Mom: It's like . . .

Dad: Tara has that trait, too. She's just, she can be just a very, very good friend.

Therapist: Um-hm. [pause] What do you miss most about Tara? [pause] Alice, what do you miss most about Tara?

Mom: Oh, let's see. I guess I miss those traits, those warm traits, you know, those traits where she's . . .

Alice: I miss Tara because you take her away. No. You want to hear why I'm saddest? Because you take everything that's important to me away. Tara's important to me and you just take her away from me.

Dad: And you feel a great deal of loss.

Alice: And you take ballet away from me. You take everything away!

Mom: Well, I really wish Tara would come home. I mean . . .

Alice: Sure you do! That's why you sent her away!

Mom: I've asked her . . .

Alice: Think!!!

Therapist: It's actually the doctor that did it.

Alice: Actually, Mom wanted to put her in there.

Dad: Tara chose it. That was Tara that came up with the idea . . .

Therapist: And it was Tara . . .

Dad: . . . that, that she wanted to be with family, but she felt it was very difficult to be in this family right now because of the way that it was before . . .

Alice: Yeah, that's what I think . . .

Dad: . . . and with the children before and now for Tara, it's hard to give up being the Mom kind of a person because she wants to be a child again.

Therapist: Um-hm.

Dad: So she only gets another year or two to be a child.

Therapist: People get to be teenagers, they want to go on and do things.

>•◄

Alice: Here you go, Dad, this is for you.

Mom: Um, her caring . . .

Alice: That's Chelsy!

Dad: Um-hm.

Alice: Don't put that away! Mommy, you like Chelsy?

Mom: Oh, yeah, there's a smile on Chelsy?

Alice: [giggles]

Mom: That's sweet. I'm thinking . . .

Alice: Tear her eyes off!

Mom: Well, she's very sweet. You know, she can be really a good person. She can . . . you know, what else I'm thinking, in really hard situations, situations where everybody else is just, just doesn't quite know what to do about how to organize, or how to do this or that, Tara just right away knows what to do.

>•◄

Mom: I wish we could just tell you that. I wish I could hug you right now.

Dad: I wish you could believe it!

Alice: Why don't you let me eat anything, why do you keep consequences for everything because . . .

Dad: Come tell us how you feel about consequences.

Alice: Well, you won't change it.

Dad: Well, just tell us how you feel.

Mom: Consequences . . .

Alice: No.

Mom: But we do care.

Therapist: And that's what parents talk about, talk about ballet and, and at what point . . .

Alice: I'm not interested in it anymore.

Therapist: You know, things can . . . can . . . things will settle down in your lives and when everything's back on track . . .

Alice: I'll tell you how I feel about consequences, 'cause it's the only time you'll listen to me.

Dad: Come on.

Alice: No.

Mom: Well, tell us, yeah. Tell us how you feel about consequences.

Alice: It's not fair to us about how, that, you . . . well, the reason we, we scream at you and stuff and call you names is because you don't listen to us and I've tried to tell you about this before, but you don't listen. And neither do you. You don't listen to me.

Dad: Have we ever explained why there are consequences?

Alice: Yeah!

Dad: Do . . .

Alice: To try and make us learn, but that, that's better. But instead of consequences, you said you'd use consequences instead of spanking.

Dad: Um-hm.

Therapist: And, and what is it that you'd like your, your parents—ask her what, what she'd like you to hear. What is it that you hear, don't hear, or don't understand?

Dad: I know that you said sometimes we don't listen. What is it you want to get us to understand?

Alice: I want to get you to understand that I don't, I don't like some of the stuff you guys do.

Dad: Um-hm.

Alice: You make consequences and, and then we have to stay in and we don't get our freedom. We have to go to school all day, we have to come home and do jobs and homework, that we do jobs every day.

Dad: Um-hm.

Alice: Just like you do. But we come home and we have consequences that we've done from like the day before.

Dad: Um-hm.

Alice: Or like refusing to go to bed . . .

Dad: Um-hm.

Alice: . . . 'cause everybody else gets to stays up, stay up, and you guys don't listen.

Dad: Do we not listen to everything or just some things?

Alice: You don't listen, you say, "Oh, take a five-minute time-out." I take it and then I start talking to you, and you guys, you just ignore me.

Dad: And there's some important things that you want us to hear that we haven't heard?

Alice: No.

Dad: So, we've . . .

Alice: 'Cause I'm not telling you anything.

Therapist: Is there anything—ask her if there's anything, if there's anything, 'cause, you know, sometimes conversations don't happen just 'cause it's not the right time or the right place and tell her, this is a right time and a right place.

Dad: That's true. This is, when we come here, this is a good time to talk about what's important. Sometimes, I think, what Jim is, is, uh, reminding me of . . .

Alice: You know what *she* does?

Dad: . . . is that there are inappropriate times . . .

Alice: You know what she does? When you're not home . . .

Dad: . . . and when you take a time-out or when you're interrupting somebody, that's a time that's usually, we don't listen because it's not appropriate.

Alice: I wasn't interrupting you most of the times you ignore me.

Therapist: But now, now we're talking about things—ask her to tell you, talk about . . .

Mom: What is it that bothers you, 'cause we want to hear it, honey.

Therapist: Ask here what it is that, that she was just starting to talk about.

Mom: Oh yeah.

Alice: Lying!

Mom: What were you going to tell me, what, what, what do I do when Dad's not there?

Alice: You lie!

Mom: So like about the book today, you mean?

Alice: Yeah! And you lie to me other times about Santa Claus and the stupid old Easter Bunny.

Mom: I lie about that?

Alice: Yeah!

Dad: How about . . . that's an interesting . . .

Alice: The Easter Bunny's not true. And I know the tooth fairy's not true, because I'm . . . you . . . to when he lost his tooth . . .

Dad: But do you think other kids should have that? Do you think other kids should have that chance to believe in Santa Claus when they're little?

Alice: Yeah.

Dad: So, eventually, though, we have to tell them.

Mom: I might still really believe in Santa Claus and the tooth fairy. I don't know, you know.

Dad: It's a nice thing for kids, but when they get older, then they find out that it was a game that the parents play to help the kids feel good.

Alice: You lie. You call people names like selfish.

Mom: That really bothered you honey, didn't it? That really bothered you.

Alice: I'm not selfish, Mom.

Mom: I didn't . . .

Dad: I don't think you're self . . . you're not a selfish person.

Mom: You know what I think what happened with that one was that we had a misunderstanding of what the word "selfish" meant.

Alice: You shouldn't call people selfish even if it means something . . .

➤●◄

Alice: Tara . . .

Mom: I know, I know you are honey, but what I think you're thinking about is different.

Dad: Tell us, tell us what you'd like to happen if, if you had, if you could choose what would happen. And Tara wasn't making a choice for herself and we didn't have any choices. What would you choose? What would you choose with Tara?

Alice: I don't know.

Dad: Would you like to her to stay forever and ever . . .

Alice: No.

Dad: . . . and be with us always?

Therapist: Sounds nice, but . . .

Dad: She has to have everybody all the time. Would you like her to stay a little bit longer before she goes away? Would you like to be able to talk to her more?

◗◀

Therapist: Plus the kids . . . you see the parents like having them around, but it's the kids, they want to go off and explore and it's eventually, they, they want to go off on their own.

Dad: They want to be on their own.

Therapist: And it's very hard on the parents and it's very hard on the kids.

Dad: It's especially hard on our kids 'cause they've been so close all their life. There are a lot of different things and we'd like for you to be able to do a lot of different things.

Alice: Are you seeing any of the other kids today? 'Cause if you're not, I have something to say. You never see me.

Therapist: I should, I should probably spend more time with you.

Dad: Yeah. That would be nice. [pause] Jim wanted to help Mom and Dad to figure out how we can best help Tara, and so he spent a lot of time . . .

Alice: See, you're always spending time on Tara; that's another problem.

Dad: Families are like that, sometimes one person has a problem, we'll spend all of our time . . .

Alice: I have problems!

Therapist/Dad: [mumble]

Alice: And do you spend time with me?!

Therapist: And I think that's maybe one thing that would be nice to change is, that, that we ought to spend time together, not because someone's having a, a problem.

Dad: Um-hm.

Therapist: And I think it's just, I mean, I think all families have to struggle with this. That, maybe, like, the best reasons to spend time together, or time is not because there's a problem but for fun and because they're doing well.

Dad: I think we do that . . .

Alice: Oh!

Dad: . . . but we get interrupted by problems, too. We could increase it. We make sure to go out once a week and do something.

Therapist: I just had . . .

Alice: What did we do this week?

Therapist: If . . .

Alice: What did we do last week?

Therapist: If, if Alice is doing well, see, Alice, I don't mean to interrupt you, but see what you think of this. If Alice is . . .

Alice: No, no, I want them to answer me. What did we do last week? What was fun?

Therapist: Well, she was talking first, so let's, let's, let's address . . .

Alice: Who?

Therapist: You. You were talking first, so let's finish your question.

Alice: What did we do that was fun last week?

Dad: Fun for me?

Mom: We went out with Granddad. Uh . . .

Alice: That wasn't last week, that was the week before.

Dad: Well, we haven't planned our weekend yet.

Alice: No, the week.

Dad: What would you like to do? What are fun things for you?

Alice: I thought we were going to dinner?!

Dad: So going, so do you like going out to dinner?

Alice: Yeah.

Dad: Uh-huh. It is fun. I like that.

Alice: And I hate to admit it.

Conclusions

This intervention describes the soothing of a confused and angry child. Using the pragmatic concepts of the hard and soft side of hierarchy and of the sequence of behavior (process versus outcome orientation), the therapist works with the clients to bring the child back to an emotional state where she feels safe in discussing her problems. In some ways, this is very traditional family therapy that seeks to remove barriers that prevent important discussions.

Code of Ethics

The following is a list of several ethical issues that are relevant in working with clients. This code of ethics provides important guidelines for all therapists but especially for those therapists working from a strategic approach.

1. The first rule of strategic therapy is an adoption of the age-old medical maxim, "Do no harm." Simply stated, therapy should not hurt the clients, society, or therapists. One guideline recommended by Haley is that a therapist should only use therapeutic procedures that the therapist is willing to experience or have his or her children experience. No therapist may ask a client to undertake any harmful, immoral, or illegal action, even as a paradoxical inter-

vention (Haley, 1980). Part of not doing harm is the responsibility to avoid giving damaging diagnostic labels.

2. The therapist must practice in a competent manner and must accept responsibility for creating change in therapy. Not accepting responsibility for change results in blaming clients for failure in therapy. Blaming the clients results in patronizing treatment of clients, decreased effort on the part of the therapist, and perpetuation of blame cycles that are part of the pathology of the client's social context.

3. Therapists must assume that they wield tremendous influence. Clients are safest when therapists assume they yield too much rather than too little influence. The therapists must take responsibility for the intended and unintended effects of their direct and indirect influence on clients and the client's social system. A therapist is not the same as a classroom lecturer whose audience is relatively free to accept or reject his teachings. A client in therapy should be considered to be in an extraordinarily vulnerable position, much like that of a hypnotic subject in a trance, and should not be taken advantage of.

4. Therapy must be respectful of the clients. Because of their influence, therapists are in a uniquely powerful position to denigrate clients and therefore must be all the more sensitive. Live supervision is especially helpful in training therapists to notice their inadvertent insults.

5. Therapists should have a minimalist view of changing clients' world views; this ensures maximum respect of the world view of the client. In successful therapy, the therapist instigates a change in the clients' world views. However, attempts to change a client's world view should be limited to the presenting problem that the therapist has contracted to change. Consciousness raising, here defined as influencing a client for a purpose not directly related to solving the presenting problem, must not be confused with therapy. For example, the Nazi ideology of a Mr. Smith would have to be addressed when the presenting problem is the violence of the son. However, the Nazi ideology would not necessarily be addressed if Mr. Smith came to therapy for help in dealing with the death of his 80-year-old mother.

A minimalist view of changing clients is a consequence of recognizing that the therapist's construction of reality is not in general more valid than that of the clients (Haley, 1973; Watzlawick, 1984). For example, it is helpful for a therapist to view problems in terms of hierarchy and sequence; however, it could be a terrible idea for clients to view problems in these terms. Different constructs of reality can be simultaneously valid depending on the different roles of the parties involved (Watzlawick, 1984).

6. Therapists must maintain an awareness of the advantages and disadvantages of the use of overt versus indirect directives. With an overt directive, the therapist's influence is clearly identifiable to the clients. Dependence on the therapist is more likely to occur with the use of overt directives, as sometimes clients credit the therapist instead of themselves as being responsible for change. However, the intent and influence of direct directives is open to review by the clients and is thus less likely to lead to abuse. With an indirect directive, the therapist's influence is not clearly identifiable and may even be invisible to

the client. A therapist may not be consciously aware of indirect directives given to clients. The client receiving the indirect directive is more vulnerable to bad interventions because the directive is not as easily reviewed. The advantage of indirect directives is that the clients' feelings of self-determination and self-confidence tend to be increased more by indirect than by overt directives. Clients internalize more quickly and take more credit for change resulting from indirect than overt directives. Thus, both overt and indirect directives have their advantages and disadvantages that must be monitored in each case. In general, indirect interventions require more clinical skill.

7. Common sense is as important as theory when determining what might harm clients. Therapists should trust their gut feelings about the appropriateness of interventions and discuss uneasiness with a supervisor before proceeding.

8. The therapist is responsible for using the most dignified, least intrusive intervention that will work within a reasonable time frame.

9. Therapy must not be oriented toward blame, nor should it collude in irresponsible or dangerous behavior or in the forfeiture of individual responsibility.

Study Questions

1. What is the importance of hierarchy in working with parents and children from the Washington School's perspective?
2. What is your response to the Washington School's emphasis on assuming that there is a "loving motivation behind the behavior of the child"?
3. How does the therapist work with Alice's oppositional behavior in the case example?
4. How does the therapist maintain a more process-oriented position with Alice? Identify an example in the case verbatim.
5. The Washington School of Strategic Therapy takes a minimalist position concerning client change. Take a position on this view, providing support for your stance.

References

American Psychiatric Association. (1994). *Diagnostic and statistical manual of mental disorders* (4th ed.). Washington DC: Author.

Eron, J. B., & Lund, T. W. (1996). *Narrative solutions in brief therapy.* New York: Guilford Press.

Haley, J. (1973). *Uncommon therapy.* New York: Norton.

Haley, J. (1976). *Problem-Solving Therapy.* San Francisco: Jossey-Bass.

Haley, J. (1980). *Leaving home: The therapy of disturbed young people.* New York: McGraw-Hill.

Jackson, D. (1976). The myth of normality. *Medical Opinion and Review, 3,* 28–33.

Keim, I., Lentine, G., Keim, J., Madanes, C. (1990). No more John Wayne: Strategies for changing the past. In C. Madanes (Ed.), *Sex, love, and violence: Strategies for transformation* (pp. 218–247). New York: Norton.

Keim, J. (1993). *The Family Therapy Institute training handbook.* Unpublished manuscript.

Madanes, C. (1990). *Sex, love, and violence: Strategies for transformation.* New York: Norton.

Minuchin, S. (1974). *Families and family therapy.* Cambridge, MA: Harvard University Press.

Watzlawick, P. (1984). *The invented reality.* New York: Norton.

Weakland, J., Fisch, R., Watzlawick, P., & Bodin, A. (1974). Brief therapy: Focused problem resolution. *Family Process, 13,* 141–168.

Chapter Ten

Solution-Focused Brief Therapy

Herb Klar and Insoo Kim Berg

Solution-focused brief therapy was developed over the past 25 years by a team of therapists led by Steve de Shazer and Insoo Kim Berg at the Brief Family Therapy Center (BFTC) in Milwaukee (de Shazer, Berg, Lipchik, Nunnally, Molnar, Gingerich, and Weiner-Davis, 1986). Solution-focused brief therapy is similar to other brief therapy models in that it focuses on the client's goals and uses homework assignments to extend the impact of sessions into the client's real life. It differs from traditional psychotherapy and from other brief therapy approaches in the way it conceptualizes therapeutic processes and implements them (Berg and De Jong, 1996; de Shazer et al., 1986).

Theoretical Underpinnings

Most therapists assume quite logically that in order for problems to be solved, they must first be analyzed and understood. Thus, a great deal of time and energy is spent assessing the problems clients bring to therapy in an effort to correct them. The therapist tries to understand what the client is doing wrong in as detailed a way as possible and develops hypotheses about what is wrong with the client or his or her family system. Problems are seen as symptomatic of underlying deficits and may be analyzed for the purpose they serve for the individual client or the family system. Based on this assessment, the therapist decides what the treatment of choice is and then suggests to the client the course of actions to be taken.

Solution-focused brief therapy regards solution building as a distinctly different process from problem solving. It assumes that it is not necessary to know the details of the problems that clients bring to therapy. It is more important to understand from the clients what their criteria for termination of therapy might be—what, in other words, needs to be different enough than when therapy began that they can confidently end therapy sessions (Berg and De Jong, 1996; de Shazer et al., 1986).

Once the therapist and the client develop a mutual understanding of what the client wants in the future, their focus turns to constructing a desirable outcome based on identifying exceptions. Solution-focused brief therapy defines these exceptions as times when some aspects of the client's life are going as the client would want (de Shazer, 1986). It assumes that all problematic situations, even ones as chronic or serious as drug and alcohol abuse (Berg and Miller, 1994), feature times when the problem could have occurred but did not. Clarifying what the client is doing different at those times and building on those differences toward the outcome the client wishes from therapy is the core of solution-focused therapy (Berg, 1994; de Shazer, 1988; de Shazer et al., 1986).

The Influence of Social Constructionism

Social constructionist maintains that people define and create their sense of what is real through interaction and conversation with others, a form of negotiation carried out within the context of language. This notion is immediately relevant to psychotherapy since, as a "talking cure," it primarily takes place within the context of language (de Shazer and Berg, 1992).

All therapists, regardless of their approach, are selective in their choice of what they ask about and what they ignore, depending on the underlying assumptions they hold about what is useful and helpful for their clients to talk about. Far from serving the "objective" purpose of "merely" gathering data, the questions therapists actually raise with clients influence and change clients' thinking about themselves (Berg and De Jong, 1996; De Jong and Miller, 1995) and invite them, in fact, to consider and highlight different versions of themselves.

Solution-focused brief therapy does not aspire to learn or confront the "truth." It is much more interested in asking questions that invite descriptions of what clients want for themselves in the richest, most detailed, and most varied ways possible. In asking about exceptions to problems and the actions clients may have taken to achieve them or in inquiring about the feasible step clients might take from their own experience and knowledge of themselves to progress to their own goals, the solution-focused therapist invites clients to think about and define themselves differently. What emerges, often tentatively at first, is a more competent or worthy side of the client—one previously unnoticed by the client because of overriding frustration with the problem.

The first and subsequent solution-focused therapy sessions follow lines of questioning that invite clients to describe the outcomes they wish to see and to identify and amplify the actions they take to move toward their definition of a successful completion of therapy.

Organization of the First Session

The first session in solution-focused brief therapy includes all or some of the following but not necessarily in the sequence presented: socializing, goal negotiation, miracle questions, exceptions to the problem, scaling questions, and the consultation break and intervention message (Klar and Coleman, 1995; Berg, 1994; de Shazer, 1988).

Socializing

All therapy, regardless of model, invariably begins with a phase of socializing and orienting clients to what is to come, described as *joining* by structural family therapists. Most approaches view this initial phase as a prelude to therapy—a kind of warm-up and a time for the therapist to begin developing hunches about the client's problems and their causes.

Since solution-focused brief therapy is interested in building on what is working for the client, the initial moments of first meetings are oriented to identifying issues the therapist and the client agree are going well for the client. Initial questions are directed at areas in which clients are successful or from which they draw satisfaction or esteem. These might include their job, academic interests, hobbies, special talents, past achievements, or ambitions for the future (Berg, 1994; Lipchik and de Shazer, 1986).

Constructing Goals

Clients generally begin therapy with much more knowledge about their problems and what they do not want their lives to be than about their goals and the ways they would like their lives to be different. The process of building well-formed goals might begin by simply asking the client, "In what ways do things need to begin to change in your life so you know that coming to talk to me has been useful?"

Goals are best described in concrete, specific, first-step, behavioral, self-referenced, and interactional ways because these kinds of descriptions help both the client and the therapist to identify progress as it occurs and to agree when therapy is completed (De Jong and Miller, 1995; Klar and Coleman, 1995; Berg, 1994).

Miracle Question

The miracle question way be used to help the client imagine what life would be like without the problem. Asking it in the following way draws a particularly rich response: "Suppose (pause) after we talk today, you go home (pause) and sometime in the evening you go to bed (pause) and the whole house is very quiet. And in the middle of the night (pause) while you are sleeping, a miracle happens and the problem that brought you here today is solved. (pause) But because this happens while you are sleeping, you won't know that the miracle happened until you awake tomorrow morning. So when you wake up, what will make you wonder, 'Maybe there was a miracle last night and the problem was solved'? What will tell you this happened?" Thinking about solutions requires a shift in time frame and focus from a preoccupation with the problem to a consideration of how the client might want life to be. The therapist's follow-up questioning should be detailed because it is crucial for the client to describe the "miracle" in as much detail as possible. The miracle question and the discussion that ensues elicits aspirations, hopes, and dreams. Contrary to what therapists might fear, clients' answers are usually realistic and rarely "pie in the sky" since the details of their responses are based on their own actual life experiences and on "normal" or successful periods in their lives.

Exceptions

Solution-focused brief therapy is extremely interested in eliciting, amplifying, and reinforcing exceptions to the problem and other variations clients say make a difference in their lives. One way this can be done is by asking about any ways things have gone better in the period of time between the first phone contact with the agency or therapist and the first appointment (Weiner-Davis, de Shazer, and Gingerich, 1987). Another way to elicit exceptions is to simply ask the client to describe times when the problem is not happening. Another method of identifying exceptions is to follow the miracle question by asking the client, "Tell me about times when some pieces of the miracle were happening."

Clients often refer to exceptions without being asked, citing "good times" or "good days" and "bad times" (de Shazer et al., 1986; Molnar and de Shazer, 1987). Solution-focused therapists are avidly interested in what is different during times when the problem is not occurring and in what the client, in particular, is doing to make those times different.

Scaling Questions

Scaling questions are enormously useful in solution-focused therapy and serve a number of helpful purposes (Berg and de Shazer, 1993). They may be used to elicit a baseline, as when the therapist asks, "On a scale of 1 to 10, with 1 representing the worst things could be for you (the situation, problem, relationship, and so on) and 10 represents the day after the miracle or the best things could be, where on the scale would you say you are now?"

Scaling questions may be used to identify exceptions because no matter how desperately clients describe their situations, their ratings are rarely as low as 1. The solution-focused therapist builds on such discrepancies by asking clients who have rated their situation at a 3, "What is happening that makes you feel that you are two notches above a 1?" Clients may also report early in therapy on periods during which they were higher on the scale. Asking them what was different about those periods and what they might do to retrieve those successful times has the potential to elicit a great deal of discussion about exceptions to the problem, client strengths, and strategies for change that derive from the client's experience rather than the therapist's expertise.

To use scaling questions to determine an end point for therapy, the therapist merely needs to ask some variation of, "At what number on the scale will you be when things are going well enough that you no longer feel you need therapy?" To elicit the client's ideas about first steps and small changes, the therapist can simply ask clients who have said that they are currently at a 3, for example, "What will tell you that things are going one step better?"

Consultation Break and Intervention Message

The characteristic solution-focused session is interrupted five or ten minutes before the end of the session for a consultation break, during which time the therapist and the team take a break to construct an intervention message. The intervention message is generally composed of a statement or two acknowledging the situation that has brought the client into therapy, stating compliments that underscore the client's strengths, and giving suggestions for a task.

In most task-oriented therapies, the therapist collects data and makes a specific behavioral assigment designed in a direct or strategic manner to correct or interrupt the presenting problem. Since solution-focused therapy strives to identify and build on the client's expertise (de Shazer, 1985), tasks are designed to identify, confirm, or solidify what the client is doing that is working (Molnar and de Shazer, 1987).

Therapy approaches are easily confused with the techniques which with they are most associated. Solution-focused brief therapists utilize questions as the primary means of identifying clients' solutions. Therapists employ these questions in the process of solution building while allowing the following issues to guide their questions:

- Maintain a focused curiosity on the client's goals and aspirations
- Focus on times when exceptions are occurring and the client's life is more similar to the way he or she would like it to be
- Focus on what the client is doing to make those times occur

This inevitably leads to a different, more competent version of the client's experience than would occur if the therapist focused on exploring the problem followed by attempts to solve the problem.

Problems that are chronic and seemingly resistant to solutions affect relationships throughout a family and undermine the family members' confidence that change can occur. Solution-focused brief therapy with such families begins slowly with a discussion of exceptions to the problem. Bringing families together, including children or other persons who have not been heard or heeded, is sometimes helpful for such discussions because they often have noticed small successes that more influential family members have not noticed or appreciated.

On the other hand, it is often difficult to uncover differences that actually matter with such families. They have reason to doubt the possibility of desirable change because they have experienced repeated past disappointment. Families dealing with such problems often appear to have given up on themselves and their own solutions. They may look eagerly to the therapist to advise them and may just as eagerly dismiss the therapist's advice because it seems too easy and removed from their experience. Family members who have felt the most disappointment may be quick to dismiss any attempts to identify successes as misguided, unsympathetic, or trivializing of their long-term suffering. It takes considerable patience and skill to draw the whole family system into a collaborative discussion of potential solutions.

Outcome Studies

An early outcome study of 164 clients conducted at the BFTC (Kiser, 1988; Kiser and Nunnally, 1990) reported success rates of 80.3% in response to follow-up questionnaires six and twelve months after the completion of therapy (65.6% of the 164 clients reported meeting their goals and 14.7% reported making significant progress). When contacted at eighteen months, the overall success rate had increased to 80.3%.

In a second outcome study of 275 clients conducted in 1995 (Berg and De Jong, 1996), 45% of those who responded said their treatment goals had been met and 32% indicated "some progress" had been made, as reported on telephone interviews conducted seven and nine months after treatment ended. The average number of sessions per course of treatment in that study was 3. The overall average number of sessions at the Brief Family Therapy Center is 4.3 (de Shazer, 1988).

The Case: A Substance-Abusing Father and the Family

The following is a transcript from a case consultation demonstrating solution-focused brief therapy conducted with Bob, a recently released convict with a long-standing history of drug and alcohol abuse; Mary, his wife; and their two oldest children, Susie and Alicia, ages 8 and 6. Bob is discouraged about repeated setbacks in his attempts to abstain from drugs and alcohol. Mary is skeptical about his ability to put the drugs and alcohol behind him and reintegrate with the family. The therapist spends most of the first session identifying exceptions to the problem by relying heavily on scaling questions. She uses the questions developed at the BFTC in a manner more similar to choosing from a menu than following a step-by-step blueprint. She relies almost exclusively on the clients' language and frames of reference to guide her in this process. The sessions demonstrate the model's emphasis on respect for the client's experience.

Therapist: Hello.

Mary: I'm Mary.

Bob: I'm Bob.

Therapist: And who's this?

Bob: Alicia.

Therapist: That's a different name. It's not Alice, it's Alicia. How old are you, Alicia?

Alicia: Six.

Therapist: Six years old. So you've finished kindergarten, or did you finish first grade?

Alicia: Kindergarten.

Therapist: And what's your name?

Susie: Susie.

Therapist: Your name is Susie. And how old are you, Susie?

Susie: Eight.

Therapist: So does that make you third grade, second grade, fourth grade?

Susie: I'm going to be 9.

Therapist: That's next month. So you're starting fourth grade? You just finished third grade.

Susie: I just finished third grade.

Therapist: So you're going to start fourth grade in September. How in the world did you manage to get up so early on Sunday morning?

Bob: I don't know. [He and Mary laugh.]

Therapist: And got the kids up and dressed and got over here. Your name's again—Mary.

Mary: Right.

Therapist: Mom's name is Mary. Dad's name is Bob. Your name is Alicia, and your name is Susie. Do you have other children besides these two?

Bob: I have a 2-year-old and a 4-year-old also.

Therapist: Two and four-year-old. You're busy, aren't you?

Mary: Yes.

Therapist: What do you do for a living, Bob?

Bob: I've been in building supplies sales.

Therapist: That must be a good business here. There's a building boom, isn't there?

Bob: Yes.

Therapist: So business is good?

Bob: Yes.

Therapist: Good and, [turning to Mary] I imagine you're very busy.

Mary: I've got two jobs—I'm a mother of four and I'm a waitress.

Therapist: You have two jobs. My gosh. You work outside the home with four kids?

Mary: Yes.

Therapist: How do you do that? I'm sure it's hard.

Mary: It's hard.

The first part of the session is devoted to joining, or socializing. Aside from inquiring about the names and ages of family members involved in the session or at home, the therapist spends very little time exploring the problems that bring the family to therapy. The questions about school with their emphasis on completed grades and those about livelihood convey an interest in areas of family competence. All of these remarks are examples of what solution-focused brief therapists describe as indirect compliments. In offering them, the therapist suggests that even before the family begins to discuss their problems, she is interested in learning more about parts of their lives and experience that are not contaminated by their problems.

Even the therapist's reference to the couple's success at getting to an appointment scheduled for "so early on Sunday" recognizes indirectly that this family has priorities and a capacity to organize around them and that they are invested in getting help and bettering their lives. It suggests that Bob and Mary might be good parents in spite of the undisclosed problems that bring them to therapy. The therapist's acknowledgment that Mary must be "busy" having four young children to raise and her appreciation, a few moments later, of Mary's capacity to work outside the home at the same time convey respect for their areas of competence.

Following a discussion of the organization of the session, the therapist returns to Bob.

Therapist: So you've been seeing your therapist for some time.

Bob: On and off.

Therapist: Let's say on a scale of 1 to 10—10 means that you feel like meetings with her have been very helpful for you and you feel like you can go on with your life on your own without having to meet with your therapist—that stands for 10. One stands for how bad things were when you first decided to start talking with a therapist. Where would you say things are at, between 1 and 10 now?

Mary: Right now?

Therapist: Right now. As of today.

Mary: Three.

Therapist: [to Bob] How about you? What would you say?

Bob: Six.

Therapist: Okay.

Bob: Compared to where I was at.

Therapist: Compared to where you were at, right. That's what I'm talking about. [to Mary] Are you talking about the family life in general or are you talking about yourself? The 3. Is that 3 for everybody or for yourself?

Mary: I don't know. I think maybe for myself.

Therapist: For yourself. [to Bob] And I suspect you were talking about yourself as well.

Bob: Correct.

Therapist: If I were to ask you to put a number on family life as a whole, on a 1-to-10 scale, where would you say things are at right now?

Bob: About a 6.
Therapist: [to Mary] How about for you?
Mary: I'd say about a 5.
Therapist: So as a family as a whole, you are pretty much in agreement. It
   sounds like you are more than halfway there, for you.
Bob: Right.
Therapist: And you feel like you're about halfway there.
Mary: Yes.

Informal scaling questions provide the therapist with a highly flexible language in which to ask clients the ways they would like their lives to be different, the degree to which they have changed, and the small steps they might take to make their lives better. Scales involve numbers in progression. Numbers are extremely helpful because they are concrete enough to place a client's sense of their situation at a specific point, yet they are abstract enough to allow the therapist to ask for a limitless description of their meaning for the client. Numbers in progression are very helpful in therapy because they offer clients another way to inform the therapist about goals in their lives and, potentially, the end point of therapy. In this instance, because the therapist is acting as a consultant to the therapy as well as the client, she utilizes scaling questions to estimate their progress to date in therapy.

Scaling questions allow the therapist a great deal of flexibility in identifying goals and describing progress. The therapist shifts to asking about "family life in general" because that question invites the couple to shift their focus from their individual experiences and concerns to their aspirations for the family—a different area in which to explore aims and successes. The discrepancy between Bob's and Mary's individual ratings (6 and 3, respectively) is wide and suggests a need to negotiate the difference and attempt to build consensus. The term "halfway there" anchors a midpoint in a way that surprises and serves to motivate family members. They only need to cover as much ground as they have already.

Scaling questions are also useful for eliciting descriptions of competence and a sense of personal agency from clients. In response to scaling questions, clients usually rate themselves as better than 1. This provides multiple opportunities to detect times when things are going better, what clients feel are different about those times, and what they might be doing to make those differences occur. Scaling questions also provide another means to uncover and expand possible exceptions to the problem.

Therapist: I wonder what you would say, Susie. You know about 1 to 10,
   don't you?
Susie: [quietly] No.
Therapist: No? Okay, let me explain it this way. [softly, slowly, and very gently] This is 10 and this is 1. Ten means your family of six is how you want it to be. That's 10. One is how you don't want it to be. Where would you say things are at between 1 and 10 right now? [pause] You don't know? You don't have any idea.

Susie: No.

Therapist: You haven't thought about this. Okay. How about you, Alicia? Have you thought about that?

Alicia: [quietly] No.

Therapist: No, you haven't thought about that. Okay. [turning to Bob] How do you explain yourself, that you have come all the way up to 6?

The usefulness of scaling questions is not restricted to adults, although here the therapist drops the question quickly when she sees the children are unable to answer it. A helpful way to tailor scaling questions for children is to draw or have the children draw a continuum of simple faces, from very sad or frowning to very happy, and ask the children to match their own sense of how things are going for themselves or their family to the drawing rather than by number.

Although the therapist conducts virtually all of the rest of the interview with Bob and Mary, she returns to the children at the end of the session and inquires about their views in a manner that amplifies the shift that has occurred in their parents' perspective.

Bob: I was pretty low down. I was drinking vodka and other things. I really slowed down. I'd been at a complete stop for quite awhile there. I had a few setbacks.

Therapist: How long did you stop completely?

Bob: About nine weeks.

Therapist: Wow.

Bob: Yes. And the last couple of weeks I've had a couple of small setbacks. Nothing like I used to be.

Therapist: Really? You mean your setbacks are different than they used to be.

Bob: Correct.

Therapist: Wow.

Bob: I've been separated from my family about four months now. We just got back together.

Therapist: You just got back together? When?

Bob: About two weeks ago.

Therapist: Is that right?

Mary: Yes.

Therapist: So you must have seen some signs that Bob is doing better?

Mary: I did. I did. He was in jail for 30 days and of course he couldn't have setbacks. And of course things were really good. He was sober, he was clean. He promised me that was it—no more, and as soon as he moves in we have a couple of setbacks.

Therapist: So it's been about two weeks, you said.

Mary: Yes.

Therapist: And in that time you had a couple of setbacks.

Mary: Yes.

Therapist: Would you agree with Bob that these are small setbacks compared to what he used to do before that?

Mary: They're small setbacks, but I feel that they lead to bigger things.

Therapist: So you're concerned about that.
Mary: Yes.
Therapist: Sure. You're worried that this might lead into a big setback.
Mary: Right. One turns into two, two turns into four.

In families and between couples, complaints do not stand in isolation. Problems are constructed as one family member complains about another. Any changes that are making a difference will need to be acknowledged and confirmed by the person voicing the complaint. Complaints are resolved when the person who is complaining acknowledges that the problematic behavior is not occurring or it is no longer a problem.

This is another reason why, in solution-focused brief therapy, it is important to encourage clients to describe their goals in interactional terms whenever possible. The therapist returns to Mary because Bob must be seen as acting differently by her before the problem is seen as resolved. The therapist proceeds very carefully throughout this exchange because what sounds like small but important differences for Bob—the setbacks have been "small" in some as yet undefined way—are viewed as setbacks by Mary. Because Bob's past setbacks led to increasingly problematic behavior, they do not make a meaningful difference to Mary.

Therapist: [turning to Bob] You seem to be pretty convinced that this was a small setback.
Bob: Compared to what I used to be.
Therapist: How is it that you are able to have small setbacks instead of big setbacks?
Bob: I was working on trying to stay with my family, get back together with them. It was pretty hard being without them for that period of time.
Therapist: How long were you separated?
Bob: Four months.
Mary: Four months.
Therapist: Right. So the four months was hard for you.
Bob: Very hard. Things just got worse instead of better when I was separated from them.
Therapist: So you do better when you're with your family.
Bob: Not in the past, but hopefully now in the future. Before I used to take off for a few days. The family life wasn't that great then, but I'm trying to improve on it.

The therapist returns to Bob because although she guesses that his small setbacks might be understood as exceptions to big setbacks, Mary is skeptical about the distinction. Bob regards them differently, and talking about that difference may generate information that will shift Mary's views somewhat.

Solution-focused therapy is interested in any behavior that marks an exception to the problem, no matter how small. Such small differences may turn out to be first steps in the resolution of the problem. In this case, the therapist's question about what made the difference reveals that Bob's desire to be with his family is a major motivation in his thinking about changing his behavior.

Therapist: I want to come back to this. Mary, how do you explain that you are up to 3?

Mary: As far as family life?

Therapist: As far as you go—the family was about 5.

Mary: I guess because I have a lot of doubts, a lot of insecurities.

Therapist: About . . .

Mary: About everything in general. Life without alcoholism, drugs.

Therapist: And somehow, in spite of that, you moved up to 3. How? How did that happen?

Mary: Because I saw a little bit of improvement.

Therapist: In Bob?

Mary: Right.

Therapist: Is that right? She saw some improvement in you?

Bob: I think so. I could communicate a little better. Before I was just shutting off and I didn't want to talk. I like to talk to her a little bit more now.

Therapist: Is that right? [turning to Mary] You communicate a little bit better?

Mary: [pause] Yes. [laughs hesitantly]

Therapist: Yes? But you have a long way to go.

Mary: [emphatically] A long ways to go.

Rather than exploring Mary's "insecurities," the therapist is interested in how it is that even with those insecurities Mary sees herself at a 3. How, in other words, is Mary coping with her insecurities, and what might she learn from her ability to do that?

This line of questioning causes Mary to agree with Bob that communication between the two of them is a bit better. Noting Mary's caution and attempting to respect and work within it, the therapist notes that they "have a long way to go."

Therapist: Right. What did Mary do that was helpful so that you were able to communicate with her even a little bit better? What did she do to be helpful to you?

Bob: By leaving me, it made me want to communicate more because I want to work things out.

Therapist: So leaving was helpful.

Bringing up the question about what Mary might have done to encourage the family to think about exceptions and goals in interactional terms conveys the notion that family members have made and can make a difference.

Asking Bob what Mary has done "to be helpful" implies to both of them that whatever Mary has attempted in reaction to her husband's substance abuse, including their separation, is her way of trying to be helpful. In the same vein, other behaviors that have previously been regarded as parts of the problem are reframed as attempted solutions.

Bob: Yes. It hurt me a lot, and I wanted to express my feelings to her.

Therapist: Is that right?

Mary: I think so. To me it's like a cycle. It's like I left so he wanted to communicate more, he wanted to work things out. He was also in jail during
that time and everything else. Once he's back in our family again, it
seems like the communication has gone down. Sometimes I think we got
along better when he was out of the home.

Therapist: So I guess you have a reason to be cautious about the future.

Mary: Yes.

Therapist: Because you have had many of these.

Mary: Right.

Therapist: So what do you need to see from Bob for you to say maybe this
time it's different? Maybe there is a little more hope than in the past—
this time. What do you need to see from Bob so that you can say that to
yourself?

In couples and family work, it is essential that all those who identify complaints begin to define ways they would know their complaints had been resolved. When exceptions are identified, it is important for family members to
agree that those noted differences make a difference for each of them. As the
therapist moves through the session, she is careful to move back and forth between Bob and Mary building agreement and consensus, exploring and expanding exceptions, and looking for differences that might make a difference to
both of them.

Couples who have problems do not think about or define their problems
contextually. They place the responsibility for things going badly or well on
their spouses. The therapist's question of Bob regarding what Mary does to help
him communicate invites the couple in an indirect way to shift their energies
from looking for reasons to blame each other to looking for ways they help each
other.

Mary, however, has been so wounded by past disappointments that she is not
ready to look at any ways the relationship may have begun to improve. She at-
tributes times the couple communicates better to "cycles" outside of their control.

Following the dictum of solution-focused therapy that the client is the expert and the imperative of all therapy is to "be where the client is," the therapist backs up and validates Mary's right to be "cautious about the future"
because she's had so many disappointments. In her responses, the therapist empathizes with Mary's apprehension about a permanent change in Bob's behavior and yet her need to see Bob change. A gentle shift then occurs to a search for
potential exceptions, with the therapist asking Mary what changes she needs to
see from Bob to feel like "maybe it's different" and "there's a little more hope
than in the past." The emphasis on small, tentative changes is realistic and fits
with Mary's reservations.

Mary: What I need personally is I need Bob to completely give up alcohol.

Therapist: Altogether.

Mary: Altogether. Not one sip, one beer, nothing. That's not acceptable to
me anymore because I've seen in the past eight and a half years that it
doesn't ever stop with one. And communicating more.

Therapist: So no more alcohol, communicating with you more. What else?

Mary: Be attentive to my feelings and my needs. When I say I want to talk, "Well, we'll talk tomorrow." Then tomorrow I'll say, "Can we talk?" "Let's just drop it." When something is bothering me, I need him to listen to me and be attentive to me.

Mary begins to describe some of the changes she wants to see in interactional terms. This is a promising development from a solution-building point of view because it offers a new goal and a new lens through which to look for exceptions and actions Bob and Mary might have taken to cause those changes to occur.

Therapist: So that's gotten a little bit better? Up to 3?

Mary: A little bit.

Therapist: Just a little bit. About 3. So what will push it up to 4? Maybe a 3.5? [laughs]

Scaling questions are particularly useful for defining goals in small, first-step terms. This is very helpful because clients often seek therapy desperately looking for the kind of definitive answers they have not found or are not yet ready to put into practice. This is likely to lead to failure and disappointment. The therapist's focus throughout the session is not on coming up with ultimate strategies for Bob and Mary but to help them develop their own solutions by taking small, realistic steps that result in discernible successes.

Mary: How I feel at this point today is I have no trust. I have no trust. I hate to say that, it hurts me to say that, and I think the only way that I can trust him and move it up to possibly a 4 is for him to be on medication for alcoholism.

Therapist: You mean something like Antibuse?

Mary: Yes.

Therapist: So that will move you up to about a 3.5 or a 4?

Mary: Maybe about a 5.

Therapist: About a 5. Okay. [to Bob] What do you think about that?

Bob: I agree with that.

Therapist: So what do you have to do so that happens?

Bob: Give up my friends.

Therapist: Oh. That's not going to be easy.

Bob: If I lose them again, it will be pretty tough.

Therapist: But how are you going to do that? Giving up all your friends is not going to be easy.

Bob: No. Just staying home. My family will be my friends.

The therapist asks Mary to describe how things will be different when they are a half or full step better. Interestingly, Mary describes how things will be when they are two steps better. The therapist does not challenge her answer in an attempt to remain in Mary's frame of reference. Change, however, often takes place in steps, and big steps often take small steps in between.

The therapist's question about what it will take for Bob to go on medication invites him to define steps that he will need to take to meet his goal. Solution-focused brief therapy has long held that clients are best motivated by goals they perceive as hard to achieve. Insoo's statement that Bob's task "won't be easy" challenges his best intentions. The steps he defines—giving up his drinking buddies and, more positively, rebuilding his relationship with his family—are described in interactional terms.

Therapist: Suppose if this past couple of weeks since you've gotten back to-gether, if that were to maintain, what would that be like? Let's say if it maintained ten months or so?

Mary: The way the past two weeks have been?

Therapist: Yes.

Mary: I don't like the way the past two weeks have been.

Therapist: You don't.

Therapist: So what about the past two weeks was good and what was not good?

The therapist appears to misunderstand Mary's meaning as she is attempt-ing to define actions Mary and/or Bob could take to "maintain" improvements. In order to remain focused on the issue and to expand Mary's frame of refer-ence, the therapist inquires about what was both bad and good about the past two weeks.

Mary: He made empty promises to me, empty promises like, "I'm not drink-ing anymore. I'm not going to hang around these people anymore. We're going to talk more. We're going to do things together as a family." It's like he's had two or three setbacks since he moved in, which totally blew my hope. And just the attitude he has towards me. I feel he doesn't like being there with us. I feel he's angry; we get into verbal fights in front of the kids. That's uncalled for. That's the reason I left four months ago; a lot of fighting, him not coming home for days at a time, not calling me, it was none of my business where he was at. And we're talking days at a time. Of course, while he was doing that, I was being angry with the kids. I was taking it out on the kids because there was no one else there to take it out on. I feel us going back into that same cycle again, and I'm not putting my kids through that for another . . . I was in it for almost nine years. I'm not going to do it for another nine.

Therapist: Of course. [looking at Bob] So it sounds like you have a tough job.

Bob: Yes.

Therapist: To convince Mary that it's different this time.

It is important for any therapist to remember that the onus for change is on the client. Mary's experience has rightfully convinced her to be skeptical even of times when some aspect of her life with Bob is going better. It is not the ther-apist's job to get Bob to comply with Mary's wishes, hold him accountable for his past setbacks and mistakes, or convince Mary the situation is getting better or Bob is doing better. It is up to Bob to do that.

Bob: It's just been real stressful the last couple of weeks with four real young children.

Mary: But we're still going to have four children in three months. Whether it's been stressful because we've had four children this past two weeks, we're still going to have them.

Bob: [laughs] I don't know. It's just something I'll have to work on.

Therapist: Do you have some plans about how you're going to do this?

Bob: Yes.

Therapist: You do?

Bob: I'm going to go on Antibuse.

Therapist: So you agree with Mary on that. So that's the first step you want to take. What else?

Eliciting workable goals from individual clients can be a slow and painstaking process. It is even more difficult identifying shared goals with couples and family members. In any case, it is important to set goals that the client has determined rather than the therapist's goals for the client. It is easy for therapists to confuse the two.

Here the therapist is very careful to be clear that Bob shares Mary's goal, although it will take considerable effort by Bob to achieve the goal. While Mary has remained very focused on Bob's consenting to Antibuse maintenance, his accomplishing that goal will demand changes on his part and may involve more effort than his wife imagines. The therapist's line of questioning attempts to uncover undiscovered competencies Bob will need to accomplish what sounds like a misleadingly easy change.

Bob: Just by staying home with the family and doing more things with them.

Therapist: You sound confident about that.

Bob: I do.

Therapist: You do. That you can do this. Stay home and sort of get rid of your old friends.

Bob: Right. I have said that in the past too, but I'm a little bit more confident this time than the last.

Therapist: Really? What's changed this time?

Bob: I saw what it's like being by myself now. It's a lot more enjoyable being with my family than it was out drinking with my friends. It's a lot more lonely by myself.

Bob reports a small improvement in confidence. The therapist regards it as a small but potentially significant exception for both Bob and Mary. She then asks Bob for more details and learns once again that, regardless of his past difficulties, being with the family is very important and thus motivating for Bob.

The most helpful exceptions are credible to all family members; thus, to prevent her discussion with Bob from getting too far ahead of Mary's concerns, the therapist invites Mary to reflect on Bob's statements. Mary's response demonstrates that it will take a lot for Bob to prove that he is credible.

Therapist: What do you think about what he said?

Mary: Right now I'm kind of at "I'll believe it when I see it." I mean he'd be gone for four days and he'd walk in the door, "Hi! I'll never do this again, I promise." Then a week later he goes; "I'll never do this again, I promise." It's my fault because I let it go on for that long. I kept saying, "Okay, next time this is it." And then it would happen again and I'd be like, "Okay, next time this is it."

Therapist: So what's different about it this time?

Mary: I don't think there's anything different about it this time yet.

Therapist: About Bob?

Mary: Yes. He says that he's going to stay in with the family and la-dee-da-dee-da. He said all this before and never did anything about it. If he gets on the Antibuse and stays with it and goes to AA meetings, then I'd feel good about it.

Therapist: So you want him to what? Go on Antibuse, go to AA meetings, and that will make you feel better?

Solution-focused brief therapy is most interested in eliciting ideas about changes clients want to see rather than convincing the client of the therapist's recommendations. In this case, it is clear that Bob's use of Antibuse and becoming involved in AA are seen as crucial by Mary. It is Mary, not the therapist, who defines these commitments as helpful. It is Bob, not the therapist, who must find some way to convince his wife that he is committed to this course if he is to achieve his goal of rejoining the family.

Mary: Yes.

Therapist: Has he done this before? Going on Antibuse?

Mary: There was always a reason why he couldn't do it. He went to AA meetings a couple of times. I don't know if he had to go.

Bob: It's part of my therapy program. I haven't gone to AA meetings for about a week. They do help me quite a bit. I've never gone in the past with this.

Mary: There's a difference if it's court ordered that you have to go or if it's because you want to go.

Therapist: So you've been ordered by the court?

Bob: This is part of my therapy program.

Therapist: So you are on probation then.

Bob: No.

Therapist: You served your time and you're done with that.

Bob: I am court ordered to go through the alcohol program, but I'm not on any probation.

Therapist: You're not on parole.

Bob: No.

Therapist: Is that part of the attempt you're making to try and follow what the court says? Get on Antibuse and get into AA and so on?

Bob: The court really hasn't ordered me to do a whole lot. They did originally, but they don't follow up on anything I do.

Therapist: You say that going to AA was helpful.

Bob: Very helpful.
Therapist: What about it?

Since Bob agrees with Mary that involvement in AA would make a difference, the therapist attempts to identify times he has been successfully involved with AA. Since it is easy to confuse ends with means in therapy, the therapist is particularly interested in what Bob gained from his involvement in AA. The information her questions elicit gives Mary an opportunity to reconsider or confirm her suspicion that Bob's current interest in AA is mandated by the court and is insincere. It is important to note that the therapist does not try to convince Mary one way or the other but leaves it to her to make up her own mind.

Bob: Just talking to people of all walks of life that are just like me. They weren't just a lot of drunks sitting at the corner. There were professional people of all different ages lending a lot of support. People that stopped for years. I had no desires at all to drink then, and like I said, I was in a work release program and I didn't drink, of course, then. I started to hang out with my friends again, and I drank a couple of times since then. Nothing real bad or nothing major. To her, one drink is bad enough. But it's not compared to what I used to be. I need to get back into going to AA. I'd like to go every night, but she works at night sometimes.
Therapist: So that means you have to watch the kids then?
Bob: Correct.

As helpful as AA may be in Mary's and many professionals' view, it has yet to be determined whether meetings will be feasible because of her schedule. Clients and professionals often have good ideas about plausible solutions, but those will not work if they do not fit the small, important details of a client's life. This is a very important reason to do the painstaking work of eliciting goals in small, realistic ways from the client's experience.

Therapist: [to Bob] I'm curious about a couple of things. You said this time your setback was smaller than in the past. How did you manage to have a smaller setback this time than other times?
Mary: Because it was only for one night instead of two or three.

Note that Mary answers for Bob in a way that suggests that, having had her ideas about goals taken seriously by the therapist, she is a bit more willing to consider the potential positive significance of Bob's smaller setbacks. This encourages the therapist to examine this potential exception in detail.

Therapist: [to Bob] How come it was only one night?
Bob: I just don't want to get back into that cycle. I went out and had a few beers with some friends. It wasn't anything. I didn't get involved with any other drugs. I was usually doing drugs like cocaine that would keep me gone for three days.
Therapist: So this time you didn't do any drugs, just alcohol.
Bob: Correct.
Therapist: And that's a change for you.

Bob: Correct.

Therapist: Wow. So you decided this time you're not going to do any drugs.

Bob: I don't ever intend to do that.

Therapist: Is that right?

Bob: Right. That's really cost me a lot financially and emotionally and my family stability.

While many approaches to substance abuse argue for abstinence, solution-focused brief therapy values any step clients take in their preferred direction and the idiosyncratic strategies clients employ to achieve even the smallest of those steps.

The therapist checks back with Mary on this because, if these steps do not represent meaningful progress to her, Bob's achievement of them will not make a difference that counts.

Therapist: (to Mary) Are you convinced about that? That Bob does not want to do any cocaine?

Mary: No.

Therapist: You're not convinced about that. Did you know about this? That he did not want to do any drugs this time.

Mary: I've heard that.

Therapist: You heard that before.

Mary: I mean I'd like to support him and have confidence in him. I want to. But like I said, I don't have any trust. I don't have any trust. But I know if he's on Antibuse and he's not drinking, then I know he's not going to do cocaine.

Therapist: [to Bob] There are a couple of other things I'm curious about. How come you didn't do drugs or alcohol for thirty days while you were in jail?

No exception is too small if it has significance for the clients. While many might forget that substance abuse occurs in correctional and treatment facilities, the therapist does not and invites Bob to say whether he did or did not use while incarcerated and whether useful information might be gleaned from his decision to abstain while incarcerated.

Bob: There was a big incentive there because they do random tests. Also, just not being with friends. I was a lot more lonely in jail and on work release program, knowing I wanted to get out and be with them [the family]. That's something I had to do.

Therapist: So you were able to stick with that.

Bob: Correct. After doing it for 20 years, I was hoping there wouldn't be any setbacks, and I thought there would be. It's not easy. Especially with the people I hang out with.

Therapist: So you seem to think that it's the people you hang out with.

Bob: I'm one of them too, so.

Therapist: [turning to Mary] Would you agree with that? It's the people that he hangs out with that's more difficult for him than himself?

Mary: Bob falls into a lot of peer pressure. He's a follower. I don't know if he's afraid to say, "No, I don't do that anymore."

Therapist: Somehow you managed only one day of drinking.

Bob: Right.

Therapist: So you must have said no to somebody.

Bob: Right.

Therapist: How?

Bob: Because of the cocaine. That always turns into three days.

Therapist: So you know that about yourself.

Bob: Right.

Therapist: So how were you able to say no to cocaine? I'm sure the pressure was there, too.

Bob: Yes. I'm just stronger about not doing that right now. I've been my best enemy.

Therapist: You're more certain about the cocaine.

Bob: Correct. If there was a drug that would make me stop doing that, I would do that, too.

Therapist: So you think that going on Antibuse will also help you say no to cocaine?

Bob: That's the only time I ever do, that is, if I drink. Once I start drinking—I have a few beers and then it leads to it.

Therapist: So the alcohol is a road to cocaine.

Bob: For me. I think I'm a little bit straighter than if I'm drinking and stuff, of course.

Therapist: So this is how you're thinking about things. So you're sort of thinking things out for yourself.

Bob: Correct.

Bob and Mary redefine the problem as saying no to peers. This invites the therapist to question about exceptions—times the problem did not occur—first in reference to drinking, then in reference to cocaine. Though the therapist has no opinion on whether Bob should or should not begin taking Antibuse, the discussion with the couple about their ideas of what has helped and what would help solidifies their mutual commitment to Antibuse.

Therapist: [to Mary] You know about that. It's the alcohol that makes him say yes to cocaine. I see. So you agree with Bob that once he says no to alcohol he's less likely to . . .

Mary: Right. I agree with that.

Therapist: And when he does cocaine, then that's when he stays out longer, many more days.

Mary: Right.

Therapist: So it seems like both of you know about this very well—about what happens.

Bob: Yes. We've gone through it.

Mary: Too well.

In developing consensus on possible solutions, it becomes necessary to first develop agreement on a definition of the problem and its impact. The therapist pursues this direction not because she wants to understand the problem better but because she is looking to build consensus. This is the first time in the session the couple seems to agree in a heartfelt way.

The therapist now invites discussion of ideas the couple might share about what they need to do to address the problem.

Therapist: So you also have some ideas of what you need to do about that.
Bob: Right.
Therapist: How confident are you that you can do it this time? On a scale of 1 to 10.

Scaling questions can be used to set small goals in ways that are highly responsive to the client's frame of reference. Since the task at hand for this couple is developing a plan both can trust, in spite of past disappointments, the therapist utilizes scaling questions to generate some ideas that might create more confidence for both.

Bob: I'd say a 7 right now. I'd say two weeks ago I was on a 9; now I'm back to about a 7.
Therapist: [to Mary] How about you? How confident are you that he can do it this time? On a scale of 1 to 10.
Mary: I don't know. Right now I'm not confident at all. You have to understand I have no trust. I want to trust him, I want to believe in him, I want to support him. I want to, but he's given me no reason to want to.
Therapist: So are you at 1, would you say?
Mary: I don't know. Maybe about a 4 because I see that he can do it.
Therapist: You know that he can do it.
Mary: I think he can. I don't know if he wants to, though.
Therapist: He did it for 30 days.
Mary: That's right. He was a much nicer person, too.
Therapist: So you see a glimpse of what he can be like.
Mary: Yes.
Therapist: Is that what keeps you hanging in there with Bob?
Mary: Yes.
Therapist: You imagine. You see some glimmer of what he can be like. [to Bob] So you know how to do that.
Bob: I'm trying to learn.
Therapist: You know how to do it, sounds like. You've shown Mary that you can.

The therapist turns to Mary to ask her the same question she has asked Bob. In couples work, both parties involved must have the opportunity to voice their ideas about what needs to be different.

The exchange between Insoo and Mary about the difference between the client's description of her level of confidence and her scaled rating marks a subtle but dramatic shift in the session. Using the lowest rating possible—a 1—to reflect back what Mary has put into words invites a correction on her part. Explaining the difference between 4 and 1, Mary reveals the beginnings of a different version of Bob and a "glimmer of what he can be like." He is redefined as a person with potential, someone who "can do it" and has done it for 30 days; and when he is able to overcome his substance abuse, he is seen as "a much nicer person."

Mary spontaneously begins to acknowledge Bob's potential competence on her own accord. The therapist has remained with the client's position rather than arguing against it, utilizing very simple questions to join with, clarify, and expand Mary's version of the couple's hope for change; that is, what keeps her "hanging in there with Bob." The discussion that ensues has a much softer, more hopeful, and more trusting quality.

Bob: Right. I was a lot less angrier person. I expressed my emotions a lot better. It just seems like the tables turned. She was a lot harder to communicate to and I wanted to communicate and you couldn't shut me up.

Mary: It was a shock to me. He always wanted to talk, talk, talk; I was like, "get away." He's like, "You always wanted to talk." I said, "I don't want to anymore." I just had this wall up. It was like I was him now and he was me. He was always,"Let's talk. Let's talk." I'm like, "I don't want to talk. Nothing to talk about." I've got a wall up there so high.

Therapist: Is that wall still up there?

Mary: It was gradually coming down and then he pulled a couple of stunts.

Therapist: And that's why you are up to a 4 in your confidence.

Mary: Yes.

Therapist: That's a lot. [to Bob] That's a lot for somebody who went through what she went through with you.

Bob: Yes.

Therapist: You said your confidence is about 7 or so. What gives you that much confidence?

Bob: I think if I lose it this time, lose my family, it's going to be forever. I don't want to go back to how the last four months were. I have my own apartment still, I have a lease on it. It's just a horrible place for me to go. I have bad feelings when I go there. It's a real lonely place. A lot of bad memories from that.

Therapist: About the apartment.

Bob: Right.

Therapist: So you don't want that.

Bob: No. I went through a period of time where I didn't see my children for probably six weeks. That was real hard.

Therapist: It seems like when you're remembering how bad it is to be in that apartment and how difficult it is for you not to see your children, that's when you do better.

Bob: I always remember it, it's just sometimes other things will block it. Like I said, if I hang out with my friends—certain people I hang out with—and they start in, my mind can be switched to different things pretty fast. I really need to stay away from all that stuff for now until I'm completely out. I won't be drinking or anything anymore.

Instead of discussing how Bob's "stunts" brought her down to a 4 and further exploring the problem, the therapist questions Mary about what brings her up to 4, returning the discussion to potential solutions. By turning to Bob and noting that it's "a lot" for Mary to be at a 4 having gone through so much with him, she expresses both empathy for Mary's hurt and admiration for her capacity to rise above it, and she utilizes both to motivate Bob.

Likewise with Bob, rather than focusing on his problematic shift from 9 to 7, she utilizes the flexibility of scaling questions to ask him why he is as confident as a 7. This elicits a powerfully sobering statement by Bob of the high stakes of failing. The idea of losing his family will help him maintain his sobriety and his resolve.

Therapist: Is there something that Mary and the children can do to be helpful to you so that you can be reminded of that? What can they do to be helpful for you so that you can keep remembering that?

Bob: I don't think they can do anything. I think it's all got to be myself now. They've done everything they can. I would like a little bit more confidence from her. That would help. A little bit more support. But I guess she's done that over the years and now . . . I should have taken advantage of it when she was giving it to me.

Therapist: Suppose she was more supportive, gave you more encouragement. What difference is it going to make for you?

Bob: It would make a lot.

Therapist: How?

Bob: I think if she also didn't drink. That would be a lot more supportive. She doesn't drink around me, but she drinks.

Therapist: So her not drinking would be helpful.

Bob: Right. I don't like it when she drinks either, but she's nothing like I was.

Therapist: So what difference would that make? Her not drinking.

Bob: It would make a minor—not a whole lot—but it would make somewhat of a difference.

Therapist: Somewhat of a difference.

Bob: Right. Around me I don't want her drinking at all, but it would make a small difference if she didn't drink. Her drinking doesn't affect me as far as my drinking at the least. I would just like a little bit more support, like, "I believe in you." But like I said, she's done that over the past and I've let her down. So a lot of it's on my own this time.

Therapist: So her saying that to you would be helpful.

Bob: Yes.

Therapist: What difference would that make?

Bob: It would help me believe in myself a little bit more.

Picking up on both Bob's and Mary's shift in tone and content toward a more positive, interactional conversation, the therapist follows their lead and asks Bob to identify some changes and strategies in interactional and systemic terms: What could his wife and family do to help? Bob seems to shake off the therapist's question in a positive way by taking full responsibility for resolving his problem but returns quickly to the question, describing ways his wife could support his efforts at sobriety. His reference to Mary's support helping him be able to "believe in myself a little bit more" resonates with Mary's earlier remarks that she has seen "that he can do it" and to his being a "much nicer person" when he is sober and with the therapist's reference to a "glimpse of what he can be like."

The session has moved decisively away from "problem talk" to "solution talk" and the social construction of a different, more progressive version of Bob and his potential. Bob's spontaneous statements of responsibility substantiate and expand this evolving construction.

Therapist: I see. So you need to believe in yourself more.
Bob: Right. It's like when I go to the AA meetings, the people lend me support. That really helps me believe in myself a lot more.
Therapist: So you can get that from AA. And you're saying getting that from Mary would make more of a difference.
Bob: Correct.
Therapist: So what do you have to do to get that kind of support from her?
Bob: Show her that she can believe in me. Prove it to her.
Therapist: You have to prove it to her. What do you have to do?
Bob: Just be there all the time and prove that I won't be out drinking and things like that. Give it a little bit of time.

It's helpful to define goals and the actions that might lead to their achievement in terms that are both interactional and self-referenced—in other words, what others can do to help and what clients can do to help themselves. The therapist winds down the session by asking Bob what he will have to do to get Mary's support.

Therapist: I have a lot more to ask you, but I realize we are running out of time so I can't ask you a lot more. [to Mary] Do you have any questions of either Bob or of me at this point?
Mary: No.
Therapist: Okay. [looking over at the kids] I realize that kids get pretty bored.
Bob: [nodding toward Susie] She's probably a lot more interested in it. It affects her a lot more than it does the younger ones.
Therapist: Is that right?
Bob: Yes.
Therapist: How does it affect her?
Bob: She mentioned to me—actually, she has, too [pointing to Alicia]—that they don't like me drinking. They've seen what it's done.
Therapist: Let me ask you, Susie, how is your dad different when he doesn't drink?
Susie: He's nicer. He takes us places.
Therapist: You like that, going places with your dad.
Susie: Yesterday we went to the beach.
Therapist: You went to the beach.

Susie: My dad is always nice, but I don't like when he drinks. I can tell. My mom always tells me when he drinks, but I can tell sometimes by myself because I can tell when he gets home in the morning.

Therapist: That's how you can tell Dad's been drinking. And you don't like that when he does drink. How come?

Susie: I don't know.

Therapist: You just don't like him to get drunk. How is Dad different when he's not drinking?

Susie: He's nicer.

Therapist: When you say he's nicer, what does he do when he's nicer?

Susie: He takes us places.

Therapist: And you went to the beach yesterday. How was it?

Susie: Fun.

Therapist: [to Bob] How did you manage to take the kids to the beach yesterday? How did that happen?

Susie: We went jet skiing, but I took a friend to the beach. It was just my dad and me and my friend. He went jet skiing with my uncle.

Therapist: So you and Dad and your friend went to the beach. I'll bet that was very special for you. [to Bob] Was it your idea? How did that happen?

Bob: It was mine, yes. I take them a lot of places and enjoy it. We're always going places together, just me and the kids.

Susie: To the park.

Therapist: So how come you like going places with Dad?

Susie: [inaudible]

Therapist: You just like it.

Bob: I usually take them a lot more places because she works late nights. I take them in the daytime and try to let her relax a little bit.

Therapist: So that gives her some time.

Susie: Sometimes my dad will take us to the pool. My mom does fun stuff, too. Mostly she likes to hang around the pool all day while my dad's at work.

Bob picks up on the therapist's seemingly casual reference to the children's state of mind. Having respected the children's shyness, the therapist utilizes the last moments of the session to get back to them. Their answers to her questions further solidify the "glimpse" of Bob as a loving, involved father. Having answered the question of ways in which Mary might support his sobriety, Bob hears the children offer a version of him they believe in that he might keep in mind and aim for.

Conclusions

The problems that clients bring to therapy define a part of their experience and their lives. While it seems entirely logical that therapists ought to focus on the problems since clients come to therapy to resolve them, therapeutic discussions that focus heavily on the problematic parts of the client's or the family's life risk ignoring the resources and competencies that allows individuals and families to identify and develop their own solutions.

Solution-focused brief therapy proposes a different kind of conversation, one based heavily on respect for the client's language, frame of reference, expertise, and self-defined goals. Additionally, the approach's focus on moments when the problem is not occurring and when the client's life is going the way he or she prefers and its willingness to build on those moments in small, feasible steps leads to a therapeutic conversation. The therapist's discussion with Bob, Mary, and their children elicits and solidifies the best that even the most compromised client and the most depleted family support system have to offer.

Study Questions

1. Describe this family's goals.
2. As a member of the team observing the session, responsible for developing an intervention message
   a. What strengths, achievements, or exceptions would you want to highlight or compliment the family for at the end of the session?
   b. What would you ask them to observe between sessions as a task?
3. Imagine you are the therapist who brought the case for this therapist's consultation. In what different direction would you hope to take your work as a result of the consult?
4. At the end of the session you just read, the family was asked what they found most helpful about the session. What do you imagine they said?

References

Berg, I. K. (1994). *Family based services: A solution-focused approach.* New York: Norton.

Berg, I. K., & De Jong, P. (1996). Solution-building conversations: Co-constructing a sense of competence with clients. *Families in Society: The Journal of Contemporary Human Service, 77*(8), 376–391.

Berg, I. K., & deShazer, S. (1993). Making numbers talk: Language in therapy. In S. Friedman (Ed.), *The new language of change: Constructive collaboration in psychotherapy* (pp. 5–24). New York: Guilford Press.

Berg, I. K., & Miller, S. D. (1992). *Working with the problem drinker: A solution-focused approach.* New York: Norton.

De Jong, P., & Miller, S. (1995). How to interview for client strengths. *Social Work, 40,* 729–736.

deShazer, S. (1985). *Keys to solutions in brief therapy.* New York: Norton.

deShazer, S. (1988). *Clues: Investigating solutions in brief therapy.* New York: Norton.

deShazer, S., & Berg, I. K. (1992). Doing therapy: A poststructural revision. *Journal of Marriage and Family Therapy, 18*(1), 71–81.

deShazer, S., Berg, I. K., Lipchik, E., Nunnally, E., Molnar, A., Gingerich, W., & Weiner-Davis, M. (1986). Brief therapy: Focused solution development. *Family Process, 25,* 207–221.

Hoffman, L. (1990). Constructing realities: An art of lenses. *Family Process, 29,* 1–12.

Hoffman, L. (1992). A reflexive stance for family therapy. In S. McNamee and K. J. Gergen (Eds.), *Therapy as social construction* (pp. 7–24). Newbury Park, CA: Sage.

Kiser, D. (1988). *A follow-up study conducted at the Brief Family Therapy Center.* Unpublished manuscript. Milwaukee, WI: Brief Family Therapy Center.

Kiser, D., & Nunnally, E. (1990). *The relationship between treatment length and goal achievement in solution-focused therapy.* Unpublished manuscript. Milwaukee, WI: Brief Family Therapy Center.

Klar, H., & Coleman, W. L. (1995). Brief, solution-focused strategies for behavioral pediatrics. *Pediatric Clinics of North America, 42*(1), 131–141.

Lipchik, E., & de Shazer, S. (1986). The purposeful interview. *Journal of Strategic and Systemic Therapies, 5*(1/2), 88–99.

Molnar, A., & de Shazer, S. (1987). Solution-focused therapy: Toward the identification of therapeutic tasks. *Journal of Marital and Family Therapy, 13*(4), 349–358.

Weiner-Davis, M., de Shazer, S., & Gingerich, W. J. (1987). Building on pretreatment change to construct the therapeutic solution: An exploratory study. *Journal of Marital and Family Therapy, 13*(4), 359–363.

Chapter Eleven

A Postmodern Collaborative Approach to Therapy

Harlene Anderson, J. Paul Burney, and Susan B. Levin

Our postmodern collaborative approach to therapy has evolved over the past three decades. The approach reflects the initiatives of Harlene Anderson and Harry Goolishian and their colleagues at the Houston Galveston Institute and reflects its roots in the Galveston group's Multiple Impact Therapy research project (Goolishian and Anderson, 1987; Anderson and Goolishian, 1988, 1992; Anderson, 1997). In this chapter we discuss our current philosophy of therapy, the conversations that we had with a family during a course of therapy, and our reflections on that process.

Theoretical Underpinnings

Our postmodern philosophy reflects a conceptual collage of social construction, contemporary hermeneutic, and narrative theories,[1] providing a metaphorical framework for our experiences in the therapy room. The common threads are

We thank Ann Andras for her assistance in transcribing the videotapes and Becky Weaver for her editorial assistance.

[1] We make a distinction between social constructionism and constructivism. Both reject the notion of knowledge as reflecting an objective reality and argue that knowledge is a construction. Constructivism emphasizes the individual constructing mind. Social constructionism, however, emphasizes the interactional and communal constructing nature. See Anderson (1997, pp. 43–44) and Gergen (1994, pp. 68–69). We also distinguish between narrative in a postmodern and a modern perspective. Narrative is the substance of all therapy; it is not a distinction. The distinction is in the biases and intentions therapists bring to the relationship, how therapists position their narrative vis-à-vis another person's narrative. See Anderson (1997, pp. 211–234).

as follows: the meanings and understandings that we attribute to the events and experiences in our lives are socially, culturally, and historically embedded; the world of meanings and understandings are socially created and shaped through language; a move away from individual authorship to multiple authorship is necessary among a community of persons and relationships; what is created is only one of multiple perspectives and possibilities; language and knowledge are relational and generative; transformation is inherent in the inventive and creative aspects of language, dialogue, and narrative; therefore, the potential for transformation and change[2] is as infinite in variety and expression as the individuals who realize it (Anderson, 1995, 1997; Anderson and Goolishian, 1988).

This philosophy has several implications for how a therapist conceptualizes and acts regarding a therapy system, its process, and its relationships:

- Therapy systems are language, meaning-generating systems that are a product of social communication.
- Therapy systems form and are organized around a particular relevance.
- All members of the therapy system participate in determining its membership and focus.
- The membership is fluid, can change as the conversation changes, and is determined on a session-by-session basis.
- The essence of the therapy process is dialogic conversation in which a client and therapist are conversational partners.
- The conversation is characterized by shared inquiry.
- Shared inquiry is a collaborative exploration between people with different perspectives and expertise.
- Clients are the experts on their lives.
- A therapist has expertise in, and responsibility for, creating a space for conversation and facilitating a conversational process.
- Opportunities for change come from within the conversation, are generated by the combined membership, and are inherent in the creative aspects of language, dialogue, and narrative.
- Responsibility and accountability are shared.
- Both client and therapist experience transformation within this kind of system, conversation, and relationship (Anderson, 1995, 1997; Anderson and Goolishian, 1988).

Conversation becomes the essence of therapy that is informed or characterized by these premises (Anderson, 1995, 1997). By *conversation,* we mean a particular kind of conversation—a dialogue. In dialogue, participants are engaged in a shared inquiry, a mutual search for understanding of the familiar (for example, a problem), and a mutual search for the new (for example, meanings,

---

[2]We hesitate to use the word *change* because in therapy discourse it has acquired the connotation of a therapist as a change agent.

behaviors, attitudes). It is a conversation where participants are engaged in talking with each other rather than to each other. It is a conversation characterized by back-and-forth exchanges and crisscrossing utterances.

Our philosophical stance is critical to establishing this kind of collaborative conversation and relationship. By *philosophical stance*, we mean a way of being in relationship with, thinking about, and responding to people both inside and outside the therapy room. The stance is a natural, spontaneous way of positioning ourselves that is unique to each relationship and each conversation. In action, this stance is an attitude and tone that involves *not-knowing* (Anderson and Goolishian, 1988), which refers to maintaining coherence, respectful listening, staying in sync, and believing (Anderson, 1995, 1997).

In our experience, the collaborative approach represents a respectful way of being helpful to a variety of clients with a wide range of dilemmas. For therapists, this approach is energizing, dynamic, and engaging—eliminating an element of stagnation often encountered in other therapy approaches. Clients have commented that working in a collaborative manner with the therapist provides an experience, and models new ways, in which they may interact (talk, be) with each other. These shifts in interaction and thus in relationships epitomize an emphasis on process over content and the transformative nature of dialogue.

To illustrate our philosophy in action, we narrate our experiences, separately and together, about a course of therapy with the Roberts family.[3] Throughout the narrative, we weave in reflections on our experiences at the time and relate them to our philosophy. At the end of the chapter, we offer our after-reflections and those of the family members on this therapy experience. Although we shift between first- and third-person narratives, session summaries and comments reflect our combined voices. Our narration draws from our collective memories and the verbatim transcripts of three videotaped sessions. We present our account of the family's story and the therapy in chronological order, beginning with Sue Levin's memory of her first meeting with the Roberts family.

The Case: Conversation with a Family and Its Members

I think it's going to be okay . . . being stuck together. Sam doesn't drink anymore. I don't know that it [therapy] helped. I always seem to change and get things out of it. Sam and I have learned how to sit down and calmly discuss what to do about this. We have finally bound together to raise Ann now that she's grown. And we do it all the time now; it's not just a one-time thing. It's amusing, I find myself smiling, because we've fought so much, and now we finally agree. Now don't you think that's strange?

[3] We have changed the names of the family members to protect their identity.

Conversation 1: Sam Roberts and Sue

The Robertses are a middle-class family living in a rural area near Houston. Sam and Martha have been married 19 years, the first marriage for him and the second for her. Martha has two grown children, both married with children of their own. Sam and Martha have two children, Dylan (age 19), and Ann (age 16). Sam has worked as an engineering contractor in oil-related industry all of his adult life. He has had overseas assignments that lasted from one month to one year. Martha was a full-time homemaker until her children were in school and then took a job as a school bus aide working with special education students, which allowed her to be available to her children after school, summers, and holidays.

I first met the Roberts family after an incident where Sam was caught secretly watching his daughter, Ann, through her window while she was dressing. Martha called and requested that I see Sam and Ann. She reported that Ann did not want to be around her father, and, therefore, we should not schedule family sessions at this time. Sam agreed. Several separate sessions were held with Sam and Ann and with Martha, who seemed the most alarmed and distressed. Martha described struggling with anger and disgust with her husband and wondered if she could ever get over this incident and trust him again. She saw his behavior as an outgrowth of other "perversions"[4] that she attributed to Sam, including his use of pornography and sporadic visiting of topless bars. Martha alternated between hopelessness and optimism, thinking that maybe I could "fix" her husband, if he would just open up in therapy.

Comment: The decision to see the Robertses separately was theirs. As collaborative therapists, we do not consider ourselves experts on how people work best nor do we know how therapy will be helpful. All we know is what clients tell us. If we have an opinion we will express it, but they decide who comes, whether they come alone or not, how often, and when to stop.

Sam attended therapy cautiously, stating in the first session that he was "not sure how a woman could possibly understand me" and that he expected to be "condemned" for what had happened. Sam was clear that although he had a strong interest in his daughter that crossed the line with his watching her dress, his interest in her was "loving, not evil." Sam did not feel that anyone understood him and described his wife as seeing him as a "rapist" rather than an intensely "loving father." Sam said he deeply regretted what he did and reported that he had greatly damaged his relationship with Ann as well as with Martha. He was more concerned about Ann and learning how he could be a better father to her than about working on his marriage, which he considered unlikely to change. He believed the marital problems were rooted in Martha's "history of bad relationships" and supported his theory with reports of her repeated victimization by men. He believed that this history set her up to "reject and distrust men," dooming his efforts at intimacy with failure.

---

[4]Quotation marks indicate words used by the person referred to.

Ann, an attractive, energetic, serious 16-year-old, agreed to come to therapy only to "pacify my mother." She reported that although the incident with her father upset her, she had confronted him, said what she needed to say, and wanted to get on with her life. She was involved in many activities (school, Future Farmers of America, barrel racing, and her boyfriend, H. L.) that kept her busy and away from the house. She, her mother, and father had organized their schedules so that Ann would not have to be alone with her father.

This decision for Sam to be away from the house when Martha was not there was reported by each family member, though each expressed different reasons why this arrangement was helpful. Martha reported having major issues trusting Sam and did not know if she would ever be comfortable with his having a father-daughter relationship with Ann again. Sam said he was glad to find ways to help Ann feel safe and hoped that staying away from the house would show her that he was cooperating and had her best interests at heart. Ann said that as long as she did not have to deal with her father, she would be fine. She voiced annoyances and frustrations about her mother's continuing attempts to get her to talk about her feelings, about her father, and about her parents' marriage, which she reported hearing complaints about from both parents for many years. Through continuing sessions to appease her mother, Ann talked about discomforts she had felt with her father, who she said "looks at me funny" and "always wants to know my business."

Comment: Some of the descriptions that Ann used in talking about her discomfort were similar to phrases and comments that Martha made. Instead of interpreting this echoing as a sign of untoward influence, it could be seen as having a variety of meanings, for instance, as a sign of how much this mother and daughter discussed various ideas and concerns with each other.

At one of the twelve sessions held over a three-month period, the family decided to discontinue therapy, with each member reporting that his or her concerns related to the window-peeking incident had subsided. Ann was feeling more comfortable with her father, stating that she had begun to deal with him on certain things. She was okay approaching him directly for help and advice about her horses or when she needed help with something and Martha was not available. Ann reported that Sam was respecting more of her boundaries, would not come into her room without knocking, and would leave when she requested.

I talked with Sam and Martha about Ann feeling comfortable and wondered if they wanted to continue talking, with the possibility of working on their marriage. Both agreed that it might be a good idea. Sam, however, suggested that they take a break from therapy for awhile. Martha seemed disappointed but resigned, stating that as long as things were okay with the kids, that was maybe the "best I can hope for" at this time.

Eight months later Sam called me and came in to talk about a new family crisis. I saw Sam alone at his request. He reported that his relationships with Martha and Ann were becoming more difficult and distant. He recounted the situation that led to his call. Ann, almost finished with her junior year in high school, was asked by her boyfriend, H. L., to his senior prom. She was very excited about going and asked her mother if she could spend the night at H. L.'s home after the prom. Sam was angry that Martha had said yes but neglected to tell him about the plan. He seemed to believe that this was a "deliberate" strategy by Martha and Ann to keep him out of the decision, and he felt that they were regularly circumventing his participation in the family.

The afternoon of the prom, suspecting that Ann planned to spend the night with H. L., Sam asked what Ann's plans were for the evening but said her response was vague. He did not press her, telling me that he knew that she was "avoiding" telling him the truth. There was no further interaction about this issue until much later in the evening when Sam, who had stayed up alone drinking beer, said he "lost it." At about one o'clock in the morning, he awoke Martha and demanded to know where Ann was. Martha told him about the plan for Ann to stay at H. L.'s, and he called H. L.'s house demanding that Ann come home. Ann refused, and in fear of her father's anger, did not come home the following day. As the session unfolded, it appeared that Ann was still positioned not to come home and that Martha blamed Sam for "running off" their daughter.

My conversation with Sam revolved around what he hoped might happen next and how he might get that to happen. Sam's greatest hope was that Ann would return home and "get her life back on track." Sam said he was very concerned about Ann and the direction her life had taken in the past year. He seemed convinced that Ann had "lost her focus and priorities," spending too much time with her boyfriend and not enough time on school and family responsibilities. He connected some of these changes to her first long-term serious relationship with a boy, as well as to her mother's undue influence.

Sam discussed his continuing frustration and confusion over what he considered a "deep, individual problem" that Martha had carried around for years. Sam viewed her "problem" as generated by childhood abuse, physical and emotional abuse in her first marriage, and a violent stranger rape in 1991. This history, he believed, led her to distrust him and to try to protect Ann from him. Sam believed that this mother-daughter alliance was based on the false premise that he was dangerous to Ann. He believed that Martha needed "intensive psychotherapy" to address these issues and to keep Ann from becoming totally "infected" by Martha's fears.

The session ended with Sam stating that Martha was talking about leaving with Ann unless "things changed." He proposed a family session since they had not done that before and since things were so desperate. I agreed that a new tack would be a good idea and offered to invite Harlene Anderson and Paul Burney to join us, hoping additional input would be helpful. I also described the writing project that Harlene, Paul, and I were beginning and explained, if the family agreed, that we might decide to write about our work with them. We agreed that I would call Martha.

Comment: Sam's suggestion of a family session was a bit of a surprise, as that had never been his preferred format for therapy. I took this seriously as a sign of just how worried he was about the current family crisis. Knowing that

Harlene, Paul, and I had an interest in working together, this seemed like a wonderful opportunity for doing something different with this family. Although teamwork is not an unusual idea in family therapy, our approach involves working with other therapists—visiting therapists—in some unusual ways. Visiting therapists are different than traditional family therapy teams in that (1) they are in the room, not behind a mirror; (2) they are free to participate during each session, as they, the clients, and the therapist prefer rather than, for instance, waiting for a break to share ideas or designating a specified time to offer reflections; and (3) they are invited for a particular reason.[5] The reason for inviting Paul and Harlene to visit with the Robertses was twofold: first, to add new voices to our conversation, and second, to have a mutual clinical experience to write about for this chapter.

The Phone Call to Martha

I called Martha to discuss the idea of a family session, the visiting therapists, and the possibility of our writing about our work with them. Martha was very excited about having Harlene and Paul join in and viewed their participation as added help. She was also interested in the writing project and wanted to read whatever we wrote. Through her work with special education students, Martha had developed a strong interest in psychology. Although not college educated, she had learned much about the field through her own psychotherapy, reading, and employment. Martha agreed to talk with Ann (as well as with Dylan, who had not been involved in the previous therapy) about a family session, the visiting therapists, and the possibility of our writing about them. Martha called back to schedule the session, saying Ann agreed to come and Dylan would if he was able to get off from work and not miss college classes. We now turn to the first family session with Paul and Harlene.

Conversation 2: Sam, Martha, and Ann; Sue, Harlene, and Paul

Sue and Paul talked with the family; Harlene operated the camera and joined in on occasion.[6] After very brief introductions of all the participants, the family began talking about a close family friend who had recently been killed in a car

---

[5] An example of a specific reason for bringing in a visiting therapist occurred when Sue worked with a man, Jim, who was struggling to keep his marriage from ending in divorce. In exploring his ideas about marriage and divorce, Jim reported that he had been raised an active and dedicated Catholic but no longer attended church. Though wanting to return to church, Jim stated that he was sexually abused by a priest as a young boy and that he felt he had to deal with that before he could return to church. He reported "not knowing how to deal with this." Since we have several colleagues who are both Catholic nuns and family therapists, Sue asked Jim's permission to invite them to join us.

[6] We decided to organize this session with Paul joining Sue in active talk with the family, while Harlene managed the video camera and offered her thoughts and questions intermittently throughout the meeting. We continued with this format for the two subsequent sessions.

accident. They had been to the funeral the day before. As it turned out, Dylan was not able to take off from work for the session because he had missed work the day before because of the funeral. Martha described that she was still filled with emotion. This friend had been a police officer, 25 years old, and was a horse fanatic like Ann. He and the family had become good friends through their mutual interest in horses. He had helped transport Ann and her horses to competitions, and Ann had just recently given him a prize saddle she had won in appreciation of their special relationship. Martha and Sam both felt like they had "lost one of our own children." Martha felt that his death seemed to "pull the family together" and predicted that they might not want to talk about "deep" things today because they were so worn out.

Paul talked with Ann about Future Farmers of America and her lambs and horses as he attempted to learn about her and her interests. Each person jumped in to respond as Paul's curiosity turned to "what brings you here today?" Martha expressed concerns for Ann and her feelings about her father while emphasizing that she believed Sam had a "big problem" and that their marriage was in "terrible trouble." To illustrate her belief that Sam was more involved in relating to the children than to her, Martha went back to their early history, saying that Sam was not interested in "marrying me unless I could bear children." They had, in fact, gone through fertility treatment before she became pregnant and they were married. Martha described Sam as having "addiction problems" and characterized him as a "workaholic," an "alcoholic," and a "sex-aholic." She was worried that Sam was currently not working much and was drinking more than usual. Martha said she felt like "an abused woman," asking Sam, "Do you know the mental, the verbal abuse you put me through? It's enough to drive me crazy—the mind games you play with me. I'm terrified of you."

Sam acknowledged his "addictive tendencies" but did not believe that he was ever "out of control." He said he recognized when his life was too much "out of balance" and was always able to "self-correct." Sam described his interest in his daughter as appropriate; it was his job as a father, one that he would never relinquish. Sam emphasized how responsible he felt for his family, stressing, "I work hard to support my family; I've given them everything; they come first."

Comment: Both Sam and Martha, from the beginning of our work together, used psychological diagnostic language to describe each other and themselves. Rather than assume we knew what these short-cut descriptions implied, we explored what they were trying to communicate as they used them. That is, from our learning position, we clarified and expanded their meanings, which prevented us from misunderstandings. These new descriptions led to distinctions that complicated their self- and other diagnostic labeling. Both Martha and Sam agreed, for instance, that some of the characteristics of alcoholism "fit Sam" and "others did not." On some levels Martha saw herself as "emotionally abused," and on others she did not. Continuing to explore and understand Martha's and Sam's meanings led to the creation of new and different language, subsequently leading to new and different options for behavior.

The session continued with Ann talking about how things had been difficult between her and Sam. The following dialogue illustrates how Ann described the problem.

Ann: I don't know, it's just weird ever since he was standing outside my window watching me, I don't know. I mean, I love Dad and I trust him. I don't mean trust, but I respect him. I love Dad. He's my father, you know, but he drills me. I don't like being drilled. He hammers me all the time, asking questions, "Why are you doing this?" [turning to Sam] When you get this way, Dad, I can't stand it. I can't talk to you.

Sue: Can you say more about what you mean about your dad getting "this way?"

Martha: He's the expert, he knows the answers. He won't listen to anything you have to say.

Ann: I haven't been able to be comfortable in the house. It's gotten to the point where I've put up a latch on my door. He bothers me. I don't like that. I can't stand the way he tries to make me talk to him. He won't leave and I can't leave. I can't do anything, I have to stand there and talk to him. I don't like that.

Sam: I left you alone that Saturday [the day of the prom], I didn't interrogate you then.

Martha: See, that's his thing. You never know when he's going to strike. That's his thing, the element of surprise. You walk around on eggshells. I'm afraid about today. What are going to be the repercussions of this [session]?

Ann grew more tense as she returned to what had happened the day of the prom.

Martha: You've driven her out, Sam. She's leaving home when she goes to college and I hold it against you. I hold it against you. I can't help it, she's my baby. I'm a mother, how else am I supposed to feel?

Ann: I've asked Mom why she stays, what's in it for her? I don't know why she stays. You say you've given me everything, but I'll tell you, Dad, it's not worth going crazy over. It's not worth the mind games.

Sam: I'm not playing mind games with you, Ann. All I've tried to do is give you everything you want.

Sue: Sam, how do you understand that your intentions get so misunderstood?

Sam: One of the things I try to tell them is that it's all for them. If they don't want to come home, if they don't want the house the way it is, if they don't want the family the way it is, if it's just so bad that they don't want any of it, then that's the way it'll be.

Comment: Family members tell their stories that are familiar to them but new to the therapists. The telling of their stories takes place in a particular environment, a conversational space cocreated by the therapists with the participants. That is, the therapists' stance encourages questioning and wondering and acts as a natural invitation to the family members to join with them in a shared inquiry.

Throughout the consultation the therapists are engaged, actively and carefully listening with interest and enthusiasm for each person's description of his or her understanding of the family's dilemmas as they unfold. The therapists' questions about what is being told expand, extend, and clarify their ideas and understandings of the family's story pieces. Catching the therapists' curiosity, each family member begins to listen and hear in different ways. They hear the unheard (Levin, 1992). Each description extends other voiced ideas. All combine to create a dialogue among the family members and between them and the therapists— advancing the narratives of their story. Here, with many questions and curiosities about what was being said, a new understanding begins to emerge as Martha decided that Ann had manipulated her about spending the night at H. L.'s and as she asked Sam and Ann questions about this event.

Following this interchange, Paul commented that even though this issue was a difficult one that had led to all kinds of upset and distress in the family, they seemed to be able to talk about it in a way that was productive. He asked the family what they thought made that possible. Martha clarified that she and Sam knew Ann was being manipulative. It was important for Ann's development, Martha believed, for Ann to know that she and her father knew what was going on. Martha reported that things having to do with the kids were of utmost importance.

Martha: It's so bizarre. People compliment us on our kids all the time, not just now and then. Everybody does. The doctors that have seen her for years, they want me to write a book about how to raise children. Do you know how that makes me feel? I think, if you only knew . . . I want her not to be where I'm at right now. I really don't. I don't want you to be like me. I want her to be secure, I want her to know right from wrong.

Martha went on to describe how she and Sam "raise children well" but "we don't do marriage well." She said that they live like roommates and have no intimate relationship but come together to parent. This led to a question about what they thought would happen to them when the kids moved out. Sam responded that the kids would never go away. They talked about their two grandchildren by Martha's oldest child who were keeping them busy. The session ended and an appointment was scheduled for two weeks.

Comment: Ideas and questions were left hanging in the air as Harlene wondered what Dylan might have added had he been at the session. This led to more positive comments about what a great kid Dylan was and how much he wanted to help the family with these struggles. They wanted to try to find a time so Dylan could come to the next meeting.

Conversation 3: Sam, Martha, Ann, and Dylan; Sue, Harlene, and Paul

Dylan, who we met for the first time, came with Sam, Martha, and Ann to the third session. He lives at home, works full-time, attends college, and therefore does not spend much time at the house with the other family members.

Sam, Martha, and Ann began the session humorously commenting on their tendency to sit in the same place. We joined in their laughter, adding that we as therapists often do the same.

Comment: In our experience, sessions often begin in a general and light-hearted manner as the family members and the therapists get to know one another, reconnect from the absence between sessions, and ease into the session.

We asked how things were going, and they talked about what was currently happening in their lives. Sam, Martha, and Ann described their thoughts and feelings, appearing to dance around each other in a tentative manner (our observation), sharing a story with some laughter or at times becoming tense as other areas were explored. Their stories unfolded with a wide range of emotional intensity. Ann began.

Ann: Things are fine at home. Things at home have changed since I am never at home and when I'm not at school, I spend my time at the barn working with my horses.

She described her recent involvement in the high school rodeo.

Sam: How do you plan to get to the rodeos since most of them are out of town?
Ann: H. L. volunteered to take me and trailer my horse. We've decided to be just best friends, like we used to be.

Ann added that for awhile they were best friends as well as boyfriend and girlfriend, but they seemed to have fought a lot lately. Sam commented that H. L. was an important part of Ann's life and that he may have felt left out of the family and that could be part of Ann's problem. He thought that it might be good if H. L. came to the sessions. Ann agreed, saying she knew that H. L. wanted to understand what the family was going through and that he had asked her if they discussed him at the sessions.

Sue: Ann, what do you think about your father bringing up inviting H. L?
Ann: My father and I do not talk with each other. I think H. L. would like to come, but I'm not surprised that he mentioned bringing H. L. I am open to suggestions, especially if they might be helpful to Dad. H. L. thinks Dad is jealous of my relationship with him, and I think Dad might be jealous because H. L. is doing things he once did.
Paul: Ann, how do you think your father feels about not being invited to go to the rodeo or do things with you since you became involved with H. L.? What do you think your father would say if you asked him if he is jealous?

Their conversation centered around how H. L. really helps Sam by taking care of Ann, "cutting me some slack" so that he could work. Ann turned to her father and asked, "Are you jealous?" They began talking about H. L. Sam stated that "H. L. takes the load off of me and helps protect Ann." He said that he always tried to protect both Martha and Ann. They talked about Ann, her horse, the rodeo, and how Sam felt about Ann not wanting him there. Sam said that he wanted to go but felt Ann would rather have H. L. helping her. At times, he felt Ann did not want him or Martha at the events.

Paul: Will you still go to the events?
Sam: We haven't talked about it.
Martha: We just found out about it last night!

The discussion turned to entry fees, trailering costs, and how Ann planned to pay for them. Martha broke in at that point.

Martha: Since we are in a safe environment, Ann should tell us how much this is going to cost.

Martha said she "came apart" the night before when she heard the cost. She continued, saying the more she thought about it that morning the more she had rationalized the cost in her mind as being no different than paying for dance lessons or costumes. Ann said she realized it would cost a "chunk of money." Because she knew her parents were concerned about money, she had borrowed $150 from her grandmother who was happy to help her. Ann planned to repay her from her rodeo winnings. Martha said she would be willing to "pitch in" and help Ann with the rodeo costs, but there were things that Ann would have to do to help.

Sam then detailed the costs as he understood them and why he believed Ann's plan would not work. This led to a discussion about "our money," the money he earned "for the family," and "her money," the money Martha earned that was hers to do "anything she wants to with." He wanted Ann to go to the rodeos, but he did not want Ann and Martha to resent him for not being able to afford it.

Sue: Sam, what do you mean by resentment?
Sam: When I provide funds for things, they see it as leverage.
Sue: What created those feelings?
Sam: That is what they tell me. It is my responsibility to provide for my family by going out and earning money, and it is Martha's responsibility to raise the kids. Suddenly all of that has changed around and anything I do seems resented. I don't do it for fun, guys, I do it for you all. You're looking at an alcoholic here. I would much rather go out, get drunk, party, kick back, and blow everything off. That is the tendency for someone with my kind of personality. That is why we are looking for $20,000 by January because I laid back for two months.
Sue: What would you see as different if they stopped being resentful? What would be the change?
Sam: Ann would need a different attitude, like she had a year and a half ago.
Sue: What was that like?
Sam: A positive attitude.

Ann said she still wanted to get involved in the rodeo. Sam agreed with her about the importance of the experience of raising horses and lambs and said she was still trying to "go for it all." He questioned her negative attitudes about school, him, and H. L., seeing the attitude as perhaps a result of many things, including just growing up.

Ann: Y'all are always saying how you are hurting about money.
Sam: Careful about y'all! Careful about y'all because you haven't come and talked to me in a long time.
Paul: If Ann would have talked to you about this, what would you have said to her? How would you have discussed this with Ann?
Sam: If she had come in with the right attitude, I would have said "let's go for it."
Paul: And what do you think Ann would have said?
Sam: I don't know.
Ann: I would have said "fine, let's go for it."

She then turned to her mother.

Ann: Dad says things, but I check it out with Mom to make sure we have the money. Maybe he has the money? Maybe he has some money hidden?
Sam and Martha: [in unison, with emphasis] It's not there, Ann.

Sam, Martha, and Ann became involved in a heated discussion about the topic of money.

Paul: My guess is that you often do this at home, and it is probably not very productive for you. It would help me understand more about your situation if you could talk in a less heated way and allow each person to have their turn. Is there another way you might be able to discuss this rather than argue?

Comment: This might be considered an intervention by some therapists. In collaborative therapy, however, as here, it was offered as a natural and tentative comment about the way the family seemed to be communicating. The comment, made not as a pronouncement or mandate, led to a discussion of how they might do it differently. The family members, however, could have agreed or disagreed with Paul's question and comment or could have ignored it entirely. Paul had no investment in the comment nor hidden intention.

As each responded to Paul's questions, tensions calmed and the tone shifted from argumentative to one that allowed each to listen to the others' perspectives. Sam expressed his feelings that Ann was "worth everything I do for her" but that "she turns around and treats me badly." Ann commented that she realized she often took things for granted, adding that she did not know how to tell them she appreciated what they did and began to cry. Martha suggested that the way Ann could acknowledge their efforts was not by telling them "thank you, thank you" but by her attitude.

Sue: Martha, do you feel some of the same lack of appreciation that Sam does?
Martha: Yes, Ann complains about everything—her old truck, for instance. She has everything. She is 17 and has everything. [Martha gives an

illustration of an occasion at a barrel race.] Ann not only ignored us but got up and walked off. We had been up there working for her and she treated us badly. Some of it I contributed to normal teenageism.

Ann responded that she was easily frustrated when working with her horse.

Ann: I don't want anyone telling me what I did wrong, I already know. It has to do more about my parents than anyone else. I will sometimes listen to someone else.

Paul: [turning to Ann] Does it have to do with your parents or is it more about your perception that they have no expertise in barrel racing?

Ann: Sometimes they seem like idiots.

Sam: You are right, Ann, we are idiots for going through all of this and providing you with opportunities. We are all at an event and you win a saddle, go out and pick it up, and don't say one word of thanks to us or anyone. Ann, you are right, we are idiots. This is not my Ann. You did that to purposely hurt me.

Sue: I was curious to know how that makes you feel like "an idiot."

Sam: Ann needs a way to do it [compete in the rodeo], and she feels like she does not owe any responsibility to anyone. She came back and disassociated herself from us. The old Ann would have appreciated us for providing her with the opportunity. She never said thank you, wrote a card, or anything.

Ann: I was going to but I just forgot. I did not mean to not thank them and it wasn't that I didn't feel thankful. I just didn't do it. [distraught cries] What? With Doug [the family friend and policeman who had been killed], you did't have to thank him, he just knew!

Sam: She was all over Doug. [referring to the occasion when Ann won a belt buckle]

Ann: [still crying] I don't feel I told Doug how much I appreciated him before he died.

The discussion returned to the upcoming high school rodeo and whether Ann wanted her mother and father to attend. Ann said that it was not that she did not want them there but that she felt as though it was an imposition on the family and a sacrifice for her to be there. She said that H. L. also felt she did not appreciate him either and that she was more focused on the goal of getting to the rodeo. People, she admitted, had not been the important issue. All agreed that "balance" was a "key word for our family." When they were happy, it was fun to be together as a family. When they were unhappy, it became "a chore" and the fun was lost.

Paul: With the information you have now as a family, how could you make the upcoming new school semester and the high school rodeo more fun? What might you do differently?

Martha: Sam and I could go to the rodeo alone and not make it a threesome. Sam and I could have a relationship, and we could be in the audience.

Harlene joined in expressing curiosity about what Dylan had been thinking as the others talked. Dylan, referring to Ann's attitude, said, "That's just the way she is." He added that he thought his parents were a little jealous of Ann's relationship with H. L., but he understood.

Sam: I feel like it's about me.

Harlene wanted to hear more but wondered if we might continue the discussion at the next session because of time constraints. Sue, almost simultaneously, had the same question.

Sue: It sounds as though there is a lot to think about. Could we possibly begin the conversation at this point at the next session?

All agreed.

Comment: Families find the collaborative approach challenges their expectations that the therapist will provide "a cure or answer for our problems" as they experience innovative ways to discuss their dilemmas and arrive at solutions of their own design. In our experience, individuals become more able or willing to listen to each other's ideas and appreciate others' points of view—something that may not take place while in emotionally escalating conversations at home. Clients often comment that they talk about the same things in the context of the therapy session that they do at home, but somehow the style of talking is different. That is not to say they had no differences or misunderstandings—only that they seemed to talk about these intense issues, as the family stated, "different from the usual way we talk at home." New kinds of relationships are created within the family as members experience new kinds of conversations.

Conversation 4: Sam, Martha, Dylan, and Ann; Sue, Harlene, and Paul

Our next meeting with the family was two weeks later. The mood seemed tense as they walked in the room and took their seats. Martha, who seemed annoyed (our observation), asserted, "Somebody start this." Sue responded addressing the whole family.

Sue: If you describe your goal for our meeting today or if you waved your magic wand . . . ?

Sam: If I had a magic wand, these guys would be happy. I'm not sure I have any other goals.

Dylan added that he thought Sam's goal was repairing their house, which had been severely damaged by a flood. Sam and Dylan continued talking about the house repairs and Ann joined in, suggesting they should move out of the house. She offered several reasons, including the need for a larger yard and a barn for her horse. She also thought both Sam and Martha would be happier with less expense and less work.

Paul: Would you be happier? Would moving make a difference?

Martha, whose annoyance at Sam seemed to have been building, instructed Paul, "Ask him," nodding toward Sam. Before Sam could respond, Martha, with what seemed a disillusioned and blaming tone, continued.

Martha: Sam makes all the decisions, particularly about the houses we have lived in.

Sue: So how do you understand the difference between the way you look at it and Sam's way?

Martha reacted quickly and strongly.

Martha: It's called a value system. I've developed one!

Martha talked for several minutes, elaborating on her values with lots of feeling.

Martha: It's [her value system] not going to be compromised!

Sue continued to be curious about Martha's thoughts on the differences between her values and Sam's. Martha shared her earlier feelings of "guilt and shame" about things she had done in the past, how they had ruled her life, and how important church had been in helping her "get rid of these feelings" and "grow."

Martha: But I had so much of it, and I just don't see any over here, and I don't understand.

An observer would assume Martha was talking about Sam, but she does not look or nod at him.

Paul: Could you tell me more about that? Maybe I'm a little confused at understanding how you're not seeing shame. Are you talking about Sam?

Martha: [turning toward Sam and responding emphatically] Oh yes, I'm talking about Sam. I don't understand how he can talk about houses and decks with the immense pain going on. There's a lot of pain. Let's get to the bottom of the pain and figure out what's happening.

Sue: How could he help you get to the bottom of the pain? Or am I misunderstanding?

Martha: I don't want them [Ann and Dylan] to question for years, I wonder where I stand with my parents? I wonder if they love me? Why did my father do that to me? Why didn't my mother do something about that? I don't want these two burdened with that.

Martha was distressed that time was running out, and she didn't want the children to go through life "carrying the burden I've carried and maybe what their father has carried."

Sue: Would it help you to know that they weren't carrying that load?

Martha was crying as she and Sue continued. She spoke about spending time and talking with the children, saying "we [referring to herself and the children] talk about deep things." She wondered if the kids just want "to go about their business" and then declared, "It's really my and Sam's problem. But it is not just our problem." She felt that Ann had a lot of pain and anger. She cried for her, fearing that she would be "just like me and I don't want her to be like that." As Martha talked, Ann began crying; both Sam and Dylan were looking down.

Comment: In therapy emotions and feelings are always present, at some times stronger than at others. We do not automatically ask about emotions and feelings the way that most therapists are trained to do. We do not believe there is one way or a right way to talk about them. We do not make silent or out-loud interpretations, nor do we ignore them. Instead, they are talked about in and as part of the conversation; how that is accomplished is specific to the persons involved and the circumstance.

Martha said that Ann wanted to run away from home. Ann had also encouraged Martha to leave and does not understand why she does not. Running from a situation, Martha advised, does not teach you anything and even though she wants to run she will not. She wants peace but believes that the reality of the situation is that she cannot leave.

Sue: Can I interrupt? If there is something that needs to happen to help with the feeling, what do you think that would be?
Martha: For him to start talking with feeling.

Martha expressed frustration that she does not know how to reach Sam.

Martha: He doesn't know anything about me, and I sure as heck don't know anything about him. He dances around with words and only talks about the safe things. I don't get any comfort from him. We don't hold hands or embrace or do any of these things.

Sue wondered, remembering that both Martha and Ann had referred to Sam as "not real."

Sue: Would that be something that would feel more real to you?
Martha: Yes, sometimes. But that's not going to come. That's not going to happen. That doesn't happen with people you don't trust.
Paul: What kinds of things would Sam have to do differently so that you could trust him? If I heard you right, trust is a real strong point for you.

Martha said that at this point in her life she has "shut down" and really does not care if she trusts Sam or not. She believes that he will leave soon after the children leave home. Then she said that she wants "shame" and "remorse" from him.

Sam, who had been listening intently, interjected that he feels the problem with Ann is not resolved. He tells Paul and Sue that Ann has not talked with him since "then" (referring to the window-peeking incident) and feels that she has "the wrong attitude." Martha breaks in with intensity.

Martha: I'm coming to Ann's defense. Why is it always us that are wrong and you are always right? [pointing to Ann, who is no longer crying] You better speak up for yourself. You had better talk *now* and get out—what you're feeling.

Sam breaks in to declare his love for his family. A conversational cross fire develops as Martha quickly returns to the window-peeking incident. Sue interrupts, expressing how fast the conversation is moving, and wonders if Ann wants to respond to her mother's request to talk and say how she is feeling. Ann, crying again, accuses Sam.

Ann: He is sitting there glaring at me. All I see is hatred . . . I don't see love, I don't feel it.

Sam: I don't hate you!

Ann: Your words don't mean anything to me.

Ann then describes how she tries to avoid Sam because she is afraid he will "try to strike up a conversation."

Ann: There's nothing he can do to fix it as far as I am concerned.

She continues talking about Sam, saying that she has a lot of anger for him but she doesn't know why. Ann glares at Sam.

Ann: I just don't understand you. You sit there trying to explain yourself and that just confuses me more. That's why I don't like listening to you. I feel like you are playing with my head.

Sue: What do you think makes it so hard for Sam to explain himself?

Ann: He explains himself okay, but it's just that I have quit listening.

Sue: I wonder if at this point any explanation would be helpful.

Ann agreed. After a long pause in the conversation, Sam, who had been looking at Ann as she talked and seemed to be absorbed in the talk, asserted, "I am the problem, Ann. Don't make my problem your problem."

At this point, Sam abruptly said he needed to get some coffee and left the room. Paul suggested a quick break. The rest of the group agreed. The family mingled in the coffee room with each other and with Sue and Paul.

Comment: Paul's response to Sam's leaving the room was spontaneous, informed by the circumstances. We do not interpret or have preset ideas about these kinds of exchanges and behaviors, nor do we have routine ways of responding to them. How we respond at any one time depends on the conversation, the situation, and the relationship. Therapy sessions occur in unfamiliar places where the environment is, if not sterile and formal, at least different from the clients' everyday settings. We think therapy should approximate everyday life as much as possible. This includes not only the trappings of our offices but the way we relate with our clients. We think of our clients as our guests and treat them as such, likewise, we are guests in their lives. We do not think of boundaries in the traditional sense. If we invite our clients to have coffee, for instance, we may or may not join them but we would not try to avoid interacting with them in the coffee room.

All returned to the therapy room spontaneously. Once seated, Paul turned to Sam.

Paul: What were your thoughts on what Ann was saying?

After a long pause, Sam responded.

Sam: The parents shouldn't pass down their problems to their children.

Sam started to talk to Ann, but Paul interceded.

Paul: Sam. Sam, let me interrupt you a minute. I'm going to ask you to do something a little bit different, if that would be okay. One of the things I've heard is that when you say things to Ann, she doesn't listen maybe the way you want her to.

Sam agreed as Paul continued.

Paul: I'm curious if you would just tell me what you're saying and let Ann listen to your conversation with me, if that might make a difference. Would you mind trying that?

Sam and Paul talked together for several minutes. Sam spoke about his and Martha's problems—how he has given up, drinks a lot, and has a bad attitude. He spoke about feeling unappreciated, how the kids take the opportunities that he provides them for granted.

Sam: When Martha and Ann come down on me and hate me, I cease to function.

Sam felt he then loses sight of the whole purpose of the marriage. Ann and Martha joined defensively in the discussion.

Martha: I don't hate you. I feel sorry for you.

Martha questioned what he was saying, and Sam felt misunderstood.

Sam: That's not what I'm saying at all.

Sam looked at Paul and wondered what Paul had heard. Before Paul could respond, Sue broke in.

Sue: I'm curious, Sam, if you could describe your understanding of how you end up feeling at the same time very—and I'm just going to throw this word out—victimized by them in terms of the way they make you feel hated, and then also are accused of victimizing.

Comment: Sue's breaking in comes with the territory of conversation, with its inherent ebbing and flowing, with its crisscrossing nature. If Paul thought what he had to say was important and could not wait, he would have said so out loud to Sue. Paul could always return to Sam's question or his thoughts about it later, or he could drop it. We would not give meaning to a therapist's or to a family member's interruption. In our experience, people become absorbed in the conversation and spontaneously contribute. Sue was merely curious about Sam's feeling misunderstood.

Martha interrupted, "You did it!" Dylan gestured to Martha to be quiet.

Sam: She is accusing me of incest!
Martha: No, I'm not!

Sam continued, expressing distress that Martha tells other people (referring to the incest) who then hate him and that she influences Ann. Ann, now with no sign of tears and sitting straight in her chair, chimed in, "I can think for myself." She continued, expressing her belief about the importance of talking, of talking with friends, and how that helps. Sue expressed her confusion about the different understandings in the room. In response, Ann paused and then began talking about her own confusion—not so sure of her thoughts about her father.

Sue: So what would you hope that your dad would understand better?
Ann: That you need people. [looking directly at Sam] You're not discussing, you're not asking for help . . . he needs to express his feelings.
Sue: So you're hoping that your dad will learn to deal with things the same way you and your mother are?

The discussion between Sue and Ann continued.

Sue: Ann, what do you think are the biggest problems?
Ann: Dad's too sure of himself . . . he's so certain . . . never seen him wonder about what's going on.

Ann does not see her father as a "real person" but has no idea why he does not act like one. Sue wondered what Dylan's thoughts were, given his indications that his relationship with Sam is different.

Comment: We do not place value on who speaks or the duration of the speaking. We do not make assumptions, judgments, or interpretations about "silence" or about the amount a person speaks. We do not think it was unusual, for instance, for Dylan to participate in the spoken conversation less than the others. He seemed naturally quiet and although what was being talked about was familiar to him, it was not familiar in this context. We are not surprised or bothered. When a person arrives in the middle of a conversation, like the middle of a play, it may take some time to catch up or cause hesitancy to join in.

Dylan: I've seen both certainty and uncertainty [referring to confidence and a lack of it] in Dad. I feel like I'm in the middle between Mom and Dad.

Dylan talked about himself—having a problem with control, not wanting to engage in "deep, emotional, gut-wrenching communication."

Dylan: I don't want a relationship like Mom and Dad's. Mom's got to change and Dad's got to change, if they're going to talk.

He continued, describing how he sees their communication problem. He believed that in the end it will be the two of them and they will still love each other no matter what. He went on to share some of the difficulties that he has had communicating with his mother.

Dylan: You have to be careful what you ask her because she's a "radioactive mom." It has come to the point of stay-away-from-Mom type of thing.

Ann joined in, resonating with Dylan's experiences.

Ann: She's liable to explode. It's his fault [referring to Sam] that she's "radioactive."

Dylan: It's Mom *and* Dad's fault. It's solid two-way.

Martha was smiling, and both she and Sam were listening intently as their children talked.

Paul: Well, it sounds like you have some radioactivity here—that possibly you're suggesting building some containment cells around it, in moderation. You're suggesting some change, and you really see that there's a possibility for that to happen.

Dylan: [enthusiastically] Yeah, I definitely think there is. I have faith in them.

Sue and Paul glanced at the clock and realized that time was up. The tension had dissipated, and the meeting ended on an encouraging note. As the next appointment was discussed, all agreed that it would be more convenient for Sue to see the family in her office, nearer their home. Paul and Harlene wished them well and expressed an interest in keeping up with them through Sue. All agreed that they were open to adding Paul and Harlene back into the conversation in the future if it seemed useful.

Conversation 5: Sam, Martha, Ann, H. L., and Sue

As suggested by Sam and Ann in an earlier session, H. L., Ann's boyfriend, came with the family. H. L. and Sue chatted a bit at the beginning of the meeting, with his filling her in on beginning college and his hope to major in criminal psychology.

H. L.:   I'm applying for a job since I'm only going to school two days a week. I applied at the hardware store where Dylan works, and I hope Dylan can help me get hired.

The chatting tone shifted to a serious one.

Sue: H. L., I was wondering what you have heard about the meetings. Do you have some things in particular that you would like to talk about?

H. L.:   No.

The conversation was broadened to the rest of the group. After a bit of hemming and hawing, Martha wondered if maybe they were a "real happy bunch today" and then announced that she had a new job at a nursing home. This seemed to be news to Sam and Ann as well, and we all asked questions and learned about the job together. There were questions about what would change, if anything, for everyone as Martha added a second job to her day. This led to a conversation about Ann's chores and how she and her mother communicate about what needs to be done around the house.

Ann told about a lamb show that had not gone well. Martha asked her who the judge was at the show.

Sue: [to Martha and Sam] So this was a contest that you didn't go to?
Ann: No, they didn't go.
Martha: Now wait a minute, we came by; in fact, we came by twice.
Ann: They came and then they left.
Martha: [sarcastically] And I felt guilty, real guilty, but it was okay. We went to the movies.
Ann: And I didn't care that they weren't there.
Martha: He wanted to go to a movie, and I followed him.
Sam: We went. Ann wasn't showing, she was just fooling around, so there wasn't anything going on.
Sue: So what movie did you see?

The conversation shifted again.

Sam: Let's talk about your horses, Ann.

Ann explained that she might have to move her horses to a new stable that was much closer to their home. They agreed that moving the horses would reduce Ann's driving time. Sam addressed his ongoing concerns about her paying for gas and driving at night. The conversation broadened to Ann's extracurricular activities and how she might round out her academics, making it possible for her to be admitted to a state university. Following a lot of laughter and lighthearted comments, Ann turned to her father and asked a more serious question.

Ann: I want to know why you wanted H. L. to be here. Cause I know you have a reason.
Sam: I pretty much gave my reasons at the last session. Well, Ann, it's because H. L.'s real important in your life and there's other reasons; so that H. L. doesn't have to question you, so if he's here, then he knows what is said. Also, if something comes up in here that upsets you, then you two can talk about it. He knows what's going on. That's why I've wanted Dylan to be here, too.
Sue: It's been nice to have Dylan here.
Ann: Dylan sheds light.
Sam: But really, H. L., and Dylan too, you're not just visiting, you're a part of this.

Sam described their financial situation to Ann so that she would not continue to believe that they have endless resources. Ann described that she had ended up believing that they have some hidden money "because every time I tell you that I need something, you say "don't worry, we can do it." Sam said that the reason he could do that was that he used credit. He has a $40,000 credit line, which runs up when he does not work much, and then he works really hard to pay it off. Martha described panicking when they use the credit, as she doesn't view this as a resource but rather another obligation.

Shifting the topic some, Sam asked H. L. whether or not it seemed like Ann was spoiled, and H. L. described his own family as spoiling him much more than Ann's spoiled her. This led to a conversation about Ann using Sam's credit card to fill H. L.'s truck when hauling her trailer to a horse show. Ann suggested Sam take the credit card away, saying she could not handle the responsibility. Sam wanted Ann to do all of the things she does but said that she needed to understand where the money comes from to pay for the cost.

Sam stated that Martha wanted him to get a "steady job," meaning full-time employment. Sam described that working as a contractor allowed him to make almost twice as much per hour as what he would make in a "steady job." Martha raised the need to cut down on expenses, which led to a discussion of how they could cut back. Martha recommended setting up a budget, which they had not had since they were first married. Martha and Sam had different memories about how the finances worked early in their marriage. Though their descriptions conflicted, Sam and Martha listened to each other intently, while Ann and H. L. seemed to be losing interest.

This conversation continued through the end of the session with Martha complaining that she did not know anything about their finances because Sam kept the checkbook and had a separate business account that she never saw. Though Martha did not want to manage the checkbook, she believed that a budget and having concrete information about their financial situation would ease her mind. Sue's continued questioning returned to the discussion of Sam's current work situation in which he was bringing home 50% less than usual. He reported spending a lot of time looking for work and doing paperwork.

The session ended with Martha saying that she did not want to talk about the financial situation any longer since she believed that Sam would never change his work or do a budget. Martha felt that he did not understand her feelings and did not seem to care to understand. Ann got reinvolved in the conversation, pointing out that Sam seemed to have "an attitude" with Martha and that neither one of them were listening to the other. Ann suggested that they were both "set in their ways." Sue wondered if Martha and Sam would like to meet sometime to talk about "their ways" and the "attitudes" that might be blocking them. They agreed.

Conversation 6: Sam and Martha and Sue

Martha called to cancel the appointment and reschedule, reporting that they could not come in because H. L. and Ann had an accident while they were hauling a horse to Sam's mother's farm. Sam, who was also hauling a trailer, was ahead of them by just a few minutes and was able to return to the scene quickly when Ann called him on a cellular phone. Although neither Ann nor H. L. was injured, the horse sustained serious injuries.

In the next session, they focused on the events of the accident and what it represented for them about Ann and H. L.'s relationship. Both Sam and Martha had similar reactions and concerns, and they seemed very unified at the time.

Sam, having been at the accident, did much of the talking this session, predominantly about what he saw in H. L. and Ann's relationship during the process of handling the accident. Sam said since H. L. was driving, he took it very hard and blamed himself for the accident. Though this seemed legitimate to Sam, he was disappointed that H. L. did not seem concerned enough for the horse to "pull himself together." H. L. reportedly sat on the side of the road crying. As soon as Sam arrived, Ann left the horse and went to "care for" H. L. Sam viewed this as a serious weakness on H. L.'s part and an error in judgment for Ann. Both Martha and Sam agreed that H. L. should have been strong enough to be "taking care" of Ann rather than the other way around.

Martha and Sam talked positively about the example Sam set for Ann, and he reiterated that he has always put the family's needs above his own. If Martha disagreed with this description, she did not indicate it but rather joined in enthusiastically to talk about the values and beliefs that they have tried to instill in their daughter. Both Martha and Sam were proud of Ann's strength, being able to comfort H. L. and care for the horse as well. They both feared "the day that something would happen that Ann would not be strong enough for" and hoped that she would have "a man that she could lean on for support." We discussed that so much came up regarding the accident that it did not make sense to go back to the issues that were raised at the last session. They decided not to set another appointment, as Martha's new job was starting and it was so difficult to get everyone's schedule together.

Comment: A feminist family therapist colleague expressed concerns that Sue should have challenged Sam and Martha's belief system regarding gender roles and should have taken responsibility to intervene in patriarchal cultural practices. Although aware of a difference in values that she holds compared to the family, Sue did not feel obliged or entitled to inject them into therapy. We do not hold specific content or outcome agendas. Instead, we work with clients where they are, on the problems they describe. The intent is to engage with family members in a dialogue rather than assume a position of authority, expertise, or knowledge—whether that be about family values, individual roles, or cultural disclosures. We might note that we are sensitive to cultural discourses and believe that all local therapy takes place within them. Therapy and its environment cannot be separated. We do not expect clients to take on our values. Clients come in a variety of packages, shapes, and sizes, and we do not see our role in therapy as trying to get them to fit our values. The questions Sue asked were relevant to the conversation—intending to help the family members discuss, explore, and clarify the values that were important to them. Gender roles and values were talked about: however, this family did not view their own gender roles and expectations as problematic.

At the conclusion of therapy, Sue sensed that the family members were more comfortable with each other and that the issues they were struggling with had shifted from sex, alcohol, and trust to finances, raising teenagers, and the future empty nest. These issues appeared more "normal" and more manageable to them. They decided what they wanted consultation on, when they needed it, and when they no longer needed it.

Conclusions
Our Reflections

How do we understand the shift from a tense, blaming, and defending exchange filled with pain, misery, and hopelessness to one filled with hope, peace, and caring? How did Sue and Paul create a space for and facilitate a conversation in which possibilities, or at least a sense of possibilities, emerged?

Through their presence, their actions, and their words, Sue and Paul established an inviting environment where family members could relate their stories, ones that were familiar to them but new to the therapists. By an inviting environment, we mean a "psychologically safe" space and process where people can freely contribute to the conversation and influence its direction and outcome, or in John Shotter's words, "a conversation in which people feel they belong" (Shotter and Gergen, 1993). In our experience, clients in this environment, like these family members, become eager to participate. They connect, collaborate, and construct with each other and the therapists toward newness or simply the possibilities for newness—transformation of thoughts, feelings, emotions, and actions. There is also transformation in relationships; put differently, inherent in new forms of conversation are new forms of relationships. People begin to think about and experience each other and themselves differently; therefore, their relationships with each other change.

Each person is an integral part of the conversational process and its dynamic complex web of interchanges. No one person can be identified as the source of the newness. The process enhances self-agency: Each person has a sense of authorship, self-competency, and responsibility for the therapy and for the future. Each participant's circumstance is distinct, each course of therapy is novel, and how each therapy experience transfers outside of the therapy room is often unique and surprising.

To help establish this kind of environment and process with the Roberts family, permitting the family members to teach them, Sue and Paul were learners giving each one a chance to talk, a chance to tell his or her version of the story. They were interested in what each person had to say; they wanted to learn about each person's concerns, feelings, emotions, and perceptions. They were curious about strong opinions and passions, about what each person was troubled by, and about what each person deemed problematic—past, present, and future talk. Sue and Paul related to each family member as an equal and valid member of the family—showing interest, respect, and sensitivity to each and what they said. They engaged actively, inviting each person's story fragment, listening with interest, checking to determine if they had heard what each person intended them to hear, and valuing each perspective. They questioned, commented, and wondered. Importantly, all therapist utterances came from within the local conversation and developed around it. Each therapist's contribution, whether question or comment, was formed by the conversation at the moment and by the experiences that the therapists and clients were having with each other. All therapists' actions combined to help the family members tell their story and to help the therapists' understandings of them.

The process that begins with the therapist's learning position naturally shifts to one that is more mutual, one where all engage in shared inquiry. Each voice—therapist and client—adds ingredients to the conversation that extend, modify, or support other voices and mutually influences its direction. In turn, in our experience, as with this family, members begin to listen and hear each other differently, becoming less defensive, more interested in what the others have to say. A student observer described it this way: "Talking to Paul or Sue [rather than to each other] seemed to help get them [the family members] out of the old conversations and seemed to shift something, or at least contain or limit the finger pointing." Another description of the process was offered by two Swedish therapists who viewed all three of the videotaped sessions:

> We were thinking about the way the therapists were handling this bloody mess. So much bitterness, so much resentment, so much pain. One way that they handled it was to direct the talk to the therapists. They asked questions to learn about the differences; they asked curious [wondering questions] "what would be different if," and "how would he handle this differently." The therapists' questions engaged the family and led to a less, nonblaming story. The family members had to talk about themselves and had to be creative for another person. The mother said, "It doesn't matter what he says, I am not in touch with him anymore, I don't care, I shut him off." But the way that they asked the questions, questions that allowed another way of thinking about something . . . they were questions that opened up the conversation rather than kept it closed.

The family members determined what issues were important to talk about. An eavesdropper might think the father's expressed alcoholism and accusations of his sexual voyeurism were important things to pursue, but this family did not necessarily see them as urgent issues they wished to discuss at length. And, although an observer commented that "the family didn't listen and didn't always answer the questions that the therapist asked," we did not experience or conceptualize it this way. We do not characterize certain issues as "problems" or have preconceived ideas about what clients should or should not talk about. We focus on areas the family identifies as important in their ongoing discussions rather than eliciting information unrelated to the focus of their energies. In our experience, when family members lead, they talk about things that are important to them and do it at their pace. In the end, we find they talk about the issues in a way that works for them, as the Roberts family did.

In this vein, we have not found it helpful to think that not talking about certain issues represents, for instance, denial or collusion. Such judgments remind us of a quotation attributed to Gregory Bateson, that in order to entertain the new and the novel there must be room for the familiar. As therapists, for us to lead or focus the discussion on these issues while the family's attention and interest is elsewhere might not have been helpful. In line with Bateson's notion, we have found that therapists' agendas, for instance, choosing what is important to talk about or statements of fact made with authority, can stifle conversation. This does not mean that we withhold. We express our opinions. We hold our inner and expressed thoughts, however, without judgments about content, without ranking issues according to importance, and without maintaining the conversation within certain parameters or channeling its direction. We offer them as food for thought and as open to challenge. In our experience, in order to hear another person's utterance—question, comment, opinion—there must be room for each family member to say what he or she wants and to feel heard.

Equally important to what Sue and Paul did is what they did not do. They did not judge, interpret, or correct. They did not choose sides or favor one narrative over another. They did not try to discover, uncover, or lead toward any content. They did not try to maintain the conversation within any parameter or steer it in one direction (for instance, solutions or the future) or away from another (for instant, problems or the past). They did not withhold. They did not provide solutions.

We work without a specific content agenda or outcome. Instead, the focus is on creating an environment conducive to open expression, ideas, and thoughts in which participants are freed from repercussions by others, including the therapists. The intent of the therapists, as cocreators of the discussion, is to engage with the family rather than to assume a position of authority, expertise, or knowledge. The therapists' expertise lies in the art of creating and maintaining conversation rather than in providing correct solutions to the family's dilemmas or in determining the outcome.

Through conversation, perspectives and relationships shift. Interestingly, clients often report that between consultations changes in their thinking and interactions occur that they often view as permanent changes in the way in which they interrelate. In this fashion, collaborative therapy can be viewed as a context for new possibilities within families.

The Family's Reflections

An aspect of our collaborative approach is to include the client's voice in the evaluation of therapy and to learn from their experiences and feedback. Toward this aim, we continually seek a client's reflections both during the course of therapy and afterward. We want to know their experiences of therapy—its usefulness, our actions, and their suggestions about what, if anything, could be or could have been more helpful.[7] In keeping with this practice, Sue called the Roberts family six months after the last meeting. She left a message on their answering machine about the purpose of her call. The next week Sue talked with

[7]We believe that research should be part of a therapist's everyday practice. For an expanded discussion, see Anderson (1997, pp. 101–102).

Martha, who had been thinking about her call and talking with the other family members about it. Here are Martha's words.

> I asked everyone and nobody had anything to add—well, of course, Sam said he didn't have anything to add, and Ann is very busy, Dylan is home for spring break and he was only at one session.[8] Dylan's been away at college since September . . . I think [our work together] gave us some insight to each other. Sam doesn't drink anymore. I don't know that it [therapy] helped. I always seem to change and get things out of it. It just helps me along the way, dealing with Sam. He seems to have learned about boundaries; I think there was some boundary setting. I think it's strange that Ann's 18 now; she's driving us crazy and that's normal. It's funny now that she's grown, Sam and I have learned how to sit down and calmly discuss what to do about this. We have finally bound together to raise Ann now that she's grown. And we do it all the time now; it's not just a one-time thing. It's amusing, I find myself smiling, because we've fought so much, and now we finally agree. Now don't you think that's strange? And he listens to me, and he'll hear what I'll say, and he says "Do you think . . . ?" So I think that's nifty, kind of goes along the lines of trust. It's just he and I, we're both starting to realize that "it's just us." Everybody's saying, "You'll have empty nest," and *I don't have it*. Ann's been accepted at [a local university] and is planning for the prom. We've cut her off financially; she's earning her own money. We decided we had done her an injustice. Sam and I agreed about this. She started off coming to me, and I said, "Go to your father, we agreed about this, don't come to me" . . . Sam's got lots of problems and they are not very socially acceptable. I don't think he'll ever accept that he's got them. He thinks that now that he's not drinking it's fixed, but . . . it does help a lot, his not drinking; his personality is pleasant now. I think it's going to be okay . . . being stuck together.

In summary, the essence of our philosophy of therapy is to create a space and an opportunity for dialogic conversation—a process. Our expertise lies in the art of creating and maintaining this process. In the natural ebb and flow of such conversations, space for possibilities emerge, allowing for transformation in thoughts, feelings, emotions, actions, communications, and relationships. These possibilities, as illustrated by Martha's words, are often unpredicatable.

Study Questions

1. Compare and contrast modern and postmodern philosophies.
2. Describe social construction.
3. Compare and contrast the differences between a collaborative approach and a less or noncollaborative approach.
4. Describe the difference between a dialogical conversation and a monological conversation.

---

[8]Our memories and the videotapes indicate that Dylan was at two sessions; we mention this for the reader's information.

References

Anderson, H. (1995). Collaborative language systems: Toward a post-modern therapy. In R. Mikesell, D. D. Lusterman, & S. McDaniel (Eds.), *Integrating family therapy: Family psychology and systems theory.* Washington, DC: American Psychological Association.

Anderson, H. (1997). *Conversation, language, and possibilities: A postmodern approach to therapy.* New York: HarperCollins.

Anderson, H., & Goolishian, H. (1988). Human systems as linguistic systems: Evolving ideas about the implications for theory and practice. *Family Process, 27*(4), 371–393.

Anderson, H., & Goolishian, H. (1992). The client is the expert: A not-knowing approach to therapy. In S. McNamee & K. Gergen (Eds.). *Social construction and the therapeutic process* (pp. 25–39). Newbury Park, CA: Sage.

Gergen, K. (1994). *Realities and relationships: Soundings in social construction.* Cambridge, MA: Harvard University Press.

Goolishian, H. A., & Anderson, H. (1987). Language Systems and therapy: An evolving idea. *Psychotherapy, 24,* 529–538.

Shotter, J., & Gergen, K. (1993). Social construction: Knowledge, self, others and continuing the conversation. In *Communication yearbook* (pp. 3–33). Thousand Oaks, CA: Sage.

Chapter Twelve

Narrative Therapy: The Work of Michael White

Bruce C. Prevatt

The work of Michael White has been termed an emergent family therapy model of the nineties (Goldenberg and Goldenberg, 1996). Generally considered to be postmodern constructivism, White's model engages families in conversations designed to externalize problems (Nichols and Schwartz, 1995). This story-based conversation theory assumes that people create stories about their lives. These stories are based on a combination of truth and narrative: Truths can be logically deduced, whereas narratives are created by people in a way that makes sense to them based on their own experiences over time. According to White (White and Epston, 1990), people ascribe meaning to their lives by creating these narratives, which in turn shape future perceptions. (This is very similar to the Milan view that a created reality is a filter through which individuals view their world.) White further proposes that since no single story can adequately describe an individual's complex life, there is always room to alter stories. Thus, White's focus in therapy is to re-create stories in a way that contradicts the individual's negative, self-defeating views and substitutes positive experiences in dealing with problems.

Theoretical Underpinnings

One of the major techniques used by Michael White is *externalization* of the problem. Oftentimes, families become overwhelmed by a situation, blaming both themselves and an identified patient for a problem, feeling helpless to act in new ways. Interventions can become bogged down with a litany of complaints regarding the problem and a focus on finding fault for the problem. This is referred to as a *problem-saturated* narrative about the situation. Externalization helps to overcome this tendency by treating the problem as a separate entity, which the family can work together to overcome.

The process of externalization begins in the first session, when the therapist asks two sets of questions. The first group of questions maps the influence of the problem on the family members: How does your husband's drug abuse affect you, your children, his job, your job, your relationship with your husband? How does everyone in the family feel about his drug abuse? How do family members react? These questions set the stage with a problem-saturated description. Next, questions are posed that contradict this description: Was there ever a time when your husband successfully avoided drug use? Was there a time when you did not allow his drug use to affect you in the way it does at this time? Were there times you or the children acted in a different way? These positive or different ways of approaching the problem are highlighted, with in-depth discussion of alternative ways of thinking about and responding to the problem. Externalization comes into play by defining the problem as another object, which all family members can join forces against. For example, rather than seeing the husband as the problem, the drug abuse is viewed as the problem. Thus, instead of a series of discussions regarding what the husband did, the discussions turn to how drug abuse has caused problems for each individual in the family as well as for each relationship in the family (husband-wife, father-son, father-daughter, mother-grandmother, and so on). According to Goldenberg and Goldenberg (1996), this creates a nonblaming view of the situation in which clients no longer feel they are to blame. Rather, they can go on to create new stories in which they have roles overcoming the problem.

White has defined several other techniques used in his model. *Unique outcomes* are experiences identified by the clients in which they acted in a positive way regarding the problem. There are several types of positive outcomes: *historical* unique outcomes are times in the past when the client behaved in a positive way. *Current* unique outcomes refer to events during the therapy session in which family members act positively. In these cases, the therapist immediately points out the occurrence and asks, "How did you do that just now?" Alternately, *future* unique outcomes refer to plans or intentions to act more positively in the future.

White's technique is similar to the social constructivism espoused by theorists such as Harlene Anderson and Sue White. His questioning also bears resemblance to the Milan technique of circular questioning. A major difference is that White is more focused, or directive, in his conversations. Social constructivism tends to utilize unstructured, empathetic questions (Nichols and Schwartz, 1995). Likewise, the Milan school emphasizes the concept of neutrality, in which the therapist accepts, without judgment, the positions of all family members and believes that nondirective questioning leads families to their own range of alternative solutions. White, on the other hand, is more politically motivated, believing that the individual narratives molded by the dominant

culture entrap individuals and that he can actively help to "liberate" individuals into creating alternative stories (Nichols and Schwartz, 1995).

White also emphasizes that problems cannot exist without effects. There are
numerous effects, and these must be identified for each individual and for each
relationship. Dad's drug abuse has affected his daughter in that she is reluctant
to engage in intimate relationships of her own for fear that she will suffer like
her mother has. Dad's drug abuse has affected his relationship with his daughter in that she rarely trusts that he will do what he promises. These identifiable
effects of the problem are the lifeblood by which the problem survives. If family members can prevent these events from occurring, they can "kill off the life
support system" of the problem. It is the job of the therapist to continually monitor these effects and to help the family identify and reconstruct new ways of
dealing with them.

White and Epston (1990) identify several other techniques that are commonly utilized in therapy:

- *Letters of invitation.* This is a technique used when someone (perhaps a
  family member) is reluctant to come to therapy. The therapist meets with
  the other family members, and together they write a "story" that is sent
  to the reluctant member. This story, of course, may trigger many unique
  outcomes.
- *Redundancy letters.* These are letters that illustrate to people the redundancy in their roles (for example, parent-watcher, brother's father).
  These are oftentimes written by the client to inform a family member that
  they no longer need for them to take on such a role. The client thanks
  them for their service and their sacrifice and explains why it is no longer
  needed.
- *Letters of prediction.* These letters are often written by the therapist at the
  end of therapy. They might predict what will happen in the next six
  months. This prediction is always for continued health (they do not use
  counterparadox as Milan might).
- *Counterreferral letters.* These are written to the person who referred the
  client. This is done with the therapist and client together, although the
  letter actually comes from the therapist with a copy sent to the family.
  The letter explains how the client is starting to change and how the therapist predicts that the client will continue to behave positively.
- *Letters of reference.* These are written by the therapist "to whom it may
  concern." They are given to the family with the therapist's impression of
  positive aspects of the family.
- *Brief Letters* These include end-of-session thoughts, inquiries about
  nonattendance, shared thoughts, disclosures by the therapist about feeling stuck, or contemplations the therapist has about something concerning the family.

According to White and Epston (1990), letters such as these are used primarily for the purpose of rendering lived experiences into a narrative or story

that makes sense according to the criteria of coherence and lifelikeness. Some-times, the therapist will actually substitute them for case notes. The advantage of letters is that the therapist's thoughts are not kept secret from the family. The letters, once received, can be amended, contested, or confirmed by the family. These letters tend to be evolving in nature, moving forward in time and creating excitement for both the therapist and client. Letters can also expand the influence of the therapist so that contact is not limited to 50 minutes per week.

The case that is presented here illustrates the following aspects of Michael White's approach:

1. An initial session in which both problem saturation and problem externalization are utilized
2. Creation of a narrative
3. Utilization of the narrative to decrease fault finding and family members' sense of failure
4. Utilization of the narrative to create new possibilities and solutions
5. Utilization of letters to expand the narrative

The Case: Alcoholism Undermines a Marriage

Tom and Judy are a married couple in their early thirties with two daughters, ages 2 and 5. Both parents are employed in quasi-professional positions. Judy holds a bachelor's degree in social work and, until the situation that brought them into therapy, was employed as a Child Protective Services caseworker. Because of the circumstances surrounding their domestic difficulty, Judy was terminated from her job. She then obtained a job with another social work–related focus. Tom completed three years of college before becoming a specialist in emergency management.

The couple was referred to therapy by Tom's father following a domestic dispute that involved a physical altercation and resulted in both parties being arrested. At the time of our first visit, both parties had been released from jail and were living apart. Judy was residing in the family residence with the two daughters while Tom was staying with a family friend. A restraining order prohibited the couple from being together except in therapy.

The first session involved Tom and his father. Tom shared his perspective of the events leading up to the most recent domestic altercation. The presentation was mostly documentable facts by Tom and his father and was followed by a request for Tom and Judy to be seen as a couple. The case study begins with the first couples session.

Session 1

Therapist: I want to welcome you, Judy ,and thank you both for coming in. As you know, Tom and I met together with his father last week. At that time, Tom presented only a brief overview of his concerns and what he perceived as your probable concerns. However, we intentionally didn't get into any significant detail since I really prefer to do that when we're all together. Perhaps the best way to begin today would be to have Tom recap our conversation of last week and share his concerns. Would you be comfortable with that, Judy?

Judy: Sure. I guess so.

Therapist: Tom, what would you like to share with us at this time?

Tom: Well, you know pretty much the events of the other night. I came home after working late to find the kids in the living room watching TV and Judy in the kitchen. Our oldest daughter was crying and said "Mommy" had been screaming at her and had spanked her. When I spoke to Judy, it was obvious that she was drunk. Judy can be a wonderful mother when she is sober, but when she drinks, she gets mean and takes out everything on me and the kids. I asked her what happened, and she started screaming at me about working late and leaving her with all of the responsibility for the house and kids. I tried to defend myself and get her calmed down at the same time, but it just resulted in an intense argument. We went to the bedroom to be away from the kids. Once there I remember Judy slapping me, and I reacted by throwing her on the bed. From there, I don't remember much. The next thing I remember is our oldest daughter standing next to the bed crying and pushing against me. I was on top of Judy, holding her by the throat, and she was hitting me. I came to my senses and backed away, going into the kitchen to get some control of myself. I guess Judy called 9-1-1 because the next thing I know, the police are knocking at the front door. We were both arrested and taken to jail. My parents came for the children and kept them for the night. My parents posted bail for both of us the next day. Now we're here. I have some real concerns about my temper, and I want to get more control over it. But I have even more concern for the safety of the children when Judy is drunk. When she drinks, she either ignores the children or screams at them. I have some real concerns that someday she'll pass out on the sofa and one of the children will get hurt. She is like a Jekyll and Hyde where alcohol is concerned. I just don't know what to do except try to protect the kids.

Therapist: Judy, you've heard Tom describe the events of the other night. Do you think that is a pretty accurate description?

Judy: Yeah, pretty much so. It's just that I can't have even one drink without it setting him off. Just because his mother is an alcoholic, he thinks I am too and that I'll screw up our kids' lives like his mother did his. I really like his dad, but his mother is one sick bitch. I admit I drink too much at times, but I love my children and I'd never do anything to hurt them. If he thinks I'm a bad mother, he ought to see some of the homes I've had to investigate.

Therapist: Oh, you do investigations?

Judy: Well, I did until I got fired over getting arrested. I'm looking for another job now.

Therapist: I see. Well, good luck on finding something you enjoy. Now, based on what you've told me, you've both identified alcohol and temper as being concerns in the family. Are there any other major concerns we should address?

Judy: Yeah. Sometimes Tom stays gone the entire day with his buddies playing golf and leaves me with everything to do around the house as well as take care of the kids. Besides, he drinks with his buddies, so why should he come down so heavy on me for drinking?

Tom: Come on, Judy, I don't get drunk and pass out while I'm watching the kids. I never said I don't drink, but I only drink with my friends or at a party. I haven't had a drink at home in a couple of years.

Therapist: OK. If it's all right with you, I'd like to get a bit more of a handle on each of these concerns so we can better see how they affect each of you. Since alcohol seems to be a major issue, perhaps we can start there. Can each of you tell me a little about your families of origin and the role alcohol has played in your respective lives and the lives of your family members?

At this point, Tom shared what it was like growing up in an alcoholic family. His mother drank heavily and verbally abused everyone. He saw his father as a gentle, caring person who let his mother get away with anything. Although he liked his father, he didn't have a great deal of respect for him when it came to standing up for himself. Another concern was the mother's ongoing attempt to interfere with how Tom and Judy were raising their children, constantly undermining them and sending the grandchildren mixed messages. He no longer was comfortable with leaving the children with his parents unless his father was present. He admits that he drank heavily at one point in his late teens and early twenties, but he stopped when he recognized that he was becoming like his mother. This was shortly before he started dating Judy.

Judy had a history of alcoholism in her family of origin. Her father was a policeman in a major metropolitan area and had been a heavy drinker for years. However, he had stopped several years previously. He had always been overly protective of his children and an extreme disciplinarian. Judy grew up feeling she could do nothing right to please her father. As a teenager, she also found herself rebelling against what she perceived as having her father dictate her every move. As soon as she could leave home for college, she did so. At school, she became a "party animal" and began heavy consumption of alcohol.

Therapist: As we come to a close on this first session, I would like to thank both of you for sharing your concerns. I also get the impression that in spite of your difficulties, you both want the marriage to work. Is that right?

Tom: Yes—I love Judy and want us to stay together, but I need some assurance that she'll stop drinking. I'm really afraid for the kids.

Judy: I think so. I don't like the way I get blamed for everything, but Tom is a good dad and I'm pretty sure I still love him. I'm not ready for him to come home yet. You see, I got pregnant before we got married and we rushed into this marriage thing. I think we need to become friends and build some trust before he can come home. We have to kind of start over and do a better job of building a relationship that doesn't involve fighting all of the time.

Therapist: I can see that the two of you care very much for each other in spite of some of the negative patterns and beliefs or stories that have developed. My hope for you is that by working together, we can build on the strengths and begin to look at some of the negative beliefs in a new light.

The therapist begins the session with a history, which is very problem saturated. He quickly begins the process of externalization, asking how alcohol has affected Tom and Judy and their families. The couple each tells the story of how alcohol has played a major role in their lives. These stories reveal patterns and beliefs that set the stage for further externalization of the problem in the next session.

Session 2

The second interview begins with a recap of the week's events. Tom had seen the children twice and reported having an enjoyable time with them. He and Judy had spoken on the phone several times, during which time they focused for the most part on the children.

Therapist: It sounds as though the two of you have had a relatively calm week.
Tom: Uh huh.
Judy: Yeah . . . it's been a lot calmer.
Therapist: How is the job search coming along, Judy?
Judy: Believe it or not, I actually have an offer. It's more administrative than what I was doing, but I think it will be a lot less stressful. I used to get so bummed out on my other job. I think that's why I drank so much.
Therapist: You used the work "drank." Does that mean you haven't been drinking this week?
Judy: Yeah . . . not a drop.
Therapist: You talk about drinking when you're bummed out. When else do you drink?
Judy: When I'm lonely or sad. Yeah . . . anytime I'm lonely or sad or depressed or seem stressed.
Therapist: It sounds like you use alcohol as a friend.
Judy: I guess so. Yeah . . . I guess you could call alcohol my friend. That's where I usually turn when I'm bummed.
Therapist: I wonder . . . do you think we could give your alcohol friend a name?

At this point, the therapist continues the process of externalizing the problem by giving it a persona of its own. The goal of this intervention is to move away from seeing alcohol as a failing of Judy's. Instead, alcohol can be seen as the shared problem that Tom and Judy can work together to overcome.

Tom: I'm not sure I understand.
Therapist: Well, if Judy sees alcohol as a friend to turn to in times of trouble or when she's feeling bummed out, maybe this friend should have a name. Something like Al. You know . . . for Al K. Hall. What do you think?

Judy: Makes sense to me. Yeah . . . Al sounds good to me.

Tom: I wish she would come to me rather than Al when she was down. It sure would make things a lot easier.

Therapist: Well, Tom, Al has been around a lot longer than you. Judy commented at the end of the last session that she wanted to do a better job of developing a friendship with you. Perhaps the two of you can explore how you can become better friends and Al won't have to be in the picture. Does that sound reasonable?

Tom: I guess so. I'll give anything a try.

Therapist: What do you think, Judy?

Judy: Uh . . . yeah . . . OK.

Therapist: Let's stay with this topic for awhile. Judy . . . you said last week that there were times when you had stopped drinking. Is that right?

Judy: Yeah. A couple of times.

Therapist: So, you didn't need Al as a friend at those times. How did Al convince you to take him back each time?

Judy: Well, I guess I just got to feeling lonely and depressed. I'd just go out and get a bottle and drink. I always drank alone. I'd go on a binge for several days . . . like a weekend . . . and then slow down. I never went for long periods of drinking. I might not drink for days. But give me an excuse like a party or when I was feeling bad and I would get a bottle.

Therapist: So, you might say that Al was a good friend at a party as well as when you were feeling down. He's pretty seductive. Do you still enjoy having Al around?

Judy: At times. But I have to admit that he does cause some problems. I would really like to stop. But if things go wrong, I always seem to go back. I guess I'm just weak. Yeah—that's how I see myself—a weakling. I don't seem to have any willpower or self-control.

Therapist: Do you agree with Judy, Tom? Do you think she's weak?

Tom: Maybe. I don't know . . . at times she is really strong. She worked really hard at her job and had to deal with some tough situations. But then she would drink to handle the stress. I think she can be strong but just gives up too easily. I don't think she's as weak as she thinks she is.

Judy: How come you never told me you thought I could be strong?

Tom: I guess I just assumed you knew.

Therapist: Judy . . . you talk about your friend Al coming to take care of you when you're down or feeling needy. Have there been times when you were strong enough to not invite him or allow him in, even though you were bummed out?

Here the therapist is looking for ways to rewrite the narrative that Judy has written for herself—that of a weakling and a victim. By heading in the direction of strength, the therapist hopes to bring out those times when she showed strength and self-control. He believes that everyone has those times and that it is a matter of finding each person's experience of strength and reinforcing it.

This is followed immediately by querying Judy for historical unique outcomes: times in the past when she did not turn to alcohol.

Judy: I'm not sure . . . let me think. Yeah, I guess there have been a few times. I think I wanted to drink, but I knew I couldn't so I didn't. You know, like when I had an important meeting or a final exam. I really wanted to drink, but I couldn't.

Therapist: So . . . what did you do?

Judy: Once, before I started going with Tom, I went to an AA meeting, but I wasn't comfortable there. Everyone smoked, and they were a lot older than me. Besides, they were alcoholics and I didn't believe I was. Usually, I just shopped. I would go to the mall and just walk around. I would get out in a crowd and lose myself. As long as I wasn't alone, I didn't have to drink. It's only when I'm bummed out and alone that I tend to drink.

Therapist: So there are times when you're down that you wanted to drink, but you were strong enough to resist the temptations of your friend Al.

Judy: Yeah, I guess so.

Therapist: You know, we have been describing Al as a friend, and I'm sure there have been times when he has seemed like a friend. But from the problems that the drinking has caused, it seems he is more like a lover that you have been having an affair with. Does it ever seem that way to you?

Judy: I'm not sure I like that analogy.

Therapist: Why not? What seems troublesome about that analogy?

Tom: I think I can field that question. Last year, I had a brief fling with a lady that works with me. As you can imagine, it caused a lot of problems with Judy. We've really had to work hard at getting past it. But now that you mention it, it does seem like Judy has turned to the bottle in much the same way I turned to another woman. The only difference is that mine was a brief fling and I stopped almost as quickly as I started. But Judy keeps going back to her lover.

Therapist: Judy, does that make any sense to you?

Judy: Yeah, but at least I didn't get into bed with the bottle. God, that hurt. It still hurts. But I keep trying to believe that it was a slip or a moment of weakness for Tom. After all, he did stop and he was honest with me. At least, I think he was.

Therapist: So the affair was very painful to you. I can sure understand that. Tom, it seems that Judy has worked hard at understanding your affair with a co-worker. Do you think you could work just as hard at forgiving her affair with Al?

Tom: I think so, but she keeps going back time and again. Sooner or later, I have to say enough is enough. If I knew what to do to really help her stay away, I would.

Judy: But Tom, the times I start drinking are when I'm really stressed or bummed out, and when I try to talk to you, you just tell me to get over it or try to tell me how to solve my problems. Has it ever occurred to you that I might need a friend and that I find more comfort in the bottle than in you? If you really want to help, try being there for me sometimes.

Therapist: Are you saying that Tom isn't as emotionally available as you would like?

Judy: Not always. He can be very emotional and close at times, but he can also be very judgmental and distant.

Tom: But sometimes I just get so damn tired of the same old excuses and whining. You know, Judy, you are one smart and sharp lady. But I get frustrated when you crawl into the bottle and start feeling sorry for yourself. Then you try to blame everyone else for your problems. You're just like Mom when you do that.

Judy: See, there you go again—comparing me to your mom. I'm not your mother.

Tom: I know that. But when you feel sorry for yourself and drink and lash out at others, you sure act like her. Thank God you don't do it as much as she does. For her, it's an everyday thing.

Therapist: I would like to bring some closure to this session if I may. Let me try to summarize some of what I've heard. Judy, you admit that you have relied on the bottle—uh, Al—to be a friend, even though a destructive one. And, if you'll allow me to draw on an uncomfortable analogy, it is like having a lover that brings disruption to the family. Now, you have indicated that if Tom were more emotionally available during your tough times, perhaps you wouldn't have to turn to the bottle. Is that fairly accurate?

Judy: OK. I'll go along with that.

Therapist: And Tom—even though Judy says that you can be very sensitive and close, you pull away when you perceive her engaging in self-pity and using that as an excuse to visit her lover. Would that be fairly accurate?

Tom: Close enough.

Therapist: OK, I'd like for the two of you to give some thought as to what your individual needs are and how the other person has effectively attended to those needs in a positive manner in the past. Think about what they have done that made you feel understood and just better in general. I would like to gather my own thoughts, and I'll drop you each a note sharing those with you.

The session ended on a somewhat upbeat note. Through beginning to externalize the problems and draw some parallels between drinking and an affair, Tom and Judy began to seem less under attack or blamed. The therapist made the decision not to dwell on the past affair of Tom's since this did not seem to be a present concern for the couple, with the exception of some normal residual emotional bruising that was continuing to heal. Rather, he only used the affair as an analogy of Judy's drinking. One interesting note is that the couple seemed at times to be very playful, having the ability to have fun together. Approximately three days later, the therapist sent the following note to Tom and Judy. (Since they were still under court order not to be together except in therapy, a separate letter was mailed to each of them.)

Dear Judy and Tom:

Based on our first two sessions, I want to briefly share some of my observations with you. I have been very impressed with the apparent love you two seem to share. Although you have experienced some difficult times that have brought you into therapy, you still seem committed to work on building a stronger marriage and a renewed relationship. Just the ways each of you will physically reach out to the other or the way you look at each other and the occasional humor you use indicates to me that there is probably a stronger foundation to your relationship than either of you have perhaps recognized. I believe that Tom sees Judy's ongoing relationship with the bottle (Al) as just as much an affair as what he briefly engaged in. Judy, perhaps you can think of how you dealt with your sense of pain and betrayal at Tom's affair and be prepared to help him come to terms with your ongoing relationship with "Al." Likewise, Tom, since you successfully ended your extramarital relationship, could you think of ways to help Judy break away from her affair?

   You have both shown remarkable strength and forgiveness in the past. Can we build on that now and in the future? I think you can, and I look forward to sharing that journey with you.

This letter serves to share with the couple the therapist's thoughts about the session. The therapist begins by mentioning the couple's strengths (commitment, nurturance of one another, ability to use humor). Next he suggests an alternate way of viewing the problems they have identified. He follows by giving each individual a task to work on during the week. This brief letter serves to reinforce an alternate belief system. It also extends the positive effects of therapy by increasing the likelihood that the couple will think about positive solutions in between sessions.

Session 3

When Tom and Judy returned for the third session, Judy started the session by stating that she had a slip the past week and had gotten drunk. Feeling stressed and anxious about the family difficulties, she had left work early, stopped by a store, purchased beer, and had gone home to drink. On the positive side, she had called Tom and asked him to pick up the children and keep them for the night.

Therapist: I appreciate your honesty about your drinking, Judy. I think there are at least two issues we need to focus on today. The first is to explore how you have been trying to deal with the alcohol and your moods and stress. The other is to explore what's worked and how to proceed from here. Let me start by asking Tom how you reacted to Judy's call.

Tom: Well, I was angry, but I tried to not get into an argument. Actually, I was probably more disappointed than angry. I had really felt encouraged after the first two sessions, but this was a setback. Anyway, I went and got the children and took them with me to my place for the evening.

Therapist: How did you interact with Judy? Was it the same way you have in the past?

Tom: No, I think I dealt with her differently, although not consciously. Usually, I would try to talk her into not drinking, try to use logic, and usually end up in an argument with her trying to blame me. I always tried to be the logical one with Mom growing up, and I guess I did the same with Judy. This time, though, I simply got the kids, thanked her for calling me, and told her I was disappointed but hoped she would be feeling better in the morning. I've been doing some reading, and I think I've tried to be the rescuer in the past. I didn't want to do that again.

Therapist: How did this strike you, Judy?

Judy: It surprised me. I was waiting for the blaming and scolding, but it never came. By the time I realized what he had said, he was gone.

Therapist: What did you do then?

Judy: Then I sat around feeling sorry for myself that I was such a weakling. That I had once again turned to the bottle to handle my stress. I had another beer, which finished the six-pack, watched some TV, and went to bed.

Therapist: Let's explore that for a moment. You said you were a weakling. But you did call Tom to come get the children and you didn't get into an argument. Isn't this a more positive approach than the way you usually handle your drinking bouts?

Judy: Yeah—I guess so.

Therapist: So you do have ways of exercising strength and restraint, even when you've been drinking. Right?

Judy: Yeah.

Therapist: So even though we won't condone the drinking, you have shown some real positive changes in how you dealt with your intoxication. Rather than lashing out at Tom, you requested his help. I see that as a very encouraging step.

Judy: Thanks. I sure didn't see anything positive about it at the time, though.

Therapist: Now, Judy, the other area I wanted to explore with you is how you are approaching your drinking; or more accurately, your abstinence. First, do you see your drinking as a problem and do you want to stop?

Judy: I don't know if it's the problem that Tom thinks it is, but I have to admit that most of our problems happen when I've been drinking.

The therapist had a discussion with Tom and Judy about various treatment plans available to help Judy stop drinking and to help Tom deal with his reactions. Judy refused to admit that she could be an alcoholic, so the therapist settled on the term "problem drinker" as a compromise. Because Judy frequently didn't feel understood or supported by Tom during periods of stress or blue moods and therefore turned to the bottle, the therapist discussed the advantages of groups like AA. Even with her previous negative opinions of AA, she agreed to try several different groups. Tom was encouraged to attend Al-Anon meetings to help him develop new ways of dealing with those times when Judy did drink.

Tom: You know, there are other times when Judy can get really hard to live with. She has bad PMS and is impossible to live with for a couple of days each month.

Judy: Boy, is he ever right about that. But he doesn't make it any easier by yelling at me. No, that's not exactly right. He tries to reason with me, and that just infuriates me. Damn it, when I feel bad or uptight, don't try to be the voice of reason. Just leave me alone.

Tom: That's what I try to do anymore—just leave her alone. It's hard at times because she is being so bitchy, but I keep my distance. Unfortunately, the kids can't keep their distance when I'm not there, so they are getting emotionally wounded.

This revelation was followed by a discussion in which the therapist recommended several physicians who could be consulted. The session ended with Judy agreeing to try at least four different AA meetings during the coming two weeks and for Tom to attend four Al-Anon meetings during the same period. In addition, Judy agreed to make an appointment with a physician. It seemed to the therapist that Judy had viewed her drinking and PMS problems in much the same light—as being out of her control. To see her agree to take some positive steps and see this as a new sense of personal control was a major goal of the therapist. It served to take her out of the victim role and into one of control. The next day, the therapist mailed the following note:

Dear Judy and Tom:

I believe we had an excellent session yesterday and feel you are making major strides. I find the honesty with which each of you is approaching therapy is most refreshing. Judy is developing an awareness of her contributions to the marital difficulties, especially her relationship to the bottle, and is willing to make some difficult choices. I see this as a real display of strength. As I've said several times, I believe you are a much stronger person than you've given yourself credit for, Judy, and I believe you're beginning to develop a sense of that.

Tom, you too are making a real effort to do things differently. Your ability to disengage from Judy at certain times, but to be able to respond to her when she needs that from you, is encouraging. I agree that you can't be a total support system to Judy, and I'm hopeful that each of you will find the extra support you want from AA/Al-Anon or other groups. I also believe that as Judy continues to develop an appreciation of her own strengths, she'll depend on you less for that role. This, coupled with your ability to not assume the caretaker or rescuer role for her, can open new avenues for the two of you to relate on a healthier level. I'm enjoying working with each of you and look forward to our next session.

Session 4

At the beginning of the fourth session, the therapist reviewed the previous week with Tom and Judy. They had attended the AA/Al-Anon meetings, and each had found a couple that they could return to. Judy had actually begun working the steps and had been befriended by someone she thought could be her sponsor. She was more willing to acknowledge her alcohol problem and to openly deal with it. Both of them saw this in a positive light. The therapist praised them in their accomplishments and encouraged them to keep with the programs. In addition, Judy had scheduled an appointment to see a physician in approximately one month. At this point, the therapist decided to shift the focus from the conflicts revolving around alcohol and PMS difficulties to working with the couple on building their basic relationship and dealing with Tom's temper.

Therapist: Judy, if I remember correctly, you said that you didn't want Tom to return to the home until you could begin to build on a relationship based on friendship and trust. Could you elaborate a bit more on that?

Judy: I think so. As I mentioned before, when Tom and I got married, I was already pregnant. Although we were living together at the time, I don't believe either of us had any desire to get married. In fact, we had even discussed living apart for awhile. But after I found out I was pregnant, we decided to get married. I don't think we had really become good friends at that point. We had simply been playing house. I didn't trust him when he went out with his friends, and he didn't trust me to not drink. We also fought a lot. I love Tom and think we can have a good marriage, but I want to kind of start over and build a friendship rather than just jump back to the way we were. We met with the judge this week and he said we could move in together again, but I don't want to rush things.

Therapist: How do you feel about that, Tom?

Tom: Well, I guess I'd prefer to move back in so I can be with my family, but I'm trying to see things Judy's way and I think she has made some good points. So I'm willing to work on building a more solid foundation first. What I'd like to know, though, is how do we do that.

Therapist: That's a valid point. Judy, how will you know when you and Tom are good enough friends and that there has been a good enough start on a new foundation to move back in together?

Judy: I'm not sure, but I think I'll know it when the time comes.

Therapist: In the area of trust, have there been times when you believe Tom was less than honest with you?

Judy: Sure, there have been times he lied to me. Nothing big, you know, just little things. I think I'm pretty good at knowing when he does. But that doesn't really bother me. Heck, I'm guilty of little white lies myself. What bothers me more is not trusting him to lose his temper with me. His unpredictability. I'm never quite sure if he'll say a few words and walk away when he's angry or if he'll get really mad.

Therapist: What happens when he really gets mad?

Judy: It's like he's a different person. More of a raging animal. I really get scared for my safety.

Therapist: Does this usually turn physical, like the most recent sequence of events that brought you here?

Judy: No, not really. There have been a couple of times when there has been some shoving or holding my arms so I couldn't get away, but not as bad as this last time.

Therapist: So even though the arguments of this magnitude are rare and have never left either of you physically injured, until this most recent episode, there is enough there to raise some fear and trust issues. Is that right?

Judy: Yeah.

Tom: I'd like to put in my two cents worth here. There have been very few times when I've gotten physical. I don't believe in that. In fact, I think Judy would have to agree that I'm pretty easygoing. The times when things seem to have gotten out of control were those times she had been drinking or suffering from a particularly bad case of PMS, or probably both at the same time, and she becomes absolutely irrational. In fact, she is usually the one that slaps or pushes me first. I'm usually trying to just defend myself or calm her down.

Judy: I'm not sure that's entirely true. There are times you have really verbally attacked me and I've been afraid that you may get physical. There are times that you're the one acting really irrational and out of control.

Tom: I know, but there are times that you push me to the edge.

Therapist: So Tom, there are times you can handle things calmly and other times you really blow a fuse. Is that what I'm hearing?

Tom: I think so. Yeah.

Therapist: And Judy, you say you're really scared when you think Tom is losing control—right?

Judy: Right. It's almost like living with my father again. He ruled with an iron fist, and I never knew when I'd get a whipping or not. He was very moody and unpredictable. That's what Tom reminds me of when he gets that mad. And frankly, I don't want to live my life in fear, never knowing when he might explode. Until I can trust his moods more, I don't think we should be living together.

Therapist: You talk of Tom's moods as being unpredictable. Yet he describes himself as pretty easygoing. I'm getting a mixed view of Tom here. Can you two help me get a clearer picture?

Judy: Well, he usually is pretty calm and even tempered. It's just that I don't know when he might have one of those rare explosions.

Therapist: Like your dad?

Judy: Right.

Tom: I can tell you when I get really angry. I think I'm pretty predictable. I usually stay calm and try to discuss things with you but sometimes when you've been drinking and/or have a bad case of PMS, you get really mean. You call me names and scream and threaten. When you do that, it just sets me off. I get really angry. I don't deserve that kind of treatment.

Judy: I don't think I'm always to blame for the bad arguments. I think there are times that you've had a bad day and you just blow up quicker.

Therapist: It seems as though both of you have the ability to lose control at times. It that a safe observation?

Tom: Yeah.

Judy: I'd say so.

Therapist: Would it also be a safe assumption to make that each of you have also acted more rationally and in control in situations that at other times you might lose your temper or—in your words—lose control?

Tom: Yes.

Judy: Yeah.

Therapist: And also, Judy, that your issues of trust are more one of being able to better predict Tom's behavior than what we might typically think of as trust?

Judy: I guess so, but it's all pretty much the same to me.

Therapist: The fact that you have both been able to control your temper at times when you might lose it under similar circumstances tells me that you have the ability but don't always exercise it. When I look at it like this, it looks more like a matter of choice rather than uncontrollable behavior. Does that make any sense?

Here the therapist is beginning to open the door to viewing the fits of anger and rage as an external problem rather than a character fault. He proceeds from here to query for unique outcomes.

Therapist: Tom, can you remember times when you were really angry but didn't blow up?

Tom: Sure. Usually, I don't blow up. I just walk away. Maybe there is some truth to what Judy says in that I'm probably more prone to blow up if I've had a stressful day.

Therapist: So if we look at extreme anger as an object sitting here on the shelf, you have the ability to reach out and take it or leave it. And when you've had a bad day and something happens between you and Judy, you're more inclined to reach out and grab it. Does that seem to fit?

Tom: Yeah, that pretty well nails it. But I think I wouldn't grab it if Judy wouldn't get so mean. If we could just talk, I wouldn't feel so much like I'm being attacked and wouldn't get so angry.

Therapist: So what I'm hearing is that even though rage is sitting on the shelf ready to be picked up, there wouldn't be a need to do so if the two of you could work out a way to engage in disagreement without name calling and meanness. Is that right?

Tom: Yeah. Pretty close.

Therapist: How about it, Judy, does that seem fairly accurate?

Judy: I guess so. Sometimes, though, he comes in and treats me like a kid and I get really angry. Like he's talking down to me. I guess I reach for the anger and there we go. If he would just talk to me like a wife and not a kid, I think I'd do a lot better.

Therapist: Ah, more shades of the past and your father. Right?

Judy: I guess so.

Although the therapist acknowledges the triggers from the past, he intentionally does not dwell on them. Rather, he looks for successes the couple has had in handling differences and conflicts and starts to build on these. In other words, he tries to stay focused on strengths and solutions rather than history and negative narratives. He goes on to explore examples in their relationship where they have not gotten uncontrollably angry and builds on these. He has also looked for triggers for each one and made these more obvious to both parties.

Therapist: We are coming to the close of this session. I would like to propose some homework for the two of you for the coming week. Would you two be agreeable to spending some time together? Some of it would be with the children, as a family, just doing some enjoyable activities. Also, I'd like for the two of you to spend some time exploring further what we have discussed today. That is, what are some of the triggers that set you off? When do you tend to lose control and when have you been able to maintain control? How can you, in the future, recognize the triggers and take steps to more effectively maintain control? How can you help each other with your challenges? OK?

Tom: I'd like that. I really miss the kids and Judy. And I'd like to try to figure out how to handle our conflicts better. I really don't like it when either of us lose control.

Judy: Yeah—I could do that. Truthfully, I've missed the fun times we often had and Tom's companionship. I'd like to spend some time together. But that doesn't mean I'm ready for him to return full-time. I really don't want to rush that. Let's just start out by having some fun and some quiet time together.

Tom: Agreed.

Session 5

Tom and Judy returned to this session in obviously better spirits. They had gotten together over the weekend and had enjoyed time with the children, going on a picnic at the lake. They appeared to be more relaxed and playful.

Therapist: Well, it looks as though you two are in pretty good spirits today. How did the past week go?

Tom: I think it went real well. In fact, a lot better than I expected. I took Judy to supper Friday night, and we had a good talk. On Saturday, we packed a picnic lunch and took the kids to the lake. We have a lot there but haven't been able to afford to build a home there. We swam and actually did a little work clearing out some of the underbrush. When we went home, we put the kids to bed and talked some more. In fact, I actually ended up spending the night. The one thing Judy and I have always enjoyed is our sex life together, even in the worst of times, and it was great sharing a bed with her again. It seems like everything is OK when we're together in bed.

Therapist: Wow. It sounds like things moved at a pretty rapid pace. How about you, Judy, was the weekend as enjoyable for you as Tom says it was for him?

Judy: I think so. I hadn't planned on him spending the night, but things were going so well that it just seemed like the right thing to do. I have to admit, it was really nice to have him hold me again. I remembered that most of our times together have been pretty darn good. It seems lately that we've focused mostly on the negative. Tom is really a great father and can be a good friend. But I still don't want to rush things. I'm still scared that if we rush back into living together, we'll start repeating our old mistakes. So, at least for now, he's still living with his friend. But we've made plans to get together a couple of nights this week as well as next weekend.

Therapist: Well, what a great report. You two have obviously done some good work. I almost hate to get into the issues we discussed last week, but I think we should keep working, at least for now, on some of these concerns. When you were together with time to talk, what issues did you discuss?

Tom: The main thing on my mind was how I could stay in control when we had a disagreement. I really don't like losing control. I think we agreed that the only times I ever lost it was when she had been drinking and I felt a combination of hopelessness for her and a sense of fear for the children. She finally agreed that she became most belligerent and combative when she was drunk.

Therapist: Is that right, Judy?

Judy: As much as I hate to admit it, I have to agree. When we thought back on the really bad arguments, it was when I was drunk and really mean. I think if I can stay away from the bottle, things will improve.

Therapist: OK. Are you staying sober?

Judy: Most of the time. I had another slip this week, but I called the lady I had met at AA and talked with her. Also, since Tom wasn't home, I was able to get the children in bed and sleep it off without an argument. I'm still going to AA, and I think that's helping.

Therapist: Let me stay with the drinking a bit longer. The last two times you've gotten drunk, you've managed to call someone. While that is certainly a huge step forward, I wonder, is there a way that you can keep from getting drunk in the first place? That is, if you feel like drinking, is there something you can do instead?

Judy: Well, I guess I could call someone. But usually when I feel like drinking, it's because I'm already stressed or feeling bad and I don't really want to talk.

Therapist: Several weeks ago, you mentioned going shopping. Is it possible to go someplace in a crowd, like a mall, so that you're not alone but you don't have to really talk with anyone?

Judy: Yeah, something like that may work. It's sure worth trying.

The therapist is exploring situations that have worked for Judy in the past as a means of emphasizing those times when she exerted control and realized positive outcomes. This is a continuation of building on the theme that she is not helpless or a victim to her moods but has the capability to handle situations in a positive manner.

Therapist: OK. Try that next time and see how that works. And don't stop there—think of other things you can do other than losing yourself in the mall.

Judy: You know, now that I think about it, there is something I used to do when I felt my life was out of control with my parents. If I did something for someone else—someone in need—I tended to forget my own problems and got relief by helping them. I know it sounds really hokey, but it seemed to work then. Maybe that's why I became a social worker. Maybe I could find a way to help others when I'm really down or stressed. Maybe then I wouldn't drink. I really would like to stop.

Therapist: That sounds like some excellent possible alternatives to me. I'd say give them a shot and see what happens. Now, to shift gears again, tell me more about your discussions this past week and any other ideas you two have generated.

Tom: Well, as I said earlier, I really believe that alcohol is a major factor. I really believe if Judy doesn't drink, we can handle matters better. For now, we've agreed that if we get into a heated argument, I'm going to leave the house for an hour or two and let things cool down. If Judy has been drinking and the children are awake, I'll take them with me. Judy has agreed with this plan and has also agreed to call her AA friend and talk with her. You know—I think we can really work things out if we can stick with a plan.

Therapist: Sounds good. What are your thoughts, Judy?

Judy: I have to agree. Tom is no angel, but I have to admit that the drinking seems to be the root of most of our problems. Not all of them, but most of the worst ones. I think if I can get a handle on that, we can work out everything else. I don't like thinking of myself as an alcoholic, but when I can think of the bottle as someone I'm having an affair with, it's easier to think of giving it up. Maybe I'm kidding myself, but if I can make it work, who cares?

Therapist: I agree. Think of it any way you want if it helps in overcoming the temptation. And Tom, it sounds as though you two have developed some ideas on coping with the demon temper. Are there other ideas you have come up with?

Tom: I don't think so. I guess I'm so convinced of the impact of the alcohol that I have trouble coming up with any other ideas. I believe so strongly in it that I haven't had a drink at home for the past three years. I'll have a couple of beers when I play golf but never more than three. And I can't remember the last time I was even tipsy. I would like to help Judy get there, too. So, for now, just leaving the scene of the argument seems like the best solution. The long and the short of it is, I think I can leave "Mr. Temper" on the shelf if Judy can leave "Mr. Bottle" or "Al" there.

Judy: I agree. We've even agreed to move back in together at the end of this month. For now, we're going to see each other a couple of evenings during the week and on weekends. I think we'll be able to make things work after all.

At this point, the therapist agreed to conclude regular appointments with the understanding that they could return if they felt they needed to. However, the therapist gave them considerable credit for their hard work and for their ability to see themselves in a new light. They both seemed less focused on being victims to life circumstances and better able to see themselves as having the ability to make choices that positively impacted their lives. The following letter was written to them at the conclusion of the final session.

Dear Judy and Tom:

Following our final session, I gave a great deal of thought to areas we had covered, where you had been, and where you're going. I would like to share some thoughts with you.

When the two of you first came in, I was concerned that yours might be one of those marriages that might best be dissolved. Between the alcohol, the general communications difficulties, and especially the physical violence, you had a great deal to overcome. However, after spending the past six weeks with you, I've definitely changed my mind.

I've been very impressed with the strengths and maturity each of you have exhibited. You have worked hard at identifying patterns of behavior that have created problems in your marriage and in your personal lives. You've approached counseling from a position of recognizing the problems and trying to work together to resolve them rather than being overly defensive and blaming. This has been most unusual and refreshing.

Judy—I admire your ability to acknowledge the difficulties that alcohol has played in your life and in your relationship with Tom. You have worked hard at what draws you to the bottle and have mobilized the strengths to make positive changes. Even though the work has been, and will remain, difficult, you have chosen to face it head-on. Yes, there have been some relapses. However, your trying to understand them and deal with them in a healthy, positive way rather than playing the victim role takes strength and determination. I have every confidence that if you continue to grow in the way you presently are doing, you'll find that you are stronger than the seductive bottle and you'll win the battle. However, don't overlook the help you can get from support groups. To do this on your own or to expect Tom to be your sole support would make the challenge much more difficult. You've also worked hard at identifying some issues from your family of origin and how these have helped shape who you are and perhaps interfere with who you want to be. You've begun to identify your strengths and modify some of your old, dysfunctional beliefs.

As for you, Tom, you've worked hard at taking a personal inventory and making some changes that will enhance your marriage. Your willingness to recognize your anger/rage behaviors and to change the ways you interact with Judy is encouraging. Further, your ability to acknowledge Judy's needs for more direct, nonjudgmental support from you speaks volumes for your dedication to Judy and the family and your willingness to conduct some major self-examination. Judy will continue to need your support in her battle with the bottle, and from the first rounds you've seemed to have a good sense of how to support and encourage her without taking responsibility for her changes. You have recognized that not all of the problems are due to the drinking but also some of the other behaviors you've each brought to and developed in the marriage. I'm very impressed at your work in this area of personal awareness and change.

I believe we are seeing a "new" and healthier Tom and Judy emerge. You have worked together to enhance the way in which you communicate and deal with conflict. You've also been able to identify the strengths each of you possess and how these strengths can help you as your efforts continue. I've enjoyed watching the evolution begin and look forward to seeing these changes solidify into a strong marital foundation as well as increased self-esteem for both of you.

Conclusions

In this case, the therapist attempted to incorporate many of the elements of narrative therapy as developed by Michael White, while acknowledging that after years of conducting therapy, each therapist develops a unique style and rarely adheres to a "pure" model.

There were two main elements at play in this case example. The first was the externalization of difficulties such as Judy's drinking, physical and emotional complications from her monthly cycle, and Tom's occasional fits of rage. The second element involved highlighting unique outcomes: times when the couple was successful in dealing with their difficulties. This was accomplished by helping them begin to rewrite the scripts by which they lived their lives. The couple's old narrative pictured Judy as being weak and out of control, a hapless victim to her father's legacy of abusiveness and alcoholism. Tom continued in the role Judy's father had begun, becoming abusively out of control when angered. Furthermore, Tom injured Judy emotionally by his lack of support, with the final injury being his affair with another woman. The therapist focused new scripts on being in control and successful rather than on negativism or seeing themselves as powerless victims. A new narrative emerged in which they could be seen as having strengths both as individuals and as a couple. This narrative helped them view alcoholism and an uncontrollable temper as foes that could be jointly overcome by identifying triggers that got them in trouble and by taking effective steps to avoid those triggers. They were encouraged to view their relationship as a burgeoning friendship that needed to be nurtured. Letters were written after several of the sessions both as a way of sharing some additional thoughts with the couple as well as having them feel the presence of the therapist with them between sessions. The sessions were at times one week apart and at other times two weeks apart, depending on what the therapist hoped they could accomplish between sessions.

Although not a unique view, I believe that most of the real work in marital therapy is done external to the actual sessions, based on information generated during the sessions. Because some of this information can become "muddied" in the days following a session, letters help to jog memories and offer clarity. Although I, as the therapist in this case, have practiced various forms of systems therapy over the years, I attempted to remain true to the principles set forth by Michael White as much as possible while working with this couple.

I also believe that if an alcohol or drug problem is present in one or both parties, it must be addressed and dealt with from the outset. If it is not, then the rest of the work will be an exercise in futility. However, I also believe that the least intrusive method is best for the individual. Unless there is a long history of frequent abuse, I usually work with the clients and support groups such as AA, NA, and so on. I have found that, for the most part, continued recovery without the help of one of these groups is extremely difficult. In this particular case, both parties were willing to use the support groups and, in fact, found good support from them.

Study Questions

1. Practice narrative therapy letter writing by composing two of the following, based on this case example: letter of invitation, redundancy, prediction, counterreferral, or reference.
2. Discuss the therapist's decision not to deal directly with Tom's past extramarital affair. Do you agree with this decision?
3. What did you learn from this case about dealing with drug or alcohol abuse that you feel might be applicable to any model of therapy?
4. Create a brief description of a problem that might be encountered in therapy. Describe some ways you could externalize this problem.

References

Goldenberg, I., & Goldenberg, H. (1996). *Family therapy: An overview* (4th ed.). Pacific Grove, CA: Brooks/Cole.

Nichols, M. P., & Schwartz, R. C. (1995). *Family therapy: Concepts and methods*. Boston: Allyn & Bacon.

White, M., & Epston, D. (1990). *Narrative means to therapeutic ends*. New York: Norton.

Chapter Thirteen

Psychoeducational Family Therapy

Constance J. Fournier and William A. Rae

Psychoeducational family therapy is a family-focused pragmatic approach to therapy in which educational training is the key intervention. While psychoeducational family therapy utilizes many of the skills seen in more traditional family therapies, such as building alliances, it also has the unique focus of intervention that is educationally based. Psychoeducational family therapy differs from typical educational approaches in that it uses family therapy techniques such as joining and identifying resistance factors in order to facilitate the educational intervention. It requires the therapist to function as a teacher, yet it also requires going beyond the traditional teacher's role. In psychoeducational family therapy, therapists not only evaluate the family's understanding of factual material; they must also assess how the information might best be incorporated into the family system as well as how it affects the affective and emotional tenor of the family.

Within the realm of psychoeducational family therapy is a specialized application called *medical family therapy*. Whereas some have argued that these are different therapies (Doherty, McDaniel, and Hepworth, 1994), in fact, each incorporates the same concepts (Lask, 1994; Nichols and Schwartz, 1995). Psychoeducational family therapy has been distinctly associated with schizophrenia (Nichols and Schwartz, 1995), while the medical family therapy literature has focused on chronic medical illnesses (Doherty et al., 1994). Despite these distinctions, in practice psychoeducational family therapy appears to provide the elements that transcend differences and foster positive outcomes in family functioning, whether used with mental illness or with chronic medical illness family issues.

For the purposes of this chapter, the term *psychoeducational family therapy* is used to include medical family therapy applications. Descriptions of differences in approach between mainstream psychoeducational family therapy and the specialized applications of medical family therapy are provided as needed. The case study has a medical family therapy emphasis as a way of illustrating psychoeducational family therapy processes.

Theoretical Underpinnings

Psychoeducational family therapy incorporates perspectives and techniques from several arenas, including systems theory, behavioral interventions, and educational psychology. There is a strong developmental focus with recognition of the family life cycle. When incorporating prevention orientations (such as premarriage counseling) and early intervention (such as parent training) in psychoeducational family therapy, education has always been a strong element (Levant, 1986). Furthermore, psychoeducational family therapy has a multidisciplinary history that transcends even the usual eclectic psychology literature, encompassing social work, ministry, nursing, and education. This adds a richness and depth to psychoeducational family therapy. Because it is described in the literature of many disciplines, it is also accessible to a large variety of therapists.

With the diverse background of psychoeducational family therapy, elements have been developed that differentiate it from other family therapies. Psychoeducational family therapy is defined as an approach that emphasizes health, in addition to amelioration of dysfunction, with education as an integral aspect of the therapy (Levant, 1986). Compared with other types of family therapy, a subtle yet significant shift occurs in psychoeducational family therapy in that families are not seen as "causing" the problem of mental or medical illnesses. Although blame can be an aspect of other family therapies, psychoeducational family therapy does not blame families for dysfunction; rather, the focus is on how families can overcome obstacles to positive functioning (Goldenberg and Goldenberg, 1996). One of the hallmarks of psychoeducational family therapy is the empowerment of the family (Nichols and Schwartz, 1995). Psychoeducational family therapy views families as the experts in knowledge of themselves and uses this expertise to enhance the family's ability to function capably outside the family unit. In the application of medical family therapy, families are conceptualized utilizing chronic medical illness, rather than mental illness, as the central focus.

Psychoeducational family therapy is adaptable to a wide variety of families with different levels of functioning. The blended family, with a need to enhance communication skills, is a good candidate for psychoeducational family therapy. A family that is considered "typical" in functioning but in which one of the family members is dealing with a chronic medical condition such as asthma is likely to benefit from psychoeducational family therapy. The family that may be considered more "pathological" in functioning, such as a family with a schizophrenic member, may also gain from psychoeducational family therapy.

Levant (1986) developed a framework of understanding psychoeducational family therapy that delineates four dimensions: the objective, the focus, the field of orientation, and the theoretical orientation. In Levant's model (1986), the *objective* of psychoeducational family therapy varies according to the needs of the family. Objectives are on a continuum, ranging from enhancement of already existing skills to amelioration of an identified problem. With the highlight on prevention and early intervention, identifying strengths as well as potential problem areas are central in determining the objectives of the psychoeducational family therapy as it applies to a particular situation.

Levant (1986) describes the *focus* of psychoeducational family therapy as being where the intervention is directed. The focus can be within the family life cycle, such as dealing with the current situation or dealing with a transition from one situation to another. The focus can also be on relationships within the family, such as the marital dyad, the parental relationship, or the parent-child relationship. Finally, the focus can be on a problem as it affects the family, such as assisting the family member with a chronic illness diagnosis.

According to Levant (1986), the *field of orientation* represents psychoeducational family therapy origins and current application. This includes the more traditional settings, such as single family therapy, or more educational contexts, such as parent or marriage counseling. The field can also be thought of as occurring in more diverse settings, such as multifamily therapy, or in nontraditional places and times, such as in community centers or during hospitalization of a family member.

Levant's description (1986) of *theoretical orientation* refers to the manner in which the therapist delivers psychoeducational family therapy. This may be based on more traditional family therapy theoretical approaches or schools of thought; however, the application of psychoeducational family therapy utilizes the objectives and foci described by Levant (1986) that are germane to the psychoeducational family therapy approach. For example, in exploring the family of origin, the psychoeducational family therapy approach may have the objective of enhancing current functioning rather than providing "insight," which is utilized in many traditional family therapy approaches.

Currently, a context that appears to be promising for psychoeducational family therapy is in the area of chronic mental illnesses such as schizophrenia (Goldenberg and Goldenberg, 1996; Nichols and Schwartz, 1995). Psychoeducational family therapy can be delivered to individual families or used in a multifamily setting. Programs typically use education-based interventions for increasing the family's knowledge about the disorder, encouraging communication skills, and enhancing practical problem solving. When used as part of the treatment for persons with a diagnosis of schizophrenia and their families, psychoeducational family therapy appears to have significant contributions in several areas. One such area is patient and family satisfaction with services

(Brennan, 1995). Perhaps more important, especially in this era of cost containment and treatment efficacy, psychoeducational family therapy shows increased treatment compliance and decreased relapse (Goldstein and Miklowitz, 1995; McFarlane, Lukens, Link, Dushay, Deakins, and Newmark, 1995). Psychoeducational family therapy appears to work well in different delivery models, such as a multifamily approach (McFarlane, Dushay, Stastny, Deakins, and Link, 1996), within a short-term focus (Brennan, 1995), and even across cultures (Wiedemann, Halweg, Hank, Feinstein, Muller, and Dose, 1994). While psychoeducational family therapy is not the only variable that produces positive results, it does appear to produce an additive effect that can be seen across time and settings (McFarlane et al., 1996; Wiedemann et al., 1994).

In the psychoeducational family therapy literature relating to medical family therapy, chronic medical illnesses are the focus of research. Conditions such as childhood diabetes, asthma, obesity, and some neurologic and cardiovascular disorders appear to respond positively to medical family therapy, while other conditions such as smoking cessation do not (Campbell and Patterson, 1995). Utilizing medical family therapy in conditions such as somatization and infertility has also been promising (McDaniel, Hepworth, and Doherty, 1992, 1995).

Psychoeducational family therapy has much to offer, yet it must be recognized that it also includes aspects seen in most, if not all, family therapies, such as building alliances, maintaining neutrality, reframing, and recognizing family process (Goldstein and Miklowitz, 1995). Thus, the psychoeducational family therapist is challenged to be well versed in general family therapy techniques and versatile in educational techniques. The therapist must also have a solid knowledge base in the factual material that is a focus of the intervention. In medical family therapy, the therapist must have a working knowledge and understanding of the medical condition.

As useful as psychoeducational family therapy can be, there are situations in which it is not appropriate. It is not suitable for highly resistant families because extreme resistance would make it difficult, if not impossible, to conduct educational training. Psychoeducational family therapy is not appropriate for families where endangerment of members is likely to occur. For example, a family with a member who is imminently suicidal, homicidal, or abusive to others is not a good candidate for psychoeducational family therapy. For this situation, crisis management is more suitable. It is also not appropriate to continue using psychoeducational family therapy with a family who is not able to gain from the educational intervention, despite accommodation by the therapist. This includes families whose style is to avoid information and families with poor language comprehension skills. In medical family therapy, if the family member is too physically ill to participate, the therapy may need to be postponed. For families already working in another therapy model, the transition to or addition of psychoeducational family therapy must be considered carefully. The family may not be able to make the change successfully, and this may impact their functioning. Finally, psychoeducational family therapy is not appropriate for families unwilling to participate in therapy, even though it may be recommended by others involved with the family. When psychoeducational family therapy is contraindicated, other approaches such as individual therapy, other family therapies, crisis management, or educational instruction may need to be considered.

Key Concepts

Although psychoeducational family therapy is distinct in providing educational training as the primary therapeutic intervention, it is similar to other family therapies in many respects. Aspects such as the phases of therapy (engagement, intervention, and termination), a time-limited family format, and clear, identified goals and objectives are common to both psychoeducational and other types of family therapy. This section examines these elements of psychoeducational family therapy, as well as how these elements may be similar to or different from typical family therapy approaches.

Engagement is the first step in the sequence of psychoeducational family therapy. This process occurs when the therapist connects with the family on an emotional as well as social level. Alliance building and acceptance of the family are basic to this phase across all therapeutic approaches. Negotiating the contract with the family regarding confidentiality, payment issues, length of treatment, and emergency procedures is likewise similar, although with psychoeducational family therapy the therapist emphasizes the educational training component. The therapist also identifies the family's current life cycle and evaluates how it might affect educational training and understanding. In addition, the therapist identifies family strengths. Identification of possible resistance to intervention, while in some ways similar to typical family therapies, must also include how resistance may interfere with the educational training. For example, resistance due to lack of knowledge or lack of skills can often be addressed within psychoeducational family therapy by employing appropriate teaching approaches. Resistance due to significant personality disorders may not be amenable to psychoeducational family therapy, as the family must be open on some level to intervention and to accepting the collegial role rather than playing out personality disorders as the focus of therapy.

The therapist must also consider other aspects of the family that would impact educational training. These can include issues such as the formal educational histories of family members, the family's current level of knowledge of the educational topics, the family's primary learning style, the presentation style of learning materials, and the age of the children in the family. These particular issues will be discussed in more detail shortly.

One key difference between psychoeducational family therapy and other family therapies at the engagement level is that the family may not have sought assistance. Psychoeducational family therapy may be part of a multidisciplinary, multitask team approach, especially with families dealing with chronic medical illness. This may serve as an advantage, as the therapist has the tacit approval and endorsement of the total team caring for the family or family member. This multiteam approach can also be a disadvantage, as the family may feel somewhat coerced into psychoeducational family therapy rather than being there by choice. This feeling of coercion can lead to resistance later.

While psychoeducational family therapy can occur in diverse settings, the first contact for some families may be during a hospital stay, which can again affect the engagement process. One example of this is that the family may assume that the therapist is a medical doctor. Another example is that the therapist may need to time visits around other patient activities. An explanation of the therapist's role is essential in this situation. The therapist must consider the impact of the setting and how psychoeducational family therapy is introduced to the family. Joining with the family and developing therapeutic alliances is critical during this phase.

Intervention in psychoeducational family therapy is educational training and skills building. In educational training, the therapist can be identified as the expert in the area of content, whereas the family is clearly the expert in knowledge of the family and its functioning. The family is also the expert in determining how the educational training will affect them. As the therapist, utilizing both family therapy and educational techniques can more precisely match the needs of the family. There are several specific educational aspects that the therapist can consider in this intervention.

The therapist must assess the educational histories, general experiences, and expectations of the family when designing the educational training. Matching the language of the family and using related metaphors and relevant examples enhances the educational process. For example, using a sports metaphor with a family who is not interested in sports is confusing and may even be distancing for the family. On the other hand, using examples and applications directly related to the family's needs maximizes the impact of the intervention. For example, the therapist can help the family problem-solve in anticipation of a medical crisis, assisting family members in deciding what role each should take during the emergency.

The family's experience with the topics of the educational training is also important. For example, in helping families with newly diagnosed schizophrenia, some families may be having their first experience with the disorder, while others may have years of experience from other family members. It is important to assess current levels of knowledge, as even "experienced" families may have dated or inappropriate information.

Looking at the proper educational approach is also important. While the therapist should be providing educational training that incorporates auditory, visual, and kinesthetic (hands-on) approaches, there may be a preferred style that can be emphasized for the family. Certainly, family therapy techniques such as role playing, modeling, and reflective listening, which use multiple sensory approaches, can be incorporated into the educational training.

Another avenue that can be tailored to meet the needs of the family is the style of presentation. Some families may be information seekers, wanting to know everything possible; other families may be information avoiders, wanting only to process small pieces of information at a time. One presentation style initially gives the family the "big picture," explaining first what the end product will be and then explaining in detail the elements related to the overall concept. This approach may best match the information seekers. Another presentation style introduces skills incrementally in a slower "building-up" process. This approach may best match the information avoiders. Most families are likely to benefit from both styles, yet they may have a preference that can be fostered by the therapist.

The ages of family members must also be considered. Families with younger children may benefit from more hands-on approaches, while families with grown children may prefer a more didactic approach. The therapist must consider how the educational training will be understood by the different age groups. At certain points in psychoeducational family therapy, the intervention may need to target specific family members, such as parents or siblings.

While problem solving and communication training are typical interventions generic to family therapy, these elements are central to educational training in the psychoeducational family therapy model. Many psychoeducational family therapy programs incorporate these interventions, which initially appear to be similar to other family therapies. Differences occur in the acquisition and application of these skills. In many family therapies, these skills would be used within the family setting. In psychoeducational family therapy, they are used both within the family and within the community. For example, communication training may emphasize helping the family communicate more effectively with outside agencies such as hospitals, schools, and governmental agencies. The communication training may target specific problem areas, such as how to be assertive without "turning off" agency helpers. In addition to teaching general skills, training also covers situations specific to the needs of the family, such as calling for and setting up appointments.

In psychoeducational family therapy, the therapist delivering educational training matches the pace, level, and style of the family. While this is usual for most joining techniques seen in family therapies, there are differences with psychoeducational family therapy. Typically, both the therapist and the family share a vision of what the educational training goals and specific objectives of skills and behaviors will be in advance. The educational training can also be problem focused, with more overt direction from the therapist as compared with other therapies. Unlike more traditional educational approaches, psychoeducational family therapy puts the therapist in a collegial position with the family rather than in an "expert" role.

The *termination* phase of psychoeducational family therapy is similar to other family therapies in that it is considered from the engagement phase and throughout the intervention phase. As in other family therapies, termination is typically a mutual decision between the therapist and the family. In typical education-only approaches, termination usually occurs when the content has been delivered or when a time frame has been completed. In psychoeducation, there are markers of skills acquired through the intervention that may provide the natural termination point. The therapist and the family can both point to skills that the family has developed and can utilize these skills for establishing appropriate follow-up procedures. During termination, the therapist should insure that the family can use their skills both inside and outside the family setting, that the family has an established mechanism for handling crisis situations, and that the family is connected with appropriate support networks. In addition, plans for further follow-up with the therapist should also be mutually decided.

Psychoeducational family therapy has many potential uses. The ability of a psychoeducational family therapist to adapt to families at virtually any level of education, skill development, and life cycle makes this approach useful in a variety of situations. Psychoeducational family therapy works well in a team approach by including other fields such as medicine and education. This is especially helpful for families addressing chronic mental and medical illnesses. The efficacy of psychoeducational family therapy in situations involving chronic illness is a current topic in the family therapy literature. Psychoeducational family therapy can also be helpful for families dealing with single issues such as adoption and for transition and life cycle issues such as parenting or stepparenting. It may also serve as a catalyst in establishing an alliance with more resistant families so that they can address other issues once certain skills have been developed.

Psychoeducational family therapy focuses on the current family members, with a special emphasis on prevention or early intervention. With the evolution of family therapy (Boss, 1990), psychoeducational family therapy may perhaps best represent the melding of various fields and orientations to a system of intervention that is producing exciting results.

The Case: A Child with Diabetes

The following case describes the application of medical family therapy in the initial session of psychoeducational family therapy with a family referred to the therapist by a multidisciplinary team. It should be pointed out that this family represents a fairly healthy, well-functioning family whose prime difficulty involves dealing with a diagnosis of chronic illness in their child. This case was chosen to illustrate key elements of engagement and intervention. Termination is briefly touched upon, as this is the initial session.

The therapist is a Ph.D. psychologist employed within a medical center. She works with the diabetes care team, seeing families during the hospitalization of a family member after a new diagnosis of insulin-dependent diabetes mellitus (IDDM). She also follows the family on an outpatient basis after the hospitalization.

Background

Alli Thane is an 8-year-old who has just been diagnosed with IDDM. Alli had been in generally good health until the previous week when she began feeling ill. When her symptoms worsened, she was taken to her family physician. She was diagnosed with diabetes and was hospitalized for a few days to stabilize her condition and to develop a comprehensive treatment plan.

Alli lives with her biological parents and her brother. Her father, Jeff, age 42, is a CPA; her mother, Patty, age 41, is a substitute teacher and is working on her master's degree in education; and her brother, Jack, age 14, is in the eighth grade in a gifted and talented program in math. Prior to her IDDM diagnosis, Alli was generally doing well. Described by her parents to other diabetes care team members as "strong willed," she is an average student who is a very talented soccer player. In fact, she is playing in a premiere league in her city and is a regional star as well.

The family has been seeing other members of the diabetes care team, including an endocrinologist, dietician, nurse clinician, social worker, and the hospital-based classroom teacher. As a member of the diabetes care team, the therapist will utilize psychoeducational family therapy in this medical illness case. The therapist will be making initial contact with the family (engagement), during which time she will be looking for any issues that may affect adherence to the IDDM regimen. This will include assessment of current levels of knowledge, communication skills, and problem-solving ability. Identification of potential resistance factors will also occur. This information is essential in developing appropriate intervention techniques and goals. During the contact, the therapist will also be establishing follow-up for the family. These steps follow the basic sequence of psychoeducational family therapy and may overlap with each other as contact with the family continues.

In terms of a psychoeducational perspective, the focus is initially on prevention by looking at ways to enhance current functioning. A change in focus may occur if there is identification of potential problem areas and resistance, which then would be targeted for early intervention. If significant problems are found, then amelioration of dysfunction would become a focus.

With this case, the focus would most likely be directed at dealing with newly diagnosed IDDM. Roles in the family and family relationships would also be considered. The therapist would also need to consider the life cycle phase of the family. As is typical of psychoeducational therapy, educational training and skills building will occur throughout the encounters.

Case Transcript

The scene is the hospital room, 24 hours after admission. In the room are Alli and her parents. Alli is fully dressed in street clothes and is playing a game with her parents while seated in her bed. The therapist has received general information about the family from other members of the diabetes care team. They indicate no pressing issues or obvious dysfunction.

Therapist: Hello, I'm Dr. Sue Jones. I'm a member of the diabetes care team. Is this a good time to meet with you?

Jeff: Sure. Dr. Smith [pediatric endocrinologist] said you would be by. I'm Jeff Thane, this is my wife, Patty, and this is our daughter, Alli.

Therapist: Nice to meet you. How are you surviving the hospital experience so far?

Alli: The food stinks, and they are going to make me give myself shots.

Jeff: It's been pretty upsetting, but we're glad we know what made Alli sick.

Patty: Everyone has been so nice, but I'm worried about when we go home and try to make all of this work.

Therapist: What you are experiencing is pretty normal for this point in getting a diabetes diagnosis. There's a lot to deal with and sort through when you have a new experience like this. What I'd like to do is explain my role on the diabetes care team, then work with you on solving problem issues that come up. Would that be okay?

Alli: I want to watch TV instead.

Patty: Alli, we'll watch later. This is important.

Therapist: Alli, I need your help especially. After all, you are the expert about how you feel about all of this. Could you help for a few minutes?

Alli: I guess so.

Jeff: Of course she will; she's really a good problem solver.

Therapist: Thanks, Alli. I'm here to help with the emotional side of being newly diagnosed with diabetes. Today I'll be getting a brief family history from you to see if there are any issues that we should be concerned with right now, and talk with you about typical issues for families in your situation. Together we'll figure out if any of these issues might be a potential problem area for your family and work together to start problem solving. At the end today, we'll set up a follow-up appointment. Does that sound okay to you?

Here the therapist is setting the stage for an educational perspective and collegial style, including everyone in the process. This session has the objective of identifying issues and taking a problem-oriented focus, with a behavioral skills orientation. The therapist is hypothesizing possible strengths and resistance factors that will be investigated further in the engagement process and incorporated in the intervention. In this family, the parents appear to be open to therapy and have already picked up on the problem-solving subtext through the initial conversation. These parents appear to be highly educated, based on their careers and vocabulary. The family also seems to be functioning well, as evidenced by the parents' responses to Alli's negative comments. Possible resistance factors include Alli's negative feelings about aspects of her care (shots), the question of parent roles in the management of the diabetes regimen, and Alli's "strong will."

The therapist elicits a brief family history, in which no significant issues are found. The family has no history of mood disorders, anxiety disorders, psychotic disorders, or major illnesses except for a paternal grandmother, age 88, who was diagnosed five years ago with type II diabetes (which is usually controlled through diet). A review of Alli's development is unremarkable.

The therapist then describes typical issues for families at this stage of diagnosis of a chronic illness. These include shock (no one in the family has had insulin-dependent diabetes), feeling overwhelmed and worried about how the family will deal with the illness (especially in terms of time and money), feeling angry (why Alli?), and feeling grief (Alli won't be the same, won't be able to do the same things she used to, and so on). The therapist then proceeds with the session.

Therapist: At this point, you may be feeling overwhelmed with all the information you have been getting.

Patty: Yes—how are we going to do all of this? The consequences for not keeping her diabetes in control are devastating. And she is already so strong willed, how will we be able to make sure that she will do what she is supposed to? Maybe I should quit work.

Alli: I don't want to give shots.

Jeff: Maybe we should cancel our spring vacation and stay at home.

Therapist: Yes, you do sound like this has been overwhelming. We'll take one point at a time.

First, you should know that how you are feeling is very typical. It takes awhile to sort through all the information and figure out how the new routines will work in your family. That's why the care team is here, to answer questions and offer advice. And you will be able to do all of this, including giving yourself shots when you are ready. What usually happens is that at first, families stick to the routine precisely. Then, as you get more familiar with the routine, it may slip a little. Then what usually happens is that you develop a routine that works for your family and in the different situations. While you have to change routines to care for the diabetes, you want to hold off on making other major changes for awhile.

Patty: But if the routine slips, won't that have major consequences down the road?

Therapist: There is a little room for tolerance in the routine. We'll make sure you have time to talk with Dr. Smith regarding the short-term and long-term consequences. Would that be helpful?

Patty: Yes, thanks.

Therapist: Are there any areas that you feel might be a problem?

Alli: Shots!

Therapist: Wow, that really seems to be worrying you. What are you doing for your care right now?

Alli: I am doing finger sticks. I did two today.

Patty: Yes, she did, and she read the meter as well.

Therapist: How do you do a finger stick? Can you show me?

Alli: Sure. [demonstrates]

Patty: And she only had to be shown this once.

Therapist: Really. You sure are a fast learner.

Jeff: Yes, she can be.

Therapist: What else have you been learning?

Alli: About diet. The diet lady brought by fake food for us to see.

Therapist: There is a lot to learn about that too.

Alli: Yep.

Comment: The therapist has gained important information about the family learning style. It appears that, while they need to understand the big picture at first, breaking tasks down into manageable components would fit this family's style. In addition, Alli clearly responds to a hands-on approach and enjoys showing off her new skills. These learning styles will need to be incorporated in the sessions with the family. The therapist empathizes with the parent's sense of feeling overwhelmed and responds to their concerns about making major life changes by directly informing them that they should delay these decisions. It does not appear that the "shot" issue is a specific needle phobia, as evidenced by the blood draw and by Alli allowing her mother to give the shots. If it were, then intervention for the phobia would take priority. It is suspected that the shot issue may be a way for Alli to maintain some control over all the changes that are occurring. In terms of education, the family would be advised that many 8-year-old children do not yet administer their own injections and that this skill is one that evolves on the child's individual time line.

Therapist: So what is diabetes anyway?
Alli: Where the pancreas doesn't make enough insulin, so you have to help with diet and outside insulin.
Therapist: Did you know this before?
Alli: Only a little because of my grandma.
Jeff: Really, all we knew is that my mother's diabetes is controlled through diet.
Patty: We were hoping that's all that Alli would need.
Therapist: So this has been especially hard since you haven't had much experience with diabetes.

Comment: The therapist learns that, although the general educational level of the family is high, their knowledge about diabetes and the regimens associated with it is less than some families and typical for most families dealing with a new diagnosis. Thus, it will be important not to make assumptions about the family's knowledge of diabetes but, rather, to make specific inquiries regarding their understanding of diabetes.

Therapist: Well, there is one good thing about this.
Alli: What?
Therapist: Soon you'll be able to get an A on a science project about diabetes because you will know a lot about it—probably even more than your teacher!
Patty: Well, that's one way of thinking about this.
Therapist: What do you parents see as potential problem areas?
Patty: Getting Alli to do what she needs to in order to follow the routine.
Jeff: And learning all we need to know.
Therapist: And what do you see as strengths of your family?
Alli: We all love and care about each other.
Patty: Thank you, honey.
Jeff: That's so nice, Alli, and true. And Patty is a great organizer. She will be able to put a routine together.

Therapist: And it seems like when Alli decides to do something, she can really do it well.

Parents: That's true.

Therapist: It sounds like everyone in the family will be able to help. Has Jack been able to get information too?

Jeff: Yes, yesterday, and he'll be back tonight. We decided that since he had a special field trip today that he should go to school.

Comment: Including all members of the family, and understanding their current and future roles, is important. It is well documented that chronic illness can have a significant impact on siblings, thus the therapist will be careful to include Alli's brother in future sessions. The therapist then introduces another potential resistance factor for the family and incorporates it as educational information.

Therapist: So you are sticking with as normal a routine as possible. That's a wonderful start. And you are getting the whole family involved from the beginning. One problem that can occur in families is that one person—usually the mom—takes on all the responsibility. While that can work well for awhile, it can also cause problems later, especially since there are so many skills to learn.

Patty: I can see myself in that situation.

Jeff: So can I—we'll have to watch for it.

Therapist: One practical thing the family can do is decide who is responsible for what when, and who is the back-up person. For example, who should be responsible for checking the morning blood sugars, and would that person be the best for the afternoon blood sugars?

Patty: Since I sometimes go to teach early, Jeff, maybe you should do it with Jack as the back-up.

Jeff: That makes sense, and you can take the afternoon shift with Jack as the back-up again.

Therapist: Alli, what will you be doing?

Alli: Nothing.

Therapist: Doing the finger stick?

Alli: Oh, yeah.

Therapist: Good work! How about in another situation, such as getting snacks to school?

Comment: The therapist elicits Alli's comments and makes sure she is included. The therapist will then see if the family can apply problem solving to other activities and will offer coaching and additional training if necessary. Note that this problem solving also involves an outside agency, in this case the school. The session continues with discussion of a resistance factor that has been verbally identified by the family.

Therapist: I haven't forgotten about you, Alli, and your worry about shots. Is it more getting shots or giving shots?

Alli: Giving shots.

Therapist: Have you given yourself one yet?

Alli: Almost, in my leg.

Therapist: What do you think—are you ready to do it by yourself yet?

Alli: Not yet.

Therapist: What do you think you can do?

Alli: I can learn to draw up the insulin levels.

Therapist: That's good! Does it bother you if someone else gives the shot?

Alli: I don't like it at all.

Patty: She's been pretty good about this.

Jeff: Except with me!

Patty: That's because she has him wrapped around her little finger. [Parents laugh.]

Jeff: That's true, but I know it's something I need to do.

Comment: Here is a situation that can be a continuing resistance factor, especially regarding the father's role in the family. While this may bear further exploration in future sessions, helping the family deal with the current situation is the priority at this point. The therapist will help the family in setting up a routine for injections, using the same problem-solving strategies as the blood-level checks. Note that Alli will not be fully responsible for the injections yet; rather, that will be a future goal of the family.

Therapist: So maybe three goals for this family are to get into a routine, for Alli to do as much as she can by herself, and to learn to get shots from Mom and Dad.

Jeff: That sounds good.

Patty: We'll work on it.

Alli: I want to watch TV now.

Therapist: You sure were helpful. I'll set up a return appointment for one month. That will give you some time to get a routine established and see where any problems pop up. If you have any problems before then, you can call me and I'll see you sooner. Will that be okay?

The Thane family is responsive to psychoeducational family therapy on many levels. This family is relatively "easy" by family therapy standards, with no overwhelming resistance factors, a high education level, good problem-solving abilities, and therefore a good prognosis. It should be noted that psychoeducational family therapy includes families with relatively fewer resistance issues as compared with other family therapies. Dealing with circumscribed situations such as a new illness is one example where there is involvement of some relatively "healthy" families in psychoeducational family therapy.

In other families, the interventions may need to focus on different issues. In the family with less developed problem-solving ability, the goal would be to develop these skills in the context of specific situations. For example, in the snacks-for-school situation, the therapist might need to present the family with a rubric such as "who, what, when, where, and how" in order to facilitate the problem solving. For more resistant families, more negotiation and family ownership of the specific objectives would need to occur when building therapeutic alliances.

These situations point out why the therapist using psychoeducational family therapy must have a solid knowledge of general family therapy.

For the Thane family, the engagement phase will continue in the next few sessions. In the first session, the therapist met with the family, indicated the themes of the psychoeducational family therapy, and probed for strengths and possible resistances of the family. The intervention in this session included practical problem solving regarding monitoring of the IDDM regimen and looked at communication between the family and Alli's school. The therapist highlighted potential problems that would be explored further in future sessions. One potential problem is seen in the delineation of roles, such as ensuring that the mother does not assume full responsibility for the care of Alli's IDDM regimen. Other potential problem areas include Alli's resistance to some of her own care and the family's anxiety about long-term consequences. It should be noted that follow-up was scheduled in this first session. The groundwork was established regarding what goals would be set by the family that would determine the termination of the therapy.

In the subsequent sessions, the Thane family continued to work on problem solving around the issue of Alli's IDDM regimen. The family continued to be supportive of each other and was able to utilize and generalize problem-solving techniques. Alli's "strong will" appeared to be mild oppositional behavior that was in evidence before the IDDM diagnosis and exacerbated after the diagnosis. When Alli was included in the problem solving, she tended to do somewhat better although she tested the limits of every situation. Patty initially tried to control her own feelings by keeping tight control on the diabetes regimen. At first, Jeff let Patty set up the routines. It then became clear that Patty was the "bad cop," while Jeff had little responsibility. With some discussion and setting up specific schedules in the sessions, the parents were able to develop more equal roles. Although Patty continued to take the lead in most situations, this was done in agreement with Jeff. Jeff took on the lead role in helping Alli administer her own injections. This served to take Patty out of the "bad cop" role in the situation where Alli was showing much oppositional behavior.

As a family, the Thanes had several adjustments to make. They had to learn new information and new skills to manage the IDDM regimen. They had to apply the information and skills in various situations, including working with outside agencies such as the school and the soccer team. They had to make contingency plans and ensure that family members' roles were clear. Throughout all of these changes, they also had to work through their feelings, not only about the IDDM diagnosis but also about its impact on each family member and on family functioning.

Conclusions

While the family therapist has many orientations to choose from, psychoeducational family therapy in this case appears to be an especially appropriate choice. The family's need for enhanced functioning when faced with new challenges, the incorporation of educational, behavioral, and systems perspectives, and the traditional techniques of family therapy combine to provide a powerful and effective system of intervention. Psychoeducational family therapy has been found to be helpful for families in transition, both with mental illness and with chronic medical conditions. While psychoeducational family therapy may not be appropriate for every situation, it certainly should be a consideration when a family is facing one of these situations.

Study Questions

1. Using the resistance to shots as the example, what further psychoeducational family therapy interventions would you work on with the family?
2. Using a psychoeducational family therapy perspective, what might be other reasons that Alli is "strong willed"?
3. What might be future resistance factors in this family?
4. How would you conceptualize this case differently if you were taking other family therapy perspectives?
5. Would you continue with psychoeducational family therapy or change perspectives with this family? Why would you make this choice?

References

Boss, P. (1990). Family therapy and family research: Intertwined parts of the whole. In F. W. Kaslow (Ed.), *Voices in family psychology* (pp. 17–32). Newbury Park, CA: Sage.

Brennan, J. W. (1995). A short-term psychoeducational multiple-family group for bipolar patients and their families. *Social Work, 40,* 737–743.

Campbell, T. L., & Patterson, J. M. (1995). The effectiveness of family interventions in the treatment of physical illness. *Journal of Marital and Family Therapy, 21,* 545–583.

Doherty, W. J., McDaniel, S. H., & Hepworth, J. (1994). Medical family therapy: An emerging arena for family therapy. *Journal of Family Therapy, 16,* 31–46.

Goldenberg, I., & Goldenberg, H. (1996). *Family therapy: An overview* (4th ed.). Pacific Grove, CA: Brooks/Cole.

Goldstein, M. J., & Miklowitz, D. J. (1995). The effectiveness of psychoeducational family therapy in the treatment of schizophrenic disorders. *Journal of Marital and Family Therapy, 21,* 361–376.

Lask, B. (1994). The illness network: Commentary on Doherty et al. *Journal of Family Therapy, 16,* 47–51.

Levant, R. F. (1986). An overview of psychoeducational family programs. In R. F. Levant (Ed.), *Psychoeducational approaches to family therapy and counseling* (pp. 1–51). New York: Springer.

McDaniel, S. H., Hepworth, J., & Doherty, W. (1992). Medical family therapy with couples facing infertility. *American Journal of Family Therapy, 20,* 101–122.

McDaniel, S. H., Hepworth, J., & Doherty, W. (1995). Medical family therapy with somaticizing patients: The co-creation of therapeutic stories. *Family Process, 34,* 349–361.

McFarlane, W. R., Dushay, R. A., Stastny, P., Deakins, S. M., & Link, B. (1996). A comparison of two levels of family-aided assertive community treatment. *Psychiatric Services, 47,* 744–750.

McFarlane, W. R., Lukens, E., Link, B., Dushay, R., Deakins, S. A., & Newmark, M. (1995). Multiple-family groups and psychoeducation in the treatment of schizophrenia. *Archives of General Psychiatry, 52,* 679–687.

Nichols, M. P., & Schwartz, R. C. (1995). *Family therapy: Concepts and methods.* Boston: Allyn & Bacon.

Wiedemann, G., Halweg, K., Hank, G., Feinstien, E., Muller, U., & Dose, M. (1994). Deliverability of psychoeducational family management. *Schizophrenia Bulletin, 20,* 547–556.

Chapter Fourteen

Current Issues and Trends in Family Therapy

Herbert Goldenberg and Irene Goldenberg

Final chapters in textbooks (to say nothing of final years of a century) offer an irresistible opportunity to sum up and look ahead to the future of a field. Where do we go from here? What have we learned—from theoretical formulations, research efforts, clinical experiences—that sheds light on family functioning and the most effective ways to intervene with temporarily troubled or otherwise more chronically destabilized families? Family therapy, begun as an outcry against static, linear explanations of behavior, continues to evolve, as exciting theoretical and clinical ideas challenge the field to assess many of its basic concepts (such as systems theory) and to rethink how most effectively to reach and serve a broad range of client populations.

How best to capture these provocative developments? We cannot adequately depict the current state of a field, as in a static photograph, but we can try to identify ongoing trends and suggest likely future research areas. As a result, we've organized this chapter around what we believe are some contemporary movements in family therapy, which together may begin to offer a picture of the field's current stirrings. To that end, we present the following topics: (1) postmodern outlooks, (2) population diversity, (3) qualitative research methodology, and (4) outcome studies regarding the effectiveness of family therapy.

Postmodern Outlooks

Very much in tune with current philosophical controversies about the knowability of the universe, postmodern views challenge our taken-for-granted assumptions regarding the existence of an absolute reality. In sharp contrast to the modernist view, with its heavy reliance on systematic observations and rigorous reasoning in order to discover objective truths, the postmodern view is skeptical about questions of truth, meaning, and historical interpretation (Norris, 1990). That is, while modernists contend that truth can be uncovered and that universal principles underlying human behavior can be revealed, postmodernists insist that we do not live in a world where irreducible universal principles explaining all human behavior can be discovered and neatly classified, laid out in cause-and-effect terms, and measured by a detached observer.

Deconstructing familiar scientific undertakings in which the researcher strives to control as many variables as possible, except for the single independent variable under scrutiny, postmodernists invite the proposition that there exist alternate routes to knowledge, that there are a multitude of personal perspectives and no necessarily correct or objective views of a situation or event, and that the values and biases of the observer inevitably influence or color what is being observed. In short, truth is relative—there exist an assortment of subjective outlooks or points of view of how things really are; what is out there is not objective but rather the result of each of our perceptions and inventions. Put another way, to the postmodernist, reality exists only in the context of each person's set of constructs for thinking about it (Guba, 1990).

What has this to do with family therapy, and why is it becoming so influential in the thinking and procedures of many of today's family therapists? As Doherty (1991) points out, family therapy—particularly its theory of family systems—is a by-product of mid-20th-century modernist culture. As he notes, both Freud and the behaviorists early in the century, although focusing on different sets of data (dreams and free associations for the former, stimulus-response cycles for the latter), searched for minuscule details in analyzing the roots of a problem. In doing so, they minimized the larger social context in which that problem was a part. Just as Freud, for example, divided the topographic structure of personality into neat components (id, ego, superego) in order to study its conflicting reactions, so early family therapy systems theories focused on interactions within a family, by and large ignoring the impact of outside social and historical forces on the behavior of family members. Specifically, such factors as client ethnicity, gender, socioeconomic status, or sexual orientation were given short shrift, if attended to at all, in the haste to discover universal truths regarding human behavior. Although the early family therapists, mostly trained in psychoanalysis, broke with the content of that theory (individually focused study of unconscious processes), Doherty maintains that they embraced the same intellectual form, namely, modernism.

By way of contrast, postmodernist theorists point out that our views or constructions of reality are based on the belief system we bring to the situation;

thus, a diversity of perspectives exists from which to view life. People from differing cultures may see the world differently; gender, too, often slants perceptions. Rather than searching for the "right" and "wrong" ways of thinking or behaving within a family, the postmodern challenge is to help families recognize how their belief systems have created their reality for them. That is, that system of beliefs, which has guided them in giving meaning to their lives—constructing their views of reality—has also inevitably limited their options. Since there are multiple ways of viewing a problem situation, are there other ways of looking at their situation? Other assumptions or language they might call upon to organize and define how they see themselves? Other choices of behavior than the ones that have led them to their present state?

One ramification of postmodern thinking has been the proliferation of *social constructionist family therapies*. Solution-focused therapy (deShazer, 1991), narrative therapy (White and Epston, 1990), a collaborative language systems approach (Anderson and Goolishian, 1992), and the use of a reflecting team (Andersen, 1991) are just some examples of an overall set of therapeutic approaches emphasizing that what we perceive as real is not objective but is based upon the dominant set of beliefs in ourselves and in society (Parry and Doan, 1994). As Gergen (1985) observes, the assumptions each of us makes regarding reality arise through communication—language and conversation with others—so that our knowledge about the world develops out of a social context. Language is the key here, since it provides the process for consensual agreement between people and thus is the basis for our views of reality (Campbell, Draper, and Crutchley, 1991).

For the social constructionist, the therapist is no longer the outside observer or expert but rather plays a part in constructing the reality being observed (Goldenberg and Goldenberg, 1996). Neither the therapist nor any one family member can reveal the "truth" about the family and its problems. Instead, what the therapist sees as taking place within the family is simply a product of the therapist's own set of assumptions about families and their problems and is not imposed upon the family, lest such an intervention close the door to new and possibly unique ways the family may discover for themselves for viewing and solving their problems (Wetchler, 1996). The family therapist with a social constructionist view is more interested in the language and the stories families tell about themselves than they are about describing the family's underlying psychological structure (Doherty, 1991). In the process, they collaborate with family members in reauthoring their lives (White, 1995) or, put another way, in generating a new, nonpathological narrative about themselves (Anderson and Goolishian, 1992).

Why does social constructionism have such an important impact on the practice of family therapy?

1. *The therapist has permission to be a nonexpert.* Here the client is the expert and the therapist can relax, become the "learner," and expand his or her perspectives. That is not to say the therapist lacks therapeutic skills but rather that he or she does not bring preconceived ideas of what the family should or should not

change. Put another way, the therapist learns to do something *with* the family rather than *to* the family and is a part of the process rather than an outside observer.

2. *There is greater acceptance of eclecticism.* Moving beyond adherence to a specific school of thought or set of intervention techniques, therapists can more easily combine techniques (for example, cognitive and systems) or modalities (individual, couples, families). With less slavish dedication to one viewpoint, outlooks regarding family problems can be expanded; for example, in seeking biological contributions, as in medical family therapy (McDaniel, Hepworth, and Doherty, 1992), or in making interventions that combine psychological and educational efforts with families (Anderson, Reiss, and Hogarty, 1986).

3. *There is increased recognition of the need to attend to diversity issues among clients.* (See section that follows.)

4. *Clients and therapists are empowered by believing their situation is changeable.* If accounts of misery or personal failure that troubled families bring to therapy are redefined not as "truths" but rather as social constructions, the hope for developing alternate accounts of their lives—and future possibilities—becomes more attainable as families give new meanings to their situation.

Population Diversity

We in North America live in a society that is rapidly increasing in diversity, made up of people from varied ethnic backgrounds and with different lifestyles. By the early part of the 21st century, it is expected that fully one-third of the U.S. population will be composed of racial and ethnic minority groups (Jones, 1991). Although acknowledged by the early family theorists (circa 1950s), insufficient attention was paid to the values and customs that families of different racial or ethnic backgrounds transmitted to their children and the subsequent influence of those factors on family functioning. We now recognize that a more comprehensive view of family functioning requires a wider lens and that, in trying to understand families, we must take into account their kinship networks, socialization experiences, communication styles, typical male-female interactive patterns, roles of the extended family, and similar culturally linked attitudinal and behavioral arrangements (Goldenberg and Goldenberg, 1996). One of the biggest changes in direction in the field today is how best to provide useful and effective counseling services that utilize this broader perspective.

Similarly, the feminist challenge in family therapy, stemming largely from the expansion of the women's movement in the 1970s, helped deconstruct early models of family functioning, pointing out that family therapists—mostly male—knowingly or unknowingly adopted patriarchal assumptions regarding desirable family functioning and role playing. The impact of this feminist critique has been a powerful one, not merely in forcing family therapists to reassess their assumptions about "healthy" family functioning and to examine their own biases but also in advocating a set of therapeutic attitudes that, consistent with the postmodernist position, promote collaborative and egalitarian relationships with client families. The growing feminist literature will undoubtedly continue to have a powerful bearing on the field of family therapy in the 21st century.

A third social force, gaining momentum and eventuating in the gay liberation movement in the 1970s, called attention to another bias in our definitions of healthy family functioning, built upon the "truth" of unchallenged assumptions equating normality with a heterosexual orientation. As has been the case with the feminist critique of customary practice, this movement—taking homosexuality out of the closet—has forced mainstream therapists to look at their own attitudes, at the same time helping gay and lesbian clients to accept and value their sexual orientation and to achieve, embrace, and integrate a gay identity (Goldenberg and Goldenberg, 1997).

Together these forces, emerging during the postmodern period of skepticism about fixed notions of absolute truths, forced a reexamination of some basic family therapy assumptions, leading to a new set of ideas regarding diversity in our society.

Multiculturalism

Family functioning cannot be understood in isolation from a consideration of the family's cultural background. Just as family therapy theories in the 1950s broke out of the individually focused restrictions of searching for intrapsychic problems, so the more recent effort to attend to a larger sociocultural context broadens our understanding of factors—race, ethnicity, socioeconomic conditions—that influence behavior. Unless prepared and informed about a family's cultural history, today's family therapist runs the risk of *cultural dissonance* with client families (Goldenberg and Goldenberg, 1997). Stated more positively, family therapists today must try to understand the cultural backgrounds of their clients in their assessment or therapeutic or basic communication efforts to avoid misdiagnosing or mislabeling family behavior and, in the process, pathologizing ethnic minority families whose behavior is unfamiliar. At the same time, therapists must also be aware of their own cultural heritage and the inevitable influence of values, attitudes, and expressive styles on their own perceptions and outlooks.

As we move into the 21st century, family therapists need to be culturally competent and culturally literate before working with ethnically diverse families. Typically, this calls for a two-pronged effort: (1) adopting a *multicultural outlook* in order to become more sensitive to general cultural issues (generational relations, acculturation problems, attitudes toward seeking help outside the immediate culture), including those brought into the consultation room by the therapist; and (2) developing a *culture-specific outlook* in which the therapist becomes better informed about specific racial or ethnic groups (African American, Cuban, Iranian, Soviet Jews, and so forth) before undertaking work with members of that group.

The multicultural view emphasizes that therapists not just learn about the client's culture but also learn about their own cultural background and the culture of the agency where the therapy is practiced, to say nothing of the dominant culture of the society where therapists and client families work together (Fontes and Thomas, 1996). Culture-specific approaches are exemplified in McGoldrick, Giordano, and Pearce's collection of background information (1996), along with some implications for clinical intervention strategies, covering over 40 groups of Americans originating in other countries. These efforts provide an invaluable aid; Fontes and Thomas liken it to a travel guide into relatively unknown territory for avoiding errors due to ignorance or ethnocentrism. The danger here is of stereotyping—assuming all members of a specific group are alike, thus responding to the family as a cultural prototype. One helpful reminder comes from Falicov (1995), who points out that, among members of any group, a variety of factors—educational level, social class, religion, stage of family acculturation—also influence family behavior patterns. In addition, the impact of socioeconomic and political factors, such as poverty, discrimination, racism, and so on need to be noted (Sue, 1994). These factors have not as yet been sufficiently explored and will hopefully lead to new insights in the near future.

Gender-Sensitive Family Therapy

One major impact of the women's movement on family therapy has been the call for a reexamination of the entrenched values and attitudes of a sexist society, one which feminists argue family therapy theory and practice have helped to perpetuate. Contending that the values and attitudes about gender and gender relations lead to unequal power at best and domination of women by men at worst, feminist family therapists (for example, Avis, 1996) call for a deconstruction of established ways of family power distribution that have reinforced roles often oppressive to women. Instead, they offer a reconstructed view—a "feminine voice" rather than a new set of therapeutic intervention techniques—in which, collaboratively, therapists and couples examine ways that society's sex-role expectations confine and hinder their fulfillment together, helping couples change those transactions where power differentials have retarded growth in their relationship (Worell and Remer, 1992).

As Brooks (1996) notes, women and men at the turn of the century are facing a period of dramatic "gender role strain," challenging traditional gender formulations. Soaring divorce rates, the multitude of one-parent families led by women and remarried families together have caused upheaval in the traditional ways in which we have defined normal family life. Brooks suggests that while it may appear that men have benefited from traditional gender role arrangements, any such benefits often have come at the price of estrangement from their children, loneliness and emotional alienation, and sometimes early death.

One challenge for the practice of family therapy is how best to help client families achieve gender equity. Brooks (1996) urges therapists to move beyond past declarations of "neutrality"—with its implication of being value-free and apolitical—since doing so only perpetuates society's traditional and powerful gender messages. The ramifications here are monumental, not merely for clinical practice but also for liberating future generations from confining, gender-stereotyped roles in society.

Same-Sex Coupling

Gay and lesbian partners are becoming more visible in many parts of our society as heterosexist attitudes (that heterosexuality is the only acceptable sexual orientation) are receding. Looking beyond identifying labels based solely on sexual preference, many in our society are beginning to look at an individual's personal qualities, ways of relating to others, and so on. Thanks in large measure to the efforts of gay liberation advocates, the once secret and taboo behavior of same-sex couples has come out of the closet for many (although by no means all) homosexual men and women, as a significant portion of the population has become less marginalized.

As in the case of the multiculturalist and feminist movements, the greater prominence of gay and lesbian issues has helped educate family therapists (along with many in the general population) regarding their own attitudes about what constitutes normal behavior. A body of literature is beginning to appear regarding gay and lesbian family life (Scrivner and Eldridge, 1995; D'Augelli and Garnets, 1995), as are publications describing specialized services that such groups may require. Books and articles dedicated to counseling same-sex couples (Laird and Green, 1996), gay and lesbian parenting (Martin, 1993; Silverstein and Quartironi, 1996), and HIV/AIDS victims (Rosenthal, Boyd-Franklin, Steiner, and Tunnell, 1996) attest to increased awareness among therapists after a long period of neglect.

To deal with these issues and others (for example, gay marriages, adoption of children), family therapists in the 21st century need to learn more about the experience of growing up gay or lesbian. They need to be aware of their own possible heterosexist biases and how to seek help from more knowledgeable consultants, such as gay therapists, regarding gay and lesbian issues when planning treatment strategies. As in the case of multicultural considerations or those concerning gender, they need to broaden their outlook and attempt to shed narrow and outdated attitudes and beliefs.

Qualitative Research Methodology

One major breakthrough within the last decade in making research in family therapy more applicable for clinical practitioners has come about as a result of the increased acceptability of qualitative research methods. Long dominated by traditional quantitative methodologies (hypothesis generation, large samples, use of control groups, search for statistically significant differences), many published research findings in the past have by and large seemed to many family therapists inconsequential and thus irrelevant to their real-world needs. Conversely, the clinical introduction of new family therapy techniques without authenticating research support for their effectiveness has long seemed unacceptable to research-trained and research-minded psychologists. One encouraging effort to narrow this clinician-researcher gap has come about through the increased adoption of qualitative investigations—exploratory and open ended—aimed more at exploration and discovery than at objectivity and verification. Sprenkle (1994) suggests that qualitative research methodologies are especially well suited for describing complex phenomena, defining new constructs, discovering new relationships among variables, and trying to answer "why" questions. Data for qualitative studies may come from in-depth interviewing, document analysis, the intense examination of a small number of case studies, and so on.

One appealing contribution of qualitative methods for clinicians is the utilization of *clinically* significant criteria (for example, the extent to which a previously dysfunctional family develops specific skills in the functional range) rather than the more customary *statistically* significant criteria (for example, differences in improvement between a treatment and no-treatment group) for evaluating therapeutic outcomes. In some cases, differences between the groups may be significantly different statistically, but those who improved statistically may not have become functional as a result of the treatment. Thus, the two methodologies are synergistic: qualitative methods offer a useful tool for the pragmatic clinician by providing contextual data that enriches and expands quantitative findings.

Quantitative methods are consistent with the modernist view that an absolute reality exists and that it can be objectively studied and measured. The relativistic postmodern viewpoint, on the other hand, is that there are no fixed realities, only points of view; at any point, there may be several equally accurate ways of describing events in the social world (Atkinson, Heath, and Chenail, 1991). Thus, the act of measuring can hardly be objective since it imposes a viewpoint that inevitably influences what is being measured. Rather than believing a researcher can approach a problem from a neutral, detached, unbiased, and thus objective stance, the postmodern view is that the researcher's subjective values, beliefs, and attitudes inevitably influence what and how a phenomenon is studied. Abandoning traditional means of utilizing reliability and validity measures, however, does not let qualitative researchers off the hook; they must collect and analyze data in a rigorous manner.

Will qualitative methods replace quantitative methods in family therapy research? No. Research into the 21st century will undoubtedly utilize both quantitative and qualitative methodologies. The former continue to be necessary for hypothesis testing or verification, and empirical findings ("hard evidence") will continue to be the scientifically acceptable standard by which we attempt to answer basic questions regarding a technique's ultimate effectiveness, as is the case with all psychotherapy research. Funding from governmental and private agencies, insurance program administrators, and other policy setters will continue to expect results verified by traditional research methods (Cavell and Snyder, 1991). However, as Piercy and Sprenkle (1990) note, necessary as they are, quantitative methods often fall short when called upon to discover relationships among variables. As they become more scientifically respectable, qualitative methods will receive wider acceptability and will complement quantitative undertakings by providing a greater contextual understanding of the meaning of quantitative results.

Outcome Studies: The Effectiveness of Family Therapy

How effective is family therapy? Always an important issue, the question takes on special significance in a health care age of increased pressures from consumers, third-party health insurance payers, legislators, and fellow professionals for greater accountability. Issues of efficiency, cost-effectiveness, durability of results, and so forth need to be addressed, and comparisons need to be made with other treatment modalities or no treatment at all. Investigating the effectiveness of family therapy is especially hazardous since the researcher must determine the complex set of conditions under which family therapy is effective—the types of families, their ethnic and social class background, the category of problems or situations, the level of family functioning, the therapeutic technique, the treatment objectives or goals, and so on (Goldenberg and Goldenberg, 1996). Nevertheless, current demands on therapists will undoubtedly continue into the new century to provide the briefest, most effective, and most cost-effective ways (for example, individual? conjoint? conjoint with multiple families? with or without medication?) of serving troubled clients.

Published outcome studies today are typically of two kinds: (1) *efficacy studies*—whether a treatment approach works under controlled experimental ("laboratory") conditions; or (2) *effectiveness studies*—whether a treatment approach works under normal ("field") conditions, as in the everyday practice of providing family therapy services (Pinsof and Wynne, 1995). The former, often in a university, clinic, or hospital setting, form the basis for most of our knowledge regarding therapeutic outcomes in family therapy at this time, since specific conditions (such as recruitment of subjects by the researcher; training of all participating therapists in a specific technique before the study; use of standardized therapeutic procedures, often following a treatment manual; independent treatment evaluation; and so on) are easier to control and institutional studies are more likely to be funded. However, although often illuminating, efficacy studies sometimes are difficult to translate into specific recommendations for therapy under more real-world, consultation room conditions. One bright note for the future is some shift in National Institute of Mental Health research grant funding into service settings (such as mental health centers), acknowledging the necessity to supplement efficacy studies with more real-world clinical effectiveness research. This shift provides a better opportunity particularly for cost-effectiveness evaluations—comparing the results of alternate interventions as to their costs as well as their effects—which is especially important in an age of greater scrutiny of health care expenditures.

Overall, the efficacy for marital and family therapy for specific disorders in specific populations has been established; it is as good or better than most other areas of psychotherapy. To date, however, no single therapeutic orientation in marital or family therapy has proven superior to any other (although almost all proved better than no treatment), according to a quantitative, multiproject, meta-analysis of 163 outcome studies reviewed by Shadish, Ragsdale, Glaser, and Montgomery (1995). Employing the rigorous criterion of clinical significance as opposed to statistical significance, these researchers found that marital therapy returned close to half of the distressed couples to a nondistressed status, according to the usual measures of marital adjustment. Overall, family therapy clients did better than a comparison control group in dealing with such problems as general child conduct disorders, child aggression, global family problems, communication and problem solving, phobias, and schizophrenic symptoms.

However, according to a survey of published results by Pinsof and Wynne (1995), marital/family therapy has not been demonstrated in and of itself to effectively treat severe disorders; such a therapeutic approach needs to be supplemented, in the case of schizophrenia, for example, with psychoeducational programs involving a combined medication and educational program and, in the case of adult or adolescent drug use, with group and/or individual and/or medication treatment along with an educational component.

Research methodology, particularly for efficacy studies, is growing increasingly sophisticated. Future studies are likely to improve further as methodological and conceptual problems are better defined. One practical suggestion offered by Pinsof and Wynne (1995) is for the creation of a set of core outcome batteries in order to facilitate the comparison of various outcome studies. Standardized measures of marital/family therapy outcomes, as yet undeveloped, will go a long way in determining what works, for which clients, and in what ways. Awareness of cost-effectiveness and performance of cost-benefit analysis are certain to be increasingly important variables in any future outcome research.

Future Perspectives

What can we expect from the next generation of family researchers? Certainly, racial and ethnic minority families need to be included in the populations being studied; their participation will not only lead to more representative results but should also facilitate the development of measuring instruments that better appraise the functioning of a wide variety of family patterns. Moreover, more culturally sensitive explanations for family diversity should emerge. Similarly, overgeneralizations and extrapolations from research findings can be more easily avoided if subject populations include gay and straight members, men and women, younger and older participants, and so forth.

The use of multiple outcome measures is likely to become more common in the 21st century, as researchers attempt to better approximate the totality of family member experiences without breaking them down into meaningless parts. Cook, Pickett, and Cohler (1997) suggest that family researchers move beyond the study of parent-offspring bonds to attend also to other intrafamilial patterns (brother-sister, grandparent-grandchild).

Finally, we must come to grips with what interventions help in family therapy, for what populations or categories of problems, under what conditions, for what level of family functioning, at what cost, and so forth. Ultimately, the lasting effectiveness of specific techniques delivered in a real-world field situation (as opposed to a laboratory) by existing practitioners needs to be determined if we are to effectively facilitate family recovery and growth.

References

Andersen, T. (Ed.). (1991). *The reflecting team: Dialogues and dialogues about dialogues.* New York: Norton.

Anderson, C. M., Reiss, D., & Hogarty, B. (1986). *Schizophrenia and the family.* New York: Guilford Press.

Anderson, H., & Goolishian, H. A. (1992). The client is the expert: A not-knowing approach to therapy. In S. McNamee & K. J. Gergen (Eds.), *Therapy as social construction.* Newbury Park, CA: Sage.

Atkinson, B., Heath, A., & Chenail, R. (1991). Qualitative research: Response to Moon, Dillon, & Sprenkle (1990), "Qualitative research and the legitimization of knowledge." *Journal of Marital and Family Therapy, 17,* 161–166.

Avis, J. M. (1996). Deconstructing gender in family therapy. In F. P. Piercy, D. H. Sprenkle, J. L. Wetchler, & Associates (Eds.), *Family therapy sourcebook* (2nd ed.). New York: Guilford Press.

Brooks, G. (1996). Gender equity in families: A promise worth keeping. *The Family Psychologist, 12*(4), 5–6.

Campbell, D., Draper, R., & Crutchley, E. (1991). The Milan systemic approach to family therapy. In A. S. Gurman & D. P. Kniskern (Eds.), *Handbook of family therapy* (Vol. II). New York: Brunner/Mazel.

Cavell, T. A., & Snyder, D. K. (1991). Iconoclasm versus innovation: Building a science of family therapy—comments on Moon, Dillon, and Sprenkle. *Journal of Marital and Family Therapy, 17,* 181–185.

Cook, J. A., Pickett, S. A., & Cohler, B. J. (1997). Families of adults with mental illness—the next generation of research: Introduction. *American Journal of Orthopsychiatry, 67*(2), 172–176.

D'Augelli, A. R., & Garnets, L. D. (1995). Lesbian, gay, and bisexual communities. In A. R. D'Augelli & C. J. Patterson (Eds.), *Lesbian and gay identities over the lifespan: Psychological perspectives on personal, relational, and community processes.* New York: Oxford University Press.

deShazer, S. (1991). *Putting differences to work.* New York: Norton.

Doherty, W. J. (1991). Family therapy goes postmodern. *Family Networker, 15*(5), 36–42.

Falicov, C. (1995). Training to think culturally; a multidimensional comparative framework. *Family Process, 34,* 373–388.

Fontes, L. A., & Thomas, V. (1996). Cultural issues in family therapy. In F. P. Piercy, D. H. Sprenkle, J. L. Wetchler, & associates (Eds.), *Family therapy sourcebook* (2nd ed.). New York: Guilford Press.

Gergen, K. J. (1985). The social construction movement in modern psychology. *American Psychologist, 40,* 266–275.

Goldenberg, H., & Goldenberg, I. (1997). *Counseling Today's Families* (3rd ed.). Pacific Grove, CA: Brooks/Cole.

Goldenberg, I., & Goldenberg, H. (1996). *Family therapy: An overview* (4th ed.). Pacific Grove, CA: Brooks/Cole.

Guba, E. (Ed.). (1990). *The paradigm dialogue.* Newbury Park, CA: Sage.

Jones, J. M. (1991). Psychological models of race. In J. D. Goodchilds (Ed.), *Psychological perspectives on human diversity in America.* Washington, DC: American Psychological Association.

Laird, J., & Green, R. J. (Eds.). (1996). Lesbians and gays in couples and families: A handbook for therapists. San Francisco: Jossey-Bass.

Martin, A. (1993). *The lesbian and gay parenting handbook: Creating and raising our families.* New York: HarperCollins.

McDaniel, S. H., Hepworth, J., & Doherty, W. J. (1992). *Medical family therapy: A biopsychosocial approach to families and health problems.* New York: Basic Books.

McGoldrick, M., Giordano, J., & Pearce, J. K. (Eds.). (1996). *Ethnicity and family therapy* (2nd ed.). New York: Guilford Press.

Norris, C. (1990). *What's wrong with postmodernism: Critical theory and the ends of philosophy.* Baltimore: Johns Hopkins University Press.

Parry, A., & Doan, R. E. (1994). *Story re-visions: Narrative therapy in the postmodern world.* New York: Guilford Press.

Piercy, F. P., & Sprenkle, D. H. (1990). Marriage and family therapy: A decade review. *Journal of Marriage and the Family, 52,* 1116–1126.

Pinsof, W. M., & Wynne, L. C. (1995). The efficiency of marital and family therapy: An empirical overview, conclusions, and recommendations. *Journal of Marital and Family Therapy, 21,* 585–613.

Rosenthal, J. M., Boyd-Franklin, N., Steiner, G., & Tunnell, G. (1996). Families with HIV illness. In M. Harway (Ed.), *Treating the changing family: Handling normative and unusual events.* New York: Wiley.

Scrivner, R., & Eldridge, N. S. (1995). Lesbian and gay family psychology. In R. H. Mikesell, D. D. Lusterman, & S. H. McDaniel (Eds.), *Integrating family therapy: Handbook of family psychology and systems theory.* Washington, DC: American Psychological Association.

Shadish, W. R., Ragsdale, K., Glaser, R. R., & Montgomery, L. M. (1995). The efficacy and effectiveness of marital and family therapy: A perspective from meta-analysis. *Journal of Marital and Family Therapy, 21,* 345–360.

Silverstein, L. B., & Quartironi, B. (1996). Gay fathers. *The Family Psychologist, 12*(1), 23–24.

Sprenkle, D. H. (1994). Editorial: The role of qualitative research and a few suggestions for aspiring authors. *Journal of Marital and Family Therapy, 20,* 227–229.

Sue, S. (1994). Incorporating cultural diversity in family therapy. *The Family Psychologist, 10,* 19–21.

Wetchler, J. L. (1996). Social constructionist family therapies. In F. P. Piercy, D. H. Sprenkle, J. L. Wetchler, & associates (Eds.), *Family therapy sourcebook* (2nd ed.). New York: Guilford Press.

White, M. (1995). *Re-authoring lives: Interviews and essays.* Adelaide, Australia: Dulwich Centre Publications.

White, M., & Epston, D. (1990). *Narrative means to therapeutic ends.* New York: Norton.

Worrell, J., & Remer, P. (1992). *Feminist perspectives in therapy: An empowerment model for women.* New York: Wiley.

Name Index

Addis, M., 52, 79, 83, 108
Alexander, A., 52, 79
Alexander, F., 91, 107
American Psychiatric Association, 216, 230
Andersen, T., 329, 337
Anderson, C., 330, 337
Anderson, H., 227, 259, 260–261, 285, 287, 289, 329
Andreas, S., 172, 186
Anger-Díaz, B., 146
Aniol, J., 87, 107
Atkinson, B., 334, 337
Auerback, A., 60, 79
Avis, J., 332, 337
Aylmer, R., 90, 107

Babcock, J., 52, 79, 87, 107
Baines, M., 50
Baldwin, M., 169, 170–172, 180
Bandler, R., 172, 186
Barrett, M., 179, 187
Bateson, G., 146–147, 168, 188–189, 209, 211–212, 217, 230, 284
Baucom, D., 28, 49, 52, 79, 83, 88, 107–108
Beavin, J., 1, 188, 209
Beck, A., 27–28, 49
Bedrosian, R., 28–29, 49
Behrens, B., 83, 108
Berg, I., 232–235, 237, 246, 252, 257
Bergin, A., 79
Binder, J., 89, 92, 109
Birchler, G., 57, 80
Bodin, A., 212, 231
Borduin, C., 11, 145

Bornstein, M., 86, 107
Bornstein, P., 86, 107
Boscolo, L., 188–190, 192, 209
Boss, P., 317, 325
Boszormenyi-Nagy, I., 1–5, 10, 25–26
Bouma, R., 86, 108
Bowen, M., 27–29, 49, 50
Bowlby, J., 89, 107
Boyd-Franklin, N., 333, 338
Boziacs, G., 28–29, 49
Bradbury, T., 88, 107–108
Bradshaw, D., 29, 50
Bray, J., 27–29, 49, 109
Brengelmann, J., 52, 79
Brennan, J., 313, 325
Bright, I., 109
Brody, C., 52, 79
Brooks, G., 332, 337
Brown, M., 60, 79
Browne, A., 179, 186
Buber, M., 3
Burney, J., 259

Campbell, D., 329, 337
Campbell, T., 6, 30
Cardarelli, A., 187
Cavell, T., 81, 109, 313, 325
Cecchin, G., 188–189, 192, 209
Chambless, D., 52, 79
Chenail, R., 334, 337
Christensen, A., 51–57, 60–61, 78–80, 87, 107
Cohler, B., 336–337
Colapinto, J., 112–113, 115, 117, 144–145
Coleman, L., 179, 186

Subject Index

TO THE OWNER OF THIS BOOK:

We hope that you have found *Casebook in Family Therapy* useful. So that this book can be improved in a future edition, would you take the time to complete this sheet and return it? Thank you.

School and address: ———————————————————————————————

Department: ———————————————————————————————————

Instructor's name: ——————————————————————————————

1. What I like most about this book is: ————————————————————

——

——

2. What I like least about this book is: ———————————————————

——

——

3. My general reaction to this book is: —————————————————————

——

4. The name of the course in which I used this book is: ————————————

——

5. Were all of the chapters of the book assigned for you to read? —————————

    If not, which ones weren't? —————————————————————

6. In the space below, or on a separate sheet of paper, please write specific suggestions for improving this book and anything else you'd care to share about your experience in using the book.

——

——

——

——

Optional:

Your name: _____ Date: _____

May Wadsworth quote you, either in promotion for *Casebook in Family Therapy* or in future publishing ventures?

Yes: _____ No: _____

Sincerely,

David M. Lawson
Frances F. Prevatt

FOLD HERE

FOLD HERE